ARCO

TOP LAW SCHOOLS

THE ULTIMATE GUIDE

Bruce S. Stuart ■ *Kim D. Stuart, Esq.*

Prentice Hall
New York • London • Toronto • Sydney • Tokyo • Singapore

Other books by Bruce Stuart and Kim Stuart, Esq.:
—**The Insider's Guide to Medical and Dental Schools**
—**Top Business Schools: The Ultimate Guide**

Prentice Hall General Reference
15 Columbus Circle
New York, NY 10023

An Arco Book

Arco, Prentice Hall and colophons are
registered trademarks of Simon & Schuster, Inc.

Manufactured in the United States of America

4   5   6   7   8   9   10

Library of Congress Cataloging-in-Publication Data

Stuart, Bruce S.
   Top law schools: the ultimate guide / by Bruce S. Stuart and
   Kim D. Stuart.
      p.   cm.
   ISBN 0-13-949967-9
   1. Law schools—United States—Directories. I. Stuart, Kim D.
II. Title.
KF266.S78   1990   90-42886
340'.071'173—dc20   CIP

To

Our Parents

ACKNOWLEDGMENTS

The authors wish to acknowledge:

Our parents, Vernon and Suellen Stuart for their unwavering support and love throughout this project and throughout our lives.

Pamela Byers, Chuck Wall, and Linda Bernbach for their support throughout this project.

Barbara Gilson, who came back from the hospital invigorated to oversee the editing of more than 700 pages of manuscript.

All the recruiters, law school administrators, pre-law advisors, and law students who guided us and provided essential information necessary for the completion of this book.

CONTENTS

University of Alabama, American University, Baylor, Boston College, Boston University, University of California at Berkeley, University of California at Davis, University of California at Hastings, UCLA, California Western, Case Western, University of Chicago, Columbia, University of Connecticut, Cornell, University of Denver, Duke, Emory, University of Florida, Fordham, Georgetown, George Washington University, Harvard, University of Houston, Illinois Institute of Technology, University of Illinois at Urbana-Champaign, Indiana, University of Iowa, University of Maryland, University of Michigan, University of Minnesota, New York University, University of North Carolina, Northwestern, Notre Dame, Pace University, University of the Pacific, University of Pennsylvania, University of Pittsburgh, University of Puget Sound, University of San Diego, U.S.C., Stanford, Syracuse, University of Texas at Austin, Tulane, Vanderbilt, University of Virginia, Wake Forest, University of Washington, Washington University, College of William and Mary, Union University, University of Wisconsin at Madison, Yale, Yeshiva

INTRODUCTION

WHY A GUIDE TO LAW SCHOOLS?

The decision to become a lawyer and the decision that accompanies it, to apply to law school, are two of the most important choices you can make in your life; decisions that will affect you significantly in all the years ahead. A book designed to guide you through evaluating law schools should be clear about just what benefits you can expect from using it. How this book can be useful to you will vary according to your background and your needs in choosing and applying to law schools.

If you are a straight A applicant with LSAT scores in the top 99th percentile, have many achievements on the undergraduate level, and can write an application essay to delight any admissions officer, this book will provide you with a comparative analysis of the law schools you are likely to consider attending. Given that you have a wider choice of schools than most applicants, this guide offers detailed descriptions of many of the country's most prominent law schools, which should help you to distinguish and discriminate among the qualities that will make one institution preferable to another. The analyses are based on the opinions of students currently attending the schools, administrators of the schools, and legal employment recruiters who are familiar over time with the graduates of these schools.

If, like most applicants, you have not aced every course or given a stellar performance on the LSAT, and your application essays are adequate but not cause for admissions officers to seek you out, then this book will show you how to maximize your strengths and minimize your weaknesses. The pointers in the law school profiles are taken from admissions officers at these schools, many of whom offer admissions tips, and from the opinions of students as to why they think their applications led to acceptance.

Perhaps most important is the fact that we are here to make your life a little easier right now when you need it most. Although there are no 100% guarantees of acceptance into the school of your choice, we hope to keep you better informed about easier methods for navigating the maze of applications and admissions and coming out at the end with a satisfactory place in a school that satisfies your needs. On page xv a step-by-step guide begins to the different procedures in getting into law school—and paying for it.

HOW THIS BOOK WAS COMPILED

When you first decided that law school was to be your destination, it is likely that you began your research into the subject by sending for a selection of catalogs from any law schools that looked like feasible choices. Many of these catalogs are glossy and inviting enough for display in a travel agency, and you must remember, as you read their glowing descriptions of schools, that they have been created essentially as a marketing device.

They were designed to give the most favorable impression of their schools. Just as an advertising agency sets out to market jeans or the latest car, these institutions are selling their product to you, the potential consumer. This guide is meant to provide a more detached and objective view of the schools, to enable you to make an informed choice of a product that will consume thousands of dollars and at least three years of your life.

In putting together this book, we too began by reviewing the catalogs. To obtain a student perspective on each school, we interviewed many of those individuals who have spent years at these institutions and who have gone through what you intend to go through. They have cleared the admissions hurdle, sat through classes you will attend, and have seen firsthand what their schools can do for them—and eventually you—in terms of placement.

We sent thousands of detailed questionnaires to law students throughout the country. After analyzing the responses, we contacted as many students as possible by phone to ask them to expand on their responses. With their answers in mind, we forwarded another set of questionnaires across the country requesting more specific information on matters that we thought intrinsic to legal education at the schools.

We contacted the admissions office of each law school under consideration and asked them to fill out questionnaires on admissions and financial information. We visited a number of conferences where we spoke with representatives of the schools. Many of these admissions officers took time out from their busy schedules to grant us interviews and add suggestions on how we might improve our book. Most administrators provided us with essential information, including top recruiters' names, phone numbers, and addresses.

Using this recruiter information, we sent questionnaires to these individuals asking for their comments about things like tier ranking of the law schools on a basis of one to five, one being lowest and five being the highest evaluation. We supplemented our written recruiter findings by phoning many recruiters as well.

Finally, we visited the schools to check them out for ourselves. At times we notified the administration before our visits and at times we didn't. We continued our student interviews, preferably in a confidential setting. From our experience, students are less likely to talk openly about their law schools in the company of administrators. On these visits, we also followed up with administration interviews whenever possible.

A WORD ABOUT NUKING

Whenever we visit campuses, we encounter many expressions law students have developed that are indigenous to their school. Some of these expressions are common to many schools, words like *gunner,* a student who "shoots down the curve." Recently, a term has cropped up among law students that we hear often—*nuking.*

"Hey, have you come here to *nuke* the school?" a skeptical student would ask us as we posed questions about his or her future alma mater. *Nuking,* or dropping a nuclear bomb, has come to mean putting down or ripping something apart, in this case, law schools. Since it's a common practice, we've had to develop ways to evaluate *nuking,* starting with considering its source.

There are three types of people who tend to nuke law schools:

■ Administrators at other law schools who will slyly drop a "tidbit" about the shortcomings of School X. "That School X. Let me tell you, that school's nothing but a new building and a good PR job." Then they will add the caveat, "But you never heard it from me!"

■ Students who have highly charged, often negative comments about their own schools. "Boy, if I'd only known what a fleabag dump this place was before I got here I sure as heck would have headed elsewhere."

■ Students at other law schools, particularly students in the same geographical or tier ranking as the "nukee." "Have you been to School X yet? They are the biggest bunch of cutthroats you'd ever want to meet. I hear there was one student who had gotten into a car accident and had some book the rest of the class needed. Well, to make a long story short, they found him in his hospital room with the cord to his respirator 'accidentally' knocked out of its socket."

After sifting through the negatives, we concluded that some criticisms warrant investigation while others can be ignored. We sorted out the quality of commentary as follows:

1. *Administrators.* It is important to examine criticisms in light of the school issuing them. For the most part administrative criticisms are well-founded because no one wants to chance getting caught in a lie. We will investigate any claim from an administrator, regardless of its source. From our observation and from those of many admissions officers, admissions officers tend to "hang out" in tiers and geographical regions, and to know the goings on of their "tier members" better than those of schools on the fringe.

2. *Students talking about their own schools.* Timing is everything when you encounter a law student. A bad day, a difficult exam, a failing grade, or a family problem can cloud his or her comment. We don't take anything at face value. If, for instance, a student feels that the faculty is lacking in quality, we ask for reasons and examples to substantiate this judgment. We will also seek out other students to see if they agree with this claim. Our aim is to find the common threads from a variety of students in order to weave a cogent picture of each school.

3. *Students at other law schools.* This is the group to be most wary of because, unlike their colleagues at the nukee school, they have nothing to lose, and if the damaging information is placed in the right (or wrong) hands their school may unjustly gain, particularly among rival schools competing for the same recruiters. Another problem even with the most objective of these critiques is that the source is secondary at best. And if you've ever played telephone you know how distorted and exaggerated comments can become.

HOW THE LAW SCHOOLS WERE SELECTED

In choosing the law schools to be included in this guide, it was first necessary to limit the number of schools, excluding the bulk of the nearly 200 law schools in the United States. The schools selected were judged by a number of criteria. In a utopian society, all law schools would be equal in facilities, faculty, students attracted, programs, placement services, financial aid, and reputation among recruiters. But we know that is just not the case. As a first standard for consideration, there are ABA-accredited law schools and non-ABA-accredited law schools. All of the schools considered for this book were ABA accredited, because without this accreditation you cannot take the bar examination in any but one state, California. Although there has been talk of California adopting this regulation, this loophole has resulted in a large number of non-ABA-accredited law schools in California.

Then we further limited the candidates to AALS-accredited law schools, which are all ABA accredited. But that is only the beginning. There are other factors that can point to a "top" law school, such as membership in the national honorary society, Order of the Coif, to which many, but not all, of the schools in this book belong. Success in placement and recruiter satisfaction with the schools were significant too, and we looked for wide geographic distribution.

At the end of elimination and selection, we had a final roster of 56 schools, approximately one-third of ABA law schools in the United States. Although you may think other schools should have been included or left out, these 56 all have very special qualities to offer the applicant. Our list of law schools may be divided into the following categories, although you must remember that institutions do, on occasion, move from one category to another.

BLUECHIPS

These schools seem to predate Socrates, to say nothing of the Socratic method. No matter what the applicant pools bring, these law schools will be unshakeable, meaning that their scores and other criteria will remain relatively constant. As the cost of a law school diploma began to soar, and some may argue even before this, more and more public law schools began entering the ranks of this elite bastion.

Interestingly, it is among this group that admissions officers will weigh other factors besides LSATs and grades, including personal statements and achievements, more heavily because, largely sought-after, they can be very choosy. Sometimes they will take a chance on an applicant who misses it by the numbers but has something special to offer in terms of commitment, background, and promise. Among this elite group are a few law schools who invite selected applicants for evaluative interviews.

Placement from these law schools generally serves all of its graduates regardless of rank (if rankings are even assigned), which alleviates many pressures among classmates who have all worked so hard to make it this far.

TOP-TIER OUTSKIRTERS

These schools hover near the top schools but depend heavily on trends, meaning that when the applicant pools fall, so do their scores. These are schools that most of us recognize by name. They are perhaps as outstanding in almost every respect as the Bluechips, with the exception of the strength of their recruiter magnetism. This fact assumes great importance when two applicants, one from a Bluechip and the other from an Outskirter are up for the same job, with the same "on paper" credentials sitting before a recruiter who did not attend either school. There is virtually no risk in attending and graduating from any school in this category. Their graduates are generally interchangeable with Bluechips, and occasionally, as mentioned above, graduates of these schools find that their school has become a Bluechip.

SECOND-TIER STRONGHOLDS

These schools may predate some Bluechips, but be it from a lack of word of mouth or because of geographical location, have failed to attract the attention of applicants and/or recruiters. Their programs tend to be highly practical. Some may refer to them as a "Black Letter Law School," meaning the school doesn't preach to higher theories of law but more to "the meat and potatoes." In a year of heavy applications, Bluechip and Outskirter applicants may count themselves fortunate to make it through these schools' admissions committees. Again, as in the Outskirter and Bluechip, you will have lost nothing by graduating from a Second-Tier Stronghold, particularly if you are in a good-sized city/ geographic region with only one law school.

UP-AND-COMING SCHOOLS

Our favorite category, these too may have been around for a century or more without becoming a law school brand name outside of their immediate area, or they may be young schools, strategically positioned in major cities, that have risen in the eclipsing shadow of a Bluechip or an Outskirter. But their programs have finally fallen into place, and these "undervalued" schools are headed for a meteoric rise, as may already have been evidenced by major upswings in applications, LSAT scores, GPAs, and/or recruiter recognition.

Many of these schools have among the most innovative curricula in the country, with young, dynamic faculties who are short on "Name" power but make up for it with charisma and an unadulterated passion for teaching law. It should be noted that many of these schools suffer from the raiding of their up-and-coming faculty members, who are lured away by Bluechips and Outskirters. They are exciting places to learn the law. However, sometimes recruiter interest hasn't caught up to that of the applicant pool, so it is wise to consider what you want from a law school before you plunge in.

HOW TO READ THE SCHOOL PROFILES

Beginning on page 1 are the detailed profiles of the law schools selected as leaders by the authors of this book. The schools appear alphabetically by name. Each profile follows a standard format, with headings and symbols indicating different categories of information. Every profile begins with a "Report Card" that summarizes the school data and includes rankings, admissions difficulty, and reputation among recruiters. The rest of the profile, organized under headings such as Admissions, Academics, and the like, discusses the information in depth. The following is a detailed outline of the profile structure.

REPORT CARD

The Report Card is both a preview of what is developed more fully in the profile and a compilation of all the essential data the reader is likely to want at a glance.

Admissions. The degree of difficulty of gaining admission to the school is rated on a scale of one to five, with five indicating the most selective schools. Figures are given for the number of applicants (in the most recent year for which data are available) and for the number who achieved acceptance. Also noted are the number of transfer applicants, the number of applicants accepted, the mean LSAT score of first-year students, and those students' mean GPA.

Academics. The most recent available figure is given for the percentage of graduating students who pass state bar exams on the first try. The faculty are given an overall grading from A+ to F with B− as a mean; these grades are based on student surveys and take into account factors such as quality of teaching and accessibility of professors after class. (Whenever student response to our surveys was too low to be statistically significant, the grade was recorded as N/A.) For schools that have been admitted to the Order of the Coif, an honorary society of law schools, the words "Order of the Coif" and the year in which the school was inducted are given.

Student Enrollment. Figures are given for the total numbers of full-time and part-time students, the percentage of women and minorities in the student body, and the average age of the entering class.

Physical Environment. The school's environment is characterized as urban (big city, medium city, or small city), suburban, rural, or college town. Campus safety is rated as excellent, very good, good, fair, or marginal, based on factors such as lighting, security guards, availability of escort services, and safety record. A handicapped accessibility rating is shown using one to five international handicapped symbols, with five being best. Factors considered include ramps, terrain, external accessibility, and interior/classroom accessibility.

Placement. From one to five stars (five being best) are awarded for the school's reputation among recruiters. Also listed is the median salary earned by graduates at their first jobs.

Law school ratings were determined by surveying 764 legal recruiters with a 39.4% response rate.

Finances. The most recent available figures are given for tuition and total costs, for both state residents and nonresidents.

Student Life. The symbols show a one-to-five ranking (with five being best) for extracurricular activities, based on student surveys. Also listed are popular "after-hours" student hangouts.

Prominent Alumni/ae. When available, names of distinguished graduates are listed, along with indications of their major achievements.

PROFILE TEXT

The text portion of each profile is divided into seven sections, several of which are introduced by graphic symbols. Each section provides an in-depth discussion of one aspect of the school, as follows:

Insider Information. This section (introduced by an "ear" logo) provides a concise "insider's" guide, combining the perspectives of students, administrators, and campus recruiters. It tells what's important to know about the school, what's current—and what's changing.

Admissions. This section shows how the admissions officers at each school rank the various criteria for admission—in other words, what factors they consider most important. It also lists application deadlines and fees, describes minority recruitment programs and tells how each admissions criterion is viewed by the admissions committee.

Physical Environment. This section gives a bird's-eye view of the law school in the context of the university. It describes the facilities, provides in-depth information about security, presents various cost-effective housing options, and tells whether students need to bring a car to school.

Financial Grid. This section shows—in graphic, chart form—the expenses students will likely face. The chart also lists different cost options for students on low, medium, and high budgets.

Academics. This section seeks to assess strengths and weaknesses of the academic programs and faculty. It also covers grading systems, joint degree programs, and other academic features.

Student Life. This section describes opportunities for social activities, sports, and the like, including school- and student-sponsored special events.

Placement. This section gives facts and figures on how the school's graduates fare in the job market. It also describes any school-sponsored job-finding programs.

CHOOSING A LAW SCHOOL

Besides reviewing catalogs and using a guide like this one, there are other avenues for exploring law school possibilities. The following sections will supply you with some pointers on investigating schools that may prove suitable to your needs and will outline the admissions procedures to be followed once you make your school selections.

Road Shows: how not to get lost in the crowd

Each year the LSAC/LSAS sponsors law school forums, held in large hotels and/or convention centers in major cities around the country, including New York, Boston, Washington, D.C., and Los Angeles. To hopeful applicants, this may be the only time to come in contact with a flesh-and-blood representative from the schools they have wanted to learn about. To harried admissions officers, many of whom bring support staffs consisting of students, alumni/ae, and/or law school professors, these frenzied settings frequently referred to as "road shows," can be high-stress experiences. Still, law school forums can be an effective way to learn something about distant or unfamiliar schools.

Believe it or not, admissions officers want you to apply to their schools as much as you want to get into them. Remember, the more applicants that apply to a school, the more the general public (at least a good percentage of the following year's applicant pool) will perceive that school as being popular and more important, worthy of that popularity.

Road shows can be an eye-opening experience to a prospective student who suddenly finds him- or herself crammed into a room with thousands of other hopefuls, all of whom are competing for the same admissions officers' attention. As you might expect, the more popular schools' tables tend to be the most difficult to get near while other tables draw little interest (this also depends on the site of the forum relative to the school), regardless of the size of the crowd. To prevent congestion, many of the more popular or "cornerstone" schools are spaced far apart from one another.

How can you make the most of these road shows? The following is a list of suggested dos and don'ts when attending a show.

■ **Don't** expect an admissions officer to know your exact chances for getting into his or her school given your raw statistics (GPA, LSAT score[s]) or based on a thumbnail sketch of yourself and your educational background. When they talk to you, they still will not know what their complete applicant pool will be like, so any determination would be premature.

Admissions is far more complicated than number cutoffs, especially in view of the volatile swings in applications over the past two years. A school whose LSAT score was 34 a year ago may have had such a dramatic increase in applicants that the number is closer to 35 or 36 for your pool. Conversely, after anticipating an increase in applications, that same school may find that the percent of students who agree to attend, or its *yield*, has shrunk below anticipated averages, forcing it to take several students off its waiting list who have LSAT scores of 34 or lower.

■ **Don't** monopolize admissions officers. As a rule of thumb, admissions officers tire quickly of students who dwell on the same questions, usually those about LSAT scores and GPAs, and chances for acceptance. Being around the admissions officer longer and even getting him or her to remember your name is unlikely to affect your chances for admission. This is particularly true of applicants who rank far below the normal admissions standards for these schools.

■ **Don't** rely exclusively on the comments of students or the rest of the support staff that the admissions officer brings along to tout the school. This doesn't mean to ignore their laudatory comments. However, realize that these students are not always what is referred to as "representative." Besides, with an admissions officer or other school administrator lurking within earshot they aren't going to discuss, if even mention, any shortcomings that their school might have. Students are best questioned one on one in a private setting, if possible. Remember you aren't looking for "nuking" (see page viii), but objectively each school has areas that could use improvement, and you should be aware of them.

■ **Do** be polite, kind, and courteous and *never* interrupt admissions officers when they're giving answers to other prospective applicants. We have seen this happen on several occasions, and it will generally draw a *yes* or *no* from the administrator, or at worst will draw open fire in response to a perceived rudeness. You are going to be a lawyer and as such you should understand the meaning of decorum.

■ Be prepared. Read up on the schools before you ask questions. Try not to ask GPA/LSAT-type questions, but know your own background and reasons for studying law. Try to get past the surface and ask thoughtful questions about each school's programs. This is far more impressive to an admissions officer than, "What's your mean LSAT score?"

■ Relax. Be yourself. Don't allow anyone at the forum to intimidate you. This includes administrators and/or other applicants who are dying to share the fact that they pulled a 46 on the LSAT. "And to think I didn't study or want to go to law school! Lucky huh?"

■ Be adventurous. Go to a table from a school you haven't considered, but might have read about in this book or others. When we first began our search for the leading law schools we looked at each and every law school. Some critics said we should have cut immediately by GPA and LSATs, but we wanted to be egalitarian. Just as no applicant wishes to be "cut by the numbers," we didn't want to eliminate schools arbitrarily. We were pleasantly surprised to find a few schools that made our list that we might not have considered had we not stepped outside of the safe perimeters of "common perception."

Pre-law Advisors and How To Use Them

What is NAPLA or MAPLA, or SAPLA for that matter? NAPLA stands for the Northeast Association of Prelaw Advisors, MAPLA is Midwest, and so on. Each of these associations has members from universities and colleges in its geographical region, including pre-law advisors and law school personnel. At a recent NAPLA conference, pre-law advisors were treated to lectures by guest speakers on subjects specific to law school such as financial aid, admissions, and the role of women in the legal profession. It is an informal setting where law school admissions officers and pre-law advisors rekindle ties, and many of the law schools take the opportunity to hand out lists of last year's accepted students to each pre-law advisor.

If you think about it properly, your pre-law advisor is the representative from your college or university who has the access code to get the attention of law school admissions officers. More experienced advisors, and those from schools known to be "feeders" to the law schools, will often have better access than advisors from lesser known schools or new advisors. Just the same, all advisors have the chance to mingle and learn more about what the law schools want in terms of applicants.

Think of your advisor (if your school has one) as an agent who is representing you to the law schools. But before you go off annoying your advisor to "push you in" you should know some facts:

■ The best way for an advisor to build his or her reputation is to call the law schools sparingly and only with good reason. This means you should have done your homework thoroughly before you entered the advisor's office, because if you're "out of reach" for a law school, your advisor will lose credibility.

■ You should get to know your advisor as soon as you can. Although there is no required pre-law curriculum, the better he or she is acquainted with you as a person and more important as a student, the better he or she will be able to make a match between you and the law schools when the time arrives.

■ For older applicants who have been away from school, don't be afraid to go back to your alma mater for help from that school's pre-law advisor.

ADMISSIONS

As a prospective law school applicant, you should know that this is one of the more difficult times to be seeking admission. Many law schools have been experiencing a surge in applicants; interest in a legal career has broadened to include groups that wouldn't have considered the field a few years ago. Last year too, many schools got a higher yield from their acceptances, and must cut that number this year to counteract crowding. You will need to focus your efforts carefully in both selection of schools and the application itself to ensure ending up with a school that fits your needs and goals.

HIGHLY COMPETITIVE SCHOOLS

No matter what your qualifications, you will encounter steep competition at what are often known as "Top Twenty" schools. Of course, more than twenty schools think of themselves as part of this elite group, but you can get an idea of who belongs more or less in that tier by checking the Difficulty of Admission portion of the Report Card in the school profile section of this book.

In any case, you cannot assume acceptance at one of these schools just because your GPA and LSAT scores match their profile in the *Official Guide.* Only to consider schools in the Top Twenty would be foolhardy. Although you should not sell yourself short, it is crucial for you to give yourself several alternatives. The number of perfect LSAT scores coming into top tier schools increased greatly in 1989.

APPLICATIONS AND YOUR STATISTICS

In the sections to follow we will be considering the different elements of applying to law school and attempting to supply some useful indicators as to how you should handle each of them. One of the first questions that the applicant is likely to ask is "How important are the numbers?" or how much emphasis do the schools place on GPAs and LSAT scores? Do the schools cut "by the numbers," eliminating applicants and making admissions decisions primarily on college transcript grades and LSATs?

This, to some degree, depends on the individual law school's admissions committee. From the admissions grids presented in the *Official Guide,* it appears acceptances are based heavily on the LSAT and GPA, yet many top law schools refuse admission to a significant number of applicants in the highest category while accepting others from lower GPA/LSAT groupings.

Clearly, other criteria are involved. Some schools use an admissions index when determining which applicants they will automatically reject and on whom they will concentrate their evaluative efforts. GPA/LSAT scores are often used to determine index numbers with other components of the admissions package, like personal statements either factored in as a scaled grade, or left out until it is decided whether the applicant is "within reach."

There is no infallible way to tell whether you're within reach. Even an admissions officer, early in the process, can't tell you, because the entire applicant pool has not been reviewed. What you can do to increase your chances of making accurate evaluations of your *candidacy* is to check carefully the admissions statistics in the Report Card for the schools that interest you. After you've narrowed your choices to ten or twelve schools that appeal to you, compare GPA/LSAT scores, difficulty of acceptance, and number of applicants accepted—both among themselves and against your own realistic review of your qualifications. Also look at the admissions information in the school profile to see what weight and order is given to different factors of the applicant's background.

When you do decide to apply, you can help yourself a bit more by observing the rules suggested below.

1. APPLY EARLY. Write this down. On your books. On your notepads. Wherever it will help you to remember! Most admissions officers will tell you that by applying early you have a better chance of admission, especially for law schools on rolling admissions. Early in the cycle the admissions committee doesn't know if it will receive a sufficient number of superior applicants. A high volume of applicants doesn't always translate into applicants with high scores. Admissions committees may be willing to accept you earlier in the cycle if you have "last year's scores" before they have seen the pool with "this year's higher scores." **Remember:** To any admissions officer except those at an elite cluster of bluechips, an applicant in the hand is worth two that may or may not apply this year.
2. Apply with a strategic plan in mind. Your strategy should focus on your GPA and LSAT score(s), your personal achievements, and what you want out of law school and a career in the law. Before you can decide which schools to apply to, you should evaluate your record just as admissions officers will.

GPA: In assessing your undergraduate academic record, admissions officers will look first at your overall GPA. If you transferred, they will look at the average of all the schools you have attended. The second review will involve going over individual courses you've taken. Don't think you can fool law school admissions officers because you aced a class in astronomy that turned out to be a quick trip to the local planetarium and a short essay on Uranus. Admissions officers know that it was a gut, or if they don't, they'll check with your school's pre-law advisor.

Courses that show aptitude for skills crucial to legal study, like writing, may carry a little extra weight, but what the admissions officer is really trying to do is to decide whether or not you will make it through law school. No one wants to admit students who have limited or no chance for success. There are too many qualified applicants to waste a seat on someone who doesn't have what it takes to make it through the rigors of law school.

Where you went to school and what you majored in are also taken into consideration when looking at your GPA. Using provided indexes, the law school admissions officer can check the percentage of applicants from your college/university who scored above or below a given score on the LSAT. Many admissions officers will resort to college guides if they've never encountered any students from the applicant's school.

The Ivy League, the "Little Three," MIT, Stanford, and highly selective schools of this caliber may give applicants a slight edge, particularly at law schools that want to boast a percentage of students from these schools. As you get closer to the top tier law schools, however, you will find that where you went will not matter as much because these name undergraduate schools are often feeders, sending off hundreds of applicants to classes that have very limited space.

Last year, Harvard Law School received 400 applications from Harvard College alone. Obviously, not every applicant from Harvard College will get into Harvard Law. In distribution statistics of where students went to college, these name schools will generally have the greatest representation. This is not simply a prestige factor but also one of numbers. The more students that apply, the greater the statistical chance that more will be accepted. You will usually notice a heavy proportion of students from the law school's undergraduate college. Many admissions officers "trust the product" from these name colleges/universities based on the successes of their past students as opposed to schools that have sent few or no students in past years.

LSAT Scores: Most law schools average LSAT scores. A few schools noted in this book, however, do take the higher score regularly or in extenuating circumstances, like illness when you took the first test, or if your scores are five or more points apart. Other schools will look at LSAT scores on a case-by-case basis.

Just like GPAs, LSAT scores are used as predictors, to determine whether you will succeed during your first year of law school. Unlike GPAs, whose worth can vary based on where they were earned, every applicant must take the LSAT, making it the only measure of the applicant's aptitude that makes use of the same yard stick.

TEST PREPARATION COURSES—YES OR NO?

The LSAT is coming increasingly under fire because more affluent students are able to afford prep courses such as Stanley Kaplan or Princeton Review, which give them a decided advantage at least in acquainting them with the format and pacing them for the exam.

One rather savvy admissions officer has remarked that he advises applicants to forgo costly test prep courses and instead pay a friend $100 to nag them at regular intervals to study for the LSAT from a stack of old tests available to any applicant.

Our recommendation is to assess your own ability to prepare for this important exam, including your ability to stick to a study plan.

- Are you a highly self-motivated individual?
- Do you need reinforcement in the practice of taking standardized exams?
- Do you have several hundred dollars to spend?

The LSAT is certainly an important factor in law school admissions. And since most of you have taken either the SAT or the ACT to get into college you know by now that standardized tests are in a dead heat with having your teeth worked on with a rusty nail. If you aren't confident that you will sit down regularly with a test prep book or some old tests, and you have the money, maybe a prep course will be beneficial to you.

RESIDENCY

Where you live is a factor in admissions when it comes to public law schools, which are often mandated by state legislation to accept a significant percentage of in-staters each year. Many of these schools acknowledge that if you are a resident you will have a better shot than a nonresident with similar scores. Take advantage of this. If there's a public law school in your state, examine it closely and consider applying there.

TRANSFERRING BETWEEN LAW SCHOOLS

Students often think that if they didn't do well in college, they can go to a lower tier law school, get good grades, and "transfer up" after the first year. There are many reasons why this is a misconception. First of all, the attrition rate at the top tier schools is generally very low, so the need for transfers to fill empty spaces is also low. Your law school grades will be used as the major source for deciding your admissibility, but don't think your undergraduate GPA and LSAT scores won't be looked at as well. You shouldn't start a law school with the sole intention of transferring "up." Rather, you should assume wherever you choose to attend will be your future alma mater. In the event that you do wish to transfer you should know that often the school you transfer from must be AALS- or at least ABA-accredited.

WHERE SHOULD YOU APPLY?

There is, as we've mentioned, no hard and fast rule about exactly where you should apply or to how many schools. To give yourself the best chance for a satisfactory outcome, however, we recommend that you apply to at least one school in each of the following categories:

1. **Reach Schools.** Schools that are a real challenge for you. Harvard or Stanford may fit here for strong but not astounding records, whereas schools far below these may be your stretches if your GPA is around 2.9 and you have LSAT scores between 30 and 32. You may have extenuating circumstances to account for these scores. But putting yourself in the running with academic Olympic gold medalists, if your academic records show that you get out of breath walking around your backyard, can be a big mistake. Above all, be honest with yourself. The most compassionate admissions officer can overlook just so many problems before being forced to move on to applicants whose scores and achievements predict their future success as law students.
2. **Fit Schools.** Schools that you feel well qualified for and have chosen based on whatever quality that strikes you as appealing about them: admissions standards, programs, placement, location, the fact that students find the faculty attentive and easily accessible, or another important factor—you think you can afford this school. These schools will have GPA and LSAT means close to your own. Even given a more competitive applicant pool, you will be in contention because you will have written a well-thought-out essay that presents you in the best possible light.
3. **Safeties.** These schools may demand less than your record and achievements, but remember, you must be prepared to attend any one of them. As law school admissions become tougher and tougher, students are finding themselves fortunate to get into schools they might not even have considered when they were starting college.

RECOMMENDATIONS

How much do they count? This depends greatly upon the individual admissions committee. To be frank, some admissions officers have told us directly that recommendations mean very little in their evaluation of the candidate. They find most sound very much alike and that many professors, particularly at larger universities, use form letters.

Other admissions officers joke about the "code" in applicant descriptions given in recommendations. A "good candidate" may be interpreted as someone who is average, while "very good" may mean above average. Occasionally more evocative language like "an insightful and highly perceptive individual, capable of deductive reasoning and with a breadth of interests almost unparalleled by any undergraduate I have encountered in several years of teaching at this university," shows that the applicant is someone special.

Make sure to start early when deciding which faculty members you want to write your recommendations. If you are just out of college, this person should be an academic and know you well. The ideal recommender is someone who has taught you within your major on both the introductory and advanced level. This person will be in a far better position to evaluate your overall performance. If you have conducted research for a faculty member at your school, he or she is also an excellent candidate for a recommendation. For applicants who transferred during college or attended a two-year college, we suggest that you use recommendations from faculty members at your final school. For older candidates, recommendations from employers and/or colleagues may also be satisfactory.

PERSONAL STATEMENTS

How much will it help? Unquestionably, personal statements are important to admissions committees at all but a few law schools. We have heard from law schools across the prestige spectrum of candidates who do not possess the "paper" qualifications, but somehow come through in an essay that rings true or touches a chord in the admissions officer's heart. Sound corny? Maybe. But it happens. In a graduate school setting where students rarely have evaluative interviews, the personal statement is that opportunity on paper. Even for law schools that do not require personal statements, we recommend that you write one anyway. It can only help you.

Don't overdo it, however. Time and time again, we hear admissions officers talk about candidates who insist on sending additional information, be it a bound thesis, a play, or even a videotape. Most admissions committees are too overburdened to have the time to evaluate these "extras." You say, "That's not fair. I'm just trying to show that I'm special." That's fine, but think of it from an admissions officer's perspective. At a highly selective law school you may have as many as three to seven thousand applications to review and pass timely decisions on. Many of your staff members are overworked, and your eyes can only handle so much reading before letters start to blur. Is it fair to read Applicant X's dissertation on life before even opening Applicant Y's academic file?

So what do you, the applicant, do? You say what you have to say and you say it with wit and economy. By now we assume you've written a good number of papers in your college career. The essay should be taken just as seriously, if not more so, than your most important final paper for a humanities class you really wanted to ace. And remember, brevity isn't just the soul of wit; it's the key to an admissions officer's heart.

Just like any other part of the application, don't put this off until the last minute. You will need time between stages to make sure everything you put down on paper is concise but long enough to convey who you are, what you have accomplished, and most important, what you are going to do for others with your law degree.

Before you sit down to write the personal statement(s) consider the following:

1. **Know the programs at the schools where you are applying.** Anything you can glean from this, or any other book, on the law schools' programs will demonstrate a more than superficial interest in these schools to admissions officers. You should be able to weave one or more elements special to the school into your reasons for wishing to attend.

   Needless to say, reasons like "I feel the prestige afforded me from attending your law school will help me make heapa big bucks" are taboo.

2. **Know what it is about yourself that sets you apart from the pack.** What makes you the wonderful, caring individual you are today? Geographic diversity may come into play here. However, if you are from a major city like L.A. and you're applying to a law school in another major city like New York, it isn't as potent as if you are applying to New York from a rural community in the Midwest.

   You needn't have climbed Mt. Everest to write about what you've done with your time until now. Connect your goals with your accomplishments. If you already have a track record as a Peace Corps worker in an underserved village in Africa, show how this achievement has helped you to focus on your present goal of serving disadvantaged groups in the United States. Now, if you find a school where the programs are strong in the areas in which you have strong interests, you're halfway there.

3. **In preparing your essay, first outline, then draft, then take a pen/pencil to it.** Once again, economy is key. If you have said something in more than one way, get rid of that extra sentence or paragraph. Don't take up room just to fill a certain space. You are not being graded on the number of words produced in your personal statement.

4. **Proofread your essay until you never want to see it again.** Spellos, typos, any mistake you can think of, will not be taken lightly by admissions officers. This is your final product. A typo or spelling mistake on your draft is one thing. The final product is you, as you are representing yourself to the school and will be interpreted rightly or wrongly as how you will present yourself once you become an attorney. Have a friend check your essay. If that's not possible, take some time off from it and read it when you're fresh or bounce a pencil on each word. Mistakes can often go unnoticed when you want something finished after you've worked on it for a long time.

FINANCING LAW SCHOOL

Ten years ago, a legal education at a private law school may have set you back thirty thousand dollars. And even back then people were complaining. Today, if you're considering a private school situated in a high-rent/high-cost-of-living city, your three years could easily approach six figures, a sobering thought. It demonstrates, however, why we devoted so much time, energy, and space in this book to costs. Much of what you read about law schools, be it books or catalogs, deemphasizes the costs of attending, leaving information gaps that can bring nasty surprises when time for payment comes. The school profiles in this guide all include a finance grid designed to break your budget down into low, medium, and high annual totals, based on individual spending patterns. Information also appears on loans, loan forgiveness programs, and any other financial policies specific to a school.

We talked at length to financial aid officers at the schools to gain an accurate perspective on the cost of attending each institution. Many schools give financial estimates in their catalogs. The budgets at many of these schools, however, are pared so close to the bone that even the most ascetic student would be hard pressed to make it on these amounts alone. Whenever there was disagreement over the cost of a variable like housing or meal options, we used the higher estimate, because if you overestimate for the purpose of taking out loans you can always repay the money, but underestimating may force you into a very precarious position.

As a general rule you should figure more rather than less for incidental expenses like supplemental textbooks or a trip to visit a family member. Even an extra phone call can mean more to you when you're bogged down in the trenches of law school than you imagined when you were meticulously figuring out your budget.

EMPLOYMENT

Most of the law schools in this book offer some form of employment for their students, though many schools will not allow working, particularly during the first year of study.

LOANS

In the 1970s loans were looked upon as a last resort for financing a legal education. Students took out small loans with the expectation of repaying them shortly after graduating from school. In the 1980s loans became a standard element in paying for an education. In the 1990s loans are not only a way of life. For most law students, they are a means of survival.

Remember, too, that many of the loans you take out will carry origination fees that can amount to hundreds of dollars borrowed that you won't see.

Listed below are several loan programs, their eligibility, amount available, and repayment requirements. Application information for the programs will be readily available from any law school's financial aid office.

STAFFORD Loan   (Formerly Guaranteed Student Loan (GSL))

Eligibility: You must be taking at least six credits, be either matriculated or non-matriculated, a U.S. citizen or legal resident, maintain good academic standing, and demonstrate financial need.

Amount: Graduate and Professional school maximum: $7500/year. The total amount that can be borrowed (including all loans accruing from undergraduate study) is $54,750.

Repayment: You must begin repaying the loan six months after you are no longer a half-time student. There is a possible fifteen-year repayment plan.

PERKINS Loan   (Formerly National Direct Student Loan (NDSL))

Eligibility: You must be taking at least six credits, be matriculated, a U.S. citizen or legal resident, maintain good academic standing, and demonstrate financial need.

Amount: Variable, interest rate 5%. The total amount that can be borrowed for professional school is $18,000.

Repayment: You must begin repaying the loan nine months after you are no longer a half-time student. There is a possible fifteen-year repayment plan.

Supplemental Loan for Students   (SLS)

Eligibility: You must be taking at least six credits, be a U.S. citizen or legal resident, maintain good academic standing, and demonstrate financial need.

Amount: This award is designed to replace the expected amount of family contribution. The maximum you can borrow annually under this program is $4,000. It carries an interest rate of between 10–12%. The total amount you can borrow under the SLS is $20,000.

Repayment: You have to make quarterly interest payments while in school. Repayment begins six months after you are no longer a half-time student. There is a possible fifteen-year repayment plan.

Law Access Loans   (LAL)

Eligibility: You must be taking at least six credits, never have defaulted on a loan, and undergo a credit check. This loan is available to students and parents of law students.

Amount: The maximum you can borrow on LAL is $10,000 a year or a total of $30,000.

Repayment: You begin paying interest while in school. Repayment begins nine months after you are no longer at least a half-time student. Parental Loan Access Repay starts sixty days after check disbursal.

Consern Loans   (1 (800) 331-5811)

Eligibility: You must be taking at least six credits. This loan is not need-based. You must undergo a credit check, and there is a $45 application fee.

Amount: Loan limits $1500 or $15,000/year.

Repayment: Variable interest rate.

THE TOP LAW SCHOOLS

UNIVERSITY OF ALABAMA
School of Law

BOX 870382
TUSCALOOSA, ALABAMA (AL) 35487-0382
(205) 348-5440

❧ REPORT CARD ❧

ADMISSIONS
SELECTIVITY

Applicants: 850; Accepted: 358
Transfer Applications: 1; Accepted: 1
LSAT Mean: 36 GPA Mean: 3.4

ACADEMICS
Order of the Coif: (1969)
Alabama State Bar Passage (first try): 90%
Faculty to Student Ratio: 1:18
Quality of Teaching: B
Faculty Accessibility: B+

PHYSICAL ENVIRONMENT
Location: Small City
Safety: Good
HA: ♿ ♿ ♿ ♿ ♿

STUDENT ENROLLMENT
Class Size: 180 (full-time)
Women: 32%   Minorities: 10%
Average Age of Entering Class: 23

PLACEMENT
REPUTATION ☆ ☆ ⚡

Recruiters: 75 +
Starting Salary Median Range: $25–30,000

FINANCES
Tuition: $2354 (R); $4890 (NR)
Average Total Cost: $7764 (R); $10,300 (NR)

STUDENT LIFE
RATING ☺ ☺ ☺ ☺ ☺

After Hours: Harry's Bar

PROMINENT ALUMNI/AE
Include: Justice Hugo Black of the U.S.
Supreme Court, 22 United States Circuit
and District Court Judges, 45 Alabama
Supreme Court and Court of Appeals
Judges, 17 Governors and Lt. Governors,
28 United States Senators and
Representatives

INSIDER INFORMATION Located on the banks of the Black Warrior River, Tuscaloosa is a small city rich in Indian history. Founded in 1872, the University of Alabama School of Law is in a multilevel building situated on a twenty-acre landscaped site adjacent to the main university campus. Recruiters have noted the fine research capabilities of Alabama graduates. This is undoubtedly due in part to student participation in the Alabama Lawyer's Research

Service (ALRS), which operates through the school's Clinical Law Program. The ALRS provides research services for members of the Bar throughout the state. The Research Service has positions available to law students, the nature of the job and pay based on the students' academic achievements and research experience. The Clinical Program also allows students to practice law under the supervision of an attorney.

The school offers a surprising diversity of courses, including Sports Law, World Peace and Conflict Resolution, and Air Pollution. In The Law in Literature, students study works of literary merit from such authors as Dostoyevesky, Miller, Faulkner, Kafka, and Tolstoy. Courses on Real Estate Practice Law and Food and Drug Law are offered as well.

Students find the school's placement capabilities to be good, but regional, with 91% of graduates practicing law in the South.

ADMISSIONS

CRITERIA

LEVEL 1:   Grade Point Average; LSAT Score

LEVEL 2:   Quality of undergraduate curriculum/coursework completed

LEVEL 3:   Quality/reputation of college/university

LEVEL 4:   Work experience

LEVEL 5:   Recommendations; personal essay

MINORITY RECRUITMENT PROGRAM

Yes. Members of the Admissions Committee and other faculty members, working with the Black Law Student Association, visit with small groups of potential minority students, both on campus and off campus, to explain the admissions process and answer questions concerning law school and the legal profession.

ABOUT THE APPLICATION

DEADLINE FOR FILING: 3/1

FEE: $20.00

LSAT: School takes the highest of the applicant's scores.

RECOMMENDED COURSES PRIOR TO MATRICULATING: Courses that develop analytical and writing skills.

PERSONAL STATEMENT: "An exceptional personal statement may assist a border-line candidate in the admissions process."

INTERVIEW: Not required or recommended. If visiting, the Sheraton Capstone Inn, located across the street from the law school, is recommended.

ADMISSIONS TIPS: "Applicants should carefully read the application materials and Law School Catalog and early in the process contact the Admissions Office to clarify any questions they have concerning their applications. Applicants should contact their university's pre-law advisor early in their junior year and begin seriously reviewing law schools and the admissions process. A knowledgeable pre-law advisor can be invaluable in this process.

CONTACT: Steven Emens, Associate Dean.

PHYSICAL ENVIRONMENT

Located on a twenty-acre landscaped site adjacent to the University of Alabama's main campus, the law school is set apart in its own three-story facility. This law center is completely self-contained with all classrooms, library, student computer rooms, and moot court rooms located on site. The entire building is wheelchair-accessible, and currently the law school has several handicapped individuals enrolled. The area around U Alabama is considered relatively safe. There is no escort service, but the parking lot is close and it is easy to find people to walk out with you if you are there late at night.

The university's recreation center, which provides aerobics, weights, Nautilus, track, basketball, racquetball and sauna, an aquatic center, and intramural fields, is within a few blocks of the law school on the university campus.

Although on-campus accommodations are guaranteed, less than 1% of the class live in school-owned housing. There is a wide range of housing available, but students advise looking three months early for the best choices. The most cost-effective accommodations are for a single student sharing expenses with a roommate; for a married student with no children, a one-bedroom apartment; and for a married student with children, a two- or three-bedroom apartment. A car is recommended.

FINANCES

BUDGET	LOW	MEDIUM	HIGH
Tuition (Resident) **Tuition (Nonresident)**	$2354 $4890	$2354 $4890	$2354 $4890
Books	$500	$500	$500
Living Accommodations (9 months)	Shared House $1575	On-Campus* $1610	One-Bedroom Apt. $2250
Food	Meal Plan (15 wk) $1195	Groceries** $1800	Cafeteria $3024
Miscellaneous	$600	$900	$1800
Transportation	Car $600	Car $600	Cabs $800
TOTAL (R) TOTAL (NR)	$6824 $9360	$7764 $10,300	$10,728 $13,264

* Shared Apt.: $1800

** Restaurants $2520

Employment During School: Recommended only after first semester. Work-study jobs are available to eligible students at $3.45 an hour. Paid positions with the Alabama Lawyer Research Service are also available to law students.

Scholarships: The school offers merit and need-based scholarships. Merit scholarships are contingent upon remaining in the top 20% of the class.

School Loan Program (Exclusive of Perkins Money): Yes. The law school has limited loan emergency funds available, generally for students who have successfully completed at least one semester of law school.

Loan Forgiveness Program: No

Students Requesting Aid: 36%; of these, 36% receive aid.

Students Indebted Upon Graduation: 36%

Average Loan Indebtedness: $23,000

ACADEMICS

First year students attend only required courses, which are taught mainly through the case method. During the first semester of the second year, there are three required courses: Constitutional Law II, Evidence, and Federal Income Tax I; during the second semester, one required course: The Legal Profession. The third-year curriculum consists of all elective work. Included in the elective course selection is the Clinical Law Program, which was developed over fifteen years ago. The program enables third-year students to gain hands-on experience by participating in court cases while under the supervision of the program's attorneys.

Faculty members have office hours in the law school building and are considered to be generally accessible. Although the quality of lectures here varies, most are very interesting and instructive. Faculty stars include Charles Gamble (Evidence), Nathaniel Hansford (Commercial Transactions), Francis McGovern (Torts and Alternative Dispute Resolution), Peter Alces (Commercial Transactions), Harry Cohen (Property), Tom Jones (Decedent's Estates), and Manning Warren (Securities Regulations). The grading system at the school is on a scale running from 0 to 4.0. It should be noted that students who expect to receive credit for being in residence must enroll in the summer session for at least five hours.

JOINT DEGREE/GRADUATE DEGREE PROGRAMS

Joint Degrees: JD/MBA; JD/MPA (Master of Public Administration).
Graduate Degress: LLM (Taxation).

STUDENT LIFE

Students find the social life at the University of Alabama excellent. "We students are keenly aware of the traditions at this school and can be summed up thusly: When we study, we study hard and when we party, we party even harder!" There are several social events, including Homecoming Week and Law Week, which occurs in the spring and culminates in the Barrister's Ball. Other activities are organized by the Student Bar Association. There are also socials, which the students call "swaps," with undergraduate sororities.

Students find that there is a competitive, yet friendly, atmosphere. They will generally work together, and the upperclassmen will help the first-year students.

PLACEMENT

Although students consider the Placement Office to be most helpful for those in the top 10–25% of the class, 98% of graduates are employed upon graduation.

PREPARATION

Students are prepared by the Placement Office through videotaped mock interviews and résumé-writing seminars. Students are also encouraged to participate in the school's four recruiting conferences: Southeastern Law Placement Consortium (SELP), Mid-South Law Placement Consortium, Southeastern Law Schools Minority Job Fair, and Southeastern Public Interest Job Fair.

WHERE/WHAT GRADUATES PRACTICE

A. 1% Northeast; 91% South; 1% Midwest; 7% Other.
B. N/A Sole Practitioner; N/A Small Firms; N/A Medium Firms; N/A Large Firms; 18% Clerkships; 3% Graduate Degrees; 3% Military; 7% Governmental Agencies; 3% Corporations.

4400 MASSACHUSETTS AVE., N.W.
WASHINGTON, D.C. 20016-8085
(202) 885-2606

REPORT CARD

ADMISSIONS

SELECTIVITY

Applicants: 5800; Accepted: N/A
Transfer Applications: 85; Accepted: 15
LSAT Mean: 36 GPA Mean: 3.4

ACADEMICS

Faculty to Student Ratio: N/A
Quality of Teaching: **A**
Faculty Accessibility: **B+**

PHYSICAL ENVIRONMENT

Location: Suburban/Large-Sized City
Safety: Good
HA:

STUDENT ENROLLMENT

Class Size: 270 (full-time); 80 (part-time)
Women: 52%   Minorities: 18%
Average Age of Entering Class: 24

PLACEMENT

REPUTATION

Recruiters: 300
Starting Salary Median: (small firms)
$27,000; (medium firms) $42,000; (large firms) $54,500

FINANCES

Tuition: $12,866 (full-time); $477/credit hr. (part-time)
Total: $24,566 (full-time)

STUDENT LIFE

RATING ☺ ☺ ☺

After Hours: Chicago's, City's, Quigley's

PROMINENT ALUMNI/AE

Include: Senator Robert Byrd, Representative Thomas Downey, Reginald Walton, Assoc. Director of Bureau of State and Local Affairs, Office of National Drug Control Policy (second in command to "Drug Czar" William Bennett)

INSIDER INFORMATION Washington College of Law at American University has long had to contend with the eclipsing shadows of Georgetown and George Washington, but there is room for more than two strong law schools in D.C., and if you want a more suburban setting, far safer than either Georgetown or GW, WCL may be the place for you. So, let's take a cab ride together, up Embassy Row, passing the statue of Winston Churchill on the grounds of the British embassy, and through American University's sprawling campus. We have arrived at WCL.

The current law school building is dark and confining, but a new structure will be built shortly. Students here find that the school's strongest point lies in its wealth of clinics, including the Appellate Advocacy Clinic, which allows students to take an appellate case, in both state and federal courts, from start to finish under the close supervision of what students believe to be some of the school's best faculty members. Unfortunately, entry into the clinics is through a lottery, and not all students are able to get into the clinics of their choosing. WCL also has an Independent Study and Externship Program, which includes the Program for Advanced Studies in the Federal Regulatory Process offered each summer. This program is taught by sixty different senior level officials from the federal government and their private sector counterparts who formulate and implement regulatory decisions. WCL also has one of the nation's largest international law programs.

Recruiters are impressed with the most recent graduates of the school, and although many devote the bulk of their recruiting schedules to GULC and then GW, more and more are giving WCL students a chance. Says one, "They make very good candidates, particularly those at the top of their class."

ADMISSIONS

CRITERIA

LEVEL 1: Grade Point Average; quality of undergraduate curriculum/course work completed; quality/reputation of college/university; LSAT score

LEVEL 2: Work experience; personal essay; recommendations

MINORITY RECRUITMENT PROGRAM

Yes; through Minority Affairs Coordinator.

ABOUT THE APPLICATION

DEADLINE FOR FILING: 3/1

FEE: $35

LSAT: "If less than six points between highest and lowest, we use the average. If six points or more, we take the highest."

RECOMMENDED COURSES PRIOR TO MATRICULATING: N/A

PERSONAL STATEMENT: "It would be used as part of (the) total application. A poor personal statement is likely to adversely affect the reader."

INTERVIEW: Not required or recommended. However, if you visit the school, Holiday Inn-Chevy Chase and Holiday Inn-Georgetown have been recommended.

ADMISSIONS TIPS: "Pay attention to personal statement. Be sure to explain what makes you special/different/interesting. File early."

CONTACT: Ms. Mary Davis Upton, Director of Admissions

PHYSICAL ENVIRONMENT

Unlike neighboring Georgetown and George Washington law schools, this school is surrounded by not only a large university but also a very safe and affluent suburban neighborhood. Students find that the confining law school and law library facilities are one of the school's only weaknesses. However, a new law school will be built in the next two or three years; the new facility is planned to be two or three times the size of the present building. Commenting on handicapped accessibility, one administration official said, "Our school is all in one building (except for placement and admissions) and is totally accessible." Security guards are available as an escort service.

Adjacent to the law school is the recently built athletic center. There are racquetball and squash courts, a swimming pool and weight rooms, and many law students take advantage of this facility.

On-campus housing is not guaranteed, and only 8% of the students live in school-owned accommodations. The most cost-effective accommodations are for a single student, a shared house or apartment or a dorm room; for a married student with no children, an apartment in the suburbs; and for a married student with children, an apartment in suburbs. Whether or not to have a car depends on where you live.

FINANCES

BUDGET	LOW	MEDIUM	HIGH
Tuition (full-time)	$12,866	$12,866	$12,866
Books	$475	$475	$475
Living Accommodations (9 months)	Shared House* $3375	On-Campus $4700	One-Bedroom Apt. $5400
Food	Groceries** $2300	Cafeteria $2700	Restaurants $3500
Miscellaneous	$2000	$2700	$3500
Transportation	Mass Transit $900	Car $1125	Taxis $1350
TOTAL	$21,916	$24,566	$27,091

* Shared Apartment: $3800

** Meal Plan (19 meals/wk): $1966

Employment During School: Only recommended in second and third years. Work-study is a need-based program. There are other part-time jobs at the school, and many of the students work part-time in law firms and federal agencies.

Scholarships: School offers need-based scholarships. Merit scholarships are not available.

School Loan Program (Exclusive of Perkins Money): Yes. The Alumni Loan Program, a small loan program designed to help second- and third-year students for whom no other financial aid seems appropriate, makes loans averaging $1500 a year available. Interest is 7%.

Loan Forgiveness Program: The school is planning on offering it in the future, but the program has not been implement yet.

Students Requesting Aid: 45%; of these, 35% receive grants, 70% loans.

Students Indebted upon Graduation: 70%

Average Loan Indebtedness: $34,000

ACADEMICS

All first-year courses are required and are taught using the case method. Students find the first-year classes larger then they would like but still feel that they receive enough individual attention, particularly in the Legal Method seminar, which has fewer than twenty students. Most students enter the Moot Court Competition during the first year and find it to be a good experience. Students also think that the legal writing course given to first-year students is a great help. Says one second-year student, "Although the course is time consuming, it pays big dividends."

WCL excels in International Law and has a field study offshoot in this area. Other specialties or strengths are Comparative International Law, Public Interest Law, Tax Law, Trial Advocacy, and Women/Women's Rights. There is an ample number of courses to choose from during the second and third years as well as clinical opportunities in the Woman and Law Clinic and Lawyering Process, a required seminar. WCL also offers externships with government agencies and opportunities for faculty-supervised independent study.

Faculty members are considered overall very good and willing to meet with students, although at times students have found them to be somewhat intimidating, particularly during the first year. Faculty stars include Ira Robbins, Herman Schwartz, and Paul Rice (Evidence) and Burt Wechesler (Federal Courts).

JOINT DEGREE PROGRAMS

JD/MS (Justice Administration); JD/MBA (International Affairs)

STUDENT LIFE

Students feel that AU has an excellent academic atmosphere. Although people work hard, it is very noncompetitive. "People here are willing to give you notes from a missed class or to trade outlines." AU has three student-run journals—*The Law Review*, *The Journal of International Law and Policy*, and *The Administrative Law Journal*—that provide students an opportunity to become part of the publishing process.

Groups like Phi Delta Phi schedule many different events, including ski trips. The school holds an annual picnic in September, which has been found to be quite successful. Washington has a number of bars and restaurants, and often a large group gathers at a local bar in Georgetown. In addition, there are many private parties.

PLACEMENT

Approximately 60% of students are placed right after graduation.

PREPARATION

Students are prepared by the Placement Office through videotaped mock interviews, interviewing techniques sessions, and résumé-writing seminars. There are also panels in all areas of the practice of law.

WHERE/WHAT GRADUATES PRACTICE

A. 20.6% Northeast; 69.6% South; 3.3% West Coast; 3.3% Midwest; 2% Other.
B. 4% Sole Practitioner; 15% Small Firms; 20% Medium Firms; 15% Large Firms; 12% Clerkships; 2% Graduate Degrees; 1% Military; 21% Governmental Agencies; 9% Corporations.

BAYLOR UNIVERSITY
School of Law

1400 SOUTH 5TH STREET
WACO, TEXAS (TX) 76798
(817) 755-1911

REPORT CARD

ADMISSIONS
SELECTIVITY 🎓 🎓 🎓 🎓

Applicants: 939; Accepted: N/A
Transfer Applications: 40; Accepted: 6
LSAT Mean: 38 GPA Mean: 3.55

PLACEMENT
REPUTATION ★ ★ ★ ✰

Recruiters: 200
Starting Salary Range: $38,000–48,000

ACADEMICS

Texas Bar Passage (first try): 94%
Faculty to Student Ratio: N/A
Quality of Teaching: **B+**
Faculty Accessibility: **A−**

FINANCES

Tuition: $6240
Average Total Cost: $12,727.50

PHYSICAL ENVIRONMENT

Location: Small City
Safety: Fair
HA: ♿ ♿ ♿ ♿

STUDENT LIFE
RATING ☺ ☺ ☺ ☺

After Hours: George's, Bill Bill's, Kelley's

STUDENT ENROLLMENT

Class Size: 77
Women: 40%   Minorities: 1.3%
Average Age of Entering Class: 24

PROMINENT ALUMNI/AE

Include: Leon Jaworski, Governor Ride

INSIDER INFORMATION

As one third-year student stated, "Baylor's goal is essentially twofold: 1) to ensure that its students pass the Bar, and 2) to ensure that the day after graduation, a Baylor alumni has the technical ability to try a case in court." Both of these goals are fully achieved by the school. For several years, Baylor has had the highest Texas Bar passage rate of any other local law school. Its graduates are well-known and are lauded by Texas-based recruiters for their courtroom abilities. The latter is due in part to the school's Practice Court Program, which has been highly praised as aggressively giving the students tremendous hands-on legal experience.

A unique aspect of the school is that its academic year is divided into quarters, as opposed to semesters. The fact that the law school is on this system and the main campus on a semester-system does, at times, cause problems with financial aid and the bookstores. However, the students don't advocate changing this system, which, most agree, provides greater scheduling flexibility. Because the system allows them to enroll in more classes per year than schools with the semester system, students can enroll in a wide variety of classes. Students do warn, however, that the grades at Baylor are technically low and it is important to consider this if you plan on transferring.

Because the school has an open-door policy, professors don't keep office hours and are supposed to be available at all times. Approximately 90% of the professors are found to be generally available.

ADMISSIONS

CRITERIA

LEVEL 1: Grade Point Average; quality of undergraduate curriculum/course work completed; quality/reputation of college/university; LSAT score

LEVEL 2: Personal Essay

LEVEL 3: Recommendations

MINORITY RECRUITMENT PROGRAM

No.

ABOUT THE APPLICATION

DEADLINE FOR FILING: 3/1 for fall quarter; 11/1 for admission into spring quarter; 1/1 for admission into summer quarter.

FEE: $25

LSAT: School takes an applicant's highest score.

RECOMMENDED COURSES PRIOR TO MATRICULATING: Accounting, philosophy, logic and reason, and English

PERSONAL STATEMENT: The personal statement is very important in admissions. A striking essay can push a borderline applicant into the admit category. The personal statement should not exceed two pages. It should be brief and concise. You should also mention any extenuating circumstances, like being sick when you took the LSAT or having taken a semester off.

INTERVIEW: Not part of admissions. If visiting, the Sheraton Inn and the Hilton are recommended.

ADMISSIONS TIPS: Apply early and read the application thoroughly. Recommendations should come from individuals in the legal profession. If this isn't possible, then submit a recommendation from one lawyer and two professors.

CONTACT: Becky Beck, Director of Admissions

PHYSICAL ENVIRONMENT

The school is housed in its own building, Morrison Constitutional Hall, completed in 1955. The first floor of the three-story building contains a courtroom-auditorium, the Frank M. Wison Rare Book Room, four classrooms, and locker rooms; the second floor, administrative offices, the M.C. and Mattie Caston Law Library, and the student lounge; and the third level, faculty offices and faculty library. The Advocacy wing, completed in 1985, includes a placement office, four small courtrooms, and interviewing rooms.

Safety in the area of the school is considered fair, but the perimeters of the campus are more dangerous. There is no escort service for the law students, but two patrol cars travel around the campus twenty-four hours a day, and there are call boxes. Furthermore, the law school building is self-contained, and the area surrounding it is well lit.

The school does not have a shuttle bus, and public transportation will not bring you that close to the campus. Practically every student has a car; parking is a problem here because students have to compete with undergraduates for spots.

Students say that school-owned housing is not available to the law students. This is due in part to the fact that the undergraduates are required to stay in the dorms their first year. The favorite form of housing is an apartment and is more affordable outside of Waco because competition with the undergrads there pushes the prices up.

Handicapped accessibility is good. The building has ramps, elevators, and accessible restrooms. However, because of the split-level floors, a handicapped individual would find it difficult to get to some of the classrooms readily.

FINANCES

BUDGET	LOW	MEDIUM	HIGH
Tuition	$6240	$6240	$6240
Books	$500	$500	$500
Living Accommodations (9 months)	Shared House $1800	Shared Two-bdrm. Apt. $2250	One-Bedroom Apt. $3150
Food	Groceries $1950	Meal Plan (5/wk)/Groceries $2152.50	Restaurants $4914
Miscellaneous*	$800	$1000	$1200
Transportation	Car $585	Car $585	Car $585
TOTAL	$11,875	$12,727.50	$16,589

* The primary source of miscellaneous costs is "copy costs," or those expenses incurred from photocopying at a nickel a page. This can add up, especially in courses such as Constitutional Law in which the professor requires students to be as up-to-date as possible, and photocopying of recent articles is necessary.

Employment During School: Not recommended in the first year. However, college work-study is available for all eligible students.

Scholarships: Baylor law school has an extensive scholarship program, with a total scholarship budget of about $350,000 per year. The school offers scholarships, which generally range from $710 to $1420 per quarter, and are usually awarded for three quarters. Scholarships are conditional on the recipient's doing high-grade work as a law student and are usually renewed if the student has a quality record. In general, students with a GPA of 3.0 or a B receive a half-tuition scholarship. Awards for specific achievement generally range from $100 to $1000 and are awarded annually.

School Loan Program (Exclusive of Perkins Money): Yes, Baylor Revolving Loans. It should be noted that students have expressed frustration with the Financial Aid Office. The office acts as a middleman between the lending institution and the student. Substantial delays in receiving funds have been known to occur. This, however, is improving.

Loan Forgiveness Program: No

Students Requesting Aid: N/A

Average Loan Indebtedness: N/A

ACADEMICS

The course work is considered to be very defendant-oriented with an emphasis on Texas Law. Students feel the curriculum is weaker in tax and international law, stronger in litigation and advocacy. The case method is employed in the majority of the courses, particularly in the first six quarters. Other methods of instruction are used where appropriate. In practice courses, for example, students are given assignments that resemble the type of problems a practicing attorney encounters daily. Practice court, a six-month course required of each third-year student, is designed to equip the Baylor Law graduate for the complexities of practice in the Texas courts. Not only is intensive training in procedural law given, but under the guidance of an instructor, the student also has the opportunity to try cases based upon factual situations. Clinical programs are also available; they deal with legal aid work at the Waco Legal Services Office and Criminal Law through the McLennan County District Attorney's Office.

Star faculty include Angus McSwain (Property) and Michael Morrison (Torts).

As noted before, grades tend to be rather low here. The average grade given is a C+ with students finding that it is certainly not impossible to flunk out.

SPECIAL PROGRAMS

A special six-year BA/JD or BBA/JD program is available. Students who have attended the College of Arts and Sciences or School of Business at Baylor for three academic years and who have completed the prescribed courses for the BA or BBA degree, are, upon successful completion (with a graduation average) of the first year's work in the School of Law, eligible to receive the undergraduate academic degree. After that, the JD degree can be secured by completing all the requirements for that degree.

STUDENT LIFE

Small classes are considered to promote closeness. Everyone knows everyone. "You are assigned a law buddy to help you when you start. They give you outlines and notes." It should be noted, however, that although the students are "not so cutthroat that they would steal someone's books," they are very competitive. This is prompted by the relatively low grades given and the fact that any student receiving a grade point average of at least 3.0 or a B receives a half-tuition scholarship. As one student put it, "Everyone is gunning for those scholarships." The Baylor University Student Bar Association and National Law Fraternities are among the student organizations at the school.

PLACEMENT

Students consider placement good, but very regional and specifically Texas-oriented. The majority of the school's graduates practice in Texas.

The school maintains an independent Placement Office. The university's Placement Center is also available to law students. Employment interviews are primarily in the fall. Austin and Dallas are the prime opportunity areas, and they interview heavily at Baylor. Outside of the school's immediate area, Houston and San Antonio also interview extensively at Baylor.

Students express satisfaction with the office, but are frustrated that it is mostly large firms that come looking for students in the top 25% of the class. They suggest that the office work on getting small firms from medium-sized towns to interview and concentrate on the 75% of the class that are now neglected.

PREPARATION

The Placement Office maintains a bulletin board of employment listings from many law firms that are not able to interview personally at the school. Information concerning government-related law practice, legal aid, and armed services careers is also provided. Information about letter and résumé writing is available, and mock interviews are held.

Boston College
Law School

885 CENTRE STREET
NEWTON, MASSACHUSETTS (MA) 02159
(617) 552-4350

❧ REPORT CARD ❧

ADMISSIONS
SELECTIVITY 🎓 🎓 🎓 🎓

Applicants: 5813; Accepted: 1004
Transfer Applications: 75; Accepted: 6
LSAT Mean: 40 GPA Mean: 3.47

ACADEMICS
Faculty to Student Ratio: N/A
Quality of Teaching: **B**
Faculty Accessibility: **A**

PHYSICAL ENVIRONMENT
Location: Suburban/Very Large City
Safety: Very Good
HA: ♿ ♿ ♿ ♿

STUDENT ENROLLMENT
Class Size: 270 (full-time)
Women: 50% **Minorities:** 20%
Average Age of Entering Class: 26

PLACEMENT
REPUTATION ☆ ☆ ☆ ☆

Recruiters: 478
Starting Salary Mean: $43,928

FINANCES
Tuition: $11,460
Average Total Cost: $21,333

STUDENT LIFE
RATING ☺ ☺ ☺ ☺ ☹

After Hours: Buff's Pub

PROMINENT ALUMNI/AE
Include: John Conrad Geenty, Trial Court of
Massachusetts Judge; Eugene Andrew
Gordon, US District Court, North Carolina

INSIDER INFORMATION

BC Law School has the rare quality of combining a fine academic experience and great reputation with a congenial atmosphere where great friends are made. Recruiters, particularly those from Boston and New York, are pleased with the school, and many give it the edge over BU. In summing up BC, one New England recruiter says, "The law school's grads consistently perform at or above our expectations. We also find them well-rounded and personable." Established in 1929, Boston College Law School is located in the safe suburb of Newton, which gives students access to Boston, but also runs up housing bills for students who want to live near the school.

BC has one of the highest minority enrollments among U.S. law schools and boasts a diverse student body as well as diverse course offerings. All three classes have a total of 205 undergraduate schools represented.

A major strength of the administration is its flexibility concerning the education of its students. All courses in the second and third years are elective, and the students have more than one hundred diverse subjects to choose from. These courses include a wide variety of clinical courses such as the Chinatown Project, a special program providing civil legal services in the Asian Community. Courses are divided into general areas, including Business Law, Family Law, Lawyering Skills, Property, and International and Comparative Law; these subject areas are then divided into further categories.

There is flexibility in the requirements for the degree with law students encouraged to propose a program if they are interested in an independent joint degree program with another school or another department at Boston College, or even with another university in the Boston area. Approval is needed by both schools, and an average of ten students a year design this type of program. In one of these programs, a number of Boston College students have been involved in a joint International Relations Law/Law Degree program. The school has five law reviews. For the most part, placement is considered very strong, particularly for students with better grades/law review experience, but it is also known to make an extra effort for students who are in the middle and lower half of the class.

ADMISSIONS

CRITERIA

LEVEL 1:   Grade Point Average

LEVEL 2:   LSAT Score

LEVEL 3:   Recommendations; personal essay

LEVEL 4:   Quality of undergraduate curriculum/course work completed; quality/reputation of college/university; work experience

MINORITY RECRUITMENT PROGRAM

Yes; the Asian-American Law Student, Black Law Student, and Latino Law Student Associations actively recruit applicants.

ABOUT THE APPLICATION

DEADLINE FOR FILING: 3/1

FEE: $45

LSAT: School takes the average of applicant's scores.

RECOMMENDED COURSES PRIOR TO MATRICULATING: Courses that develop the applicant's analytical skills.

PERSONAL STATEMENT: "Personal essays are an important part of the admission file; however, they cannot overcome a poor GPA and LSAT."

INTERVIEW: Not required or recommended.

ADMISSIONS TIPS: "Applicants applying to high-volume schools should complete their applications early in the cycle—those files read early have a better chance for admission before the class is filled."

CONTACT: Louise M. Clark, Director of Admissions

PHYSICAL ENVIRONMENT

Boston College has a legitimate "campus," although it is located just outside of Beantown in a "city-burb." The law school is contained in four interconnected buildings—Stuart House, the James W. Smith Faculty Wing, Barat House, and the Kenny-Cottle Law Library. Stuart House, the primary law school building, is a five-story, colonial-style building, which contains academic, administrative, and service facilities. The James W. Smith Faculty Wing houses faculty offices, the law school bookstore, and offices for student organizations. Barat House contains the Alumni Relations and Development Offices and Library. Besides the many fitness centers located in the Boston area, Boston College has an excellent facility located on the main campus, which is approximately one mile from the law school. The area is found safe by the students, and escort service is provided. Handicapped accessibility is very good and accommodations are made to suit individual needs.

No campus housing is available, although dorms are being planned. The most popular form of housing is an apartment. The most cost-effective living accommodations are for a single student, shared apartment or house near a mass transit line (the more roommates, the less cost); for a married student with no children, a one-bedroom apartment off a mass transit line; and for a married student with children, an apartment off mass transit lines. Whether or not to have a car depends on where you live.

FINANCES

BUDGET	LOW	MEDIUM	HIGH
Tuition (annual first year)	$12,510	$12,510	$12,510
Books	$580	$580	$580
Living Accommoda-tions (9 months)	Shared Apt. $3825	Shared House $4950	One-Bedroom Apt. $5850
Food	Groceries $630	Cafeteria $2300	Restaurants $2750
Miscellaneous	$800	$1000	$1200
Transportation	BC Shuttle $0.00	MBTA Bus $300	Car $1125
TOTAL	$18,345	$21,640	$24,015

Employment During School: Recommended, but for no more than ten hours per week. Work-study jobs are available for eligible students. Students receive $5 to $7 an hour.

Scholarships: The school offers merit and need-based scholarships. Merit scholarships are not contingent upon maintaining a certain GPA.

School Loan Program (Exclusive of Perkins Money): Yes. This is a need-based program and the maximum amount permitted to be borrowed is based on that need. Interest is at the same rate as that for Stafford Loans.

Loan Forgiveness Program: The Willier Award Loan Forgiveness Program. Graduates who pursue law-related public interest careers shall be eligible for consideration for complimentary loan deferral and loan forgiveness mechanisms. Supports summer living expense stipends to law students who choose summer employment in low or nonpaying public interest law positions. At graduation, the Willier Award also presents honorary stipends to law graduates who directly enter public interest careers.

Students Requesting Aid: 90%; of these, 70% receive aid.

Students Indebted upon Graduation: 90%

Average Loan Indebtedness: $40,000

ACADEMICS

Boston College's strengths include: Arts/Communication Law, Sports Law, Entertainment Law; Civil Rights/Civil Liberties; Constitutional Law; Corporate Law; Energy/

Environment/Natural Resources Law; International Comparative Law; Labor Law; Legal Ethics; Public Interest Law; and Tax Law.

The first-year curriculum has recently been changed through the Introduction to Lawyering and Professional Responsibility course. In this course, the students meet in small sections to discuss the adversarial system and the professional responsibilities of lawyers operating within the system. Students experience client interviewing, client counseling, case evaluation and planning, negotiation, motion practice, and trial-level argument through various simulation exercises. Alternative dispute resolution processes, such as arbitration and mediation, are also part of the course. A special focus now has been placed on the second semester of Property, and the Legal Research and Writing course has been expanded to two semesters. Second- and third-year students are not required to take any specific courses, and they have more than fifty courses to choose from each semester, including, as noted before, a wide variety of clinical courses, the Attorney General Law Clinic and the Judicial Process, which includes placement with a specific superior court judge.

The students have a high opinion of the faculty, who are very accessible; all have posted office hours.

JOINT DEGREE PROGRAMS

JD/MBA; JD/MSW

STUDENT LIFE

The social life is considered excellent. The most popular social event scheduled by the school is Bar Review, a happy hour sponsored by the Law Student Association every Friday. In addition there are other conferences and parties. The Law Revue Show is an annual student-run musical parodying life at the law school and the roles of administration, staff, and faculty.

Boston College has an interesting selection of student organizations, including the Holocaust/Human Rights Research Project; the *Alledger*, a student-operated newspaper; and the Public Interest Law Foundation.

PLACEMENT

Although 97.8% of the class is employed after graduation, students who are not in the top 10–15% of the class feel frustration with regard to direction for help.

PREPARATION

Students are prepared through videotaped mock interviews, interviewing techniques sessions, and résumé-writing seminars.

The school is very good at helping the students obtain summer jobs. They have a full recruitment program that draws firms from all over the country. Many work experience/internship opportunities are available through on-campus jobs. Off-campus jobs are posted in Career Placement.

WHERE/WHAT GRADUATES PRACTICE

A. 62.7% New England; 21.6% Mid-Atlantic; 2.8% Southeast; 8.3% West/Southwest; 2.3% Midwest; 2.3% Foreign.
B. 63.3% Private; 8.2% Very Small Firm, 4.6% Small Firm; 6.9% Medium Firm; 13.3% Large Firm; 29.4% Very Large Firm; 0.9% Unknown; 4.6% Corporate; 5.0% Public Interest; 9.2% Government; 17.9% Judicial Clerkships.

ADMISSIONS OFFICE
765 COMMONWEALTH AVENUE
BOSTON, MASSACHUSETTS (MA) 02215
(617) 353-3100

❧ REPORT CARD ❧

ADMISSIONS
SELECTIVITY 🎓 🎓 🎓 🎓

Applicants: 6200; Accepted: 1700
LSAT Median: 40 GPA Median: 3.23

PLACEMENT
REPUTATION ☆ ☆ ☆ ☆

Recruiters: 438
Starting Salary Range: $27,000–60,000

ACADEMICS

Faculty to Student Ratio: 1:23
Quality of Teaching: A−
Faculty Accessibility: A

FINANCES

Tuition: $13,900
Average Total Cost: $24,500

PHYSICAL ENVIRONMENT

Location: Urban/Large City
Safety: Fair
HA: ♿ ♿ ♿ ♿ ♿

STUDENT LIFE
RATING ☺ ☺ ☺

After Hours: The Castle

STUDENT ENROLLMENT

Class Size: 406
Women: 50%   Minorities: 21% (includes
  Asians)
Average Age of Entering Students: 23

PROMINENT ALUMNI/AE

Include: Irving Goldblatt; Sean M. Dunphy,
  First Justice, Trial Court

INSIDER INFORMATION

BU is a skyscraper of a law school. Of course, with one of the largest law student enrollments in the country, the school needs the space. In 1989, BU decreased its class size from 430 to 406. According to Marianne Spalding, Director of Admissions, "We were always shooting for a class of around 406 students, but this was the first year we were able to actually do it." The reduced class has somewhat alleviated overcrowding, while making BU's admissions picture more competitive.

For those of you who want to have an outstanding variety of courses to choose among, BU probably has anything you could possibly want or imagine in law course offerings and the chance to take courses outside the law school in one of BU's other schools. But BU's greatest strength undoubtedly lies in its expansive clinical programs, which students praise for their thoroughness of preparation and recruiters for its graduates' "sharp presentation skills." The intense drive among students to get "the big firm jobs" rears it unsightly head in the form of an intense competition because students here realize that being in the top 25% and/or being on a journal can mean "the difference between having law firms wine and dine you across the country and having to make an incredible effort armed with your résumés and a good pair of Reeboks ready to pound the pavement." BU's Placement Office is well regarded among students who recognize that recruiting is more a function of firms' preferences than their school's lack of trying.

Students are quick to mention that there are former Harvard professors on their faculty; in reality, the school does have two former HLS faculty on a faculty of sixty, including most notably Archibald Cox. Half of the school's faculty are under 45 years old, and although there have been complaints concerning a sprinkling of good researchers and poor teachers among them, they generally receive favorable comments from students, such as one second-year student who said, "I can honestly say I was surprised at how good the faculty at BU really are. They are erudite, witty, and they really do care about their students." Accessibility appears to be good, with a little extra effort made by the student.

If BU were in any other major city, it would probably have overcome its "shadow problem" years ago. The school has been an innovator from its inception, being the first law school to raise the number of years of study from two to three years. As you take your law school finals, you can also thank BU for instituting the practice of written and graded examinations. Of course were BU not in Boston, it wouldn't be Boston University in spirit any more than in city name. The school thrives on its location in the heart of the best city in the country for students. So, if you want a solid legal education, and you don't care about that crimson H law school, set your sights high on the skyscraper of a law school named BU.

ADMISSIONS

CRITERIA

LEVEL 1: LSAT; GPA; and personal statement

LEVEL 2: Marked improvement in undergraduate scores; quality and difficulty of courses taken; demonstrated leadership abilities; motivation for law study, and outstanding nonacademic achievements.

MINORITY RECRUITMENT

Yes. The school engages in extensive efforts to attract larger numbers of men and women from minority groups into legal education.

ABOUT THE APPLICATION

DEADLINE FOR FILING: 3/1

FEE: $45

LSAT: School takes the average of applicant's scores, unless informed of extenuating circumstances serious enough to justify the consideration of a single score.

PERSONAL STATEMENT: Candidates are urged to submit written statements detailing all information that could influence the committee's decision. It is important that "applicants shouldn't string together their résumés." Says Marianne Spalding, "We have no preconceived notion of what we're looking for." However, Spalding also mentions that in the best personal statement, an applicant chooses a topic that interests him or her, "something near and dear to their heart." She cites as an example, an applicant who may have been in a divorce court as a child and who may have a special insight into families in relation to the law. It is not crucial that academic pursuits tie directly with the statement.

INTERVIEW: Not part of the evaluative process.

ADMISSIONS TIPS: Letters of recommendation are considered extremely important. The quality of the recommendation and the nature of the relationship between the recommender and the applicant are important, not the status of the recommender. Pay special attention to the personal statement; each one is read very carefully by the Admissions Office. As Marianne Spalding states, "It's [the personal statement] the first thing I look at when I open an applicant's file."

CONTACT: Marianne Spalding, Director of Admissions

PHYSICAL ENVIRONMENT

Students here claim that the eighteen-story BU is the tallest law school in the world. "Also the ugliest," says one student, "It was built in the 60s and it was supposed to be hip then." Handicapped accessibility is considered excellent. Blind students and wheel-chaired are enrolled. There is a law-school-backed group that helps the handicapped study.

BU has limited housing on campus for graduate students. Several small coeducational dormitories have been set aside for graduate housing and are located within walking distance. One university-owned apartment building, Warren Hall, is set aside for married graduate students. A car is not recommended because parking is inadequate. There is very good public transportation. The school is located near the trolley, and safety near the school is adequate, given that proper precaution is exercised.

FINANCES

BUDGET	LOW	MEDIUM	HIGH
Tuition	$13,900	$13,900	$13,900
Books	$650	$650	$650
Living Accommodations (9 months)	On-Campus $4000	Shared Apt. $5400	One-Bedroom Apt. $6210
Food	Groceries $1080	Meal Plan $2100	Restaurants $2700
Miscellaneous	$1200	$1700	$3000
Transportation	Mass Transit $450	Mass Transit/Car $750	Car $900
TOTAL	$21,280	$24,500	$27,360

Employment During School: Work-study jobs are available for continuing students who are able to demonstrate eligibility and need. Students are employed as faculty research assistants and library assistants, with some off-campus jobs, many law-related. Employment is also available to single and married students as undergraduate residence hall directors and assistants; these positions provide room and board and a stipend.

Scholarships: The school offers merit and need-based scholarships.

School Loan Program (Exclusive of Perkins Money): Yes. Various loan programs are available from the school.

Loan Forgiveness Program: No

Students Requesting Aid: N/A

Average Loan Indebtedness: N/A

ACADEMICS

BU's academic strengths are considered best in Civil Rights/Civil Liberties, Constitutional Law, Computer Technology, Corporate Law, Health/Medicine, International/Comparative Law, and Tax Law. There is much competition for grades, and although it is not as cutthroat as some here had anticipated, competition is present and felt among students. This competition is in part due to the fact that only the top 25% of the class obtains positions with the most prestigious firms and corporations. The school has two rankings: top 25% and top 6%. These rankings can be affected by as little as a hundredth of a percentage. The mean is a grade of 81. One student gave an example of this competitiveness: If an upperclassman gave you his or her old notes, you would share them with your close friends and no one else.

First-year students are required to take two year-long courses, three required one-semester courses, a one-semester elective, and a year-long research and writing seminar. The first-year student body is divided into four sections for the required year-long and one-semester courses. The Research and Writing course is taught in small group seminars. The second and third years consist of elective courses, except that all students must successfully complete a constitutional law course in the first semester of the second year and two courses in professional responsibility in the second semester of the second and third years. Each student is further required in the second or third year to complete satisfactorily a faculty-supervised major research and writing project. A wide array of clinical programs are provided, including the Criminal Law Clinical Program, the Arbitration and Mediation Clinic, and the Judicial Interns Seminar. BU also sponsors several speakers' programs that supplement the curriculum. The school has several centers and institutes, including the Center for Law and Health Services, the Institute of Jewish Law, and the Morin Center for Banking Law Studies.

Through the faculty-student advisor program, each entering student is assigned a faculty advisor who is available to discuss questions or problems related to the law school experience. Students consider the professors at BU excellent. Student-chosen faculty stars include Clark Bice and Paul Wallace (Criminal Law).

JOINT/GRADUATE DEGREE/SPECIAL PROGRAMS

Joint Degrees: JD/MBA (Law and Management); JD/MS (Law and Mass Communication); JD/MA (Law and Preservation Studies); JD/MBA (Law and Health Care Management); JD/MPH (Law and Public Health).
Graduate (Masters) Degrees: LLM in Banking Law; LLM in International Banking Law Studies; LLM in Taxation.
Special: A six-year program offering a baccalaureate degree and the JD is available with other Boston University schools.

Approximately 50% of the students have had some post-grad experience before entering law school. In conjunction with the Student Bar Association, each student is assigned an upperclass student advisor who works with the faculty advisor throughout the year. Many advisors host luncheons or other social functions for their advisees.

Students admit that BU has a reputation for being cutthroat. One student explains, "420-odd students are split into four sections. You are graded against 108 or so people. (The) school sets maximum curves and grading guidelines." The school has many organizations including the Environmental Law Society and the Women's Law Association. If a student organization doesn't exist at BU Law School, it will once students set their minds to it. BU has a large number of student-run organizations and journals, including *The American Journal of Law and Medicare; Journal of Tax Law; International Law Journal; Probate Law Journal; Boston University Law Review*, which combines articles written by professors, practicing attorneys, and student members; and *Commentaries*, the only journal in the U.S. devoted to reviewing books germane to the legal profession. Special interest groups are wide reaching, including a Communications and Entertainment Law Society, many of whose students are pursuing a JD/MS in Communications with BU's College of Communications. BU sponsors a speaker series that has hosted among others, Ralph Nader, William Kunstler, and BU Municipal Court Judge Margaret Burnham.

PLACEMENT

Grades are considered essential for placement. Only the top 25% of the class obtains positions with the most prestigious firms.

PREPARATION

The Career Planning and Placement Office aids the students through career counseling, individual résumé and cover letter writing, consultations, and specialty programs. First-year orientation programs introduce students to the staff, services, and resources of the office and present strategies for summer employment. Legal career panels highlight specific areas of specialty and feature experts in the field. There are newsletters for students and alumni, and consortium programs include the National Law Firm Program and the Graduate Recruitment Program.

WHERE/WHAT GRADUATES PRACTICE

A. 47% New England; 35% MidAtlantic; 3% Southeast; 6% Midwest; 0.75% Southwest; 7.65% Pacific; 0.3% Rocky Mountain; 0.3% Other.
B. 77.7% Private Practice; 8.5% Public Sector; 2.8% Business; 7.9% Judicial Clerkships; 0.3% Academics.

UNIVERSITY OF CALIFORNIA AT BERKELEY
Boalt Hall School of Law

BERKELEY, CALIFORNIA (CA) 94720
(415) 642-2274

❧ REPORT CARD ❧

ADMISSIONS
SELECTIVITY 🎓 🎓 🎓 🎓 🎓

Applications: 5,851; Accepted: 500
Transfer Applications: 130; Accepted: 24
LSAT Mean: 43 GPA Mean: 3.7

ACADEMICS

Order of the Coif (1927)
California Bar Passage Rate (first
  try): 92.3% (July 1989 ABA Statewide
  Average: 72.2%)
Faculty to Student ratio: 1:10
Quality of Teaching: B−/C+
Faculty Accessibility: B/B−

PHYSICAL ENVIRONMENT

Location: Large City
Safety: Very Good–Good (Escort Service)
HA: ♿ ♿ ♿ ♿

STUDENT ENROLLMENT

Class Size: 270 (full-time)
Women: 46% Minorities: 27%
Average Age of Entering Class: 24

PLACEMENT
REPUTATION: ★ ★ ★ ★ ⯨

Recruiters: 500+
Starting Salary Mean California: $55,200;
  South: $52,000; Northeast: $64,600;
  Southwest: $51,700; Midwest: $54,500;
  West Coast, excluding California:
  $41,900

FINANCES

Tuition: $1563 (R); $6069 (NR)
Average Total Cost: $11,558.50 (R);
  $17,750.50 (NR)

STUDENT LIFE
RATING: ☺ ☺

After Hours: Cafe Strada

PROMINENT ALUMNI/AE

Include: Earl Warren, past Chief Justice U.S.
  Supreme Court; Roger Traynor, past Chief
  Justice California State Supreme Court;
  Dean Rusk, former Secretary of State

INSIDER INFORMATION

Some students feel that there is something of a mismatch between the faculty and the student body at Boalt, with a more liberal student body and a somewhat more conservative faculty. (They add that the faculties of Stanford and Berkeley were switched at birth). Although students are not glowing about the faculty, they do point out that they are generally outstanding scholars. A while back there was a student strike organized at Boalt with law students striking (they weren't arrested but detained for five to six hours without being able to call a lawyer or use the bathroom) at the same time that the McBaine Moot Court Competition below was arguing Fourth Amendment rights before Justice Brennan. Diversity among faculty members is among the most heated issues at the school and at law schools across the country.

Of special interest is the fact that the school permits the students to specialize through a newly developed program that provides the option of taking one of three concentrations: Criminal Justice and Public Policy, Environmental Law, or Financial Services. This program permits students to take two to four prerequisite courses during their second year and then spend a significant portion of their third year in a year-long research seminar that deals with advanced issues in the concentration field. The School of Law also has a unique liberal arts graduate program leading to the MA and PhD in Jurisprudential and Social Policy (JSP).

Placement is excellent for mainstream or corporate law with a large number of recruiters, and there is a recent placement thrust into public service law as well. Many East coast recruiters, along with their West coast counterparts, have strong impressions of Boalt regarding its graduates, whom one megafirm recruiter describes as "skilled and high-spirited." Others will quickly add that Boalt is "just under Stanford for their top California pick." Among the public California law schools, there is a general consensus that Boalt reigns supreme.

ADMISSIONS

CRITERIA

LEVEL 1: Grade Point Average; LSAT score

LEVEL 2: Quality of undergraduate curriculum/coursework completed; quality/reputation of undergraduate university/college

LEVEL 3: Personal essay

LEVEL 4: Work experience; recommendations

MINORITY RECRUITMENT PROGRAM

Yes; national recruitment campaign via area and school visits, mailings, and campus recruitment projects. There are four minority student law groups, and admissions works with them all.

ABOUT THE APPLICATION

DEADLINE FOR FILING: 2/1

FEE: $35

LSAT: The school takes the average of applicant's scores.

RECOMMENDED COURSES IN COLLEGE: Well-rounded education.

PERSONAL STATEMENT: "As we do not conduct interviews, it is the applicant's only opportunity to relate subjective qualities."

INTERVIEW: Not required or recommended. For visitors, the Hotel Durait or Claremont Hotel is recommended.

ADMISSIONS TIPS: "Craft the personal statement to be just that—a personal statement rather than résumé—in narrative form. Include a regular résumé with the statement [as an addendum]."

CONTACT: Edward Tom, Director of Admissions and Financial Aid

PHYSICAL ENVIRONMENT

Boalt Hall is located on the Berkeley campus within easy distance of the main campus. Although the main campus is rather striking in appearance, Boalt is not as attractive. It is considered to be in a safe area, although situated at the base of wooded hills.

School housing is very limited because the campus is able to house less than 30% of the university student body; however, student housing for law students is guaranteed. 20% of the students live in student-owned accommodations. Living in Oakland (two to three miles out) is your best bet for inexpensive housing relatively near to campus, but be sure to allow at least two to three weeks to find housing in the Berkeley community or the surrounding area.

A car is not recommended because parking is limited. Public transportation, which will take you to and from the campus, is certainly good enough so that students do not need a car on campus. Bikes are a big plus. BART (Bay Area Rapid Transit) will take you to San Francisco in about half an hour.

FINANCES

BUDGET	LOW	MEDIUM	HIGH
Tuition (Resident) Tuition (Nonresident)	$1916.50 $7715.50	$1916.50 $7715.50	$1916.50 $7715.50
Books	$634	$634	$634
Living Accommodations (9 months)	Shared Apt.* $2700	On-Campus $5134	One-Bedroom Apt. $5850
Food	Cafeteria $1080	Groceries $2046	Restaurants $3500
Miscellaneous	$1000	$1328	$2444
Transportation	Mass Transit $270	Car/Bus $500	Car $650
TOTAL (R) TOTAL (NR)	$7600.50 $13,399.50	$11,558.50 $17,357.50	$14,994.50 $20,793.50

* Other options: Family student housing married only (+ dependents): $3060; Shared house: $3150

Employment During School: Recommended. Work-study jobs are available for eligible students; these positions pay $8 to 10 an hour.

Scholarships: The school offers merit and need-based scholarships. Merit scholarships are contingent upon passing.

School Loan Program (Exclusive of Perkins Money): Yes, short-term and emergency interest-free loans that must be repaid within four months or upon receipt of GSL.

Loan Forgiveness Program: Not now; pending.

Students Requesting Aid: 65%; of these, 60% receive aid.

Students Indebted upon Graduation: 60–80%

Average Loan Indebtedness: $25,000

ACADEMICS

Before the commencement of the regular first-year classes, students are required to take Legal Systems and Legal Analysis, a week-long course. Three of the four courses of the totally required curriculum students take each semester during the first year are taught in classes of about 115; the other class is taught in small sections of 25 to 30. Some students take legal research and writing in separate classes taught by recent law school graduates called Law Associates, while other students have this course combined with their other small section courses. During the second and third years, students are required to take Professional Responsibility and otherwise will have a wide selection of over 130 courses from which to choose.

There are numerous one-semester and half-semester clinical opportunities for which students can get credit. One student worked for a feminist law firm handling sexual harrassment suits. Specialized courses are available, including Advanced Tax Planning and Appellate Advocacy. Exchange programs are available in Japan, Germany, and at Harvard. Students also have opportunities to take classes at the undergraduate school for credit.

Grades are HH (High Honors–10%), H (Honors–30%), P (Pass–60%); some students received Sub-Ps but they are rare. Students volunteer to be on journals. Participation in the *California Law Review* is not based on grades, but on a writing competition.

The faculty tend to be research-oriented. The faculty do keep office hours, but many students feel they are inaccessible and therefore do not seek them out. Star faculty include Earl Warren (past Chief Justice, U. S. Supreme Court), Roger Traynor (past Chief Justice, California State Supreme Court), and Dean Rusk (former Secretary of State).

COMBINED DEGREE/SPECIAL PROGRAMS

Combined Degrees: JD/MBA; JD/MSW; JD and degrees in other fields, including library science, journalism, and public policy.
Graduate Degree: LLM (Masters in Law); JSD (Doctor of Juristic Science).

It is found that the students here are not cutthroat and are very diverse in terms of interests. The school is considered excellent for students having taken time off after college.

There are numerous organizations at Berkeley, including the International Law Society and the Boalt Hall's Women's Association. The Berkeley Law Foundation is an income-sharing organization of Boalt Hall students, graduates, and faculty. Public interest law projects are funded through this foundation.

Placement is considered excellent here. As one student said, "She (the placement director) has her heart in it." While the students have numerous offers from corporations/law firms, they also have several opportunities in the public sector and public service.

PREPARATION

The school prepares its students by résumé-writing workshops, individual résumé consultations with placement staff, and through a variety of panels and colloquia. Students may participate in videotaped mock interviews through the campus Career Planning and Placement Center. The Boalt Hall Alumni Association provides networking opportunities for the students. Graduates serve students through counseling and career colloquia.

WHERE/WHAT GRADUATES PRACTICE

A. 10.5% Northeast; 1.1% South;. 83% West Coast; 2.5% Midwest; 2.9% Southwest.
B. 3.8% Very Small Firms: (10 or fewer lawyers); 8.2% Small Firms (11–25 lawyers); 11% Medium Firms (26–50 lawyers); 18% Large Firms (51–100 lawyers); 59% Very Large Firms (over 100 lawyers); 18.4% Clerkships; 0% Graduate degrees; 0.4% Military; 3.4% Governmental Agencies; 1.9% Corporations; 3% Public Interest, Public Defender and Legal Services; 1.1% Academic.

KING HALL
DAVIS, CALIFORNIA (CA) 95616
(916) 752-6477

𝕣 REPORT CARD 𝕤

ADMISSIONS
SELECTIVITY 🎓 🎓 🎓 🎓

Applicants: 3033; Accepted: 610
Transfer Applications: 45; Accepted: 7
LSAT Mean: 40 GPA Mean: 3.43

ACADEMICS
Order of the Coif (1972)
California Bar Passage (first try): 93.7%
  (July 1989 Statewide Average: 72.2%)
Faculty to Student Ratio: 1:16
Quality of Teaching: B+
Faculty Accessibility: A

PHYSICAL ENVIRONMENT
Location: Small Community
Safety: Good
HA: ♿ ♿ ♿ ♿ ♿

STUDENT ENROLLMENT
Class Size: 167 (full-time)
Women: 51%   Minorities: 23% (excluding
  Asians)
Average Age of Entering Class: 25

PLACEMENT
REPUTATION: ★ ★ ★ ⭒

Recruiters: 282
Starting Salary Median: $40,468

FINANCES
Tuition: $1912.50 (R); $7711.50 (NR)
Average Total Cost: $10,234.50 (R);
  $16,033.50 (NR)

STUDENT LIFE
RATING: ☺ ☺ ☺ ☺ ☾

After Hours: N/A

PROMINENT ALUMNI/AE
Include: N/A

When you think about the four public law schools in California, you might lead off with Berkeley as the most elite; UCLA as the youngest and hardest driving; Hastings as the oldest school, which lacks an undergraduate university to bolster its reputation; and then, there's Davis, the smallest UC law school with what students and recruiters characterize as the warmest atmosphere. As Sharon Pinkney, Director of Admissions at Davis, says, the school stresses "cooperation over competition." Students agree that the school attempts to moderate some of the unpleasantries that exist in law school. To further the Davis' goal, the "Big Sib" program, an organization of second- and third-year students designed to assist first year students with the transition into law school, was formed. A real advantage is the size of each graduating class. Everyone knows everyone. The disadvantage of the school is that course offerings are sometimes limited.

Recruiters have been mixed in their reactions to Davis grads. Though the school has no difficulties with recruiter satisfaction and visibility on the West Coast it does not fare as well in other regions of the country.

ADMISSIONS

CRITERIA

LEVEL 1:   Grade Point Average; LSAT score

LEVEL 2:   Personal essay; recommendations; racial/ethnic background

LEVEL 3:   Quality of undergraduate curriculum/course work completed; quality/reputation of college/university; work experience

Other: Important factors in admissions are extracurricular and community activities, diversity, and residency.

MINORITY RECRUITMENT PROGRAM

Yes. Davis' recruitment activities are conducted through the Admissions Office. The school places special emphasis on attracting minority applicants through such activities as campus recruitment visits, attendance at law days, the Candidate Referral Service, and participation in and encouragement of any minority law student organization events.

ABOUT THE APPLICATION

DEADLINE FOR FILING: 2/1

FEE: $35

LSAT: Davis takes the average of the applicant's scores. Applicants are urged to take the LSAT no later than December 1 of the year prior to which admission is sought.

PERSONAL STATEMENT: "With more than eighteen applications for each first-year seat the personal statement provides information that allows us further to distinguish the strongest applicants. It is possible that information may be included that would move an applicant from 'borderline' to 'admit'."

INTERVIEW: Neither recommended nor required.

RECOMMENDATIONS: Davis prefers two letters of recommendation from faculty from upper level courses. These professors should be fully acquainted with the applicant; this is especially important for applicants who attended larger universities where faculty members might not be as familiar with students in introductory courses.

ADMISSIONS TIPS: "Applicants should obtain as much information as possible before starting the admissions process. It is extremely important to attend law days, visit law schools, and speak to law students. Early application and careful attention to all details of the admission process are essential. It is especially critical to register for and take the LSAT early and only after substantial preparation for the exam."

CONTACT: Sharon Pinkney, Director of Admissions

PHYSICAL ENVIRONMENT

The law school consists of a three-story building located in a small farmlike community. The campus is medium-sized.

On-campus accommodations are not guaranteed, and only 5% of the students live in school-owned housing. Single graduate students are offered on-campus living accommodations at the privately owned and managed Atriums, but the most popular and cost-effective accommodations for single students are shared off-campus apartments. The most cost-effective for married students, with or without children, is on-campus married student housing. On-campus apartments for student families are located in Solerno Park, Orchard Park, and Russell Park. The difficulty in locating suitable housing near the school is considered average. The school is very accessible to campus facilities by car, bike, or foot. A car is recommended because, although the city is accessible by bicycle, some students find a car useful for clinical placements off campus and summer employment.

Handicapped accessibility is excellent at UC Davis. The law school is equipped with chairlifts in the Moot Court Room, automatic door entrances, and room numbers in braille; special testing procedures and other accommodations are made available as needed.

FINANCES

BUDGET	LOW	MEDIUM	HIGH
Tuition (Resident) **Tuition (Nonresi-** **dent)**	$1912.50 $7,711.50	$1912.50 $7,711.50	$1912.50 $7,711.50
Books	$700	$700	$700
Living Accommoda- **tions (9 months)**	Shared Apt. $2930	Married Student On- Campus $3512	On-Campus $5253 (inc. board)
Food	Groceries $1355	Groceries/Rest. $1690	Restaurants $2025
Miscellaneous	$1600	$1800	$2000
Transportation	Bus $500	Car $620	Car $620
TOTAL (R) TOTAL (NR)	$8997.50 $14,796.50	$10,234.50 $16,033.50	$12,510.50 $18,309.50

Employment During School: Work-study jobs are available (need dependent); the pay is approximately $8 an hour.

Scholarships: The school offers merit, need-based, and minority scholarships. Students must meet certain grade point requirements to remain in school, but none specifically to maintain scholarships or aid.

School Loan Program (Exclusive of Perkins Money): Yes. University funding from the state has terms that duplicate the Perkins Loan.

Loan Forgiveness Program: No. A committee is currently doing research on this issue.

Students Requesting Aid: 80–90%; of these, 50–70% receive aid.

Average Loan Indebtedness: $20,000

ACADEMICS

First-year students are required to take certain set courses. During this time, students receive extra personal attention. Each student takes one of the major first-year classes in a small class of about thirty. Upperclass tutors aid the professors in providing help and guidance.

Except for required courses in legal ethics and professional responsibility, and a legal writing requirement, upperclass law students are free to choose from a good range of electives. These courses are divided into different sections, including Constitutional Law, Consumer Law, Business Law, Agricultural Law, and Public Law. Clinics include Judicial Clinicals, Clinical Program in Employment Relations, and a clinical program in Environmental Law. Second- and third-year law students are given even more flexibility by being permitted to plan their own clinics, group study seminars, and individual research. They can also receive credit for certain courses taken in other departments of the university and for summer courses taken at other accredited law schools. Energy/Environmental Law and clinical programs are considered the school's strengths.

JOINT DEGREE PROGRAMS

JD/MA (Administration); JD/MBA; other flexible programs that can be arranged.

STUDENT LIFE

Students find that there is a relatively noncompetitive atmosphere at UC Davis and that the social life is very good. The Law Student Association (LSA) funds a number of student organizations, speaker programs, and social events, including parties and other functions such as Luau and weekly social groups.

Student organizations include the Environmental Law Society, the Disabled Student Caucus, and the Law and Medicine Society. Another group is Student Lawyers for the Arts, which consists of students who may wish to explore careers in Art Law or involve themselves in art appreciation.

PLACEMENT

89% of the students are placed after graduation.

PREPARATION

Students are prepared by the Career Services Office through videotaped mock interviews, interviewing techniques sessions, and résumé-writing seminars. In addition, the office has a vast array of publications specifically designed to assist students, including *How to Write Effective Cover Letters*, *Struggles for Successful Interviewing*, and *Résumé Preparation Guide*. Alumni participate in panel discussions designed to help the job search. Every student receives a copy of the *Directory of Recruiting Employers*. Current students receive a monthly newsletter from Career Services in addition to the *Employment Opportunity Bulletin*, which goes to students and alumni.

WHERE/WHAT GRADUATES PRACTICE

A. 4.6% Northeast; 3.4% Southeast; 79.3% CA/Northwest; 1.1% Midwest; 8% Southwest, Alaska, and Hawaii (26% of the school's graduates remain in the area within one year of graduation).

B. 39% Small Firms; 22% Medium Firms; 39% Large Firms; 18% Clerkships; 3% Military; 11% Governmental Agencies; 1% Corporations.

UNIVERSITY OF CALIFORNIA
Hastings College of The Law

200 MCALLISTER STREET
SAN FRANCISCO, CALIFORNIA (CA) 94102-4978
(415) 565-4623

❧ REPORT CARD ❧

ADMISSIONS
SELECTIVITY 🎓 🎓 🎓 🎓 🎓

Applications: 5,126; Accepted: 957
Transfer Applications: 75; Accepted: 5
LSAT Mean: 42
GPA Mean: 3.56

ACADEMICS
Order of the Coif (1954)
California Bar Passage Rate (first
   try): 81.4% (July 1989 statewide average:
   72.2%)
Faculty to Student Ratio: 1:17
Quality of Teaching: A−
Faculty Accessibility: A

PHYSICAL ENVIRONMENT
Location: Large Urban City
Safety: Fair–Marginal
HA: ♿ ♿ ♿ ♿

STUDENT ENROLLMENT
Class Size: 415 (full-time)
Women: 48%   Minorities: 22%
Average Age of Entering Class: N/A

PLACEMENT
REPUTATION: ☆ ☆ ☆ ☆

Recruiters: 450 in person
Starting Salary Mean: $55,000

FINANCES
Tuition: $1476 (R); $7275 (NR)
Average Total Cost: $10,726 (R); $16,525
   (NR)

STUDENT LIFE
RATING: ☺ ☺ ☺ ☺

After Hours: Squid's, The Beach

PROMINENT ALUMNI/AE
Include: Clara Shortridge Foltz, first female
   law school graduate; Willie Brown, Jr.,
   Speaker of the California Assembly; Hon.
   Robert Matsui, Richard Dannemeyer,
   Norman Shumway, current members of the
   U.S. House of Representatives; Hon.
   Richard Bryan, U.S. Senate

INSIDER INFORMATION

As the oldest law school in the West, Hastings has strived for and maintained its integrity and high standards. Located in the heart of the San Francisco Civic Center, the Hastings campus is next door to every level of court (state and federal), except the United States Supreme Court. Although the environment may not be the best as to safety, Hastings has taken precautions by employing reliable professional security guards.

Recruiters are impressed with Hastings graduates because of their attention to detail and oral and written presentation skills. However, many larger firms, particularly outside of California, are not as attracted to Hastings students as they are to graduates of other California prestige law schools, most notably, Stanford and Berkeley. Many feel that Hastings isn't as recognizable as other "name" law schools, based on the fact that it has no university to give it added prestige. Although many Hastings students would have preferred to be Berkeley-bound, they have been very satisfied with Hastings.

Some students say that Hastings is a school that rests on its aging laurels and the aim of those who attach themselves to it to avoid retirement. Students characterize Hastings' faculty as being generally older than average (The 65 Club). Students are on both sides of the fence about this. Some feel that the faculty possesses members who experience difficulty in teaching; others, however, think that the age of the faculty helps to provide the students with a great depth and diversity of background and experiences that add significantly to the classroom experience. Where else could your professor be a former dean of Stanford Law School or have taught Sandra Day O'Connor in law school?

Of special interest is that the school greatly encourages and aids those individuals who come from disadvantaged backgrounds. Candidates for admission are divided into two categories: general candidates and those who qualify for the Legal Education Opportunity Program (LEOP). Initiated in 1969, LEOP seeks to assist highly qualified individuals from disadvantaged backgrounds to be active members of the legal community. Students admitted through LEOP are offered a number of academic support services throughout their three years of study. They begin with a one-week orientation program in August. As LEOP first year students, they participate in a first-year study group program conducted by second- and third-year students. In the second and third years, LEOP memers are eligible for colloquia in areas such as Constitutional Law, Federal Income Tax, and Evidence. Practicing attorneys, often LEOP graduates, and third-year students lead weekly and biweekly colloquia focusing on the further development and refinement of analytical skills. Finally, LEOP members preparing for the California Bar Examination are offered a supplemental program designed to augment the commercial bar review courses. Informally called "Bar None," it is taught exclusively by LEOP graduates and includes instruction in exam-taking techniques, regularly scheduled practice exams, and individual review. LEOP students may also have individual counseling with the LEOP director.

ADMISSIONS

CRITERIA

LEVEL 1: LSAT Score

LEVEL 2: GPA

LEVEL 3: Quality of undergraduate curriculum/course work completed

LEVEL 4: Quality/reputation of undergraduate university/college

LEVEL 5: Work experience

LEVEL 6: Personal essay

LEVEL 7: Recommendations

MINORITY RECRUITMENT PROGRAM

Yes; representatives of minority student associations accompany professional admissions personnel to recruitment field events.

ABOUT THE APPLICATION

DEADLINE FOR FILING: 2/1

FEE: $35

LSAT: School takes the average of the applicant's scores.

RECOMMENDED COURSES PRIOR TO MATRICULATING: Courses that train students to listen, read, comprehend, and write concisely and accurately; also courses that train students to reason analytically.

PERSONAL STATEMENT: Could possibly influence the decision on a borderline candidate.

INTERVIEW: Not required or recommended. If visiting, the Abigail Hotel (moderately priced bed and breakfast adjacent to the school) has been recommended. There are also low-cost accommodations at the Central YMCA one block from the school.

ADMISSIONS TIPS: "A) Apply early in the application period. B) Use the personal statement to 'brief' your case for admission. Why should you be selected for admission and not some other candidate? C) Don't send unrequested material [i.e., videotapes, cassettes, doctoral dissertations, etc.] with your application. D) Do check recent median data (LSAT scores/GPAs) for schools to which you are considering applying. If your personal data is far below the median or mean for the school it is probably not the right school for you."

CONTACT: Attention: Director of Admissions

PHYSICAL ENVIRONMENT

Hastings is located in the heart of San Francisco's civic center, which unfortunately is not the safest part of town. The location provides easy access to the California Supreme Court and Court of Appeal, which are virtually adjacent to the college. Two blocks away is City Hall. In 1980 the college completed its academic facility, which houses the law library, faculty offices, student services, the dining commons, and the bookstore.

In 1982, the college opened McAllister Tower, a former luxury hotel, as a student housing facility. The structure, built in 1927, is 24 stories tall and includes 250 student apartments of various types and a gymnasium. 35% of the class live in school-owned housing. On-campus housing is not guaranteed. The most cost-effective accommodations for a single student is a shared apartment, and for married students, with or without children, an on-campus apartment.

A car is definitely not recommended because of lack of available parking, high insurance costs, high garaging costs, and the fact that San Francisco offers excellent mass transit.

Handicapped accessibility is considered good.

BUDGET	LOW	MEDIUM	HIGH
Tuition (Resident) **Tuition (Nonresident)**	$1476 $7275	$1476 $7275	$1476 $7275
Books	$550	$550	$550
Living Accommodations (9 months)	Shared Apt. $2925	On-Campus* $3150	One-Bedroom Apt. $5850
Food	Groceries $2070	Cafeteria $2475	Restaurants $2925
Miscellaneous	$2475	$2475	$2475
Transportation	Mass Transit $600	Mass Transit $600	Mass Transit $600
TOTAL (R) TOTAL (NR)	$10,096 $15,895	$10,726 $16,525	$13,876 $19,675

* Shared House: $3375

Employment During School: Definitely no for the first year. Limited part-time employment in courts and agencies near the school is worthwhile second and third years. College work-study program (need-based) is available. Other jobs are open to all. These positions pay $7 to $15 an hour.

Scholarships: The school offers merit and need-based scholarships. Merit scholarships are contingent upon maintaining a 3.0 GPA for second and third years.

School Loan Program (Exclusive of Perkins Money): Yes. Short-term loans, not exceeding $250, are available to meet financial needs caused by immediate and unexpected circumstances. Repayment must be made thirty days after the loan was advanced.

Loan Forgiveness Program: School does not have one; however, a loan amnesty plan is under study and may be available to graduates selecting public service careers within a year.

Students Requesting Aid: 75%; of these, 95% receive aid.

Students Indebted upon Graduation: 70%

Average Loan Indebtedness: $20,000–30,000 (including undergraduate expenses)

ACADEMICS

The entering class is divided into sections that remain together throughout the first year. All first-year courses are required. Each entering student is assigned a faculty advisor at registration. Second- and third-year courses are elective, except for three requirements: 1) each student must pass the course in professional responsibility; 2) each must complete, with at least a C grade, either a seminar with a substantial writing component or a two-unit independent study with a substantial writing requirement; and 3) each student must successfully complete the Moot Court program or participate on the staff of one of the scholarly publications. An outstanding second- or third-year student is appointed by the academic dean to serve as a discussion group leader for each of the first-year classes. Discussion groups are also held for selected classes in the elective curriculum. Academic strengths include Admiralty Law; Arts/Communication Law; Entertainment/Sports Law; Constitutional Law; and Trial Advocacy. Clinical opportunities are available to those students who successfully complete three or four semesters. These opportunities are of two types: serving as a judicial extern for the state or federal courts or participating in a clinical seminar and practice experience under the supervision of an attorney. These seminars include the Civil Justice Clinic, the Sex Discrimination Clinic, and the Family Law Clinic.

Most professors are found to be fairly accessible outside of class. Because there are so many older faculty members, the Socratic method, although "soft," tends to run through all first-year courses. There are younger faculty members, but surprisingly they are not considered as accessible or as liberal as many of the older faculty members. Legal writing, which stretches through the first year, is taught by adjunct professors who are mostly practicing attorneys; students think that this course could be improved. Star faculty include: Jerome Hall (Jurisprudence), William Lockhart (Constitutional Law), W. Ray Forrester (Constitutional Law), and Raymond Sullivan (California Supreme Court–Constitutional Law).

JOINT DEGREE/SPECIAL PROGRAMS

A variety of flexible programs can be designed with UC Berkeley.

STUDENT LIFE

Hastings students are a rather eclectic group and highly motivated to participate in schools activities like Law Revue, spoofing law school life, and Beer on the Beach, with the front of the school referred to as "the beach," although it is cement. Competition isn't as keen among students as has been rumored, although it has been noted that there is definitely a competitive spirit here. This is because students are ranked not only by percentages but by numbers. The governing organization of the student body is the Associated Students of Hastings College of Law (ASH). There is a multitude of student organizations at Hastings, including the Dive Club, the Globetrotters, and the Personal Computer Users. The North of Market Child Development Center, a child-care center, cooperates with Hastings in an effort to meet the needs of students.

PLACEMENT

85% of the students are placed within six months of graduation. Employers are not allowed to screen Hastings students, which allows all students to interview with top law firms. Placement works best for second- and third-year students, although there are several seminars on job opportunities for all students.

PREPARATION

Students are prepared by the Career Services Office through an active program of group sessions on interview techniques, résumé writing, nonlegal sources of employment, public interest employment, and researching the employment market, combined with individual videotaped mock interviews and one-on-one counseling. A speaker series and panel discussions provide students the opportunity to meet judges and attorneys. The Northern California Public Interest/Public Sector Conference is held at Hastings to acquaint students with public interest and government legal careers.

WHERE/WHAT GRADUATES PRACTICE

A. 6% Northeast; 2% South; 85% West; 4% Southwest; (70% of students remain in the same city as the law school within one year of graduation).
B. 1% Sole Practitioner; 20% Small Firms (2–25); 18% Medium Firms (26–99); 38% Large Firms (100 +); 6% Clerkships; 1% Graduate Degrees; 1% Military; 10% Governmental Agencies; 5% Corporations.

405 HILGARD AVENUE
LOS ANGELES, CALIFORNIA (CA) 90024-1476
(213) 825-4041

☙ REPORT CARD ☙

ADMISSIONS

SELECTIVITY: 🎓 🎓 🎓 🎓 🎓

Applicants: 6,536; Accepted: 973
Transfer Applications: 120; Accepted: 10–15
GPA Mean: 3.53 LSAT Mean: 41

ACADEMICS

Order of the Coif (1954)
California Bar Passage (first try): 82.1 (July 1989 ABA Statewide Average: 72.2%)
Faculty to Student Ratio: N/A
Quality of Teaching: B+
Faculty Accessibility: A

PHYSICAL ENVIRONMENT

Location: Suburban/Big City
Safety: Very Good–Good
HA: ♿ ♿ ♿ ♿ ♿

STUDENT ENROLLMENT

Class Size: 320 (full-time)
Women: 37%   Minorities: 38%
Average Age of Entering Class: 25.5

PLACEMENT

REPUTATION: ★ ★ ★ ★ ⯨

Recruiters: 505 (on-campus interviews, fall); 65 (on-campus interviews, spring, for all students)
Starting Salary Mean: $54,740

FINANCES

Tuition: $1660 (R); $7458 (NR)
Average Total Cost: $10,595 (R); $16,393 (NR)

STUDENT LIFE

RATING: ☺ ☺ ☺ ☺

After Hours: Q's, Stratten's

PROMINENT ALUMNI/AE

Include: N/A

INSIDER INFORMATION

UCLA is the youngest member of the "prestige circle" of California law schools. You might assume that being the youngest has hampered the school in terms of recruiter or other kinds of recognition. In fact, this is not the case. UCLA may be youthful in spirit and demeanor, and the atmosphere at the school may be relaxed, but when classes begin, everyone here from students and faculty to the school's dean, who happens to be a graduate of the school, is ready and willing to roll up their sleeves and get the job of legal education done as effectively and innovatively as possible. This law school has clearly emerged as a leader in legal education and has capitalized on its location to build a strong international law program focusing on the Pacific Rim countries. UCLA's Externship Programs allow students to take a semester working in a public interest job for a semester's credit in places including London, Micronesia, China, and Washington, D.C.

The school boasts the same laid-back atmosphere found at Stanford with a good, informal relationship between faculty and students. This has something of a calming effect to counterbalance the high pressure of law school. Of course, the price is right considering UCLA's tuition, and establishing residency isn't difficult, with most second-year nonresidents coming back as in-staters. On the downside, the cost of living anywhere near the school will probably bring your tab higher than at other state schools. It's still worth the cost.

You might find UCLA law students lunching on sushi rolls at the LuValle Commons adjacent to the school. But make no mistake, the pioneering attitude is definitely present in the school's programs, particularly its emphasis on clinical and externship programs. Students are impressed with the fact that they represent real clients with full-time professors who operate the clinics. And with recently expanded clinical facilities, these programs are on the move up in terms of quality. Recruiters often mention that the presence of externships on UCLA students' résumés is a big plus and over all, recruiters outside of California are taking greater notice of the school.

Dean Michael Rappaport tells East Coast applicants considering UCLA law school, that the setting resembles a beautiful campus like Cornell set down two blocks from Wall Street. UCLA has much to offer to anyone considering law school, with a good location, outstanding clinical and externship opportunities, and a great price.

Students note that this is a relatively inexpensive tuition for a quality education and excellent job opportunities on a scenic site in a well-to-do section of Los Angeles near Beverly Hills.

One of UCLA's strengths is its Comparative Law program. A master's in Comparative Law program brings in students with foreign law degrees; this exposes UCLA's JD candidates to different perspectives on legal education. Many of the international students go back to their own countries with what they have learned and become teachers.

One of the largest drawing cards for the school is what Rappaport calls "The Los Angeles Factor." Los Angeles is a major center of international trade, and the school capitalized on its location by directing its International Law program towards Pacific Rim countries. Entertainment Law is also strong at the school, and a glimmer of Hollywood enters through its financial aid office with the Mary Pickford Foundation Graduate Scholarship Fund, which provides scholarships to needy, worthy law students doing graduate work.

ADMISSIONS

About 60% of the entering class is admitted largely on the basis of academic ability. For that group, the approximate LSAT score is 43, with an average GPA of 3.65. However, a substantial portion of the class, about 40%, is admitted not only on academic ability but also on other factors, which the Admissions Committee believes will add diverse and interesting elements to the class. Such diverse characteristics include, but are not limited to, age, interesting experiences and background, work experience, race, outstanding achievements, and disadvantages overcome. For this group of entering students, the approximate average LSAT is 37 and the approximate average GPA is 3.23. The LSAT and GPA figures for admitted applicants should be seen as only a general guideline because they can be misleading. Other academic factors like letters of recommendation and the rigor of the undergraduate program may also be considered. All applicants are assigned an index number that combines their LSAT and GPA, giving approximately equal weight to each factor. Although no applicant is admitted solely on the basis of the index number, applicants with higher scores and grades will have an advantage.

CRITERIA

LEVEL 1: LSAT; GPA; age; interesting experiences and background; work experience; race; outstanding achievements, disadvantages overcome; recommendation; and quality of undergraduate program.

MINORITY RECRUITMENT PROGRAM

Yes. "We expect to be able to admit significant numbers of minorities and other nontraditional applicants to UCLA as long as we continue to receive significant numbers of qualified applicants. Minorities are strongly urged to apply to UCLA School of Law."

ABOUT THE APPLICATION

DEADLINE FOR FILING: 2/1

FEE: $40

LSAT: Scores of tests taken prior to December 1985 are no longer acceptable. In most cases, the school takes the average of scores presented. However, if there is a large discrepancy in scores and an explanation is noted, the school may be inclined to take the higher score.

PERSONAL STATEMENT: A focused essay, which doesn't just tell why you want to be a lawyer but tells something about you as a person.

INTERVIEW: Not required or recommended.

ADMISSIONS TIPS: "Applicants will be considered without letters of recommendation. However, applicants are strongly encouraged to send two letters of recommendation from people who are familiar with their academic and other talents. It is important to discuss weaknesses in your academic record. If you had a 3.8 first, second, and fourth years and a 2.1 the third year, don't talk about the good years. Tell us what happened that third year when your grades fell."

CONTACT: Michael Rappaport, Dean of Admissions

PHYSICAL ENVIRONMENT

Located in an affluent and safe area just minutes away from Beverly Hills, the law school is housed in one modern structure on the university's sprawling campus. James E. LuValle Commons serves food from eggs and bacon to sushi at reasonable prices, and there is an outdoor eating area.

The law school building has just gained a multimillion-dollar wing of classrooms, offices, and clinical classrooms, and the UCLA campus offers the added attraction of athletic facilities and the opportunity to take classes in other divisions, including nearby Anderson School of Management. However, the law library is, in the words of one UCLA third-year student, "about as ugly as any I have seen or can imagine, and incredibly cramped." Another student adds, "The main reading room is dominated by the ugliest mural I've ever seen. In all fairness however, it provides ample research sources and one can always study in one of UCLA's many other libraries." The student lounge is also considered less than adequate. There are reports, however, that these facilities will be remodeled in a year.

Safety is considered good here, but many warn that suburban Westwood may not be as safe as it appears. Students are urged to take advantage of the escort service that is readily available by using a campus phone. On-campus housing is available and parking is very limited.

FINANCES

BUDGET	LOW	MEDIUM	HIGH
Tuition (Resident) Tuition (Nonresident)	$1660.50 $7458	$1660.50 $7458	$1660.50 $7458
Books	$775	$775	$775
Living Accommodations (9 months)	On-Campus $4400	Shared Apt. $4050	One-Bedroom Apt. $6300
Food	Meal Plan (19/wk) Included	Groceries/Cafeteria $950	Groceries/Restaurants $1750
Miscellaneous	$1500	$2360	$3500
Transportation	Mass Transit $470	Car/Bus $800	Car $1000
TOTAL (R) TOTAL (NR)	$8805.50 $14,603	$10,595.50 $16,393	$14,985.50 $20,783

Employment During School: Not recommended during first year.

Scholarships/Fellowships: A limited number of fellowships for one or more years may be awarded to applicants who show outstanding promise; the school also offers some scholarships.

School Loan Program (Exclusive of Perkins Money): N/A

Loan Forgiveness Program: No

Students Requesting Aid: N/A

ACADEMICS

UCLA believes that any student accepted should make it through the program, and it puts its resources where its mouth is, with numerous support programs, including workshops for all law students in study skills and taking exams. Although the class size is relatively large, it is divided into four groups of eighty. Two of the first year's four courses are broken up further so that the students can receive closer attention. First-year students may take an optional class in legal analysis instead of legal research and writing.

Perhaps the most unique aspect of the school's courses exists through the Extern Program open to second- and third-year students who can serve as law clerks for state and federal judges sitting on trial and appellate courts throughout the United States. UCLA also boasts strong clinical programs and a strong faculty in Communications and Entertainment Law. Students find that course offerings are flexible and keep pace with the rapidly changing legal profession. Recent course offerings have included seminars on Child Abuse, Homeless Families, and the Legal Status of the Fetus. Individualized instruction is provided in such courses as trial advocacy and negotiation techniques.

There are quite a few female faculty members, and as a whole, faculty are considered "the lifeblood of this school: outstanding communicators and caring, compassionate human beings." The Socratic method is used by many of the faculty. Grading is anonymous; 40% of the class must receive Cs and Ds. Star faculty include Grant Nelson (Real Estate Finance), Steven Munzer (Property), and William McGovern (Contracts).

JOINT DEGREE/SPECIAL PROGRAMS

Joint Degree: JD/MBA
Graduate Programs: LLM; Masters in Comparative Law

STUDENT LIFE

As one third-year student put it, "UCLA is a city school within a vast metropolitan area. The social life of law students therefore doesn't necessarily focus on the immediate vicinity." Whether it be the San Francisco Saloon on Pico Boulevard, My Father's Office in Santa Monica, or the Fig Tree in Venice, students get together in a wide variety of settings, in many instances without other law students. Although some here feel that "people tend to keep to themselves," UCLA has a good degree of student activism with the *UCLA Law Review, The Black Law Journal, The Chicano Law Review, The Federal Communications Law Journal, and the popular UCLA Pacific Basin Law Journal,* which happens to be the only law review in the country that devotes itself to the study of international and comparative law within the Pacific Basin.

Students are relatively competitive, but they feel that in each of their classes, there are many people that they can count on. Although there are some notable exceptions, most students are friendly and helpful, encouraging a laid-back atmosphere where students get serious work accomplished.

PLACEMENT

Within the immediate vicinity of the school and throughout California, placement is phenomenal. Students find that farther out, the going gets considerably tougher, with many Midwestern and Eastern firms choosing not to recruit at UCLA. "They don't take us seriously as far as moving away from sunny L.A. or California." Students feel that the placement emphasis is on corporate law with little emphasis on government work or public interest. UCLA's reputation hasn't penetrated the outside world, and out-of-state firms are underrepresented. UCLA offers the benefit of a first-year, on-campus interviewing program that attracts mostly small and medium-sized firms. Approximately two-thirds of first-year students work in law-related jobs during the summer.

WHERE/WHAT GRADUATES PRACTICE

A. 88.5% Pacific (California, Washington, Oregon, Hawaii, and Alaska); 8.5% Mid-Atlantic (New York, New Jersey, Pennsylvania); 7.9% South Atlantic (Washington, D.C. [primarily] and the Southeast); 2.4% East North Central (Primarily Chicago); 1.5% New England (Boston and Connecticut).
B. 41.1% Very Large Firms (100+ Attorneys); 16.1% Large Firms (51–100 Attorneys); 9.6% Medium Firms (26–50 Attorneys); 7% Small Firms (11–25 Attorneys); 6.5% Very Small Firms (2–10 Attorneys); 1% Self–employed; 1.3% Business/Corporate; 4.8% Public Interest (Including Public Defender); 3.5% Government; 7.4% Judicial Clerkship (State & Federal).

350 CEDAR STREET
SAN DIEGO, CALIFORNIA (CA) 92101
(619) 239-0391, (800) 443-6091 (INSIDE CA);
(800) 255-4252 (OUTSIDE CA)

REPORT CARD

ADMISSIONS
SELECTIVITY

Applicants: 2350; Accepted: 1222
LSAT Mean: 34–35 GPA Mean: 3.2

PLACEMENT
REPUTATION

Recruiters: 75
Starting Salary Median: $35,425

ACADEMICS

California Bar Passage Rate (first
  try): 75.7% (July 1989 ABA Statewide
  Average: 72.2%)
Faculty to Student Ratio: 1:22
Quality of Teaching: B+/A−
Faculty Accessibility: A

FINANCES

Tuition: $10,960
Average Total Cost: $18,824

PHYSICAL ENVIRONMENT

Location: Medium-Sized City
Safety: Fair (downtown area). No escort service.
HA:

STUDENT LIFE
RATING

After Hours: Waterfront, Diegos, The
  Beach, Lahina's

STUDENT ENROLLMENT

Class Size: 240 (full-time)
Women 40%   Minorities: 11%
Average Age of Entering Class: 26

PROMINENT ALUMNI/AE

Include: Thomas Nassif, former U.S. Ambassador to Morocco; Abbie Wolfshiemer, San
Diego City Council member; Keith
Tanaka, Attorney General, State of Hawaii

INSIDER INFORMATION

In the race among law schools, there are those schools that have been near the finish line for well over a century; others are marathon runners keeping a steady pace without much fanfare, attention, or advancement. California Western is undoubtedly a sprinter that has quickly hit its stride. And with courses in cutting-edge areas of the law, including sports law, biotechnology and the law, entertainment law, and telecommunications and the law, guided by nationally recognized faculty in these fields, there is a strong probability of California Western's continued momentum.

Of course, California Western's location in a city with 325 sun days annually and temperatures from 65 degrees in January to 77 degrees in August could leave applicants with the idea that this is a place to pick up your law degree after spending a day at the beach. To be honest, California Western will provide you with far more than the chance to pick up a good tan. It will provide you with the opportunity to concentrate in areas such as Real Estate Law, Corporate-Business Law, Constitutional Law and Civil Rights, Advocacy and Dispute Resolution, and International and Comparative Law.

Living in what one student calls "America's finest city" tends to become rather costly. Students feel the library is somewhat crowded. They further bemoan the fact that the school is not part of a larger university and therefore doesn't have any of the associated benefits like housing or a collegiate atmosphere.

The school's extensive Clinical (internship) Program, which provides on-the-job training for credit, was cited at a recent National Conference of Law Schools as a model program in legal education. Its trimester system allows students the flexibility to go through law school in six consecutive terms without summers off. This affords students the chance to graduate in two or two-and-one-half years. However, students strongly advise prospective applicants to apply for the fall, rather than January, trimester, because they believe it helps with scholarships, financial aid, law review, and summer jobs.

Students find one of California Western's strongest assets to be its highly energetic faculty and a very family-type atmosphere. The entire school has an open-door policy. Approachability is a key point at the school. Most recently, the faculty baked cakes for an auction benefitting the San Francisco earthquake relief and raised over $1500 from students, faculty, and staff.

CRITERIA

LEVEL 1: LSAT score; Grade Point Average; quality of undergraduate curriculum/ course work completed

LEVEL 2: Quality/reputation of college/university; personal essay

LEVEL 3: Work experience

LEVEL 4: Recommendations

MINORITY RECRUITMENT PROGRAM

No; no formal program, but the school gives special consideration to minorities and offers scholarships to most who are accepted; the Multicultural Association provides tutoring and special support.

DEADLINE FOR FILING: Rolling

FEE: $35

LSAT: The school takes the average of applicant's scores.

RECOMMENDED COURSES PRIOR TO MATRICULATING: None

PERSONAL STATEMENT: "It will rarely help the candidate with low credentials. The essay will often help the borderline to be accepted, or, if the personal statement is poor, be denied. This is the interview and the applicant needs to build his or her own case—tell us what *they want us* to know, not what they *think* we want to hear, which results in a stilted piece. The striking essay is an honest, sincere, well-thought-out, technically correct essay."

INTERVIEW: Not required or recommended. "We do call applicants if we have questions while reviewing their application." For visitors, Howard Johnson Hotel, 1430 Seventh Avenue (619) 696-0911 ($45/night; mention California-Western); Embassy Hotel (619) 296-3141 (rates begin at $35/night; make reservations early); Budget Motels of America, 641 Camino del Rio South, San Diego 92108, (800) 624-1257 (rates begin at $30/night) are recommended.

ADMISSIONS TIPS: "Follow the directions. Fill out the application fully and accurately and sign it. We have added a checklist that has helped. Don't submit lengthy personal statements." Although there is rolling admissions, the school urges applicants to apply for the January entering class by November 1 and for the September entering class by June 1.

CONTACT: Nancy C. Ramsayer, Director of Admissions

PHYSICAL ENVIRONMENT

Cal Western is housed in a large building that was formerly an old Elk's lodge, providing the older building with some character. Located on the outskirts of downtown San Diego, it is near the courts and the local firms. As a result of its not being affiliated with a university there are no athletic facilities or campus.

The school owns no housing. The most popular form of student housing is apartments. Apartments are considered plentiful, but students should shop around for one that is clean and safe. A car is recommended, because it is the most effective means of transportation, especially for those in low-cost housing, which is at a distance from the school. However, parking can be a problem. Street parking is available for those who arrive by 7:00 am; otherwise parking lots are available for $60–100/month. The transit system is very good for those on the bus lines.

Handicapped accessibility is considered good. There is a front doorway for the use of the handicapped and an elevator that travels to all three floors. Some of the rooms may be difficult to get into, but it is a small school. The school makes arrangements and insists that all handicapped students visit first.

BUDGET	LOW	MEDIUM	HIGH
Tuition	$10,960	$10,960	$10,960
Books	$540	$540	$540
Living Accommodations (9 months)	Shared House $1800	One-Bedroom Apt. $3600	Two-Bedroom Apt. $5400
Food	Groceries $2124	Groceries $2124	Restaurants $3600
Miscellaneous	$800	$1000	$1200
Transportation	Car $600	Car $600	Car $600
TOTALS	$16,824	$18,824	$22,300

Employment During School: Work-study jobs are available; need-based.

Scholarships: The school gives merit scholarships, contingent upon maintaining a 3.0 GPA.

School Loan Program (Exclusive of Perkins Money): No

Loan Forgiveness Program: No

Students Requesting Aid: 90%; of these, 85% receive aid.

Students Indebted upon Graduation: 85%

Average Loan Indebtedness: $50,000

ACADEMICS

At many law schools, you will be assigned a faculty advisor as soon as you register. At Cal Western, a faculty mentor is assigned to you as soon as you make a deposit to hold your place in the entering class. He or she will answer any questions you have about law school or your schedule.

All the first-year courses are required and numerous upperclass courses are required as well. Included in these requirements are Business Organizations (Corporation), Professional Responsibility, and Evidence. Electives are grouped by areas of concentration, with, for example, ten electives in Entertainment Law and the opportunity to intern. In fact, each concentration area provides an internship opportunity for students. Among the programs available is the Practical Legal Education Program, an internship program that provides students with the opportunity to acquire lawyering skills. The school developed a mediation training program for Cal Western students that includes course work and actual experience as mediators with the San Diego Attorney's Office. It also hosted the annual Entertainment Law Conference. With the San Diego Trial Lawyers' Association, Cal Western co-sponsors the People's Law School, an eight-week public education program. Students are also involved in a Telecommunications Moot Court Competition.

One of the school's specialties is Biotechnology, and Cal Western is one of the first law schools in the country to offer this course. Cal Western also presents a Current Legal Issues Series for students and the community that has recently addressed Biotechnology in the Pacific Basin and Legal Issues in the AIDS Crisis.

One half of the professors use the Socratic method. Faculty stars include William Lynch (Evidence/Torts), Robert Bohrer (Biotechnology, Environmental Law), Katherine Rosenberry (Land Use, Condominium Law), Jan Stiglitz (Sports Law, Labor Law), John Noyes (International Law), Howard Berman (Human Rights Advocate, International Law), and Chin Kim (International Law).

GRADUATE/SPECIAL PROGRAMS

The School's Master of Comparative Law program is designed for persons who have earned university law degrees outside of the United States. It requires a minimum of two trimesters in residence at CWSL. Supplementary courses are available at San Diego State University for students who wish to supplement their education with graduate courses in their area of legal interest.

STUDENT LIFE

The majority of students questioned found the social life at Cal Western on the whole excellent. The school has a very family-type attitude, one of the strongest attractions it has to offer. Various functions are organized by the school, including the Barrister's Ball, game night, and a revue show put on by the students.

PLACEMENT

There are great opportunities for internships and outside work experiences through the internship program, like those through the juvenile court.

Approximately 95.5% of the students are placed after graduation. 47% of the graduates remain in the immediate vicinity within one year of graduation.

PREPARATION

Cal Western's placement office prepares its students through mock interviews with local alumni practitioners. Workshops deal with many subjects including résumé writing, researching legal employers, interview skills, and decision making. Seminars include Introduction to Law Clerking and the Wednesday Forum Program, in which practitioners discuss legal specialties.

WHERE/WHAT GRADUATES PRACTICE

A. 15% Northeast; 5% South; 70% West Coast; 10% Midwest.
B. 3.5% Sole Practitioner; 53% Small Firms; 27% Medium Firms; 16.5% Large Firms; 4% Clerkships; 2% Graduate Degrees; 1% Military; 12% Governmental Agencies; 8% Corporations; 3.5% Public Interest.

11075 EAST BOULEVARD
CLEVELAND, OHIO (OH) 44106
(216) 368-3600

REPORT CARD

ADMISSIONS
SELECTIVITY 🎓 🎓 🎓 🎓

Applicants: 1573; Accepted: 640
Transfer Applications: 9; Accepted: 4
LSAT Mean: 36 GPA Mean: 3.26

ACADEMICS

Order of the Coif (1912)
Ohio Bar Passage (first try): at or above
   statewide average
Faculty to Student Ratio: 1:18
Quality of Teaching: A−
Faculty Accessibility: A−

PHYSICAL ENVIRONMENT

Location: Urban/Big City
Safety: Fair
HA: ♿ ♿ ♿ ♿

STUDENT ENROLLMENT

Class Size: 227 (full-time); 2 (part-time)
Women: 41%   Minorities: 10%
Average Age of Entering Class: 25

PLACEMENT
REPUTATION ★ ★ ★

Recruiters: 150
Starting Salary Mean: $42,677

FINANCES

Tuition: $12,500
Average Total Cost: $19,510

STUDENT LIFE
RATING ☺ ☺ ☺ ☹

After Hours: Boarding House Restaurant,
   Licks, Arabica Coffee House.

PROMINENT ALUMNI/AE

Include: N/A

INSIDER INFORMATION When assembling material to bring to Law School Forums, most admissions officers make sure they bring enough applications, brochures, bulletins, placement statistics, and catalogs. In the case of Barbara Andelman, the dynamic Director of Admissions for Case Western Reserve School of Law, there is one more thing to add to her list: literature about Cleveland, Ohio. Singlehandedly, this one-woman committee for "I Love Cleveland" has shown prospective applicants that a city or physical environment can change for the better. She has also shown numerous applicants what it means to be excited about a law school. And for all of you Doubting Thomases and Thomasinas, there's one thing you should know: this "hidden treasure," perceived highly by both students and recruiters, who regard the school's graduates as "incredibly diverse . . .

highly insightful, possessing strong written communication skills," is well worth getting excited about.

Case's "focused curriculum" is designed to guide students in six areas of knowledge: 1) Problem Solving and Analysis; 2) Theories of Law; 3) Communication; 4) Information Management; 5) Professionalism; and 6) Preventive Law. The ideal of the school is learning founded on continual active participation by students, supported by smaller classes, frequent interaction with faculty, and immediate feedback. Case Western Reserve University has also begun an ambitious project to construct a computer network, CWRUNET, which will be among the most advanced in the country. The law school was the first academic building wired to this system, affording students tremendous capabilities for information retrieval. These services will be available to students at their dorms, homes, or apartments.

The school's student body is diverse in terms of age, experience, race, background, ethnicity, and interests. Faculty lean more heavily toward research, but most students agree, teachers who cannot convey information are the exception, rather than the rule. The safety of Case resembles an island with perimeters about three blocks away from each part of the site of the law school. Students who exercise proper safety precautions shouldn't have much difficulty and there is an escort service. If you're visiting the school looking for students to talk to about what life at Case Law is like, venture no further than across the street to an old carriage house converted into a restaurant. With a name like Licks, you can't miss it.

ADMISSIONS

CRITERIA

LEVEL 1:   Grade Point Average; LSAT score

LEVEL 2:   Quality of undergraduate curriculum/course work completed; quality/reputation of college/university; recommendations; personal essay

LEVEL 3:   Work experience and diversity in background and experience. If grade point average is not strong, we look for an upward trend in grades.

MINORITY RECRUITMENT PROGRAM

Yes. Although the school does not have a separate minority recruitment program, it is rigorous in its recruitment of minority students. Efforts are comprehensive, beginning with participation in minority recruitment fairs and special visits to predominantly minority schools to its need-based half-tuition scholarships for minority students to its Mentor Program for incoming first-year minority students.

ABOUT THE APPLICATION

DEADLINE FOR FILING: 4/1

FEE: $35

LSAT: School takes the average of applicant's scores.

RECOMMENDED COURSES PRIOR TO MATRICULATING: The school encourages undergraduates interested in law to gain a broad educational background and to choose vigorous courses requiring critical thinking and logical analysis, such as history, economics, philosophy, and accounting. The school particularly urges students to choose courses in which they will develop strong writing skills.

PERSONAL STATEMENT: "The personal statement is an important part of our admissions process, providing the committee an opportunity to learn more about the applicant and to evaluate an applicant's writing ability. Although a good personal statement is unlikely to help an applicant whose qualifications are significantly below our normal requirements, it may assist a 'borderline' candidate."

INTERVIEW: Not required or recommended. However, the school welcomes visits by prospective students who will have an opportunity to attend a first-year class, meet current students, and speak with an Admissions Office representative. The school offers an overnight stay program, which gives a prospective student the opportunity to stay one weekday night at the apartment of a current student during the school year (depending on availability). Arrangements must be made at least two weeks before the planned visit. Accommodations recommended are Glidden House (bed and breakfast directly across the street from the law school) (216)231-8900 and The Clinic Center Hotel (216)791-2710.

ADMISSIONS TIPS: "Applicants should prepare their applications carefully; errors in spelling and typing may reflect an inattentiveness to detail. If extenuating circumstances (such as illness or death in the family) affected scholastic performance, the applicant may wish to provide an explanation."

CONTACT: Barbara Andelman, Director of Admissions and Financial Aid

PHYSICAL ENVIRONMENT

Greater Cleveland is home to more than two million people. The law school is housed in George Gund Hall, a light-red modern brick building, built in 1971. The campus is located in a safe area, surrounded by less safe areas about three blocks away. Although not necessary, a car is certainly a convenience.

On-campus housing is not guaranteed, and only 3–4% of the students live in school-owned accommodations. Most Case Western Reserve students who live off campus are in apartments around the University or else just a small distance away in suburbs, such as Cleveland Heights (a twenty-minute walk) or Shaker Heights (ten minutes by car or bus).

$$$
FINANCES

BUDGET	LOW	MEDIUM	HIGH
Tuition	$12,500	$12,500	$12,500
Books	$535	$535	$535
Living Accommodations (9 months)	Shared House* $1800	On-Campus $2525	One-Bedroom Apt. $3213
Food	Groceries $1950	Meal Plan $2050	Restaurants $3500
Miscellaneous	$1000	$1200	$1500
Transportation	Bus $450	Car $700	Car $700
TOTAL	$18,235	$19,510	$21,948

* Shared Apartment: $2250

Employment During School: Not recommended.

Scholarships: School provides merit scholarships. The student must maintain a GPA required by specific scholarship.

School Loan Program (Exclusive of Perkins Money): No

Students Requesting Aid: 70%; of these, 70% receive aid.

Students Indebted upon Graduation: 70%

Average Loan Indebtedness: $47,000

ACADEMICS

The first year of legal studies at Case consists of required courses. The most valuable of these is what students call RAW: Research, Advocacy, and Writing, taught in sections of about twenty. RAW extends over two semesters. The 220-student class is divided into two or three sections, with all students having one small group class. Second- and third-year students have only two requirements: Professional Responsibility and at least one course with a substantial research paper. Second- and third-year students can register in any semester for supervised research.

Case's Law–Medicine Center's focus includes the whole range of legal, social, economic, scientific, and ethical issues in which law and medicine are interrelated. Courses at the center include Law and Medicine, Civil Law and Psychiatry, and Legal and Biomedical Ethics. The Canada–United States Law Institute is jointly sponsored by Case Western Law and the law school at the University of Western Ontario; its primary purpose is to give students a comparative perspective.

The school's Professional Skills Program includes The Lawyering Process, a simulation course in which students can practice basic legal skills like interviewing and negotiating. The Law School Clinic, a law office housed within a law school, offers two intensive courses each year—civil and criminal. The Litigation Program receives mixed reviews from students and consists of an array of courses that prepare the student for a career as a trial attorney.

Most students get Bs, with grades computed on a scale from 0.00 (F) to 4.3 (A+). Legal writing is taught in the first year by full-time faculty members. Students find the programs offered diverse. However, the primary concern for students is that the scheduling system be changed. Course offerings are excellent, but it is often difficult to get into certain courses. Faculty, apart from being published scholars, are excellent teachers. Case is small enough so that students can know their professors as well as fellow students. Faculty stars include Leon Gabinet (Federal Income Tax), Morris Shanker (Bankruptcy), and William Marshall (Civil Procedure).

JOINT DEGREE PROGRAMS

JD/MBA; JD/MA (Legal History); JD/MSSA (Master of Applied Social Science)

Students are competitive but not cutthroat. Case students feel that Cleveland has a great deal to offer culturally with museums, theater, and concerts. The class is highly eclectic, bringing with it a high energy level and excitement for learning the law.

Students are satisfied with Case Western's ability to find them jobs. They feel that placement provides numerous job opportunities to students, although the top 25% generally have the easiest time. The Placement Office actively seeks out and publicizes job openings. With other Ohio law schools, it sponsors an annual Placement Consortium, giving students access to another set of employers, many of them out of state. It organizes off-campus interview days in other cities, including Chicago, New York, Pittsburgh, and Washington, D.C. It further maintains reciprocal agreements with the placement offices of other law schools.

PREPARATION

The Placement Office prepares its students through sponsoring presentations about all varieties of career opportunities. It arranges videotaped mock interviews and critiques. It also publishes a handbook that includes sample résumés and sample letters. The placement director is available for advice, and this may include the review of résumés and letters.

WHERE/WHAT GRADUATES PRACTICE

A. 22.6% Northeast; 6.4% South; 1.3% West; 68.4% Midwest; 1.3% Other; 45% of students remain in Cleveland one year after graduation.
B. 1.9% Solo Practitioner; 23.3% Small Firms; 15.7% Medium Firms; 28.9% Large Firms; 6.3% Clerkships; 11.9% Governmental Agencies; 6.9% Corporations; 1.3% Other (includes academic, military, and nonlegal).

UNIVERSITY OF CHICAGO
Law School

1111 EAST 60TH STREET
CHICAGO, ILLINOIS (IL) 60637
(312) 702-9484

☙ REPORT CARD ❧

ADMISSIONS
SELECTIVITY 🎓 🎓 🎓 🎓 🎓

Applicants: 3350; Accepted: 550
Transfer Applicants: 50; Accepted: 10
LSAT Median: 44 GPA Median: 3.75

ACADEMICS
Order of the Coif (1912)
Illinois Bar Passage Rate (first try): 99%;
   New York Bar Passage Rate: 90%
Faculty to Student Ratio: 1:15
Quality of Teaching: B−
Faculty Accessibility: A+

PHYSICAL ENVIRONMENT
Location: Large City
Safety: Marginal–Poor
HA: ♿ ♿ ♿ ♿ ♿

STUDENT ENROLLMENT
Class Size: 178
Women: 42%   Minorities: 15%
Average Age of Entering Class: N/A

PLACEMENT
REPUTATION ☆ ☆ ☆ ☆ ☆

Recruiters: 550+
Starting Salary Mean: N/A

FINANCES
Tuition: $14,445
Average Total Cost: $24,305

STUDENT LIFE
RATING ☺ ☺ ☺ ☺

After Hours: Midici, Jimmy's

PROMINENT ALUMNI/AE
Include: James B. Parsons, Senior Judge,
   U.S. District Court, Illinois; Robert Dale
   Morgan, Senior Judge, U.S. District Court,
   Illinois

INSIDER INFORMATION

At other law schools, you may hear students talk about their faculty in terms relative to Chicago, such as "The faculty here certainly isn't as conservative as at Chicago." As was pointed out by Assistant Dean at the Law School, Richard Badger, these students are not in a position to know the nature of Chicago's faculty. He surmises that the "conservative" labeling may be due in part to two prominent alumni, Bork and Ginsburg, being nominated to the Supreme Court. Interestingly, when Bork was nominated, about ten faculty members were opposed to the nomination and ten were in favor. At the time of these nominations, Bork was teaching at Yale and Ginsburg was teaching at Harvard. Perhaps another factor in the conservative label may be the school's affiliation with Milton Friedman from the Chicago School of Economics. Given that Chicago's dean, Jeff Stone, has been labeled a "liberal," based on his work with ACLU and Free Speech, the "conservative" label appears to be overly applied. In general, students do concur that there is a definite faction of conservative faculty present at the school.

"People are pushed harder at Chicago than at other law schools. Chicago law students think, why is the law the way it is? rather than Rule X is this, apply it," says Badger. The school can create a sort of fishbowl feeling, although this can be advantageous for students who are sick or who have missed notes. Contrary to the school's reputation, there is very little competition among students because, as many point out, there is little difficulty in getting jobs. The class size is approximately 180. As a result there is an intimate atmosphere. Chicago students categorize their school as having no bureaucracy, and a good mix of people. The intimacy created by its small size and intense student body can at times be somewhat overwhelming and students here are quick to mention that safety in the area of their school is abysmal, making them feel a little more anxious because of their surroundings.

Recruiter satisfaction with recent graduates is resoundingly high at the school, with many competing for the small class. Many refer to it as the "academic's law school," but others point out that Chicago grads are highly skilled litigators, and above all, have superior legal writing skills.

ADMISSIONS

Begins in mid-November with candidates who have their files in by that time expecting to receive word by December 15th. Most (90%) candidates will be informed of an admission decision by April 15th.

CRITERIA

LEVEL 1: Grade Point Average; quality of undergraduate curriculum/course work completed; quality/reputation of college/university; LSAT score; work experience; recommendations; personal essay

MINORITY RECRUITMENT PROGRAM

N/A

ABOUT THE APPLICATION

DEADLINE FOR FILING: Rolling

FEE: $45

LSAT: School usually takes the average of applicant's scores. LSAT must be taken within four years of application. A substantially higher second or subsequent score will occasionally be used alone, if there are indications that it would be inappropriate to average all of applicant's scores.

PERSONAL STATEMENT: Although the school does not require a personal statement, it is encouraged. Statements that supply additional information about your background or explain discrepancies/shortcomings in your academic record will be most beneficial. Essays/personal statements that are narrowly focused are often better than those that explain your broad purpose or how the law fits in with your career or scholarly endeavors.

INTERVIEW: Used as an evaluative interview for approximately 10% of applicants. You must be invited for the interview after the school has completed an initial review of your application. This is an opportunity for applicants who have been placed on "hold." At times, the interview will be a major determining factor in deciding to admit an applicant; at other times, if the interview cannot compensate for weaknesses in the applicant's academic record, the applicant will not be accepted. Last year 600–700 applicants who were placed in the hold category were given the option to have a personal interview; among that group, approximately 330 applicants took this option.

ADMISSIONS TIPS: Since the school uses rolling admissions, it is best to apply as early as possible. Chicago requires three recommendation letters, and it is advised that at least one professor who writes a recommendation should know you well enough to comment about your complete academic performance, rather than just one or two classes. Additionally, Assistant Dean Badger strongly advises applicants to pay careful attention to the application instructions. Since lawyers must follow instructions carefully and pay attention to detail, the admissions committee takes into consideration any applicant failing to follow instructions. Students should refrain from sending associated material, such as term papers or videotapes, with the application.

CONTACT: Richard Badger, Assistant Dean and Dean of Students in the Law School

PHYSICAL ENVIRONMENT

Bordering the south side of Chicago around Hyde Park, the campus is considered a relatively unsafe area. However, if one is careful and alert, it can be acceptably safe. Take precautions like not walking around at night by yourself. There is no escort service, but the university does provide security.

Chicago Law is housed in the Laird Bell Quadrangle, a set of buildings built in 1959. A major expansion was completed in 1987. This collection of modern and geometric structures, which has a reflecting pool or fountain in the front where people skate in winter, is in sharp contrast to the primarily Gothic architecture of the main campus.

Although students do not find it difficult to locate suitable housing, they warn that safety should be a strong consideration when choosing a place to live. First-year students prefer living on campus, and a variety of university-owned housing units are available for both single and married graduate students. All are within walking distance of the campus or near the route of the Campus Bus, an inexpensive shuttle service run by the university. Apartments are also available in the nearby South Shore area, which has lower rents and is also served by the Campus Bus. There is single-student housing available in the three-storied Graduate Residence Hall, which houses approximately 100 first-year law students; students are advised to apply early. Housing for single students is also available at International House, an international student center on campus that accommodates approximately 250 American and 250 foreign graduate students from the university and other colleges in the Chicago area. The university has more than 1000 apartments in 30 buildings for the housing of married students. However, there is no guarantee that housing will be provided.

Good handicapped accessibility exists and ramps are evident. The school is near campus facilities such as an athletic center.

FINANCES

BUDGET	LOW	MEDIUM	HIGH
Tuition	$14,445	$14,445	$14,445
Books	$550	$550	$550
Living Accommodations (9 months)	Shared House $2700	On-Campus $3150	One-Bedroom Apt. $4050
Food	Groceries $1800	Meal Plan $3600	Restaurants $5400
Miscellaneous*	$1065	$2200	$2900
Transportation	Mass Transit $180	Taxis $360	Car $450
TOTAL	$20,740	$24,305	$27,795

* Includes Health Fee—all students pay a $165 annual fee for use of the university's Student Health Service.

Employment During School: The University House System provides opportunities for law students to serve in the staff positions of Resident Head or assistant Resident Head. The Resident Head receives a furnished suite, board, weekly maid service, telephone privileges, and, in the large houses, a cash stipend. Assistant Resident Heads receive a single room, and first year, the equivalent of one half of a board contract, in second year a full board contract. These positions are available generally for students who have been in residence for one year.

Scholarships: The school offers merit and need-based scholarships as well as research and fellowship funds.

School Loan Program (Exclusive of Perkins Money): Yes. The university offers law students short-term emergency loans of up to $500. Such loans may be obtained within forty-eight hours to meet a genuine emergency and must be repaid within three months.

Students Requesting Aid: N/A; of those requesting aid, 80% receive aid.

ACADEMICS

The first year consists of required courses, including contracts, torts, property, criminal law, and civil procedure. First-year students also take an introductory course in Elements of the Law in the fall quarter. In the spring quarter, they choose an elective from a wide variety of subject matter, including economics, legal philosophy, and history. During this year, students are split into two sections. All first-year students also take a legal writing program, which involves writing a series of memoranda and other legal documents that a lawyer would write regularly. During the spring quarter, each of six legal writing sections is divided into teams to prepare briefs for an appellate case and argues that case before a panel of judges made up of faculty and practicing lawyers. Further experience is provided by the school's mentor program, which pairs local alumni with first-year students.

Chicago places a strong emphasis on legal writing and, unlike other schools, this component of their legal education counts as 10% of the grade. Students are taught by full-time faculty, Bigelow Scholars. The Joseph Henry Beale Prize is awarded for outstanding written work in each legal section. All students are required to complete at least two substantial pieces of writing beyond what is required of the Legal Research and Writing course. This requirement can be satisfied by a paper or papers, as part of a course, through a seminar, or through a three-credit independent research program supervised by a faculty member; through comment prepared for *University of Chicago Law Review* or *University of Chicago Legal Forum;* with a brief for the semi-final or final round of the Hinton Moot Court Competition; or a brief, memorandum, or series of writings in the Mandel Legal Aid Clinic.

The Mandel Legal Aid Clinic, located on the premises of the law school, is a joint venture between the Chicago Law School and the Legal Aid Bureau of United Charities of Chicago that provides legal aid to indigent clients in civil cases. Participation in the program is planned as a two-year learning experience during which students are guided in every aspect of litigation, including interviews and representing clients under the supervision of an attorney in the United States District Court for the Northern District of Illinois and the Seventh Circuit Court of Appeals.

Chicago students are, for the most part, pleased with the diversity of courses offered, when they can be fit into the students' schedules. Teaching is accomplished primarily through case method and class discussion. Chicago is almost the antithesis of what is often referred to as the "black letter" law school. Students often find themselves digging much deeper into legal issues than they ever had anticipated. Aside from being an exceptionally well-published group, Chicago professors are shapers of legal thought. The small class size optimizes individual attention. The faculty are considered to write well but are not as good speakers. Other students found them variable in that most are superb, but some can be at times incomprehensible. The professors' offices are located in the library itself and all observe the open-door policy.

There's no need to go through a secretary to set up an appointment. They enthusiastically talk with students.

JOINT DEGREE/GRADUATE PROGRAMS

Joint Degrees: JD/MBA; JD/AM (History, Economics); JD/PhD (History, Economics); JD/MA (Public Policy)
Graduate Programs: LLM; JSD; M.Comp. Law (Master of Comparative Law); D.Comp. Law (Doctor of Comparative Law)

Social life is very good here. A weekly student/faculty "Wine Mess," a school cocktail party, and one large party every quarter are some of the social events scheduled by the school. One spring a boat cruise on Lake Michigan was organized. Another function organized by the school is "Eat Chicago," which enables the students to travel around the city sampling different ethnic foods at various restaurants. Students generally stay around campus or go to the north side of Chicago to socialize. The small class size allows students to know one another, but at times produces cliques. The atmosphere is competitive but not cutthroat. People are willing to help one other.

Students are pleased with the wealth of job offerings. The school is also considered excellent at helping students obtain summer jobs. Chicago has an on-campus interviewing program only for first-year students wishing to obtain summer jobs, that last year yielded 32 recruiters. 90% of students obtain law-related positions in the summer after their first year.

PREPARATION

The placement office employs two full-time counselors. Students find the office's information very current and readily accessible. There is no videotaping of mock interviews, but the office does offer numerous workshops on skills like writing cover letters and preparing résumés.

WHERE/WHAT GRADUATES PRACTICE

A. 36% East; 40% Midwest and Plains; 18% West; 8% South.
B. 69.1% Private Practice; 25.4% Judicial Clerkships (State/Federal); 0.6% Local Government; 1.1% Public Interest; 0.6% Corporate Legal; 6% Nonlegal; 2.6% N/A.

435 WEST 116TH STREET
NEW YORK, NEW YORK (NY) 10027-7297
(212) 854-2678

REPORT CARD

ADMISSIONS

SELECTIVITY 🎓 🎓 🎓 🎓 🎓

Applicants: 6136; Accepted: 977
Transfer Applicants: 100; Accepted: 13
LSAT Median: 44
GPA Median: 3.57

ACADEMICS

Quality of Teaching: **B**
Faculty Accessibility: **C+**

PHYSICAL ENVIRONMENT

Location: Urban/Large City
Safety: Marginal.
HA: ♿ ♿ ♿

STUDENT ENROLLMENT

Class Size: 338 (full-time)
Women: 40%   Minorities: 23%
International: 3%
Average Age of Entering Class: 23

PLACEMENT

REPUTATION: ★ ★ ★ ★ ✰

Recruiters: 600+
Starting Salary Mean: $60,667 (entire class);
   $77,075 (for those joining firms in New
   York)

FINANCES

Tuition: $14,050
Average Total Cost: $23,900

STUDENT LIFE

RATING: ☺ ☺ ☺ ☾

After Hours: Abbey Pub, Amsterdam Cafe,
   Anna Lee's

PROMINENT ALUMNI/AE

Include: Richard T. Andrias, Justice, New
   York Supreme Court; Theodore R. Kupfer-
   man, Associate Justice, New York Supreme
   Court, Appellate Division.

INSIDER INFORMATION

Columbia Law School. Think of these three words as an extremely powerful, electromagnetic force capable of drawing in students, faculty members, and recruiters from across the country. This "name magnet" has succeeded in attracting an exceptionally diverse and high-powered student body. The school boasts the fourth highest yield, behind Harvard, Yale, and Stanford, of student acceptances, ranging from 34 to 37% on its admissions offers. These students are often willing to go out on a limb for a cause they believe in, whether it involves standing up for the rights of AIDS patients in housing discrimination cases or organizing a group of fellow students to form a journal. Armed with a tenacity strengthened by their physical surroundings, these dynamic—one might even say, passionate—individuals are also resourceful enough to bring home results.

Placement at the school is also caught up in this magnetic field, although not always aided by the Placement Office, which many here have characterized as complacent, drawing recruiters from across the spectrum of legal opportunities. Be it working for a 700-lawyer firm based in midtown Manhattan or serving a public interest group on the West Coast, the chances to make ties that stick are abundant. Interestingly, recruiters at a greater geographical distance from the school are many times more enamored with Columbia graduates than are New York firms. Many recruiters comment about the school's low-key approach to placement and the accompanying nonchalance of its students. Lastly, the school has pulled in a faculty whose qualifications, based on scholarly research and publications, place them in the upper echelon of their colleagues.

Unfortunately, this same magnet, located adjacent to Columbia's undergraduate campus, has drawn other less desirable elements into its field of attraction. Columbia's faculty is described by students as highly uneven in teaching abilities: "A few [faculty] are good teachers, a large number are inaccessible and somewhat patronizing to students who have questions . . . at times they're just uncaring." Says one third-year *Law Review* member, "I was in a class and I had a question, so I went up to the professor afterward. He turned to me and said, 'It's in the book.' When I tried to explain [my question] he turned his back on me." Adds another, "It's like we're some kind of inconvenience that they have to put up with." One student puts it this way, "I would have preferred to have come back here to study as an LLM. They [the faculty] know their material. That's obvious. But they might know it too well. It's like trying to teach someone to tie their shoes." One second-year student counters that law school is ". . . not a time when students should expect to be spoon-fed." But even supporters of the school cannot help mentioning their faculty's shortcomings. One second-year student recalls one of his faculty members calling all of the students who got Es (excellent) in his class into his office. "He talked with them about their futures. The rest of us were just left out in the cold."

But Columbia law students are resilient. Many of them are streetwise or have quickly adapted to their less than hospitable surroundings, shuttling back and forth to school by New York's increasingly more expensive and unreliable subway system. Of course, one does not choose a law school for its location, but in Columbia's case, location has to be mentioned to anyone unfamiliar with the area of the school. Says one second-year student, "It is relatively safe around the campus. Outside of that are pockets of very unsafe areas." Columbia has a number of escort services for students. The law school's physical plant is in dire need of a planned overhaul, and although the library has not caused students difficulty for lack of legal references, it is rather unimpressive, particularly for a school of Columbia's reputation.

Once again we return to that magnetic Columbia name. In a candid outtake, some third-year students here actually wished they had accepted NYU's offer of admission based on its course variety and facilities. Adds yet another, "I wish that I had known about the uneven quality of the lectures provided. You have to rely on other methods of fully grasping the material, including the use of upperclassman outlines and review books." Given Columbia's polarized traits, which occupy both ends of its magnetic spectrum, applicants should consider what they are willing to forgo if they accept the irresistible attraction of the Columbia name.

CRITERIA

All of the following factors are considered in the evaluation. "There is no one factor that determines admissibility." Grade Point Average; quality of undergraduate curriculum/course work completed; quality/reputation of college/university; LSAT score(s) work experience; recommendations; personal essay; special honors and awards; fellowship opportunities; publications; extracurricular involvements, community service; political activity; and professional contributions.

MINORITY RECRUITMENT PROGRAM

N/A

DEADLINE FOR FILING: 2/15

FEE: $45

LSAT: See criteria listed above.

RECOMMENDED COURSES PRIOR TO MATRICULATING: "We recommend that applicants have a broadly based undergraduate preparation for law school."

PERSONAL STATEMENT: N/A

INTERVIEW: Neither required nor recommended.

ADMISSIONS TIPS: N/A

CONTACT: James Milligan, Dean of Admissions

In 1990, the building that houses all of the law school will be renovated. One of the improvements made will be greater handicapped accessibility. As it stands now, accessibility is considered only fair with few ramps. There is only one elevator that is handicapped-accessible. However, this elevator reaches all of the floors in the school. There are also complaints about the overcrowded athletic center located across the street. The law school has lounges in the building. The safety is marginal, but security is very evident.

A car is not recommended because public transportation is good and there are parking problems on and around the Columbia campus. 65% of both JD and graduate students live in either residence hall accommodations or a university-owned apartment. Students are guaranteed some form of university housing for all the three years provided their permanent residence is more than twenty-five miles from the campus. It is difficult to locate suitable housing unless one is eligible for Columbia-owned apartments, which are considerably less expensive than the normal housing in the area. While one of these apartments can cost approximately $556 for a one-bedroom, a normal one-bedroom apartment in the area can easily cost $1300/month.

Generally, single entering students are housed in East Campus or Harmony Hall for their first year of legal training and are then eligible to participate in a lottery during the spring term to determine the type of accommodation they will receive as upperclass students. In virtually all cases, those wanting to move into a university apartment are permitted to do so along with those wanting to continue in the residence halls. On the other hand, entering students who are married or older are almost always placed in an apartment because there are few dormitory units earmarked for married couples, and older students, who usually attend the law school direct from the work force, and cannot be expected to live among the 23- and 24-years-olds in East Campus or Harmony Hall.

FINANCES

BUDGET	LOW	MEDIUM	HIGH
Tuition	$15,160	$15,160	$15,160
Books	$500	$500	$500
Living Accommodations (9 months)	On-Campus $3600	Shared Apt. $4500	One-Bedroom Apt.* $5400
Food	Groceries $1300	Meal Plan $1440	Restaurants $3200
Miscellaneous	$1500	$1800	$2200
Transportation	Mass Transit $500	Mass Transit $500	Mass Transit $500
TOTAL	$22,560	$23,900	$26,960

* School-owned housing

Employment During School: Not recommended first year; other years, optional. Work-study jobs are available for eligible students (need-based). Some other jobs are available as well. These jobs pay $10 an hour.

Scholarships: The school offers need-based scholarships.

School Loan Program (Exclusive of Perkins Money): Yes. "Relatively small amounts of university loan money are available to law students; this is usually earmarked for aliens or others who, for various reasons, are prevented from using the loan programs normally available. The university limits any borrower to a gross total of $15,000 with no annual limit. Interest at 9% is payable after repayment begins, following a six-month grace period. Eligibility is based on need."

Loan Forgiveness Program: Yes. "Graduates apply during the fall following graduation. Qualifying employment includes full-time work as a lawyer or teacher of law in a nonprofit setting. Graduates are expected to repay 3% of their loan cost for each of the first three years; the rate rises to 10% at the rate of 1% additional per year. The balance is advanced to the graduate as a loan and begins to be forgiven for every year of covered employment following the third.

Students Requesting Aid: 64%; of these, 37% receive aid.

Students Indebted upon Graduation: 65%

Average Loan Indebtedness: $35,000

ACADEMICS

All first-year courses are required, and most of them employ case method. Columbia recently adopted a Foundation Curriculum, which replaced the required first-year curriculum. Two new courses in this program are Foundations of the Regulatory State and Perspectives on Legal Thought. The upperclass curriculum is primarily elective. To help in choosing electives, Columbia has grouped them into categories. Although no formal procedure is required to specialize, students who do wish to specialize may be given a preference when fitting courses and seminars into their schedules. The Law and the Arts program permits students to help struggling artists. The Human Rights Internship program permits the student to travel to places around the country and abroad in order to deal with human rights issues. Students can also defend AIDS patients in housing discrimination cases. There is also a Harlem Tutorial Program and signs of growing activism among the students, although says one student, "Students interested in public service are there, but they're an invisible minority."

Columbia's faculty are considered brilliant, but appear to know their material to such an extent that they neglect to teach the course on a basic level. Instead, the courses are taught as if the student has already taken the initial course and is now taking the more advanced level of the same subject matter. Students pass faculty evaluations after each class; other students take these evaluations when selecting courses; it is possible to bypass the less dazzling teachers. A student-chosen faculty star is Curtis Burger (Property and Tax).

Grading is on a five-point system: E(excellent), VG(very good), G(good), P(poor), and U(unsatisfactory). There is no ranking. However, there are honor awards, such as the Kent Scholar Award, given to those students who earn seven Es in one year.

Law Review is attainable by a combination of grades and a writing sample, and has recently added a "diversity factor" where up to 5% of students will be chosen with the additional factor of ethnicity, unusual background, and interests taken into consideration. There are unlimited opportunities for being on a journal, with new ones forming, including the *Women's Law Journal*. Students run the entire Moot Court Program, with twenty-five student editors creating cases used.

JOINT/GRADUATE DEGREES/SPECIAL PROGRAMS

Joint Degrees: JD/MBA; JD/MA; JD/M.Phil.; JD/PhD; JD/MS (Journalism); JD/MIA (Master of International Affairs); JD/MPA (Master of Public Administration, given in cooperation with Princeton); JD/MPA (with Columbia); JD/MFA (Master of Fine Arts); JD/MS (Social Work); JD/MS (Urban Planning)
Special Programs: Programs involving work with East Asian and Harriman Institutes are available as are international fellowship programs.
Graduate Degrees: JSD; LLM

It is highly recommended that the student take advantage of the extracurricular activities in the school. "Law Revue," a musical with lyrics sung to Broadway melodies, is particularly recommended. Biweekly bagel hours, happy hours, and a semi-formal Barrister's Ball are scheduled by the school. Parties are also sponsored by student activity groups. These functions are the primary means that the first-year students have to mingle with the upperclassmen, as there is otherwise little contact with them.

The atmosphere has been found to be competitive. Students will work together, however, 95% of the time. "There are a few 'hard-core' types but you learn to avoid them."

Students find placement very well organized, but some add that it has something of a "laissez-faire" attitude. 167 out of 178 students surveyed responded that they received their first choice in employment. 95% of these students responded that they got their "first choice" city. Placement will assess your qualifications and give you their realistic evaluation of your chances of obtaining certain jobs. An Alumni Advisor network encompasses all law fields designed to help students better understand what practicing law is like in different sized cities, firms, etc. 96.58% are employed by May of year of graduation.

PREPARATION

N/A

WHAT GRADUATES PRACTICE

70.81% Law Firms (74% of this number work for firms larger than 100 lawyers); 17.7% Clerkships; 0.62% Federal Government; 0.93% State/City Government; 0.62% District Attorney; 0.93% Legal Services; 0.93% Public Interest; 0.31% Corporate; 0.62% Misc.; 1.24% Further Study; 0.31% Not Seeking.

55 ELIZABETH STREET
HARTFORD, CONNECTICUT (CT) 06105-2296
(203) 241-4696

REPORT CARD

ADMISSIONS

SELECTIVITY 🎓 🎓 🎓 🎓

Applicants: (Day): 1470; **Accepted:** 326;
Applicants: (Evening): 523; **Accepted:** 114
Transfer Applicants: 10; **Accepted:** 2
LSAT Mean: 39 (full-time); 38 (part-time)
GPA Mean: 3.21 (day); 3.18 (evening)

ACADEMICS

Connecticut Bar Passage (first try): N/A
Faculty to Student Ratio: 1:20
Quality of Teaching: **B+**
Faculty Accessibility: **A−**

PHYSICAL ENVIRONMENT

Location: Medium-Sized City
Safety: Fair
HA: ♿ ♿ ♿ ♿

STUDENT ENROLLMENT

Class Size: 147 (full-time); 70 (part-time)
Women: 49%   Minorities: 11%
Average Age of Entering Class: 25 (day); 30
(evening)

PLACEMENT

REPUTATION: ★ ★ ★ ⯪

Recruiters: N/A
Starting Salary Mean: N/A

FINANCES

Tuition: $3260 (R); $6710 (NR)
Average Total Cost: $9865 (R); $13,315
(NR, not in a Compact State, see below)

STUDENT LIFE

RATING: ☺ ☺ ☺

After Hours: The Spigot, The Keg, Sisson
Tavern

PROMINENT ALUMNI/AE

Include: N/A

Driving up to Hartford, Connecticut, it isn't difficult to see why one East Coast recruiter has referred to UCONN as "the state Yale Law," and numerous others feel that the graduates coming out "are showing radical increases in quality." The school offers classical architecture similar to Yale's and a quality education at a fraction of the cost. Despite state funding problems, which students attribute to the school's forty-minute distance from the main campus in Storrs, "out of sight out of mind," UCONN is growing in popularity by leaps and bounds among applicants. Applicants are lured by the low cost, sterling faculty chosen both for teaching and scholarly record, the school's international programs, including the Exeter, England semester abroad, and the flexibility of part-time enrollment, together with several dual degree programs, including JD/MSW and JD/MBA. UCONN has Compact State agreements with Vermont, New Hampshire, Massachusetts, and Rhode Island reducing these state residents' tuition below nonresident levels.

One student best summarized the school's current situation, "UCONN needs to improve its Placement Office; and the library has suffered through state budgetary constraints. The school is on the verge of breaking into the upper echelon of law schools, but without a major overhaul of these two problem areas, UCONN will remain regional rather than a national law school."

UCONN has to its credit a very congenial atmosphere where students find there are never problems finding notes. The faculty are praised because they never force students to go "head to head" rather, they encourage working together. This may be the place for you, if you want an affordable law school on the rise where you won't have to worry about your classmates cutting pages out of books in the library.

ADMISSIONS

CRITERIA

Selection is made after a careful review of the entire admissions file. The following are given the same weight: LSAT scores; Grade Point Average; quality of undergraduate curriculum/course work completed; quality/reputation of college/university; work experience, including military service, Peace Corps, and Vista; college and community activities; academic honors and awards; writing ability; character and motivation; and recommendations from individuals who know the applicant. *Note*: Preference is given to residents of the state of Connecticut. Residents of those New England states that do not have state-supported law schools also receive some preference in admissions under the New England Higher Education Compact.

MINORITY RECRUITMENT PROGRAM

Yes.

ABOUT THE APPLICATION

DEADLINE FOR FILING: 3/1; 6/1 (advanced standing). In cases of special hardship, applications for transfer and visiting student status may be accepted for consideration for admission in January.

FEE: $30; $45 (fee for simultaneous applications to day and evening divisions)

LSAT: Looked at on a case-by-case basis.

RECOMMENDED COURSES PRIOR TO MATRICULATING: "An applicant's academic preparation should include substantive courses emphasizing critical reasoning and writing, essential skills for the study of law."

PERSONAL STATEMENT: Applicants are encouraged to bring matters to the attention of the Admissions Committee by supplementing their applications with written statements.

INTERVIEW: Not an integral part of the admissions process. The Admissions Committee does, however, reserve the right to ask that an applicant be interviewed by the Associate Dean of Admissions.

ADMISSIONS TIPS: With regard to recommendations, letters prepared by the applicant's professors in undergraduate or graduate school are generally of the greatest help to the Admissions Committee. The recommendation of a pre-law committee will satisfy this requirement.

CONTACT: Nancy Dart, Associate Dean for Admissions

PHYSICAL ENVIRONMENT

As one student puts it, "Hartford is a deadbeat town." Others concur with this estimation, adding that Hartford "becomes a ghost town after dark." However, most here find there are plenty of cultural diversions including Bushnell Civic Center and the Atheneum, which recently had an exhibit of controversial art world figure, Robert Mapplethorpe. Another benefit of its location for students wishing to practice in the Hartford area: Many Hartford firms recruit only at UCONN.

Ivy League in appearance, the law school building and, in particular, the library are in need of revamping. Students have found poor library staffing, library resources, and library funding, as well as inadequate library hours. There is a lack of parking because most students bring and recommend bringing a car to school. Cabs in the area are few and far between, and the bus system is not highly regarded. UCONN provides no on-campus living accommodations for law students, but if you have a car, you can find reasonably priced housing about a ten-minute drive from the school. This past fall the school opened a cafeteria.

FINANCES

BUDGET	LOW	MEDIUM	HIGH
Tuition (Resident) Tuition (Nonresident)	$3260 $6710	$3260 $6710	$3260 $6710
Books & Supplies	$900	$900	$900
Living Accommodations (9 months)	Shared House $2295	Shared Apt. $2520	One-Bedroom Apt. $4500
Food	Groceries $810	Groceries/Cafeteria $1170	Restaurants $1800
Miscellaneous	$900	$1395	$2500
Transportation	Car $620	Car $620	Car $620
TOTAL (R) TOTAL (NR)	$8785 $12,235	$9865 $13,315	$13,580 $17,030

Employment During School: Full-time day division students are encouraged to avoid anything other than incidental part-time work. First-year, full-time students are discouraged from engaging in outside employment at all. Work-study jobs are available. The university provides part-time employment opportunities through federal College Work-Study funds for students demonstrating financial need. The amount received is based upon the student's financial need.

Scholarships: The school offers merit, need-based, and minority scholarships.

School Loan Program (Exclusive of Perkins Money): Yes. Three short-term loan funds are available: The J. Agnes Burns Scholarship Loan Fund, The Edward Joseph White Loan Fund, and the Hartford College of Law Loan Fund. Each is administered as a revolving loan fund for law students in accordance with university policies to meet short-term financial emergencies, generally not exceeding thirty days.

Loan Forgiveness Program: Does not have, but is currently considering implementing one.

ACADEMICS

At UCONN, first-year courses are required, including courses in Legal Method and Moot Court with one small-section substantive course taught, with a class size of about twenty-five people. Moot Court is given in a four-week Inter-Term with students divided into groups of sixteen. Students find course variety at the school just enough to "pacify the masses." They agree that too many classes are scheduled for Mondays, which produces conflicts.

A minority of students here feel that some of the school's professors are quite intelligent but cannot convey any information on the student level. Most feel that faculty make a great effort, are well prepared prior to entering the classroom, and are accessible, with almost all faculty giving out home phone numbers during the first day of class. Says one second-year student, "Most, if not all, professors maintain an open-door policy. Professors are flexible and accommodating and encourage you to seek them out for help with course work, future plans, or to shoot the breeze." Students would like to see more minority faculty members hired. Student-chosen star faculty include Hon. Douglas Wright (Torts), James Lingren (Trusts & Estates), and Terry Tondro (Land Use).

Connecticut's liberal student practice rules greatly benefit UCONN's criminal and civil clinical programs, which most here consider well run and comprehensive. Students can represent indigent clients, work in a legislative clinic, participate in a judicial clerkship workshop, or represent inmates at state mental institutions. One third-year student says that the clinical programs are both good and bad, in that they are something of a "black hole," with students going into the clinics and getting so absorbed they forget all else going on around them.

JOINT DEGREE PROGRAMS

JD/MLS; JD/MSW; JD/MBA; JD/MPA (Master of Public Administration); JD/MA (Public Policy)

STUDENT LIFE

The great strength of this school is its student body. Students go out of their way to help one another. According to students, UCONN fosters a spirit of cameraderie, and cutthroats are all but nonexistent. Adds one upperclassman, "UCONN is a small school, and almost everybody attempts to be part of the social scene." Happy Hours are sponsored every two weeks courtesy of the Student Bar Association. Most of the students at UCONN treat one another as partners. Many of UCONN's students are part-time and/or older, so the class spirit is difficult to effect, but a strong effort is made to bring the class together.

PLACEMENT

The school states that 99% of the most recent class surveyed reported employment as of March 1 following graduation.

However, there has been a strong reaction against the Placement Office by the student body, and they feel that this is an area in severe need of an overhaul. One student quoted a recent article in the law school's newsletter: "God helps those who help themselves, and the Placement Office helps those who don't need any help" (i.e., the students on Law Review and in the first quintile). Another complaint has been that the Placement Office brings in major employers within the immediate location of the school but that there is very limited national recruiting. Fortunately, the market in Hartford is such that a student doesn't need to rely on the Placement Office which, they say, only focuses on the top 1/5–1/10 of the class and doesn't reach the small local firms. As one student put it, "We need to recruit more actively from mid-size and small firms. We also need to provide chances for less qualified students to have an opportunity to interview—not just the same twenty people."

PREPARATION

The school reports that the Placement Office offers a variety of informative career programs. As part of the orientation, first-year students are invited to attend "Legal Career Day" at which prominent panelists from private law firms, government, and public interest organizations share their experiences as legal practitioners and interact informally with students during question-and-answer sessions. At the beginning of the second and third years, day and evening students attend separate Placement Orientation meetings. It is then that Placement Office procedures are explained, and the special concerns of those groups are addressed. Individual counseling appointments are encouraged.

WHERE/WHAT GRADUATES PRACTICE

A. Most graduates practice in Connecticut or nearby states.
B. 60% Private Practice; 10% Corporations; 7% Governmental Work; 12% Judicial Clerkships. The remainder hold positions in teaching law or military, or pursue advanced degrees.

MYRON TAYLOR HALL
ITHACA, NEW YORK (NY) 14853-4901
(607) 255-3626

❧ REPORT CARD ❧

ADMISSIONS

SELECTIVITY 🎓 🎓 🎓 🎓 🎓

Applicants: 4000; Accepted: N/A
Transfer Applications: 75; Accepted: N/A
LSAT Mean: 42
GPA Mean: 3.5

ACADEMICS

Order of the Coif (1915)
NYS Bar Passage (first try): 95%
Quality of Teaching: A−
Faculty Accessibility: B−
Faculty to Student Ratio: 1:14

PHYSICAL ENVIRONMENT

Location: Small City/College Town
Safety: Excellent (Escort Service)
HA: ♿ ♿ ♿ ♿

STUDENT ENROLLMENT

Class Size: 180 (full-time)
Women: 39%   Minorities: 18%
International: 5%
Average Age of Entering Class: 25

PLACEMENT

REPUTATION: ☆ ☆ ☆ ☆ ☆

Recruiters: 450+
Starting Salary Range: $25,000–82,000

FINANCES

Tuition: $14,800
Average Total Cost: $21,165

STUDENT LIFE

RATING: ☺ ☺ ☺

After Hours: Ruloff's, College Town, On-
Campus Parties, The Connection, The
Chapter House

PROMINENT ALUMNI/AE

Include: Edward Muskie, former Senator and
Secretary of State; Sol Linowitz, former
Ambassador; U.S. Middle East peace
negotiator; Barber Conable, President,
World Bank

Perhaps it is fitting that Cornell Law School's strikingly beautiful Myron Taylor Hall is situated a stone's throw away from the pounding
waters of one of Cornell's many gorges. Like the driven waters racing
at a furious pace down Cascadilla Gorge, Cornell law students tend to
launch themselves into their studies. But unlike the currents racing
next to them, they can direct the flow of their individual paths. This may translate
into pushing a little harder to get what they want in terms of seeing faculty and
making an extra effort to research recruiters before making use of the Placement Office. However, to those who persevere, and most here do, the rewards are staggering.
As one second-year student puts it, "You can get an awful lot accomplished just by
pushing." In her case it was an astounding fifty interviews with top law firms. It
seems safe to assume that once the initial inertia is overcome, faculty are more than

willing to talk with students, but many agree that faculty accessibility is not something that is openly advertised as much as it is pursued.

In many ways, Cornell conforms flawlessly to the law school ideal. The school boasts picture-perfect facilities, Gothic architecture together with state-of-the-art accoutrements, including a recently completed atrium inside Myron Taylor Hall as well as videotaping equipment to help students with presentation skills. Faculty here are an accomplished group praised for their ability to teach as well as research; many can transform the most mundane subjects into a provocative discourse. Cornell's library is worth noting for its skilled librarians and extensive resources, including both WESTLAW and LEXIS. Last, but far from least, is the supportive and tightly knit student body of which one student says, "Even in one of the larger classes, if you hear a voice behind you, you'll be able to tell who it is just by the voice."

Add to this Cornell's placement, which would surprise anyone under the misconception that the law school's "geographical isolation" has hampered its ability to attract the top law firms around the country, whose commentary regarding Cornell graduates in their firms and the Cornell students they have recruited is virtually all positive, particularly regarding Cornell graduates' initiative in the workplace. One recruiter found that the school has a significant number of students with bachelor's degrees from Cornell's School of Industrial Labor Relations, which is of particular value when coupled with the Cornell JD. Many firms from New York to L.A. pick Cornell as the "big riser," but one recruiter at an East Coast megafirm adds, "It just isn't this year's riser. It's been a solid school for years. It seems like now more and more firms are finding out how good Cornell grads really are."

Those law students not totally enamored with the school tend to dwell on its location, of which even its staunchest supporters will warn applicants, "Ithaca is a small town, and although there's a lot to do, it just doesn't have everything you might find in a big city. People who want a big city like New York or Boston are going to be disappointed." In all fairness, despite the patchwork of farms, traditional red barns, and silos you will encounter on the highways and byways leading up to Ithaca, Cornell certainly has many cultural offerings associated with a nationally renowned research university, including theater, concerts, and even a five-star French restaurant in town.

The school also has the added attractions of allowing its students to specialize with a degree in International Law and a very highly regarded LLM program, which attracts a very eclectic group of students.

ADMISSIONS

CRITERIA

LEVEL 1: LSAT Score(s); Grade Point Average; quality of undergraduate curriculum/course work completed; quality/reputation of college/university; personal essay; recommendations; interview (when it becomes evaluative).

MINORITY RECRUITMENT PROGRAM

Yes, conducted by the admissions office with assistance from student organizations.

ABOUT THE APPLICATION

DEADLINE FOR FILING: 2/1

FEE: $50

LSAT: School takes the applicant's highest score, if there is a 4-or-more point difference; otherwise scores are averaged.

RECOMMENDED COURSES PRIOR TO MATRICULATING: Courses that require reading, writing, and analysis.

PERSONAL STATEMENT: *Important*: A good essay can help borderline candidates, whereas a bad essay can hurt an otherwise solid candidate.

INTERVIEW: Important for applicants to understand that the interview is informative until the applicant is actually in contention for admissions (i.e., wait-listed); at this point it becomes evaluative, so it is important for students to take it very seriously. Where to stay when visiting: Collegetown Motor Lodge, Hillside Inn, Best Western University Inn.

ADMISSIONS TIPS: "Be yourself. Don't try to 'mold' yourself into what you think we want."

CONTACT: Richard Geiger, Assistant Dean

PHYSICAL ENVIRONMENT

As you drive up and down the San Francisco–like hills in Ithaca, you will undoubtedly notice bumper tickers attesting to the fact that ITHACA IS GORGES. With its Gothic arthitecture and "moat-like" Cascadilla Gorge bordering the school, Cornell Law's Myron Taylor Hall takes on the appearance of a castle. Although the law library can at times be overcrowded, Cornell has the benefit of many libraries all across the campus, which are easily accessible to law students. The area surrounding the law school is made up of a hilly terrain. However, the building itself is highly accessible for the handicapped. Safety around the school is excellent, and an escort service is available.

Chief among Cornell's advantages as part of a university with many other colleges, is the opportunity to take courses outside of the law school in areas including business in conjunction with the Johnson Graduate School of Management. Athletic facilities are within easy walking distance of the school.

15% of Cornell law students live in Charles Hughes Hall, which is not guaranteed to incoming first-year students or transfers. Students recommend bringing a car to school although parking on campus is tight. Campus parking is by permit. Students recommend Hughes for the first year and living in College town (C-town) after the first year in a shared house or apartment.

FINANCES

BUDGET	LOW	MEDIUM	HIGH
Tuition	$14,800	$14,800	$14,800
Books	$625	$625	$625
Living Accommodations (9 months)	Shared House/Apt. $2250	On-Campus $3150	One-Bedroom Apt. $4275
Food	Meal Plan $1600	Groceries/Cafeteria $1800	Restaurants $2500
Miscellaneous	$450	$540	$630
Transportation	Walking/Bus $110	Bus $250	Car $500
TOTAL	$19,835	$21,165	$23,330

Employment During School: Only after first year. Work-study jobs are available for eligible students (need-dependent); the jobs pay approximately $6.30 an hour.

Scholarship: The school offers need-based scholarships, contingent upon maintaining a 2.0 GPA.

School Loan Program (Exclusive of Perkins Money): Yes. Very small awards to only about ten students are available; need-based. Interest is 8%.

Loan Forgiveness Program: Yes. Public Interest Low Income Protection Plan. Qualifying graduates will be expected to apply only a certain percentage of their annual incomes from public interest law jobs to repay law school education loans. (Salary must be less than $31,500 for 1989 graduates). During the first year of program participation, the law school's assistance will be in the form of an interest-free loan. During subsequent years in the program, the law school's assistance to the graduate will be in the form of an outright grant. Like all law school grants, these program grants carry with them the moral obligation to repay the law school, should future financial circumstances make repayment possible.

Students Requesting Aid: 70%; of these, 70% receive aid.

Average Loan Indebtedness: Approximately $25,000–34,000.

A C A D E M I C S

All first-year courses at Cornell Law are required. Most classes have about eighty students, and there is one class in a major subject with about twenty-five students. Legal writing is taught in the first year with classes of sixteen students each. The second- and third-year curriculum is structured, but students have a wide range of choices. Four core courses are recommended during the second year: Administrative Law, Corporations, Evidence, and Federal Income Taxation. Students are also required to take a "perspective" course, offering perspectives on current U.S. law and legal institutions through a theoretical or comparative approach or by using another discipline; this is usually taken during the second year. Cornell has a writing requirement and also requires a course dealing with issues in professional responsibility. Third-year students are able to concentrate through in-depth study in either advocacy, business law and regulation, general practice, or public law. Students find that at times it is difficult to take the courses they want due to scheduling conflicts.

Cornell's clinical program includes Cornell Legal Aid Clinic, where students provide legal assistance to indigents in Thompkins County. Some students opt to take a full clinical semester as externs either at the Center for Law and Social Policy or the National Wildlife Federation in Washington, D.C. during their fourth or fifth semester. Although this option is interesting, many students find that clinical offerings are not the strongest component of the program. Most recently, the clinics were oversubscribed and not all students got what they wanted.

Merit points are awarded from A + to F, with pluses and minuses. Students find that most students "come in near a B or B −."

JOINT DEGREE/GRADUATE/SPECIAL PROGRAMS

Specialized and Combined Degrees: JD/MBA; JD/MA (Philosophy); JD/PhD (Philosophy); JD/MILR (Master of Industrial and Labor Relations); JD/MRP (Master in Regional Planning); JD/PhD (History and Economics; flexible). A JD with a specialization in international legal affairs is also available.

Graduate Programs: LLM; JSD (Doctor of Juristic Science)

S T U D E N T   L I F E

"The social life at Cornell Law is what you make of it. If you want to sit with your books and study all the time you can; if you want to have fun you can do that too." Parties, such as Negligence Weekend, cocktail hours, and dances are organized by the school. There is a wide variety of organizations, including the Entertainment and Sports Law Union, Law Ethics and Society, the Herbert W. Briggs Society of International Law, and the Cornell Prison Project. Students here have observed that school functions tend to be underattended.

PLACEMENT

Although the Placement Office itself is not regarded by many students as one of the strongest features of the school, the Cornell name is very strong and students locate not only permanent positions but also summer jobs after the first and second years without too much difficulty.

PREPARATION

The office provides a placement manual, résumé-writing counseling, videotaped mock interviews, employment counseling, panel discussions, and video presentations.

WHERE/WHAT GRADUATES PRACTICE

A. 60% Northeast; 10% South; 25% West; 5% Midwest.
B. 5% Small Firms; 10% Medium Firms; 59% Large Firms; 20% Clerkships; 0.5% Military; 5% Government Agencies; 0.5% Other.

7039 E. 18TH AVENUE
DENVER, COLORADO (CO) 80220
(303) 871-6133

 **REPORT CARD**

ADMISSIONS

SELECTIVITY:

Applicants: 1862; Accepted: 670
Transfer Applications: 200; Accepted: 25
LSAT Mean: 37
GPA Mean: 3.21

ACADEMICS

Colorado Bar Passage (first try): 77%
Faculty to Student Ratio: 1:22
Quality of Teaching: B+
Faculty Accessibility: B+

PHYSICAL ENVIRONMENT

Location: Large City
Safety: Good
HA:

STUDENT ENROLLMENT

Class Size: 220 (full-time); 95 (part-time)
Women: 47%   Minorities: 8%
Average Age of Entering Class: 26.7

PLACEMENT

REPUTATION: ☆ ☆ ☆

Recruiters: 100
Starting Salary Mean: $32,725

FINANCES

Tuition: $12,384 (day); $9228 (evening)
Average Total Cost: $18,944 (day); $15,848
(evening)

STUDENT LIFE

RATING: ☺ ☺ ☺ ☺

After Hours: N/A

PROMINENT ALUMNI/AE

Include: Justice Byron White, United States
Supreme Court

INSIDER INFORMATION The University of Denver College of Law is a lively place, where highly qualified people work seriously in the law. The school offers a diversity of interesting courses, including one that provides a broad overview of Aviation Law and another that focuses on the complex set of rules and laws that govern Indians, tribes, and their reservations. DU is one of the law schools governing the Rocky Mountain Mineral Law Foundation, which is housed on the law center campus. This nonprofit corporation promotes legal research and the study of Mineral Law.

A prime concern of DU is the practical application of the law. To further this goal, a Lawyering Skills Program is offered in several legal specializations. Practical experience is gained by public service work in the Student Law Office or through the school's extensive internship program, which offers approximately one hundred different for-credit internships on an ongoing basis. Students may also design internships in a special area in which they may wish to practice and apply for credit. In addition, full-time externships can be arranged for an entire quarter's credit.

Recruiters find that the experience provided to the students produces good results. Graduates are praised for their strong commitment to the area, and it was felt that the top 10% at DU will do well anywhere. Graduates received highest ratings for their team playership abilities and oral/written presentation skills.

ADMISSIONS

CRITERIA

LEVEL 1: Grade Point Average; quality of undergraduate curriculum/course work completed; quality/reputation of college/university; LSAT score

LEVEL 2: Work experience; recommendations; personal essay

LEVEL 3: Personal interview

OTHER: Important factors in admissions are extracurricular and community activities, diversity, and residency.

MINORITY RECRUITMENT PROGRAM

Yes

ABOUT THE APPLICATION

DEADLINE FOR FILING: Applications are accepted anytime. It is recommended, however, that an application be submitted before May 1 unless a candidate has extremely strong credentials.

FEE: $40

LSAT: School takes the average or highest of applicant's LSAT scores, depending on the circumstances.

RECOMMENDED COURSES PRIOR TO MATRICULATING: A student should pursue the development of analytical and communication skills.

PERSONAL STATEMENT: "It may push a 'borderline' candidate into the 'admit' category."

INTERVIEW: Not required or recommended. Prospective students may stay in College of Law Campus housing (Call Bob McGee at (303)871-6829).

ADMISSIONS TIPS: "Applicants should apply and complete their applications early; the timing of applications has a large impact on financial aid."

CONTACT: Claudia Tomlin, Admissions Officer

PHYSICAL ENVIRONMENT

The law school is housed in the new Law Center. The new Westminster Law Library provides for the needs of the students and faculty as well as those of the Denver Legal Community.

Although off-campus accommodations are usually readily available, the most cost-effective living accommodations are generally on-campus housing. Two on-campus housing options are available: apartments in Curtis Hall or dormitory rooms in Dunton Hall. A Day Care Center, located in the Health Center building on the Law Center campus, is available to the students with children. Both students and the administration recommend bringing a car because public transportation may be inadequate depending upon whether one lives on a bus line. The safety in the area of DU is considered good, provided students take proper precautions.

FINANCES

BUDGET	LOW	MEDIUM	HIGH
Tuition (Day Division)	$12,384	$12,384	$12,384
Tuition (Evening Division)	$9288	$9288	$9288
Books	$650	$650	$650
Living Accommodations (9 months)	Shared Apt. $1530	On-Campus $2430	One-Bedroom Apt. $3060
Food	Groceries $1800	Meal Plan (19/wk.) $1980	Cafeteria $2340
Miscellaneous	$800	$1000	$1200
Transportation	Mass Transit $350	Car/Bus $500	Car $650
TOTAL (Day)	$17,514	$18,944	$20,284
TOTAL (Evening)	$14,418	$15,848	$17,188

Employment During School: Not recommended and strongly discouraged during the first year. Work-study jobs are available for eligible students. Students receive $2100 per year; hourly rate is flexible but total for one year cannot exceed $2100.

School Loan Program (Exclusive of Perkins Money): Yes, DU has special revolving funds to assist students with short-term financial problems. These loans are expected to be repaid during the quarter in which they were granted.

Loan Forgiveness Program: Does not have, but is currently considering implementing one.

Students Requesting Aid: 70%; of these, 70% receive aid.

Students Indebted upon Graduation: 70%

Average Loan Indebtedness: $11,500

ACADEMICS

DU's calendar is divided into quarters, and entering first-year law students are admitted only in the autumn quarter. Entering students are assigned an advisor from a list of faculty volunteers; this assignment, however, is not intended to restrict the student's access to any faculty member for advice and counseling. First-year day students are required to take certain prescribed courses, including a Legal Research and Writing course. Additional courses, required for graduation, include Basic Tax, Post-Trial Procedure, Legal Profession, Corporations, Administrative Law, and Criminal Law. As noted before, U. Denver's curriculum consists of a diversity of courses including Space Law and the Law of the Sea Seminar. Special programs include the Business Planning Program, Transportation Law, Natural Resource Law, and International Law. Students are also permitted to take graduate courses in other units of the university.

The faculty are known to have responsible office hours. Although home telephone numbers are rarely given out, office phone numbers have always been provided and receptionists are always present for messages. Star faculty include Lucy Marsh (Property), Larry Pozner (Criminal Law), and Dana Wakefield (Juvenile Law).

JOINT/GRADUATE DEGREE PROGRAMS

Dual Degrees: Numerous dual degrees are offered by DU and currently exist in Geography, Business Administration, History, International Management, Judicial Management, Professional (Clinical) Psychology, Speech Communication, and International Studies.
Graduate Degree: LLM (Taxation)

STUDENT LIFE

The Student Bar Association (SBA) sponsors speaker programs and social events throughout the year, including the Spring Revue. Special interest organizations funded by the SBA include the International Law Society, the Student Trial Lawyers' Program, and Children's Legal Issues in Perspective.

PLACEMENT

88% of graduates are placed after graduation.

PREPARATION

Students are prepared by the Placement Office through videotaped mock interviews, interviewing techniques sessions, and résumé-writing seminars.

WHERE/WHAT GRADUATES PRACTICE

A. 7% Northeast; 2% South; 4% West Coast; 12% Midwest; 75% Other. 63% of the students remain in the immediate area within one year of graduation.
B. 3% Solo Practitioner; 9% Small Firms; 4% Medium Firms; 3% Large Firms; 8% Clerkships; 1% Graduate Degrees; 1% Military; 10% Governmental Agencies.

DUKE UNIVERSITY
School of Law

ROOM 126
DURHAM, NORTH CAROLINA (NC) 27706
(919) 684-2850

REPORT CARD

ADMISSIONS
SELECTIVITY 🎓 🎓 🎓 🎓 🎓

Applicants: 3501; Accepted: 667
Transfer Applications: 34; Accepted: 10
LSAT Median: 43
GPA Median: 3.60

ACADEMICS

Order of the Coif (1933)
Quality of Teaching: A−
Faculty Accessibility: A

PHYSICAL ENVIRONMENT

Location: College Town/Small City
Safety: Good–Very Good
HA: ♿ ♿ ♿ ♿ ♿

STUDENT ENROLLMENT

Class Size: 198
Women: 42% Minorities: 12%
International: 4.5%
Average Age of Entering Class: 24

PLACEMENT
REPUTATION: ☆ ☆ ☆ ☆ ☆

Recruiters: 650
Starting Salary Range: $28,500–80,000
Starting Salary Mean: $56,000

FINANCES

Tuition: $13,300
Average Total Cost: $22,170

STUDENT LIFE
RATING: ☺ ☺ ☺ ☺

After Hours: Hide Away, Satisfaction

PROMINENT ALUMNI/AE

Include: Eugene H. Phillips, Associate
Judge, North Carolina Court of Appeals;
Eugene Andrew Gordon, Senior Judge,
U.S. District Court, North Carolina

INSIDER INFORMATION

Mind, body, and soul. Applied to Duke Law School, these three terms refer to a physical plant situated on Southern soil, a mind that addresses legal issues on a national perspective, and a soul, or goal, that stretches farther yet to the realm of international law with one of the country's strongest international law programs and among the highest numbers of international students in attendance of an American law school. Indeed, in a class of fewer than 200, there are students from seven foreign countries, including Greece, China, Japan, and India. Visiting faculty have trekked to Durham from as far away places as Ramat-Gan, Thessalonika, and Sydney, Australia. And although Alaska, the state with the largest number of attorneys per capita, has no law school of its own, Duke law students, in conjunction with the Alaska Bar Association, produce a scholarly journal focusing on issues concerning Alaska, including land-use planning, state-federal relations, and Native American rights.

Duke has emerged as a leader in legal education since, as Trinity College of Law, it was, in 1904, one of the first 39 law schools approved by the ABA. It shifted to a more national perspective in the 1950s and 1960s. Under Professor E.R. Latty, the school began reaching out to applicants across the country and has moved as rapidly as possible under financial constraint. Unlike other schools of similar stature, Duke has had to rely heavily on alumni support for expansion. There has been a 38% increase in alumni/ae giving, with approximately $1.7 million out of the needed $8 million already raised for the school's new building, and there is an associate dean whose sole responsibility is raising funds for the law school.

Critics of the school, both within and without, usually point to Duke's physical facility, but the school has begun an aggressive plan to expand the facility and has recently completed its fundraising effort. Given the heavy competition for the fairly small pool of top applicants, Duke has had to work hard to make sure it keeps the best and the brightest from among the applicant pool, and once it finds them, works doubly hard to keep them from going elsewhere. Last year alone, over 80% of admitted applicants were contacted by the school. Admitted students can enter in the summer prior to the fall semester in order to complete courses.

One student sums up her experiences at Duke Law School by alluding to Scott Turow's widely read account of life as a HLS student. "Read *One L* and then ignore it. The guy was paranoid!" And though, as many will attest, Duke, like many other leading law schools, can be "an ego-crushing experience," one third-year student states, "The level of motivation at Duke Law is incredible, but it doesn't mean we're all a bunch of cutthroats. We really work together." Still others find that the best friendships they have ever made were those formed while attending the law school.

A recent graduate describes his alma mater, "Duke is a school with a southern location; it is not really a southern law school." That characterization seems highly accurate, given that 35% to 45% of Duke's law students are from the Northeast and many of those same students choose after graduation to go back to the states from which they came. Recruiters give Duke graduates very high marks in overall satisfaction, though some among the group feel the students may need to strengthen their legal writing skills. Many recruiters argue that Duke is a "sleeper" whose time to move into the highest echelon of law schools has finally come.

ADMISSIONS

CRITERIA

LEVEL 1: LSAT, GPA; quality of undergraduate university(ies)/college(s) attended. These factors are tied to one another in the evaluation of the applicant's academic performance. Also taken into consideration are strength of courses taken and class rank.

LEVEL 2: Grade trends (such as improvement over the course of the four years or sophomore slump); personal statement.

LEVEL 3: Recommendations; significant extracurricular activities; community service; work experience; proven capacity for leadership. Important for older applicants who have been in the work place is a current résumé. On occasion special consideration is given to children of Duke University alumni/ae who are qualified to do acceptable work.

MINORITY RECRUITMENT PROGRAM

Yes. Duke makes a conscious effort to achieve broad diversity in each entering class in terms of general background, geography, and undergraduate institutions represented. The school has a faculty-initiated affirmative action plan for minority admissions.

ABOUT THE APPLICATION

DEADLINE FOR FILING: 1/15

FEE: $45

LSAT: Generally, looked at on a case-by-case basis. However, if scores presented are very wide apart, or if there are extenuating circumstances, such as the testing conditions being less than ideal as in the case of Hurricane Hugo (letter sent to each law school from Law Services), the school will probably be inclined towards taking the higher score.

RECOMMENDED COURSES PRIOR TO MATRICULATING: Courses that place a heavy emphasis on writing, philosophy, history, or other courses in the humanities.

PERSONAL STATEMENT: Like most law schools, the personal statement has been deliberately left unstructured so that the applicant can single out what is most important in conveying what he or she will bring to the school. The statement shouldn't exceed 650 words. Neatness counts. The statement is used as the primary tool in evaluating the applicant's writing skills.

INTERVIEW: Neither required nor recommended. Informational interviews are available, and if students have special circumstances like dyslexia they may request an interview to clarify their situation. Nevertheless, the interview is not evaluative.

ADMISSIONS TIPS: Don't send the same application essay (with school name on it) to Duke that you sent to another law school. Make certain that the application is typed and "packaged well."

CONTACT: Gwynn T. Swinson, Associate Dean for Admissions

"Miles and miles of suburbia." Many agree that Duke has much to offer those who want a life outside of school with a university setting and athletic facilities nearby. Duke's rather large and separate East and West campuses are connected by a forested area. Duke Law School itself may not have the most stately or state-of-the-art law building. Duke's library has been remodeled recently, and a new law school building is projected for completion in the mid 1990s, designed by Gunner Birkes, who designed Michigan's law library. Students have a food/concession stand at the school where they can eat. The school has replaced furnishings including chairs and TVs for students. Handicapped accessibility is considered excellent by both students and administration with existing ramps and handicapped-accessible bathrooms.

Safety is considered so-so. The law school is situated near a wooded area, and people can hide in woods, but there have been no instances of assaults reported in the area of the school. The campus is safe, but within one mile is downtown Durham, which is not as good. An escort service, "Safe walks," "Safe rides," and "Public Safety" will provide rides from one point to another on the campus.

Central West Apartments is located between the East and West campuses. The building is owned by the school. Apartments are approximately the same price as other noncampus apartments. Students do not find it difficult to find suitable housing.

FINANCES

BUDGET	LOW	MEDIUM	HIGH
Tuition (annual first year)	$13,300	$13,300	$13,300
Books	$750	$750	$750
Living Accommodations (9 months)	Shared House/Apt. $2700	On-Campus $2700	One-Bedroom Apt. $3600
Food	Groceries $1000	Groceries/Cafeteria $2300	Restaurants $2750
Miscellaneous	$2000	$2500	$3500
Transportation	Car $620	Car $620	Car $620
TOTAL	$20,370	$22,170	$24,520

Employment During School: Only after first year. Work-study jobs are available for all students (not need-dependent).

School Loan Program (Exclusive of Perkins Money): Yes

Loan Forgiveness Program: Yes; limited program.

Students Requesting Aid: 85%; of these, 52% receive aid.

Average Loan Indebtedness: $45,000

ACADEMICS

First-year students have "major" courses and "minor" ones, all of which are required. Legal Writing, a first-year course, is taught by full-time faculty. Second and third years are entirely elective, and Duke has a vast array of course offerings, including Jewish Law, Critical Legal Studies, and a multitude of international law courses. Students can also choose among clinics, including Child Advocacy, Antitrust Practice, and Civil/Criminal Trial Practice. Says one student, "There's something for everybody here [Duke]. If you want to go into clinics, you can do that or just concentrate on international law. It's really up to you." Grading is up to a 4.5; it appears that the mean has risen from a 2.7 to a 3.0.

Students find that Duke's faculty are generally very good, with a few instructors who are experts in their fields but not as skilled at teaching. Because of the low ratio of students to faculty, faculty members are also quite accessible. Student-chosen faculty stars include William Van Alstyne (Constitutional Law and First Amendment), James Cox (Business Association), Melvin Shimm (Commercial Law), Thomas Rowe (Civil Procedure), and John Weistart (Commercial Law).

JOINT/GRADUATE DEGREE PROGRAMS

Joint Degrees: JD/MD; JD/MBA; JD/MPPS (Master of Public Planning Systems); JD/MHA (Master of Hospital Administration); JD/MS (History, English, Humanities); JD/MA.
Graduate Degrees: LLM

STUDENT LIFE

Duke students are "not laid-back, but not cutthroat either." The feeling is that everyone will get a good job and generally everyone tries to help one other. Formals, semi-formals, and house parties are scheduled by the school. Hangouts include bars, tennis courts, and polo fields. Duke has many student organizations, including a Volunteer Income Tax Assistance Program whereby students provide preparation assistance to low-income people in the Durham community. Duke's highly regarded student-edited quarterly, *Law and Contemporary Problems*, addresses current issues using a multidisciplinary approach. Students are selected for the journal on the basis of grades and tutorial instructor evaluations. Student admissions to *Duke Law Journal*, one of the most prestigious publications of its kind, is achieved by grading for first-year students and by writing for second-year students.

PLACEMENT

Over 650 recruiters come to the school. The Placement Office does not screen by grades, and the firms are not allowed to screen either. Duke grads speak very highly of the school's Placement Office adding, "They really work for everyone in the class regardless of if they are at the top of their class or on Law Review."

PREPARATION

The Placement Office provides such advice as how to dress, what not to order at lunch, and how to guide a conversation. The Placement Office has a staff that plans numerous activities to help students. Information on legal careers is maintained. Cover letter and résumé-writing workshops are held; personal counseling is available, and career seminars are scheduled.

WHERE/WHAT GRADUATES PRACTICE:

A. 41% Northeast (Including Washington, D.C.); 26% South; 12% Midwest; 17% West.
B. 78% Private Practice; 1% Public Interest; 2% Business Concerns Legal; 0.6% Non-legal; 2% Government-Federal; 1% Government-State; 12% Judicial Clerkships-Federal; 1% Judicial Clerkships-State; 1% Military.

GAMBRELL HALL
ATLANTA, GEORGIA (GA) 30322
(404) 727-6801

REPORT CARD

ADMISSIONS
SELECTIVITY

Applicants: 3251; Accepted: 950
Transfer Applications: 27; Accepted: 15
LSAT Mean: 39
GPA Mean: 3.25

ACADEMICS
Order of the Coif (1971)
Georgia Bar Passage (first try): 90%+
Faculty to Student Ratio: 1:24
Quality of Teaching: **A**
Faculty Accessibility: **A−**

PHYSICAL ENVIRONMENT
Location: Large City
Safety: Very Good
HA:

STUDENT ENROLLMENT
Class Size: 225
Women: 43%   Minorities: 9%
Average Age of Entering Class: 22.5

PLACEMENT
REPUTATION ☆ ☆ ☆ ☆

Recruiters: 250 (off-campus); 175 (on-campus)
Starting Salary Mean: $42,135

FINANCES
Tuition: $13,200
Average Total Cost: $20,945

STUDENT LIFE
RATING ☺ ☺ ☺

After Hours: Hemingway's, Good Ole Days

PROMINENT ALUMNI/AE
Include: Sam Nunn, U.S. Senator

INSIDER INFORMATION

As put by one recruiter, "Emory places a strong emphasis on litigation/ clinical skills. A distinguishing characteristic of the school is its clinics and internships. Emory lawyers are competitive and supportive of each other's endeavors. Classes are typically fairly deep in good to high-quality law students. Emory is a safety-valve, fall-back law school for many students from other regions (particularly Northeast/Mid-Atlantic) of the country who have the qualifications to apply to the top national law schools but miss out on their admissions lottery. Good physical facilities and good utilization of local practicing lawyers as adjunct professors create a solid environment for legal learning." Regarding research abilities, students are often considered by many recruiters to possess "good workmanlike qualities," with fundamental skills well developed at the school.

When you're located in the Sunbelt you harness solar energy; Emory Law School has harnessed Atlanta Power. From the popular Atlanta Underground, an enclosed shopping and eatery area, to MARTA, Atlanta's mass transit system, comparable to the monorail in Disney World in terms of maintenance, Atlanta is booming and Emory Law is making good use of it to fuel its applicant pool, which was up 40% last year alone. Emory has succeeded in pulling vital resources from the community—namely legal adjuncts drawn from the city's wide array of law firms, many of whom teach at the school. Students find that these faculty generally bring added insight and practical experience into the classroom, although as one student here has said, "There is a problem when adjunct professors are used. These people, often active in hectic private practices, can be frustratingly unavailable." Students are kept posted on faculty's research even when they are taking time off from the school.

Many believe Emory to be faculty-driven, the past three deans having taught courses at the school. The foremost authorities in the country on Soviet Law (Harold Berman), Business Associations (William Carney), and Trial Procedure are present at the school. The National Institute for Trial Advocacy (NITA), an intensive, two-week program required of all second-year students, consistently takes top honors. Through this "legal learning submersion" students go through an entire trial from jury selection to closing arguments and are taught by more than 250 attorneys from around the country.

In Business Associations, required of first-year students, students are exposed to such areas as tax benefits, piercing the corporate veil, drafting an agreement, and the formation of a firm as a business structure. The school offers three journals so that as many students as possible can work on one, including the *Emory Law Journal,* the *Emory Journal of International Dispute Resolution,* and the *Bankruptcy Development Journal.*

As admissions becomes more selective, competition among students has risen also, with incidents of students hiding books in the library and refusing to lend notes to students who have missed a class for reasons like illness. Many here share the feeling that what sets Emory apart from other law schools is that it is a striver, not simply satisfied with increases in popularity, but pushing toward continued improvement and growth.

ADMISSIONS

CRITERIA

LEVEL 1: Grade Point Average; LSAT score

LEVEL 2: Quality of undergraduate curriculum/course work completed; quality/reputation of college/university

LEVEL 3: Recommendations; personal essay

LEVEL 4: Work experience; graduate course work completed

MINORITY RECRUITMENT PROGRAM

Yes. Minority candidates are given special consideration in the evaluation process. A portion of Emory's scholarship fund is reserved for minority students. The Black Law Students Association members assist in the recruitment of minority students.

ABOUT THE APPLICATION

DEADLINE FOR FILING: 3/1

FEE: $30

LSAT: The school takes the average or highest score. Which one the school uses depends on individual circumstances, when the test scores were taken, etc.

RECOMMENDED COURSES PRIOR TO MATRICULATING: Courses that require extensive (critical) writing, economics, and logic.

PERSONAL STATEMENT: "The personal statement helps us to differentiate among the numerous candidates with similar academic credentials. In a few instances, the statement may push a candidate from the wait list to the 'admit' category or from the 'deny' to the wait list category. In addition to the content of the essay, we are interested in the quality of the writing."

INTERVIEW: Not required or recommended. For visitors, University Inn (across the street from the law school) and Stafford Emory Inn (one-quarter mile down the street from the law school) are recommended.

ADMISSIONS TIPS: "Apply early; at the very least, complete the file by the March 1 deadline."

CONTACT: Jane DiFolco, Director of Admissions

PHYSICAL ENVIRONMENT

Emory Law School is housed in Gambrell Hall, a modern three-story building located on the southern edge of the campus. Gambrell includes a library that spans a portion of all three floors. A well-equipped student computer lab exists on the library's first floor. The law school also contains a 450-seat auditorium and a court room with studio-quality video equipment. The law school is close enough to the campus for students to take advantage of undergraduate facilities, however, there is little organized interaction between law students and undergraduates.

Housing around Emory is moderately priced, and the school is in one of the safest areas of Atlanta. Location is one of Emory's most popular features to students, due in part to the school's outstanding connections with area firms, which provide numerous opportunities for both summer and full-time employment. A car is recommended, with public transportation good but not quite as extensive as in some other major cities.

FINANCES

BUDGET	LOW	MEDIUM	HIGH
Tuition (annual first year)	$13,200	$13,200	$13,200
Books	$500	$500	$500
Living Accommodations (9 months)	Shared Apt. $2925	On-Campus* $3060	One-Bedroom Apt. $3915
Food	Groceries $1950	Groceries/Restaurants $2535	Restaurants $2925
Miscellaneous	$800	$1000	$1200
Transportation	Mass Transit $500	Car**/Mass Transit $650	Car** $750
TOTAL	$19,875	$20,945	$22,490

* Shared House $400/month

** Includes $85 to register car

Note: Tuition is three-tiered, in an effort to alleviate annual tuition increases. 1st year and Transfers: $13,200; 2nd Year: $12,000; 3rd Year: $10,750.

Employment During School: Possible after first year. Work-study jobs are available for all students (need-dependent). The Financial Aid Office assists placement of students in non-work-study positions. Average salary for work study is between $4.25 and $5.50 per hour, depending on department.

Scholarships: The school offers merit, need-based, and minority scholarships. Merit scholarships are contingent upon maintaining a GPA of 72.

School Loan Program (Exclusive of Perkins Money): Yes. Tuition can be borrowed each year with a minimum loan of $3000. Variable interest rate is significantly lower than SLS or private law loans (LAL, LSL) (8.7% for 1989). Repayment of interest begins immediately. Borrowers have a three-month grace period after graduation for repayment of principle. Maximum repayment is ten years. ESPL requires co-maker. Credit analysis is required for applicants. Loan is not based on need and can replace family contribution.

Loan Forgiveness Program: No

Students Requesting Aid: 66%; of these, 61% receive aid.

Students Indebted upon Graduation: 53%

Average Loan Indebtedness: $34,687

ACADEMICS

The first-year curriculum consists of required courses. The first-year class is split into large sections of 75 students and small sections of 25 students. Research Writing and Oral Advocacy, generally considered one of the weaker offerings at the school, is taught by adjuncts and upperclass students, whom students refer to as a "grab bag" in teaching ability. Beyond the first year, all students are required to complete successfully Evidence, Legal Profession, and Trial Techniques. In addition, there is an upper level seminar requirement. These seminars include Business in Japan, Securities Regulation, and Products Liability.

Special programs at Emory include Trial Techniques, Tax Law, Law and Economics, Corporate Law, Law and Theology, Law and Business, and International Law. The Tax Law program is particularly strong because JD students can take classes from the LLM program in taxation. Clinical programs are provided as well. Advanced students have worked as interns with the Atlanta offices of the Federal Trade Commission, the Securities Exchange Commission, the Environmental Protection Agency, and the U.S. Attorney's Office.

Emory students are very pleased with their faculty. As one third-year student says, "Although not every professor deserves an 'A+,' I was pleasantly surprised by the numbers in the excellent range in a school that also has a good professor-productivity record." She further adds, "I would give Emory's full-time professors high grades for availability." Many students did not find the use of upperclass students as Research Writing instructors to be beneficial. Student-selected faculty stars include Harold Berman (Soviet Law), Abraham P. Ordover (Trial Techniques), and Fred McChesney (Law and Economics, Corporate Law).

JOINT/GRADUATE DEGREE PROGRAMS

Joint Degrees: JD/MBA; JD/M.DIV (Master of Divinity)
Graduate Degrees: LLM (Taxation); LLM (Litigation)

STUDENT LIFE

Various student organizations exist on campus, including the International Law Society, several legal fraternities, and the Sports and Entertainment Law Society. Students describe the majority of their classmates as willing to "go that extra mile if you need help in a class," with many forming friendships with those students who were in their first-year small section. There does, however, exist a small faction of students at the top of the class and on journal who "would sooner cut your throat as look at you."

PLACEMENT

96.1% are placed after graduation. Students are generally satisfied with the Placement Office, with its ability to get recruiters on campus, particularly among Atlanta and Southeastern law firms. "After that, it's up to you to show them what you've got to offer."

PREPARATION

The Placement Office prepares students through both group and individual counseling on interviewing, cover letters, and résumés. Videotaped interview training is also available. Small group meetings regarding career choices and options and career education panel discussions, live and on videotape, are also held.

WHERE/WHAT GRADUATES PRACTICE

A. 33% Northeast; 58% South; 5% West Coast; 2% Midwest; 1% Other. (Approximately 45% remain in the immediate vicinity within one year of graduation.)
B. 1% Solo Practitioner; 16.6% Small Firms; 18.6% Medium Firms; 30.7% Large Firms; 9% Clerkships; 1% Graduate Degrees; 12.1% Governmental Agencies; 5.5% Corporations; 2.5% Other.

164C HOLLAND HALL
GAINESVILLE, FLORIDA (FL) 32611
(904) 392-2087

❧ REPORT CARD ❧

ADMISSIONS
SELECTIVITY 🎓 🎓 🎓 🎓

Applicants: 1800; Accepted: 430
Transfer Applications: 35; Accepted: 9
LSAT Mean: Fall: 38; Spring: 36
GPA Mean: Fall: 3.4; Spring: 3.2

ACADEMICS
Order of the Coif (1955)
Florida State Bar Passage (first try): 90% and above
Faculty to Student Ratio: 1:19
Quality of Teaching: A−
Faculty Accessibility: B

PHYSICAL ENVIRONMENT
Location: College Town
Safety: Very Good
HA: ♿ ♿ ♿

STUDENT ENROLLMENT
Class Size: Fall: 200; Spring: 200 (full-time)
Women: 38%   Minorities: 11%
Average Age of Entering Class: 23–24

PLACEMENT
REPUTATION ☆ ☆ ☆ ☆

Recruiters: 256
Starting Salary Mean: $43,694

FINANCES
Tuition: $1979.60 ($70.70 per credit hour for 28 hours) (R); $5712 ($204 per credit hour for 28 hours) (NR)
Average Total Cost: $7379.60 (R); $11,112 (NR)

STUDENT LIFE
RATING: ☺ ☺ ☺ ☺

After Hours: Joe's Deli, CJ's, Purple Porpoise

PROMINENT ALUMNI/AE
Include: Reece Smith, former ABA President; Chesterfield Smith, former ABA President; Ruben Askew, former Governor of Florida

INSIDER INFORMATION

Regarded by many recruiters and administrators as the premier Florida law school, UF has three principle drawing cards: costs among the lowest in the country, a good location in a fairly reasonably priced residential area, and a high-powered—some students here say "driven"—group of students drawn from among the finest schools in the country and intent on going places in both public interest law and the corporate world. Recruiters are more than satisfied with UF's preparation of its students in oral communication skills, and as one points out, "We have found that the students here (UF) are getting better and better with each passing class."

On the downside is the fact that UF tends to "grade deflate" with a 3.0 out of 4.0 putting students in the top 15–20% of their class. A new full-time class begins in the spring term; many of those entering then couldn't make it past the increasingly difficult fall admissions process. These students are required to spend a semester in the summer, but do not catch up to the class commencing in the fall, which graduates in May, as opposed to spring students who graduate in December.

UF boasts a sound faculty made up of both "older teachers born and bred in southern Florida who stick to the black letter law" and younger faculty "who present more theoretical aspects of the law." Some of the students here are interested in corporate work, but there is a substantial number of non-corporate types who are not intent on "dominating and making money" after graduation. For anyone even considering Florida as a region in which they wish to practice and/or go to law school, UF should be on your list. More and more East coasters are showing up at Holland Hall extending the school's powerful outreach farther north.

ADMISSIONS

CRITERIA

Approximately 50% of each entering class is chosen solely by reference to LSAT scores and GPA. Approximately 40% is selected from the "hold" category. In addition to GPA and LSAT scores, the following are considered: quality of undergraduate curriculum/course work completed; quality/reputation of college/university; work experience; recommendations; personal essay and applicant's race, and ethnic, cultural, and economic background and geographical origin.

MINORITY RECRUITMENT PROGRAM

Yes, through the regular admissions process with active involvement of the Assistant Dean for Student and Minority Affairs. Black Law Student Association does assist in the process.

ABOUT THE APPLICATION

DEADLINE FOR FILING: Fall: 2/1; Spring: 7/1

FEE: $15

LSAT: The school takes the average of applicant's scores.

RECOMMENDED COURSES PRIOR TO MATRICULATING: None

PERSONAL STATEMENT: "Functions as an 'interview on paper,' and thus gives the candidates the opportunity to state their case in writing."

INTERVIEW: Not required or recommended. If visiting the campus, Holiday Inn–University Center, and Student Union–J. Wayne Reitz Union have been recommended.

ADMISSIONS TIPS: Candidates should note that the February administration of the LSAT is *not used* in making fall admissions decisions. It is to the applicant's advantage to apply as early as possible. However, applications should not be filed prior to one year in advance of the intended month of entry.

CONTACT: J. Michael Patrick, Assistant Dean

PHYSICAL ENVIRONMENT

Even though UF College of Law is part of a major state university, the facilities are separate and housed in one location so that the students don't have to deal with the hassles of a huge campus. Classrooms, however, are considered crowded and noisy. The main building used to be an auditorium, which has now been divided into classrooms with movable doors. Handicapped accessibility is a big problem.

The legal information center is in the law library. The Bruton-Geer Commons Building provides a full cafeteria and student lounge in addition to housing the media area of the library, the Virgil Hawkins Legal Clinic, the Center for Governmental Responsibility, Career Planning, and the Legal Research and Writing areas.

Sharing a house off campus is the most cost-effective living accommodation. A car is recommended by both students and administration.

FINANCES

BUDGET	LOW	MEDIUM	HIGH
Tuition (Resident) **Tuition (Nonresident)**	$1979.60 $5712	$1979.60 $5712	$1979.60 $5712
Books	$500	$500	$500
Living Accommodations (9 months)	Shared House/Apt. $1350	On-Campus $1500	One-Bedroom Apt. $3375
Food	Groceries $630	Groceries/Cafeteria $2300	Restaurants $2750
Miscellaneous	$500	$600	$725
Transportation	Mass Transit $225	Car/Bus $500	Car $600
TOTAL (R) TOTAL (NR)	$5184.60 $8917	$7379.60 $11,112	$9929.60 $13,662

Employment During School: Beginning students are prohibited from employment in the first semester; otherwise students are restricted to no more than twenty hours per week. Work-study jobs are not provided to students.

Scholarships: The school offers merit and need-based scholarships. Most merit scholarships are contingent upon maintaining a 2.8/4.0 GPA. Some require that you maintain a 3.0/4.0 GPA. The Virgil Hawkins Fellowship provides $5000. Financial need and merit as well as attendance at the Summer Program are requirements for eligibility.

School Loan Program (Exclusive of Perkins Money): No

Loan Forgiveness Program: No

Students Requesting Aid: N/A; of those requesting aid, 80 + % receive aid.

ACADEMICS

In order to graduate, satisfactory completion of certain courses, including Legal Research and Writing, Appellate Advocacy, Advanced Writing Requirement, Professional Responsibility, and Legal Drafting are required. UF offers a wide range of courses, particularly in business and corporate law. The seminars offered are on a wide range of topics as well. Students feel, however, that prerequisite courses are not offered frequently enough. The school also has clinics involving actual client representation, such as the Civil and Criminal Law Clinic, and clinics based on simulated lawyering, such as the Domestic Relations Particulum and Lawyers as Negotiators.

Most faculty members are very friendly, caring, and accessible. Almost all professors are known to have an open-door policy. Star faculty include Francis Allen (Criminal Law–Huber Hurst Eminent Scholar), Joseph R. Julin (Natural Resources/Property–Chesterfield Smith Professor of Law and Dean Emeritus), Jack Freeland (Taxation–Distinguished Service Professor), Chris Slobogin (Criminal Law), and Winnie Taylor (Contracts).

JOINT DEGREE/GRADUATE PROGRAMS

Joint Degrees: JD/Master of Accounting; JD/MBA; JD/MA (Political Science and Public Administration); JD/MA (Sociology); JD/MA (Urban and Regional Planning); JD/PhD in History.
Graduate Degrees: LLM in Taxation

STUDENT LIFE

Most students at UF are willing to help each other, particularly after the first semester. People are mostly willing to share notes, work on outlines together, and talk about class. There's very little in Gainesville besides places that cater to undergrads, which suits a significant number of the students who hang out with UF undergraduates. Many students participate in extracurricular activities, such as the John Marshall Bar Association International Law Society and the Black Law Student Association. Gainesville is a classic college town. The law students are a welcome addition to all college activities and events. The bars are usually full of fun, and northern Florida abounds with parks, lakes, and nearby beaches for day or weekend excursions.

PLACEMENT

The Placement Office has a wide range of services and brings many law firms to the campus. However, there has been marked frustration from some students because, although many firms interview on campus, generally only students with very high GPAs get interviews. Also placement in smaller firms and outside Florida is very limited. Very little guidance is given by the Placement Office. This may be because their new director has had no legal placement experience. Very few out-of-state firms come for on-campus interviews. Basically those who attend UF and look for a job in Florida are pleased.

98% placed within three months of passing the bar.

PREPARATION

The Placement Office prepares the students with a variety of workshops, seminars, and job fairs. In addition, the Center for Career Planning provides an extensive career resources library for students to pursue their individual interests.

WHERE/WHAT GRADUATES PRACTICE

A. 6% Northeast; 90% South; 3% West Coast; 1% Midwest. 3–5% of the students remain in the vicinity within one year of graduation.
B. 72.7% Law Firms; 12% Government; 2% Business/Industry; 5.2% Judiciary; 2% Public Interest; 3.1% Other.

FORDHAM UNIVERSITY
School of Law

140 WEST 62ND ST.
NEW YORK, NEW YORK (NY) 10023
(212) 841-5189/90

🙠 REPORT CARD 🙡

ADMISSIONS
SELECTIVITY 🎓 🎓 🎓 🎓

Applicants: 6000 +; Accepted: N/A
LSAT Mean: 40
GPA Mean: 3.32

ACADEMICS
New York Bar Passage (first try): N/A
Faculty to Student Ratio: N/A
Quality of Teaching: B−
Faculty Accessibility: B/B+

PHYSICAL ENVIRONMENT
Location: Urban/Large City
Safety: Fair
HA: ♿ ♿ ♿

STUDENT ENROLLMENT
Class Size: 444
Women: 50%   Minorities: N/A
Average Age of Entering Class: N/A

PLACEMENT
REPUTATION ☆ ☆ ☆ ☆

Recruiters: 278
Starting Salary Mean: $53,000
Starting Salary Range: $19,500–80,000

FINANCES
Tuition: $12,500 (day); $9412 (evening)
Average Total Cost: $24,500 (day); $21,362
(evening)

STUDENT LIFE
RATING: ☺ ☺ ☺

After Hours: Houlihan's

PROMINENT ALUMNI/AE
Include: William J. Kent III, Judge, Suffolk
County District Court; William L. Kelleck,
Jr., Judge, Niagara County Family Court

INSIDER INFORMATION It has been said by more than one law school administrator that when their colleagues used to think about New York law schools, of which there are many, their collective rankings would form an "hourglass" figure with one particularly solid school joining the two halves at their crux—Fordham Law School. This may have held true up until a few years ago, but the sands of time running through that hourglass have been good to Fordham. With a location just a short walk from Lincoln Center, as opposed to the school's undergraduate campus at Rose Hill in the Bronx, Fordham has access to all of New York's cultural opportunities along with its inexhaustible business attractions. Its positioning between NYU and Columbia often helps attract recruiters who are "passing through" Manhattan. Not incidentally, many of those recruiters have been so impressed with Fordham graduates that they have come back specifically for the school. "Fordham's just behind NYU in terms of the graduates it's turning out," says one New York recruiter. Several other Manhattan recruiters value the school because they can count on the majority of its graduates staying in New York.

Grades seem to be among the most heated topics for students because of the numerical grading system that can separate vast percentages of the class by one point. One third-year student feels that placement works best for students in the top 25% of the class (grade average above 87%). Another student comments that the school teaches "black letter law, but that's because that's what the students want. It's not the faculty's fault." Another laments, "There's a lot of rule worshipping here. People tend to abide by the letter and not the spirit." For example, in the Uniformed Writing Competition for journals, students had to write their entries out and then type them over as they had written them, including all typos. Students making corrections on their finished entries were disqualified automatically.

Aside from its location in the heart of Manhattan, its adequate facilities, and growing reputation among recruiters, the school has one thing that would and does make most law schools green with envy. Fordham has alumni/ae who stick by their school as do very few others. This group supports fund drives and leads their firms and other employers right back to their alma mater. Rising scores and applicant pools demonstrate the school's growing popularity, but this remains Fordham's greatest agent of advancement.

ADMISSIONS

CRITERIA

All factors, including LSAT scores, GPA, quality of undergraduate course work completed, reputation of college or university attended, personal essay, work experience, and recommendations are considered level-one factors and are evaluated equally.

MINORITY RECRUITMENT PROGRAM

Yes; Minority Enrichment Program. Faculty remain committed to increasing the number of minority students in the school and to assisting minorities in the transition to law school.

ABOUT THE APPLICATION

DEADLINE FOR FILING: 3/1

FEE: $45

LSAT: Scores older than three years are not acceptable. The school judges on a case-by-case basis.

PERSONAL STATEMENT: Make certain you've distilled the most critical aspects of your reasons for studying law. Focus the essay and try to keep the total length to 250 words.

INTERVIEW: Not required or recommended, although the school offers tours to prospective applicants.

RECOMMENDATIONS: Fordham does not require them and limits you to three, which must be submitted with the application, if at all. It's probably best to take advantage of this opportunity, particularly if you have a recommender/recommenders who know(s) you and can comment on your abilities to perform both academically and professionally.

ADMISSIONS TIPS: As you will notice from letter (a) in your application instructions, typing and attention to detail are crucial in the application. Make sure you proofread your application before sending it off, and be as concise as possible when outlining and writing your personal statement.

CONTACT: James A. McGough, Assistant Director of Admissions

PHYSICAL ENVIRONMENT

"Bells, bells, bells." Edgar Allen Poe himself couldn't have said it better if he had been a student at Fordham Law hearing the sound of bells that announce the end and beginning of classes much like in high school. Students find the library very accommodating, with the exception of the recently built lounge adjoining it, which serves as a convocation center for Fordham functions. Unfortunately, the lounge, separated from the library by a glass wall, is not soundproofed, causing students great angst when the functions include music or a band.

Fordham has one of the better locations of New York law schools and is near both Lincoln Center and Central Park. "It's great; you can walk over to the park or take in a concert—if you can find the time." The school has begun renting rooms at a nearby hotel, and students can obtain housing at the Rose Hill campus in the Bronx, from which the school runs a shuttle for $1.50 each way.

FINANCES

BUDGET	LOW	MEDIUM	HIGH
Tuition (annual first year)	$12,550	$12,550	$12,550
Tuition (evening)	$9412	$9412	$9412
Books	$550	$550	$550
Living Accommodations (9 months)	Shared Apt. (Q) $3600	Hotel Lucerne (79th) $5000	Graduate Housing* $5000
Food	Groceries $1850	Groceries/Cafeteria $2400	Restaurants $3800
Miscellaneous	$2200 (annual)	$3500	$4300
Transportation	Mass Transit $550	Mass Transit $550	Car $950
TOTAL (Day)	$21,300	$24,550	$27,150
TOTAL (Evening)	$18,162	$21,412	$24,012

Q = Queens

* Rose Hill Campus in the Bronx

Employment During School: Not recommended

Scholarships: The school offers merit, need-based, and minority scholarships. Merit scholarships are contingent upon staying in the top 25% of the class.

School Loan Program (Exclusive of Perkins Money): Yes, an Emergency Loan and a Tuition Loan (no interest while in school, then 8% interest per annum six months after leaving school).

Loan Forgiveness Program: Does not have, but is currently considering implementing one.

Students Requesting Aid: N/A

ACADEMICS

There is a wide variety of teaching styles with many first-year faculty following a "relaxed Socratic teaching style." Faculty are considered highly approachable; says one second-year student, "They (the faculty) give us phone numbers, and any time I stopped by their offices to talk they were helpful. In fact one professor who's also a judge gave us his phone number in his judge's chamber." If there is a complaint among students, it concerns evaluations, particularly in the legal writing program. One third-year student felt that professors were not taught how to evaluate students. "When they read something, they know whether they like it, but aren't clear at marking corrections and instructing on how to improve the style of the memo/brief."

Fordham has three types of clinic offerings: In-House Clinics, which include the Litigation Skills Seminar and the Mediation Clinic where students practice civil and criminal law under the supervision of a faculty member; simulation courses, including courses in Collective Bargaining, Environmental Law, and Negotiating Deals and Disputes; and Clinical Externships Courses, whereby students witness and assist in the lawyering process under attorney supervision. Strengths and specialties of the school are Admiralty Law, Corporate Law/International Comparative Law, Labor Law, Legal Ethics, Tax Law, Trial Advocacy, and Clinical Training Programs.

The average grade at Fordham is 79%. If they could change one thing, students would like a reading period. Some feel that the highly structured first-year curriculum is good in that students are provided with a sense of direction. One second-year student counters that she "felt like a sheep being herded from class to class." Faculty present a good combination of real world/research-oriented materials in their class. And although it is virtually impossible for students to avoid the "occasional duds," these faculty members do seem to be in the minority. One woman recounts, "All of my encounters (with the faculty) have been exceptional. Anyone who's there will go out of their way to help you. It doesn't have to be a question or a topic. Just if you feel like a scared first-year law student. They can be in the middle of grading exams. They'll turn off the computers and ask you, 'What's on your mind?'" Faculty stars include Calamari & Perillo (Contracts—textbook authors).

Most of the deans recognize every person in the law school by sight and make a point of remembering students, though several students add that the downside to this is a somewhat "cliquish atmosphere." "I felt like I was back in grammar school."

JOINT/GRADUATE DEGREE PROGRAMS

Joint Degree: JD/MBA (Corporate Bank/Finance)
Graduate Degree: LLM in International Business

STUDENT LIFE

Fordham students have a regular party one Thursday a month. New York provides students with unlimited culture, entertainment, and shopping.

Fordham is located near Lincoln Center which features the New York City Ballet and the New York City Opera. The law school is also a short distance from "Museum Row." Student organizations include the Entertainment and Sports Law Council, the Pro Bono Program, and the Crowley Labor Law Guild.

PLACEMENT

Despite some complaints from students outside the "magical top 25% of the class," most agree that placement here is very well run and makes a conscientious effort. Students are able to rank-order employers of interest and can be scheduled for an interview even if not chosen by the employer.

98% of Fordham students found jobs within nine months after graduation. 278 organizations recruited on campus. 84%, law firms; 9.5%, government and public interest; 6.5%, corporations. The school also held off-campus interviewing in Washington, D.C.

The Career Center has drop-in hours as well as extensive files for summer jobs. According to students, it's more difficult for first-year students to get summer placement, but after that it's much better.

PREPARATION

Fordham offers career placement counseling, and contact with first-year students begins in November. There are numerous career seminars and workshops on how to interview, how to write a résumé, and how to network among potential employers. There is also a résumé-critiquing service, as well as alumni/student programs, including Career Dinners, which are based on students' interests and preferences in Labor, Litigation, Criminal, International, Real Estate, Public Interest, Investment Banking, Small Firm Practice, Environmental, Financial Services, Entertainment and Mass Media, and Judicial Clerkships. Students have access to alumni/ae advisors on a one-to-one basis.

WHERE/WHAT GRADUATES PRACTICE

A. 80% New York City; 20% Outside New York City.
B. 74.3% Law Firms; 9.2% Corporations; 7.5% Government; 7.5% Judicial Clerkships; 0.9% Academic; 0.6% Public Interest.

600 NEW JERSEY AVENUE, N.W.
WASHINGTON, D.C. 20001
(202) 662-9010/9020

❧ REPORT CARD ❧

ADMISSIONS
SELECTIVITY 🎓 🎓 🎓 🎓

Applicants: 9600; Accepted: 2000
Transfer Applications: 85; Accepted: 10
LSAT Mean: 42
GPA Mean: 3.55

ACADEMICS
Order of the Coif (1988)
Faculty to Student Ratio: 1:26
Quality of Teaching: B+/B
Faculty Accessibility: B/B−

PHYSICAL ENVIRONMENT
Location: Urban/Large City
Safety: Marginal–Poor
HA: ♿ ♿ ♿ ♿ ♿

STUDENT ENROLLMENT
Class Size: 628 (both full-time and part-time)
Women: 50%   Minorities: 22% (includes Asians)
International: 3%
Average Age of Entering Class: 24 (day); 29 (evening)

PLACEMENT
REPUTATION ★ ★ ★ ★ ⯪

Recruiters: 800 registered, 706 came; 1046 offers
Starting Salary Median: $52,000

FINANCES
Tuition: $13,975 (full-time)
Average Total Cost: $22,055 (full-time)

STUDENT LIFE
RATING ☺ ☺ ☺

After Hours: Union Station (Train Station); Irish Times (Bar); Kogod's Deli

PROMINENT ALUMNI/AE
Include: John P. O'Rourke, Judge, Illinois 5th Judicial Circuit Court; Norma Holloway, Judge, U.S. District Court of Columbia

INSIDER INFORMATION

"Civil liberties are a great heritage for Americans. They protect us against the excesses of totalitarian government and form a vital part of the freedoms to which we urge other nations to aspire. They guarantee Americans Freedom of Speech, Freedom of Religion, Security Against Arbitrary Police Action, a fair trial. They are not rights which the government gives to people, rather they are rights which the people carved for themselves when they created the government." This quote, "One Man's Freedom," chiseled in stone on the entrance way leading to the newly constructed Edward Bennett Williams Library at Georgetown, echoes the sentiments of a world-class law school with its eye on preserving freedom for Americans as well as people around the globe.

Given the current conservative trend in law schools across the country, Georgetown is something of an anomaly with an increasingly progressive and diverse student body. The school boasts an active chapter of Amnesty International, which concentrates many of its efforts on freeing members of the legal community who are imprisoned abroad. GULC's joint program with the School of Foreign Service affords students firsthand exposure to international issues in the law, but as one second-year student here has remarked, "You can get around the international emphasis if you really don't want it."

GULC attracts a healthy mixture of both seasoned and young, highly creative faculty members. Says one first-year student, "I was surprised to find all of the professors in my section were under 37 years old." Both self-inflicted and external competition among students ("Given our backgrounds before coming here it would be hard to avoid it") and being taught primarily by the Socratic method keeps first-year students on their toes. "You know you've got to be ready before you get to class." Says one student, "Knowing and seeing that all of your classmates are working hard makes you want to work hard, too."

Main Journal, Georgetown's Law Review equivalent, appears to carry great weight here with many students feeling they are more marketable for summer jobs with that hard-earned credential. The clinics have been so enthusiastically received that this is the first year that they have been oversubscribed. One of the more unusual of these offerings is Street Law, wherein students are able to teach in both high schools and prisons, concentrating on the issues of the law that would most affect their students' lives.

Rarely is a single individual responsible for the rise or fall in popularity of an entire law school, but in the case of Andrew Cornblatt, Georgetown's energetic Director of Admissions, one individual has certainly added steam to an already upwardly mobile school. He has proven that there are those in admissions who really care about the applicant at both Law School Forums and visits to undergraduate schools. And with the largest number of applications of any law school in the country, applicants appear to have responded favorably to this treatment.

Perhaps Georgetown's greatest drawback centers around the school's location and its safety, or the lack of it. Students have recounted incidents of being followed from the law school and a general feeling of the need to be safety aware. Students will often criticize classmates who walk alone at night because it displays a wanton neglect for their personal safety. The recently remodeled train station, Union Station, has become one of the hubs of student activities with numerous restaurants and shops.

ADMISSIONS

CRITERIA

Undergraduate GPA counts for about one-third of the admissions determination, including where you went to school and what you studied; LSAT counts for another third; and the subjective aspects of the file, including recommendations and personal statements, count for the final third.

MINORITY RECRUITMENT PROGRAM

Yes.

ABOUT THE APPLICATION

DEADLINE FOR FILING: 2/1

FEE: $45

LSAT: Judged on a case-by-case basis.

PERSONAL STATEMENT: "There's a reason why we call it the **personal** state-ment—not just statement. Tell me who you are. How you define you is your call. It's not that complicated." The admissions director further adds, "You should address your weaknesses, but **not** in the personal statement—use an addenda for that. . . . If you didn't do well on the LSAT. . . . If you were sick for a semester."

INTERVIEW: Not required or recommended.

ADMISSIONS TIPS: What applicants do wrong: Applicants tend to ignore their weaknesses hoping that if they don't mention them they will somehow go away. Others try to impress the admissions committee with how many big words they can fit per square inch in the essay. We are looking for creativity, the notion that you stand out. Writing well makes the most persuasive case for this. Applicants should also coordinate whatever it is they are writing about themselves with their recom-menders. This way it's not only you but somebody else telling us about what you're discussing.

CONTACT: Andrew Cornblatt, Director of Admissions

PHYSICAL ENVIRONMENT

Contrary to what many applicants may assume, Georgetown Law School, unlike most other divisions of the university, is not located in Georgetown, but in downtown D.C., a short distance from Capitol Hill. Georgetown Law consists of three build-ings, including the clinical building, the newly built library, and the stark and insti-tutional-looking McDonough Hall in which most classes are held. Plans are underway to move the clinics into McDonough as well. Safety is a major concern here, where it is considered dangerous to walk from McDonough to the clinics half a block away.

Foremost among the structural additions to Georgetown is the spacious Bennett Library, completed in January 1989. It has multi-tiered levels, etched glass doors, wood paneling, and comfortable student lounges where students actually "hang out," as well as office facilities for *Main Journal*. As to housing, students find that it is more cost-effective to live in suburbs such as College Park, which is accessible by Metro. There is a shuttle from the school to the Metro. Living way out is not recommended because of length of time spent commuting.

$$$

FINANCES

BUDGET	LOW	MEDIUM	HIGH
Tuition (Day)	$13,975	$13,975	$13,975
Books	$430	$430	$430
Living Accommodations (9 months)	Shared Apt. $2700	Shared House $3150	One-Bedroom Apt. $5400
Food	Groceries $1150	Cafeteria $2000	Restaurants $2570
Miscellaneous	$1000	$1300	$2000
Transportation	Bus/Metro $500	Car/Metro $1200	Car $1600
TOTAL	$19,755	$22,055	$25,975

Employment During School: It is accepted that many GULC students work part-time, although it is not encouraged for first-year day students. Each full-time faculty member can hire a research assistant. Eligible students can earn $8.00 per hour by working up to fifteen hours per week for various law center departments through College Work-Study.

School Loan Program (Exclusive of Perkins Money): Yes, the Law Center Loan I and II and short-term emergency loans.

Loan Forgiveness Program: Yes, the Loan Repayment Assistance Program (LRAP); designed to assist graduates who enter low-paying, law-related public interest employment. Graduates must enter qualifying employment within two years of graduation from GULC and receive a yearly income of $30,000 or less (if single with no dependents). In calculating the eligibility of a married graduate, a $13,000 working spouse allowance is subtracted from the spouses' combined income, and a $4,000 allowance is subtracted for each nonspousal dependent. The LRAP remains interest-free while the borrower is in the program. Following a three-month grace period after leaving the program, interest begins to accrue at a 10% rate. If the graduate participates in LRAP for a sufficient number of years, the loans are gradually forgiven and converted into grant funds.

Students Requesting Aid: N/A

ACADEMICS

"The classes first year are big. It can be a little tougher to get to know people and to get to all of the professors but it's manageable and you really get to know the people in your small section." During the first year at GULC, students take required courses in a section of approximately 125 students and one small section chosen from among these courses. Legal Writing and Research is taught in smaller sections by competitively selected upperclass students known as Law Fellows. Most here find that it's a "mixed bag" regarding who you get, but regardless, Law Fellows are supervised by full-time faculty members.

Second- and third-year courses are primarily electives. GULC students have more difficulty in selecting and fitting courses and clinics into their schedules than worrying if there are enough courses to take. Georgetown's preeminent International & Comparative Law department, offering seminars in areas including Soviet, Space, and Chinese Law, has tended to overshadow some areas in which GULC excels, most notably Constitutional Law and Taxation. Other strengths and specialties of the school are Civil Rights/Civil Liberties, Legal Ethics, Public Interest Law, Women/Women's Rights, and Patent Law. Clinical opportunities are many and are very popular, including among others, a Sex Discrimination Clinic; the Harrison Institute, which among other things provides technical assistance to the D.C. Taxi Commission; and a Juvenile Justice Clinic. Georgetown also houses several institutes that serve as springboards from academia to community involvement, including the Institute of Criminal Law & Procedure. GULC also offers students a summer program at the European University Institute in Florence, Italy.

Georgetown faculty are greatly praised by students and most were surprised that their faculty were as young, liberal, and accessible, whenever possible, as they were. "Many of them [the faculty] have written the text, but they still approach it [the material] with the same excitement as if it were all brand new." Student-chosen faculty stars include Charles Abernathy, textbook author, best known for work in civil rights, Robert Haft, who worked as a Special Consultant for the SEC, and "tax guru" Martin Ginsburg.

Grades are very competitive at Georgetown with a "B−/C+" at the mean. Students here know that they have to work as hard as their classmates. For all journals with the exception of *Main Journal*, students must be in the top 15% of their class. *Main Journal* accepts students divided into three groups. *Grade On* is for the top 4% of the class, but you have to be sure you have a high GPA (11 on a twelve-point scale), because this rank isn't available to students until after *Main Journal* membership has been determined. A *Writing On* option is available to all students regardless of grades, but says one *Main Journal* member, "You'd better be a strong writer. This is the hardest way to get on *Main Journal*." There is no limit to the number of students accepted and usually about 10–15 students get on through this option. The third option is *Writing On* in the top 15% of your class: a combination of grades and writing.

Competition is definitely present on the internal and external levels. Although the school doesn't officially rank students, you can know if you're in the top 4% (used for *Main Journal* Grade On); the top 15% (*Main Journal*); and the top one-third (used for computing the Dean's List).

STUDENT LIFE

Georgetown attracts a highly diverse student body from all areas of the political spectrum. As to socializing, students tend to hang out at Union Station, a beautifully remodeled train station with stores and an eye-popping array of restaurants serving international foods. The Gilbert and Sullivan Society recently put on a production of *Bye Bye Birdie,* with members rehearsing five days a week. GULC is convenient by Metro to many cultural opportunities in Washington.

PLACEMENT

Georgetown students find placement well-organized but would like to see additional staff members. The school draws a wide array of employers, and its location as the seat of federal government allows those students interested in governmental jobs great opportunities, although this past year, there has been a federal freeze on job hiring, so that the situation is not as good.

PREPARATION

Students are videotaped upon request. Résumé writing and preparation is gone over at the end of the first semester first year. In the second semester, World of Choices Forum on Careers in Law gives students an overview of the types of practices available to them. There has been a much greater interest among students in public interest law in the last couple of years. The school also participates in the Consortium of Washington, D.C. Area Law Schools for small firms.

WHERE/WHAT GRADUATES PRACTICE

A. 76% Northeast; 5% Southeast; 7% West Coast; 7% Midwest.
B. 72% Private Practice (majority in large firms); 10% Clerkships (both state and federal); 1% Graduate Degrees; 1% Military; 10% Governmental Agencies (majority federal); 4% Corporations; 1% Other.

GEORGE WASHINGTON UNIVERSITY

The National Law Center

716 20TH ST, N.W.
ROOM 414
WASHINGTON, D.C. 20052
(202) 676-7230

ADMISSIONS

SELECTIVITY 🎓 🎓 🎓 🎓

Applicants: 7233; Accepted: 1744 (both day and evening)
Transfer Applicants: 120; Accepted: 28
LSAT Mean: 39   GPA Mean: 3.39

ACADEMICS

Order of the Coif (1926)
Faculty to Student Ratio: N/A
Quality of Teaching: B/B+
Faculty Accesssibility: B+/A−

PHYSICAL ENVIRONMENT

Location: Urban/On-Campus/Large City
Safety: Good–Fair
HA: ♿ ♿ ♿ ♿ ♿

STUDENT ENROLLMENT

Class Size: 372 (full-time); 88 (part-time)
Women: 42%   Minorities: 16.3% (includes Asians)
Average Age of Entering Class: 24

PLACEMENT

REPUTATION ☆ ☆ ☆ ☆

Recruiters: 609
Starting Salary Range: $18,000–76,000

FINANCES

Tuition: $13,500 (full-time)
Average Total Cost: $22,650

STUDENT LIFE

RATING ☺ ☺ ☺ ☺

After Hours: 21st Amendment, Samantha's, Cafe Express

PROMINENT ALUMNI/AE

Include: N/A

George Washington is Washington's oldest law school with the distinct advantages of a liveable three-building facility and a location nestled securely on the GW campus near the university's undergraduate facilities. Though not as nationally known as another law school up the road whose name also begins with George, GW offers a solid program, and for those determined to make their mark on "The Hill" and its outskirts, GW's age works to its advantage, with an impressive number of GW alumni/ae sitting in hiring positions in Washington, and to a somewhat lesser extent, around the country. A consensus of recruiters believes that among all the law schools in the D.C. area, GW has moved the fastest over the past few years, though many share this recruiter's feelings. "It's definitely on its way up in quality of students and programs, but it just isn't in the same league with Georgetown."

This may be a factor of GW's more regional initial focus and the fact that the school's undergraduate reputation does not give it as much of a "halo effect" as at Georgetown. What GW does give its law school is a very compact city campus with easy access to other schools and athletic facilities.

Although many here feel that GW is competitive, with students talking freely and openly concerned about grades, it does not approach cutthroatism. Says one third-year student, "The school is student-oriented. It is very academic, but you get practical instruction as well."

Older students can begin their studies in either the day or night school (which takes four years), but the major benefit to those electing day session is that after the first year they can take all of their classes at night. Considering that the area around GW is navigable with proper safety precautions, night classes are a very attractive option, with applicants not indicating whether they are planning to enter evening or day classes until after they have been accepted.

ADMISSIONS

CRITERIA

All factors, including LSAT scores, GPA, quality of course work completed, quality and reputation of college or university attended, personal essay, work experience, and recommendations, are considered level-one criteria and are evaluated equally.

MINORITY RECRUITMENT PROGRAM

Yes.

ABOUT THE APPLICATION

DEADLINE FOR FILING: 3/1

FEE: $45

LSAT: Judged on a case-by-case basis.

PERSONAL STATEMENT: In the words of Assistant Dean Stannek, "When I read an essay, I am particulary unimpressed by people writing about Environmental Law or Patent Law . . . . What we're looking for is writing ability. A sense of the applicant as a person/potential student, a sense of [his or her] motivation, and a sense of background. [I am] more interested in students making an argument for their admissions rather than a 'slice of life' essay." Somewhere in the application you should explain why you had discrepancies in performance, etc.

INTERVIEW: Students are strongly encouraged to visit the school. However, personal interviews do not play a large role in admissions decisions. Try not to hard-sell yourself; it generally makes a negative impression.

RECOMMENDATIONS: Not required, but recommended for marginal applicants. For students who have been out of school for a while, it's still probably best to get academic recommendations, if at all possible. Employer recommendations tend to be the most useful when written by an employer who is also a lawyer, such as for someone who is working as a paralegal. This may show that the applicant has conducted extensive legal research and may give a better sense of the applicant as a potential student.

ADMISSIONS TIPS: The biggest problem that applicants have is that they think there's a magical formula in writing the application. Applicants think law schools are looking for a certain type of person, such as one who has an interest in public service. In essence, the school wants you to be yourself and is not concerned with gathering one group of individuals, but a diverse class that will contribute to the classroom discussion.

CONTACT: Robert Stannek, Assistant Dean

PHYSICAL ENVIRONMENT

GWLC, a three-building complex, makes up its own small quad. The main building is older and is flanked on both sides by more modern additions with a small courtyard in the front. The facades of some buildings date back to the mid 1800s. Founded in 1865, GWLC is the oldest law school in the District of Columbia and is situated four blocks from the White House.

The university does not provide on-campus housing for graduate students. As a result, you are encouraged to look for accommodations in the summer before you attend. A roommate list for first-year students is kept in the Admissions Office. Apartments are the most common form of housing. There are many apartment complexes in Foggy Bottom, a strongly recommended area to live in rather than commuting from nearby suburbs. Southwest Washington is considered inexpensive; east of Dupont Circle is not recommended, and west of it is more expensive. Handicapped accessibility is good. The area is considered relatively safe. Escort service is available.

FINANCES

BUDGET	LOW	MEDIUM	HIGH
Tuition (full-time)	$13,500	$13,500	$13,500
Books	$550	$550	$550
Living Accommoda-tions (9 months)	Shared House $3150	Shared Apartment $3600	One-Bedroom Apt. $5850
Food	Groceries $1980	Groceries/Cafeteria $2800	Restaurants $3600
Miscellaneous	$1125	$1650	$3000
Transportation	Mass Transit $460	Cabs $550	Car $700
TOTAL	$20,765	$22,650	$27,200

Scholarships: The school offers scholarships based on a combination of merit and need. Several scholarships based on merit alone are available as well.

School Loan Program (Exclusive of Perkins Money): No

Loan Forgiveness Program: Does not have, but is currently considering implementing one.

Students Requesting Aid: N/A; of those who request aid, 60% receive aid.

ACADEMICS

The first year at GW is all required courses with Legal Writing divided into sections of fourteen students taught by two different teachers—a dean's teaching fellow, selected on the basis of writing skills, and a practicing attorney alumnus. An assistant dean oversees the program.

Environmental and Government, Contracts, and Patent Law are considered chief among GW's academic strongholds. Although it is not as strong as at Georgetown, GW also has a good International Law program.

The Legal Clinic provides varied subject matter, with opportunities arising from consultationships for the federal government, contract work for the District of Columbia, and internships serving clients in the inner cities.

Students find that faculty are for the most part, "thorough in presentation of material," although accessibility after class is somewhat trickier. Says one student, "It's there, but you have to take the initiative."

JOINT DEGREE PROGRAMS

JD/MBA; JD/MA. There are a number of flexible programs that can be arranged with other graduate schools of the university.

STUDENT LIFE

"Washington, D.C. itself is a cultural mecca, with more things here to do than you could even think of, from museums and government to just having a good time." GW students have a Law Revue, a presentation that spoofs professors. Students at GW are considered competitive. Students also find classmates to be "human and as such, bonds of friendship do develop." Football tournaments, parties, and a good number of organizations are sponsored by and for GW law students. The school also has numerous older students who strongly recommend GW to older applicants because of its course structuring, particularly in the evening program, of which full-time students can take advantage during their second and third years.

PLACEMENT

97% of the students are placed by January following graduation. 80% of students have already found employment prior to graduation.

PREPARATION

Students are prepared through résumé preparation assistance, presentation of forums on legal career opportunities, newsletters, and a placement handbook.

WHERE/WHAT GRADUATES PRACTICE

A. 50% South Atlantic; 15% Mid-Atlantic; 5% New England; 2% West South Central; 8% Pacific Coast (includes Hawaii); 4% East, North Central; 2% Mountain States; 2% West North Central; 1% Foreign; 13% Unspecified.
B. 61% Law Firm Practice; 14% Government (including Military); 8% Judicial Clerkships; 6% Business and Industry; 1% Legal Services/Public Interest; 10% Other.

POUND 303
CAMBRIDGE, MASSACHUSETTS (MA) 02138
(617) 495-3102

REPORT CARD

ADMISSIONS
SELECTIVITY

Applicants: 7800; Accepted: 790
LSAT Mean: N/A   GPA Mean: N/A

ACADEMICS
Faculty to Student Ratio: N/A
Quality of Teaching: B+
Faculty Accessibility: B+

PHYSICAL ENVIRONMENT
Location: Urban/Large City
Safety: Fair–Good
HA:

STUDENT ENROLLMENT
Class Size: 500
Women: N/A   Minorities: N/A
International: 5%
Average Age of Entering Class: 24–25

PLACEMENT
REPUTATION ☆ ☆ ☆ ☆ ☆

Recruiters: 725 on-campus interviews
Starting Salary Mean: N/A

FINANCES
Tuition: $13,400
Average Total Cost: $25,240

STUDENT LIFE
RATING ☺ ☺ ☺

After Hours: The Hark–Harkness Commons

PROMINENT ALUMNI/AE
Include: William K. Reilly, Judge, U.S.
District Court, North Carolina; James
Bryan McMillan, Administrator,
Environmental Protection Agency

INSIDER INFORMATION

Freedom. As this country's first institution of higher learning, it may be fitting that the land of the free also has produced a law school where students can pick and choose the course of their legal education. Aside from rather large, required introductory level, first-year courses, Harvard Law School has virtually unlimited possibilities for students, who have the opportunity to participate in one of its many clinics or take courses in other parts of the university, including the Kennedy School of Government or the highly acclaimed Fletcher School of International Law and Diplomacy in conjunction with Tufts. Whereas a great many law school faculties are sprinkled with a few bright stars whose visionary careers grace the pages of their schools' catalogues, Harvard is one of the few that can claim a complete and unbroken constellation of pure star power.

When asked what sets their school apart, most Harvard students picked placement and the incredible job opportunities as their first reason above quality of faculty and programs offered. Indeed, although there are a "small core of public interest types," a vast majority of HLS grads opt for prime positions in top law firms encircling the globe. This may be one of the reasons why hiring partners, many of whom happen to be Harvard alumni/ae themselves, prefer the school. Unlike rival Yale, with its small class, a substantial number of whom are clerkship bound, HLS has a large enough class so that, although a significant percentage of its grads go into clerkships, firms still have a good crack at pulling students their way. Recruiter satisfaction has been resoundingly high with most sharing the feeling that, "When we have something that is particularly important to do in our firm, it's an unwritten rule that we give it to our Harvard graduates." Adds another recruiter, "Harvard students are well worth their salaries. They're handpicked by a strenuous admissions process, and it shows up in what we see when we come on campus to recruit there."

As you might expect, any school that's been around as long as Harvard, picks up its share of detractors waiting to throw rocks through the school's Ivory Tower whenever they get the chance. Students at other top law schools who were accepted at Harvard generally chose another institution because they found, as one student at Yale says, "I walked in, they [Harvard] handed me a map of the school and a class schedule and sent me on my way. That was it." Given its large class size—which does break down into small sections both in the first year and in some upperclass seminars—the school may not exude a warm feeling as you find your way among the seventeen buildings that make up HLS' complex. But in all things, with greater freedom comes greater responsibility, and at Harvard that translates into fashioning a schedule that fits your personal goals and to many here, personal dreams. "This is certainly not the place to come if you need hand holding," warns one second-year student, though many students find that if there is something that needs explaining in any course, with few exceptions the professor will be more than willing to explain it and, occasionally, if they sense mass confusion, pick up with the same point at the next class.

Although Harvard has one of the, if not the highest, yields on its acceptances, it does not "cut by the numbers," quite simply because it doesn't have to boast or even publish high GPA and high LSAT means to prove its worth. This security translates into a great deal more flexibility in admissions than is found at other schools of Harvard's caliber. Despite the fact that the school is not "numbers-driven," or as many administrators feel, projects the image of not being numbers-driven, the majority of students accepted into the school score among the top 5 to 10% of applicants in both LSAT scores and academic record. Due to its own breadth of choice, every now and then, the school is willing to pick up an interesting candidate who didn't come out with high scores.

Harvard is also the land of plenty. Plenty of alumni/ae out there will help and advise you, plenty of job offers come after graduation, and there are plenty of students, which can make some feel like a number on occasion. As one student says, "Harvard is an international status symbol." That may be an understatement, as was recently proven when the Soviet Union encountered difficulties with its minority population. Where do you think they went seeking advice about negotiation? You guessed it, Harvard's Program on Negotiation, much of which is based out of the law school.

ADMISSIONS

You might assume that a school as popular as Harvard Law School would cursorily cut students "by the numbers," given the high volume of well-qualified applicants they are deluged with annually. In actuality, this is not the case. Harvard does not give out either mean LSAT or GPA scores because the school looks for a variety of factors and does not wish candidates who may have unusual backgrounds but grades/LSATs below a norm or outside of a range not to apply. Along with GPA and LSAT, Harvard places great importance on less easily quantifiable factors, like accomplishment and the desire to help others. The school looks beyond the applicant's overall GPA and examines the academic record including such factors as the strength of courses taken and where the degree(s) was (were) received. Conceivably the school could fill its class with applicants possessing near perfect GPAs and LSAT scores, but they are more concerned with diversity and accepting what will turn out to be "an interesting class," based on both the academic records and backgrounds of the applicants.

Harvard Law tends to draw on the Ivy League, the Little Three, and other schools of similar academic reputation, not because it has a favorite group of schools as much as because these schools tend to produce the greatest number of applicants. Last year there were 400 applications to the law school from Harvard College alone. Despite this, applicants from a wide number of colleges are accepted. Each year the number of students who choose to defer admissions for a year comes close to balancing the number of students who are entering the school from the previous year's deferment.

MINORITY RECRUITMENT PROGRAM

Yes.

ABOUT THE APPLICATION

DEADLINE FOR FILING: Rolling Admissions

FEE: $50

LSAT: The school looks at each applicant's scores in light of his or her individual case.

PERSONAL STATEMENT: Harvard's essay question is rather open-ended. According to Joyce Curll, Assistant Dean for Admissions, this is the applicant's opportunity to have the equivalent of an interview where [the applicant] can control the questions asked and answered. The two pages provided should be sufficient for the majority of applicants, but if you feel you need more or less space, that is fine as well. Submitting additional information, such as a thesis, generally will not help you to gain admission.

ADMISSIONS TIPS: For those in programs described as professional, if the program is primarily an applied, as opposed to a theoretical, one, it is recommended that applicants take courses that are more theoretical in nature. For applicants in hard sciences, it is important to make an effort to take courses in the social sciences and humanities, particularly courses that emphasize written presentation skills, because there is a great deal of writing involved in the study and practice of law.

CONTACT: Joyce Curll, Assistant Dean for Admissions and Financial Aid

PHYSICAL ENVIRONMENT

You get off the Red Line "T" stop that leads you to a fast-paced Harvard Square crawling with students from all of the other Boston schools. As you make your way past the crowd and through the metal gates, which admit you to the main campus, you feel as if you've entered an educational enclave. You walk past many buildings that are a combination of both modern and classic architecture. Harvard Law School is composed of seventeen buildings, with most fully accessible for the handicapped. Facilities at the school run the gamut from breathtakingly beautiful to rather plain, with more emphasis on the former.

Dormitories are on campus and rooms are obtained by lottery. As a result, not all first-year students are able to get in; if they do get on-campus housing, students strongly recommend it, as opposed to living in Cambridge, which has "rents through the roof." Safety appears to be fair as well, and an escort service is available. Bringing a car is not recommended because transportation is readily accessible. Furthermore, it is expensive to park and insure a car in the area.

FINANCES

BUDGET	LOW	MEDIUM	HIGH
Tuition	$13,400	$13,400	$13,400
Books	$550	$550	$550
Living Accomodations (9 months)	Shared House $4050	On-Campus $5040	One-Bedroom Apt. $6300
Food	Groceries $1500	Groceries/Cafeteria $2000	Restaurants $3500
Miscellaneous	$1900	$2500	$3500
Transportation	Mass Transit $1200	Car/"T" $1750	Car $2900
TOTAL	$22,600	$25,240	$30,150

Employment During School: Not recommended. Work-study jobs are available for all students; not need-dependent.

Scholarships: The school offers need-based scholarships. Merit scholarships are not available.

School Loan Program (Exclusive of Perkins Money): Yes

Loan Forgiveness Program: Yes; the Low Income Protection Plan. Participants are allocated a calculated portion of their annual income toward repayment of all their eligible educational loans for the fiscal year (July 1–June 30) in which they participate. A new application must be made by the borrower each year.

Students Requesting Aid: 70%; of these, 66% receive aid.

Students Indebted upon Graduation: 66%

Average Loan Indebtedness: $39,385

ACADEMICS

The first year has required courses except for one elective. The last two years are almost all electives. There is a third-year writing requirement. The students here feel it is impossible to flunk out and their marks, graded from A to F, are inflated. "Everybody always gets a B or above." Courses are taught using a case method, similar to that found at Harvard Business School. This teaching methodology presents you with a narrative fact situation, which has information on social, business, political, and economic factors, integrated with legal issues, and you must decide how a party or parties should proceed in addition to identifying critical facts and legal issues. Students find that HLS does not train the students in taking the bar exam. It focuses on the thinking and reasoning of a lawyer, with many different approaches brought to tackle the same topic.

Harvard has nearly 200 courses and seminars ranging from "meat-and-potato" bar courses to courses dealing with Chinese and Islamic legal systems. Says one second-year student interested in litigation, "There are so many from which to choose with virtually every imaginable course . . . you wouldn't even have thought some of them existed." Harvard offers unlimited flexibility to second- and third-year students, with the exception of the school's writing requirement, which has to be of publishable quality. According to Joyce Curll, Assistant Dean for Admissions, "You could spend all of your upper level courses taking poverty law if that is what you wanted to do."

Harvard has numerous special programs, including the East Asian Legal Studies program, which has recently attracted full-time faculty member Bill Alford from UCLA, and the Center for Criminal Justice, which is doing breakthrough work on terrorism law. It is also possible to take a limited number of credits at the Fletcher School of International Law and Diplomacy in conjunction with Tufts and Harvard's and Kennedy School of Government.

Class size tends to be the biggest student gripe, with the class of five hundred divided into smaller sections. Says one third-year student, "They do exist, but groups of only twenty-five are pretty rare and primarily for those courses that are in specialty fields."

Harvard boasts a very diverse, revered, and high-spirited faculty. Professor Ogletree teaches Criminal Law and a Harvard graduate "Saturday School" for people of color that deals with racial matters. Only two or three faculty members employ the Socratic method. "The courses here teach you how to think rather than simply to memorize pieces of information." "When a lecture doesn't go well and the professor senses that, the next lecture will start with that point and a general recap to help those who didn't get it before." Student-selected faculty stars include Kathleen Sullivan (Criminal Law, Constitutional Law), Professor Ogletree, and Alan Dershowitz.

STUDENT LIFE

Despite the fact that grades are generally quite good and students have little trouble getting jobs, one student says, "There are some students here who have been so used to being number one from kindergarten on that it's impossible for them not to work all the time. But if you're smart, you stay away from those types, do your work, and have some fun. The pressure's what you make it out to be. You turn up the volume or you let yourself relax. It's basically your choice." HLS students hang out outside the buildings or at the "Hark," Harkness Commons, to watch "LA Law." Many of them still don't have time for TV despite their ability to devote fewer hours to academics; they pour all of their remaining energies into Harvard's somewhat overwhelming number of student organizations.

PLACEMENT

"There's a reason why Harvard calls it [placement] Career Services and Counseling. They don't have to work to get us placed. They have to help us decide what jobs to take." Adds another student concerning employment, "That's the great thing about Harvard. Once you're in you're all set. If you were in the bottom of your class at most other schools you wouldn't have a chance with most firms. Here they still want you." Although students have commented that Harvard "tends to be on the laissez-faire side" regarding placement, and many feel that it "lives and breathes off its reputation," they are satisfied with the office's organizational and counseling abilities.

PREPARATION

The Placement Office begins seeing students in March of their first year. Students are not videotaped, but their interviewing techniques are critiqued by counselors. Students are able to use the phone freely for calling about public interest positions but must report back what they have learned.

WHERE/WHAT GRADUATES PRACTICE

A. Five Major Cities: 22.5% New York; 14.8% Washington, D.C.; 12.5% Boston; 10% Los Angeles; 5.9% Chicago.
B. 1% Academics; 0.6% Banks/Investment Banking; 1.1% Corporations/Legal; 0.2% Corporations/Nonlegal; 1.3% Federal Government; 26.1% Judicial Clerkships; 1.1% Legal Services to Low Income; 65.7% Law Firms; 0.2% Local Government (City); 1.3% Public Interest; 1.3% State Government.

HOUSTON, TEXAS (TX) 77204-6391
(713) 749-4816

REPORT CARD

ADMISSIONS
SELECTIVITY

Applicants: 3100; Accepted: 888
Transfer Applicants: 78; Accepted: 12
LSAT Mean: 37   GPA Mean: 3.32

PLACEMENT
REPUTATION

Recruiters: 220
Starting Salary Median: N/A

ACADEMICS
Order of the Coif (1985)
Texas Bar Passage Rate (first try): 83%
Faculty to Student Ratio: 1:18
Quality of Teaching: B
Faculty Accessibility: A

FINANCES
Tuition: $2790 (R); $5580 (NR)
Average Total Cost: $10,025 (R): $12,815 (NR)

PHYSICAL ENVIRONMENT
Location: Urban/Large City
Safety: Good–Fair
HA:

STUDENT LIFE
RATING ☺ ☺ ☺ ☺

After Hours: Kay's, Sam's, Black-Eyed Pea

STUDENT ENROLLMENT
Class Size: 300 (full-time); 75 (part-time)
Women: 48%   Minorities: 17%
Average Age of Entering Class: 26

PROMINENT ALUMNI/AE
Include: Richard "Racehorse" Haynes; Raul Gonzalez, Texas Supreme Court Justice

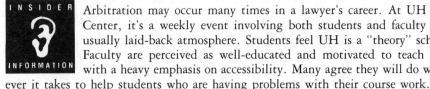

INSIDER INFORMATION   Arbitration may occur many times in a lawyer's career. At UH Law Center, it's a weekly event involving both students and faculty in a usually laid-back atmosphere. Students feel UH is a "theory" school. Faculty are perceived as well-educated and motivated to teach law, with a heavy emphasis on accessibility. Many agree they will do whatever it takes to help students who are having problems with their course work.

UH assigns first-year law students to sections, the members of which take all of their courses together, and also provide one another with a sense of support. Although the first-year curriculum is required, there is a good choice of second- and third-year electives. The school is known nationally for its strong programs, including one in Health Law. The Health Law Institute is located in the Texas Medical Center, which treats more than 2.5 million people a year and is currently Houston's largest employer. The Institute is responsible for coordinating health law courses, which provide unique opportunities for interdisciplinary study and professional interaction at UH. Taught by both full-time faculty members and adjuncts, the Law Center is reported to have the largest number of health law course offerings of any law school in the country. Specific programs of the Institute include the "Health Law Semester in Houston" and the dual JD/MPH degree program with the University of Texas School of Public Health.

UH's strength also lies in its International Law and Environmental Law specialties. In addition to a wide range of course offerings in International Law, the school also conducts a Mexican Legal Studies Program in Mexico City, has an active International Law Society, and offers an LLM in International Law. *The Houston Journal of International Law* is one of the two major journals published by the school.

The Environmental Liability program is a major research program on the topic of liability and compensation for environmental harm. The school offers an LLM in Energy and Natural Resources Law.

The Law Center has an underground law library, which many students here find second to none in the state of Texas. The roof of the library forms a spacious raised plaza with trees and plants.

Nationally, recruiters have expressed satisfaction with U.H. graduates. One says, "It's a solid school with a very sound program. . . . Quality graduates are the norm not the exception."

ADMISSIONS

CRITERIA

LEVEL 1: LSAT scores

LEVEL 2: Grade Point Average; quality of undergraduate curriculum/course work completed

LEVEL 3: Quality/reputation of college/university; work experience; personal essay; list of extracurricular activities

LEVEL 4: Recommendations

MINORITY RECRUITMENT PROGRAM

Yes; through the Law Service Candidate Referral Service (CRS), Black Law Student Association, and Hispanic Law School Student Association.

ABOUT THE APPLICATION

DEADLINE FOR FILING: 2/1

FEE: $25

LSAT: The school takes the average of applicant's scores.

RECOMMENDED COURSES PRIOR TO MATRICULATING: Philosophy-Logic. Any course work developing analytical and writing skills.

PERSONAL STATEMENT: "A quality, focused personal essay could push a 'borderline' candidate over into the 'admit' category."

INTERVIEW: Not recommended or required, but visits with the dean of admissions of permitted. It is not used as part of the evaluation procedure. University Hilton (on-campus) has been suggested for accommodations (741-2447).

ADMISSIONS TIPS: "Do not assume anything. Approach the personal essay as basically a document doing the law school interview for you. Include your work or activity résumé. Try to tailor your application to the Law Center. Research the Law Center and its location. What are the strengths? This will provide a more focused application. Try to differentiate yourself from other applicants. Packaging is not important; content is important."

CONTACT: Murray M. Nusynowitz, Assistant Dean for Admissions and Financial Aid

PHYSICAL ENVIRONMENT

The Law Center is contained in four modern interconnected buildings. Two three-story buildings serve as teaching units. A third structure contains administrative offices and a large auditorium. Of special interest is the fact that the Law Center provides a permanent study carrel for each student. The law library is housed in a separate underground structure.

The campus is designed barrier-free to integrate handicapped students. On-campus housing, while not guaranteed, is available to single students. Only 1% of students live in school-owned accommodations. Those who do live there frequently choose to live in Cougar Place, a building offering apartment-like living, which is designed for graduate and professional students. There is no university housing available to married students. The best living accommodations for single and married students, with or without children, is an apartment. A car is recommended. Even though public transportation is adequate, a car is considered a necessity. Be advised, however, that students who operate cars on campus are required to pay parking fees.

FINANCES

BUDGET	LOW	MEDIUM	HIGH
Tuition (Resident) **Tuition (Nonresident)**	$2790 $5580	$2790 $5580	$2790 $5580
Books	$500	$500	$500
Living Accomodations (9 months)	Shared Apt. $1350	Shared House On-Campus $1500	One-Bedroom Apt. $2700
Food*	Groceries $1950	Cafeteria $2535	Restaurants $3315
Miscellaneous	$1200	$1500	$1700
Transportation	Car $1200	Car $1200	Car $1200
Total (R) Total (NR)	$8990 $11,780	$10,025 $12,815	$12,205 $14,995

* Note: No Meal Plan provided.

Employment During School: Not recommended. Jobs are available for all students (not need-dependent). Students receive $5.50 an hour.

Scholarships: The school offers merit scholarships, contingent upon maintaining a 2.67 (B−) average. Need scholarships are not available.

School Loan Program (Exclusive of Perkin's Money): No

Loan Forgiveness Program: No

Students Requesting Aid: 80%; of these, 75% receive aid.

Students Indebted upon Graduation: 75%

Average Loan Indebtedness: $22,000

ACADEMICS

First-year students are divided into five sections of about seventy students each. All courses are required. Second- and third-year students have a wide selection of electives from which to choose, but are required to take Professional Responsibility and to fulfill a senior research and writing requirement. During these years, class size seldom exceeds ninety and one-half of the courses have thirty or fewer students. The electives are grouped by subject matter, including Business Organization and Regulation,

Commercial and International Law, and Dispute Resolution, Litigation, and Skills Training.

Students feel that there is enough variety in the types of courses offered, especially the Trial Advocacy course.

In addition to the programs previously mentioned, the Law Center also has the Institute for Higher Education Law and Governance. International and comparative education are one of its focuses and foreign scholars are regular participants in research activities. Clinical courses are offered in the Legal Clinic.

Students point out that the "C" curve is very strictly enforced at the law school, which, some here believe, makes it more difficult to be placed.

Star faculty include Sidney Buchanan (Constitutional Law, First Amendment Rights, Trusts and Wills), Judge Montgomery (Family Law), and Richard Alderman (DTPA).

JOINT DEGREE PROGRAMS

JD/MBA; JD/MPH (Master of Public Health); JD/MHA (Master of Health Administration)

Social life at UH is considered good. It has been noted, however, that the Student Bar Association excludes nonmembers from on-campus activities that some students feel should be open to the entire law school. Student organizations include the Health Law Organization, the Business Law Organization, and the Aeronautical and Space Law Society. This last mentioned association deals with discussions concerning legal issues stemming from the development, use, and exploitation of space and related technologies. The school has an intramural sports program. One third-year student at the school felt that "cohesiveness rather than competitive negativism" should be encouraged among the students.

Students are generally satisfied with the Placement Office at their school, but feel that there is little exposure to firms outside of the South.

PREPARATION

Students are prepared by the Placement Office through various means. There are two group presentations on résumé preparation annually. Individual assistance on résumé preparation, interview techniques, and job search is always available through placement. First-year students may participate in a videotaped mock interview.

WHERE/WHAT GRADUATES PRACTICE

A. 2% Northeast; 88% South; 1% West Coast; 2% Midwest. 75% of students remain in the vicinity of the law school within one year of graduation.

B. 3% Sole Practitioner; 27% Small Firms; 21% Medium Firms; 20% Large Firms; 4% Clerkships; 1% Graduate Degrees; 9% Governmental agencies; 5% Corporations; 8% Other.

ILLINOIS INSTITUTE OF TECHNOLOGY

I.I.T. CHICAGO-KENT COLLEGE OF LAW
77 SOUTH WACKER DRIVE
CHICAGO, ILLINOIS (IL) 60606
(312) 567-5012

REPORT CARD

ADMISSIONS
SELECTIVITY 🎓 🎓 🎓 🎓 ⚑

Applicants: 1800; Accepted: 750
Transfer Applications: 15; Accepted: 2
LSAT Mean: 37 GPA Mean: 3.1

PLACEMENT
REPUTATION ☆ ☆ ☆

Recruiters: 139 corp./law firms; 48 public
  sector employers
Starting Salary Mean: $42,000 (private
  sector); $26,000 (public sector)

ACADEMICS

Order of the Coif (1989)
Illinois Bar Passage (first try): 93%
Faculty to Student Ratio: 1:18
Quality of Teaching: `B+/A−`
Faculty Accessibility: `A−`

FINANCES

Tuition: $10,760 (full-time); $7420 (part-time)
Average Total Cost: $19,858 (full-time);
  $16,518 (part-time)

PHYSICAL ENVIRONMENT

Location: Urban/Big City
Safety: Fair
HA: ♿ ♿ ♿ ♿ ♿

STUDENT LIFE
RATING ☺ ☺ ☺

After Hours: Celtic Club for SBA functions,
  Bennigan's, Vie de France, Monday's,
  Everly Club

STUDENT ENROLLMENT

Class Size: 239 (full-time); 89 (part-time)
Women: 50% Minorities: 11%
Average Age of Entering Class: 26.5

PROMINENT ALUMNI/AE

Include: Joel Daly, News Anchor, ABC,
  Chicago Affiliate; Silas Strawn, founder,
  Winston & Strawn; Weymouth Kirkland,
  founder, Kirkland & Ellis

INSIDER INFORMATION

IIT—Perhaps the first thing that will tell you that this is not an ordinary law school is the presence of "Institute" in its name. To those who have not heard of it, it may come as a surprise that Chicago Kent is not a "new kid on the block." It happens that Kent is over one hundred years old, but as one top recruiter has said, "It was perceived as a commuter school for people already in the workplace." Only within the last ten to fifteen years, since its affiliation with the Illinois Institute of Technology, has the school taken off. Many students agree with this characterization. Adds one third-year student, "The faculty and administration are not complacent. They can't afford to be. Though Kent has been around for 100 years, it is not as well-known as some of the other schools. As a result,

ILLINOIS INSTITUTE OF TECHNOLOGY **141**

Kent will take chances in order to gain the recognition and reputation it needs to survive. This is a school where you can have some influence." As the youngest member of the Order of the Coif (1989), Kent takes its place of academic distinction among its Chicago neighbors University of Chicago and Northwestern.

Kent has capitalized on its technological bent by adding computer facilities to its program in a joint venture with Mead Data Central, Inc., which is conducting a three-year test program at Chicago-Kent to integrate Computer Assisted Legal Research (CALR) fully into the law school curriculum. From the first year on, students begin their computer instruction by using computers to outline course notes, brief cases, do computer-assisted research, and diagnose citation errors. The school also offers advanced courses teaching students, among other things, how to generate complex legal documents.

In the words of a current second-year student, "The fact that you are attending IIT-Chicago-Kent virtually guarantees you will pass the bar with flying colors. You stand to gain practical knowledge of the legal profession from a diverse faculty. You will gain invaluable exposure to computers and have the opportunity to participate in innovative projects involving the legal profession and computers."

The students consider IIT-Kent's physical environment to be nonacademic, making it less conducive to serious scholarly work. The school's downtown location, far away from residence halls, makes it more of a commuter school. However, the school will be opening a new facility in spring 1992 which, all concur, has been designed with both faculty and student concerns in mind. Another point of agreement among students and administration is that the three-year legal writing program is one of Kent's best features. Recruiters are impressed with this program and find that among law schools, graduates from IIT are very well prepared in written presentation.

ADMISSIONS

CRITERIA

LEVEL 1: Grade Point Average; quality of undergraduate curriculum/course work completed; quality/reputation of college/university; LSAT score; personal essay; recommendations

LEVEL 2: Diversity (e.g., race, geographic origin, work/graduate work experience, age, etc.)

MINORITY RECRUITMENT PROGRAM

Yes, through Admissions Committee Subcommittee, recruitment at minority student events, and programs with the Black Law Student Association and Hispanic Law Student Association.

ABOUT THE APPLICATION

DEADLINE FOR FILING: 4/1+

FEE: $25

LSAT: School takes the average of the applicant's scores. It also depends on the individual circumstances; sometimes the school takes the highest or the most recent LSAT score.

RECOMMENDED COURSES PRIOR TO MATRICULATING: Any course requiring reading, writing, and analysis: history, philosophy, English.

PERSONAL STATEMENT: "Very important—especially with regard to scholarships and borderline candidates. Yes, we do try to talk/meet with applicants whose personal statements are special."

INTERVIEW: Not required or recommended. However, the school is happy to meet with applicants to answer their questions. For visitors, the Holiday Inn-Mart Plaza, Midland Hotel, and IIT main campus are recommended.

ADMISSIONS TIPS: "Visit the school. Talk to students and alumni/ae. Research through standard reference material and own efforts. Election to the Coif is proof of rapid advances in the past 5–8 years. Proofread the application carefully; careless spelling and grammatical errors are noticed. Tell us what makes you stand out—what will you bring to the law school environment?"

CONTACT: Nancy Herman, Assistant Dean-Admissions

PHYSICAL ENVIRONMENT

The law school is contained in IIT's Downtown Center in a fairly safe and flat area in a modern six-story building in Chicago's Loop. Accessibility for the handicapped is considered very good; all of the hallways and doorways can accommodate wheelchairs.

IIT-Kent is a short walk from the federal building and La Salle Street, one of the centers of law practice in Chicago. The school has three law school computer laboratory classrooms that contain seventy personal computers connected to a local area network.

On-campus student housing is not guaranteed, but no one has ever been turned down. 1% of students live in school-owned housing. The best living accommodations are, for a single student, sharing an apartment; for a married student with no children, an apartment (apartments are also available on the main campus); for a married student with children, living in a nearby suburb and commuting by train to the law school.

A car is not recommended. Parking is expensive, and the public transportation system is efficient and affordable.

FINANCES

BUDGET	LOW	MEDIUM	HIGH
Tuition (full-time) **Tuition (part-time)**	$10,760 $7420	$10,760 $7420	$10,760 $7420
Books (first year)	$500	$500	$500
Living Accommoda- **tions (9 months)**	Dorm room $2610	Two-Bedroom Shared Apt. $3375	One-Bedroom Apt. $5625
Food	Groceries $2000	Meal Plan (21/wk) $2238	Restaurants $3900
Miscellaneous	$1950	$2535	$2925
Transportation	Bus or Train $390	Bus Pass $450	Car $700
TOTAL (full-time) TOTAL (part-time)	**$18,210** **$14,870**	**$19,858** **$16,518**	**$24,410** **$21,070**

Employment During School: Only after first year. Work-study jobs are available for students. These jobs are open with some based on need and pay $6 an hour.

Scholarships: The school offers merit and need-based scholarships. Financial-need scholarships are contingent upon maintaining a 2.90 GPA, merit scholarships on a 3.25 GPA.

School Loan Program (Exclusive of Perkins Money): No

Loan Forgiveness Program: No

Students Requesting Aid (federal financial): 65%; of these, 99% receive aid.

Students Indebted upon Graduation: 64%

Average Loan Indebtedness: Approximately $30,000 (day); $28,000 (evening)

ACADEMICS

The first year is all required courses, which begin the integration of computer programs with the study of torts and with the legal research and writing program. Students learn to brief cases with the help of the computer. Each first-year student is assigned a faculty advisor whose scholarly work interests parallel the student's law interests.

Because the law school is growing so fast there is a shortage of professors and thus a shortage of variety. However, beginning in 1989, the law school engaged in aggressive recruiting and the problem should be remedied soon. Kent is constantly offering new courses, but students have to plan their schedules well in advance in order to take a wide selection, because some courses aren't offered each semester. Course offerings include Corporate and Business Law, International Law, Environmental and Energy Law, and Public Interest Law. There are three lecture series: the Piper Lecture in Labor Law, the Green Lecture in Law and Technology, and the Morris Lecture in International and Comparative Law. School strengths include Legal Research and Writing, Computer/Technology Law, Corporate Law, Energy/Environmental/Natural Resources Law, International Comparative Law, and Trial Advocacy.

IIT's five Clinical Education Programs accommodate more than one hundred second- and third-year students each semester. These programs include In-House Civil Clinic, In-House Judicial Externship, Advanced Externship, and Advice Desk, open to third-year students, who provide counseling services to indigent defendants under a teaching attorney's supervision.

Most faculty members are enthusiastic about teaching in general and about the subjects that they teach. Kent provides students with the practical skills necessary to practice law. It also supplements those skills with the needed theoretical underpinnings. In general, the average faculty member possesses strong communication skills.

The faculty, both professors and administrators, go out of their way to make it clear to the students that they are available for help with academic, professional, and personal advice. Students find that most professors don't have to set up hours, because they are frequently in their offices. Star faculty include Joan Stienman (Civil Procedure I and II), Maggie Stewart (Federal Courts), and Howard Chapman (Personal Income Tax).

JOINT/GRADUATE DEGREE PROGRAMS

Joint Degree: JD/MBA
Graduate Programs: LLM (Tax Law); LLM (Financial Services Law); Master of American Legal Studies Program

Kent students have CLASS, the Student Computer Law Association, which also instructs students in the use of computer equipment. Other organizations include the Biotechnology and the Law Society, BREHON Law Society, and a chapter of the Student Bar Association. "Kent's overall atmosphere is exciting, informal, but professional." School-sponsored social events are generally very successful. SBA functions are frequent. Kent is not on the main campus of IIT and is something of a commuter school. The social life is there if you are interested. Although there is a lot of competition, there is also a lot of camaraderie among students at the school.

PLACEMENT

Students find the Placement Office highly effective in preparing them, as well as very well organized. 97% of graduates are placed after graduation.

PREPARATION

The Placement Office offers résumé preparation, with six workshops offered each year and individual counseling appointments available; interview training, with one interview demonstration session offered each year and individual simulated videotaped interview sessions with a professional counselor available; and job search strategy workshops, including four on attorney positions and two on research clerk positions offered each year.

WHERE/WHAT GRADUATES PRACTICE

A. 2% Northeast; 1% South; 2% West Coast; 95% Midwest.
B. 3% Sole Practitioner; 20% Small Firms; 9% Medium Firms; 19% Large Firms; 7% Clerkships; 15% Governmental Agencies; 19% Corporations; 7% Public Interest; 1% Other.

209 LAW BUILDING
504 EAST PENNSYLVANIA AVENUE
CHAMPAIGN, ILLINOIS (IL) 61820
(217) 333-0931   FAX: (217) 244-1478

REPORT CARD

ADMISSIONS
SELECTIVITY 🎓 🎓 🎓 🎓

Applicants: 1495; Accepted: 503
Transfer Applications: 44; Accepted: 5
LSAT Mean: 39   GPA Mean: 3.4

PLACEMENT
REPUTATION ☆ ☆ ☆ ☆

Recruiters: 250
Starting Salary Median: $42,000

ACADEMICS
Order of the Coif (1902)
Illinois Bar Passage (first try): 98%
Faculty to Student Ratio: 1:18
Quality of Teaching: **A**
Faculty Accessibility: **A**

FINANCES
Tuition: $3280 (R); $7376 (NR)
Average Total Cost: $9587 (R): $13,683
(NR)

PHYSICAL ENVIRONMENT
Location: Small City
Safety: Good
HA: ♿ ♿ ♿ ♿ ♿

STUDENT LIFE
RATING ☺ ☺ ☺

After Hours: Murphy's, Gulley's

STUDENT ENROLLMENT
Class Size: 202
Women: 40%   Minorities: 12%
Average Age of Entering Class: 24

PROMINENT ALUMNI/AE
Include: John B. Anderson, former U.S.
Congressman and Presidential candidate;
Hon. Harlington Wood, U.S. Court of
Appeals, Seventh Circuit; Fred Barlit,
partner, Kirkland and Ellis, noted trial
attorney

INSIDER INFORMATION

Founded in 1897, the University of Illinois is looking forward to a new century with a campaign for a new $10 million building due in part to overcrowding of the old structure. Ground breaking is expected in 1990. With about one hundred different courses from which to choose, the school provides a traditional and rigorous curriculum, and the students feel that the education given them at the University of Illinois is clearly a very good value. As one student said, "If you do reasonably well, you can get the best education." This training is enriched through various special programs, including a civil liberties lecture series, a legal history forum, and a law and economics workshop. U. Illinois further provides its students with a computer lab.

A major strength of the University of Illinois is its remarkable number of published individuals. Faculty members are well-known for their exceptional case books and treatises. The students find that their professors provide a high quality lecture and are very accessible. The faculty can easily be found in their offices when not in class.

Students feel that another asset of U. Illinois is the good relationship they have with the administration. On thing considered impressive is the school's broad method of rewarding accomplishments. "The school doesn't just recognize a select few students for their achievements. Instead they recognize many individuals by various means."

Though off the beaten path, this outstanding value in legal education has a substantial number of recruiters seeking out U. Illinois students. As might be expected, the school has a strong pull among midwestern recruiters. Satisfaction with U. Illinois grads particularly among Illinois recruiters is phenomenal with many commenting that the graduates are well versed in legal research.

ADMISSIONS

CRITERIA

LEVEL 1: Grade Point Average; LSAT score; work experience; personal essay; minority or handicapped status

LEVEL 2: Quality of undergraduate curriculum/course work completed; quality/reputation of college/university; recommendations

MINORITY RECRUITMENT PROGRAM

Yes; through the Recruiting Committee, using recruiters from the faculty, administration, and student body.

ABOUT THE APPLICATION

DEADLINE FOR FILING: 1/15

FEE: $25

LSAT: No set rule about average or highest score. Determined by reviewing the complete application.

RECOMMENDED COURSE PRIOR TO MATRICULATING: Survey of accounting.

PERSONAL STATEMENT: "Could be the determining factor in the admission of the student."

INTERVIEW: Not required or recommended. If visiting, contact the University of Illinois Housing Information Office (217) 333-1420 or the Student Union (217) 333-1241.

ADMISSIONS TIPS: "Most [applicants] do not spend enough time on their personal statements."

CONTACT: Jack Riley, Assistant Dean

PHYSICAL ENVIRONMENT

The College of Law is located on the main campus of the university in Urbana-Champaign, 130 miles south of Chicago. Champaign is a small city with a population of about 100,000.

The university is separated from the city to create a collegiate atmosphere. The law school itself is contained within a 1950s vintage building that houses all the college's facilities, including classrooms, courtroom, auditorium, staff, and activities offices, and the law library. A campaign is under way to produce a multimillion-dollar building to replace it. Campus facilities are very accessible. In fact, an elaborate athletic center is right across the street.

There has been a big push for handicapped accessibility here at U. Illinois, and it is considered excellent. The law school building is one story, and the area around it is on flat ground. Every block has a ramp. All classes are located on the ground floor, and an elevator is available for access to lower and upper level offices and lockers. The school has several handicapped students attending. Although safety is considered good, an escort service is provided.

5% of students live in school-owned housing. The most popular form of accommodations here is apartments. It has been said that there is presently a housing glut; as a result it is a buyer's/renter's market. The most cost-effective accommodations are considered to be the University Graduate Hall for single students and the Married Student Housing for married students with or without children. Whether or not to bring a car is strictly up to the student. Bus service in Champaign/Urbana is excellent.

FINANCES

BUDGET	LOW	MEDIUM	HIGH
Tuition (Resident)	$3280	$3280	$3280
Tuition (Nonresident)	$7376	$7376	$7376
Books	$575	$575	$575
Living Accommodations (9 months)	Shared House $2000	On-Campus Apt. $2247	One-Bedroom Apt. $2250
Food	Groceries $1215	Meal Plan $1800	Restaurants $2700
Miscellaneous	$1300	$1500	$1800
Transportation	Bus $97.50	Car/Bus $185	Car $270
TOTAL (R)	$8467.50	$9587	$10,875
TOTAL (NR)	$12,563.50	$13,683	$14,971

Employment During School: Only after first year. Work-study jobs are available for eligible second- and third-year students.

Scholarships: The school offers merit scholarships, contingent upon maintaining a 4.0 average on a 5.0 scale.

School Loan Program (Exclusive of Perkins Money): Yes; in accordance with student need as determined by the Scholarship Committee.

Loan Forgiveness Program: No

Students Requesting Aid: N/A; of those requesting aid, 75% receive aid.

Students Indebted upon Graduation: 84%

Average Loan Indebtedness: N/A

ACADEMICS

First-year students are taught by the Socratic method and are required to take a specified set of courses. The curriculum remains under continuous study for improvement. Second- and third-year students are taught less by the Socratic method with more lectures and learning of principles. Upperclass requirements for graduation are the successful completion of the Law of Professional Responsibility and Constitutional Law. A wide selection of courses is divided into sections and include Labor Law, Taxation Law, Business and Commercial Law and Jurisprudence, Legal History, Public International Law, and Comparative Law. The latter section deals with such topics as Roman Law, the History of Jewish Law, and International Law. International Legal Studies, Environmental and Planning Studies, and Legal History are considered special programs at the school.

As noted previously, faculty have been found to be very accessible. Faculty stars include Peter Hay (Conflict of Law), Peter Maggs (Soviet Law), and Harry Krause (Family Law).

JOINT/GRADUATE DEGREE PROGRAMS

Joint Degrees: JD/MILR (Master of Industrial Labor Relations); JD/MS; JD/MPA (Master of Public Administration); JD/MUP (Master of Urban Planning); JD/MD; JD/PhD Ed.
Graduate Degrees: MCL (Master of Comparative Law); LLM (Master of Law); SJD (Doctor of Juristic Science)

STUDENT LIFE

The student life at U. Illinois is considered to involve a competitive but not cutthroat atmosphere. It is said that the Student Bar Association spends thousands every year to sponsor functions such as SBA happy hours, Beer Gardens, Law Review show, Student-Faculty auction, Class Action Tournament, a Formal Dance, and a Student International Dinner. Most of the socializing is done at the school because students spend most of their time there. Students also hang out in the courtyard and in the athletic center. On the whole, the student body is a cohesive group subject to good-natured, competitive ribbing. It is found that the intense pressure of the course load teaches you to value your free time.

PLACEMENT

Many Chicago firm's recruiters come here. Percentage of students placed after graduation: 94.6%.

PREPARATION

Although there are no formal courses, the Placement Office prepares students through instruction on writing résumés and interviewing.

WHERE/WHAT GRADUATES PRACTICE

A. 3.4% Northeast; 4% South; 2.3% West Coast; 89.1% Midwest; 1.2% Other (79.9% stayed in state within one year of graduation).
B. 35% Small Firms; 10.1% Medium Firms; 54,6% Large Firms; 9.8% Clerkships; 0.6% Military; 8% Governmental Agencies; 10.9% Corporations; 2.3% Other.

BLOOMINGTON, INDIANA (IN) 47405-1001
(812) 335-4765

REPORT CARD

ADMISSIONS

SELECTIVITY 🎓 🎓 🎓 🎓

Applicants: 1358; Accepted: 521
Transfer Applications: N/A; Accepted: N/A
LSAT Mean: 37
GPA Mean: 3.36

ACADEMICS

Order of the Coif (1925)
Indiana State Bar Passage (first try): 85–90%
Faculty to Student Ratio: 1:17
Quality of Teaching: **B**
Faculty Accessibility: **B**

PHYSICAL ENVIRONMENT

Location: Small College Town
Safety: Very Good
HA: ♿ ♿ ♿ ♿ ♿

STUDENT ENROLLMENT

Class Size: 215
Women: 30% Minorities: 8%
Average Age of Entering Class: 24

PLACEMENT

REPUTATION ☆ ☆ ☆ ☆

Recruiters: 200
Starting Salary Mean: N/A

FINANCES

Tuition: $2960.50 (R); $8075.50 (NR)
Average Total Cost: $9885 (R); $15,000 (NR)

STUDENT LIFE

RATING ☺ ☺ ☺ ☺

After Hours: Kilroy's, Nick's

PROMINENT ALUMNI/AE

Include: N/A

INSIDER INFORMATION

Opened in 1842, Indiana University is the oldest state university law school in the Midwest. The school is made up of a diverse student body, which represents over ninety undergraduate schools. Students feel that although the social life here is good, the atmosphere is highly competitive. One student noted that his classmates were "not as close a group as what I expected." Another emphatically said that his class was competitive and described it as being a "jungle. Some work together, others are predators by nature." Yet another said that "Students do seem to work together, but, for the most part, only within their small groups."

Professors teach both analytical and courtroom skills with a great emphasis on the theoretical. This is changing, however, with more clinical and writing courses. Special attention is found in many of the electives that are taught on a small-group basis.

A broad-range curriculum is offered and includes Patent Law, International Business Transactions, the Juvenile Justice Systems, and Law and Sports. The school has a center for Law and Sports and a center for the Study of Law and Society. A Practitioner in Residence Program has been formed as well.

On the whole, recruiters are satisfied with Indiana students' performance in both research and presentation.

CRITERIA

LEVEL 1: LSAT score; Grade Point Average

LEVEL 2: Quality of undergraduate curriculum/course work completed; quality/reputation of college/university; work experience; recommendations; personal essey; extracurricular activities; educational diversity, and residency

MINORITY RECRUITMENT PROGRAM

No

DEADLINE FOR FILING: Rolling

FEE: $20

LSAT: "It is strongly recommended that applicants take the test in the preceding summer or fall of their senior year in college."

RECOMMENDED COURSES PRIOR TO MATRICULATING: At least ninety credit hours of undergraduate work must be in academic courses rather than in courses of a skills-training nature.

PERSONAL STATEMENT: "Applicants are encouraged to explain matters that may have adversely affected their undergraduate performance (e.g., necessary employment that took time from studies, initial selection of a course of study for which the applicant was not suited, illness) as well as factors indicating their potential for law study that might not be elicited by the questions on the application form. Applicants who feel that they have been disadvantaged should bring this to the Admission Committee's attention as well."

INTERVIEW: Not part of admissions procedure.

ADMISSIONS TIPS: Although there is no deadline for applications, applications received after March 1 may be at a disadvantage.

CONTACT: Frank Motley, Assistant Dean

PHYSICAL ENVIRONMENT

The School of Law is a combination of Gothic and modern architecture located on the southwest corner of the Bloomington campus. In 1985, the building that houses the law school was completely remodeled and an addition was constructed. This included a six-level law library that provides seating for 600 and has an atrium. Microcomputer work stations, small group conference rooms and carrel seats exist here. The area around the law school is considered safe, and an escort service is available. Handicapped accessibility is found to be very good. The law school building was designed so that a handicapped individual can gain access to the library, offices, and classrooms.

Campus housing is available for both married and single students. Single students may live in Eigenman, Foley, or Weatherly Halls. Married students are offered efficiency apartments. Because school-owned housing is not guaranteed, you are advised to apply as early as possible. You are also warned that because the School of Law year is longer than the university year, your housing contract may have to be modified to accommodate you. The most popular form of accommodations is sharing a house. Suitable housing is not difficult to locate. The school is approximately one-quarter mile from athletic facilities including tennis courts, track, gym, and pool.

FINANCES

BUDGET	LOW	MEDIUM	HIGH
Tuition (Resident) **Tuition (Nonresident)**	$2960.50 $8075.50	$2960.50 $8075.50	$2960.50 $8075.50
Books	$400	$400	$400
Living Accommodations (9 months)	Shared House $1800	On-Campus Apt. $2250	One-Bedroom Apt. $2700
Food	Groceries $1125	Meal Plan $1800	Restaurants $2700
Miscellaneous	$1600	$1800	$2000
Transportation	Mass Transit $225	Car $675	Cabs $1350
TOTAL (R) TOTAL (NR)	$8110.50 $13,225.50	$9885.50 $15,000.50	$12,110.50 $17,225.50

Employment During School: Work is considered inadvisable during the first year. After this, only a limited amount of work should be undertaken. Graduate assistantships are offered to students with superior records and specific skills.

Scholarships: The school offers merit, need-based, and minority scholarships.

School Loan Program (Exclusive of Perkins Money): No

Students Requesting Aid: N/A; of those requesting aid, 75% receive aid.

ACADEMICS

During the first year, students at Indiana take a certain set of required courses. In order to graduate, second-year students are required to complete a perspective course. This type of elective is one that emphasizes the perspectives of nonlegal disciplines, such as Legal History and Economics, on legal problems. The completion of a substantial research paper is also required. Upperclass law students have a diverse array of courses to choose from, including Law and Biology, which deals with such matters as genetic counseling and organ transplantation.

Special programs include the London Law Consortium in which students study in London for a semester and an accelerated or summer program, which permits the student to graduate after twenty-seven consecutive months. Students can also earn credit through independent research with an advisor. Clinics are also available; they include the Community Legal Clinic, Student Legal Services Clinic, and the Federal Law Clinic. A clinic on environmental problems is periodically offered as well. The school also provides an Independent Clinical Project, which allows students to create their own clinical experience.

The professors are said to be intelligent and well-informed in their fields. The education provided to the students is practical as well as theoretical, and the faculty relates real-world experience. Star faculty include William Hicks (Securities Regulation), Joseph Hoffmann (Real Estate Finance), and Daniel Conkle (Constitutional Law).

JOINT/GRADUATE DEGREE PROGRAMS

Joint Degrees: JD/MBA; JD/MPA (Master of Public Administration); JD/MS (Environmental Science)
Graduate Degree: LLM

Student organizations include the Inmate Legal Assistance Clinic, which is a non-credit program dealing with prisoners' intrainstitutional problems. Students are eligible for participation in the *Indiana Law Journal* by academic achievement or writing competition.

Placement is considered very good here. Approximately 95% of the students are placed within six months after graduation.

PREPARATION

Students are prepared by the Office of Career Services through career counseling, programs, workshops, and reference materials.

WHERE/WHAT GRADUATES PRACTICE

A. About one-half of each class locates in Indiana. The largest concentrations of alumni/ae appear to be found in Illinois, California, Michigan, Florida, New York, the District of Columbia, and Texas.
B. 58% Private Practice; 12% Business; 10% Government; 5% Judicial Clerkships; 3% Legal Services/Public Interest; 3% Teaching/Research; 9% Other.

IOWA CITY, IOWA (IA) 52242
(319) 335-9095

REPORT CARD

ADMISSIONS
SELECTIVITY

Applicants: 1300; Accepted: 487
Transfer Applications: 23; Accepted: 8
LSAT Mean: 37
GPA Mean: 3.46

ACADEMICS

Order of the Coif (1911)
Iowa Bar Passage Rate (first try): 80%
Faculty to Student Ratio: 1:16
Quality of Teaching: B+
Faculty Accessibility: B+

PHYSICAL ENVIRONMENT

Location: Large City
Safety: Verg Good
HA:

STUDENT ENROLLMENT

Class Size: 277
Women: 50.54%   Minorities: 16%
Average Age of Entering Class: N/A

PLACEMENT
REPUTATION: ★ ★ ★ ★

Recruiters: 300
Starting Salary Median: $30,000

FINANCES

Tuition: $2354 (R); $7402 (NR)
Average Total Cost: $7866 (R); $12,914 (NR)

STUDENT LIFE
RATING: ☺ ☺ ☺ ☾

After Hours: Fitzpatrick's, Mickey's, Airliner Bar

PROMINENT ALUMNI/AE

Include: Philip W. Tone, President, American Academy of Trial Lawyers; Thomas J. Tauke, Congressman; David Nagle, Congressman

INSIDER INFORMATION

The University of Iowa seeks to provide an equal balance of practical as well as theoretical skills for a low cost. In achieving this goal, it offers one of the most intensive programs of faculty-supervised legal writing in the country, conducted throughout all three years of law school. Iowa has a diverse course offering, which includes courses dealing with client representation and an American legal history survey. More attention is provided to first-year students through a small section program. Of special interest is the accelerated program, which permits a student to graduate in about twenty-five months. In order to broaden their experiences, students are able to study abroad in London and France. Iowa's clinical offerings are also varied.

Placement is found to be very good. The school had 300 recruiters there last year, and 95% of the students were placed within six months of graduation. Recruiters on both coasts greatly value Iowa graduates because they bring a "unique perspective and strong work ethic with them." The great majority of these individuals practice in the Midwest.

ADMISSIONS

CRITERIA

LEVEL 1: Grade Point Average; LSAT score

LEVEL 2: Personal essay; quality of undergraduate curriculum/course work completed

LEVEL 3: Recommendations; quality/reputation of college/university; quality/duration of time of outside work experience, including work and internships.

MINORITY RECRUITMENT PROGRAM

No. Although there is no separate program, there is emphasis placed on recruitment of minorities.

ABOUT THE APPLICATION

DEADLINE FOR FILING: 3/1

FEE: $20

LSAT: School takes the average of applicant's scores.

RECOMMENDED COURSES PRIOR TO MATRICULATING: Mathematics, English, Sciences, Logic, Philosophy, Business

PERSONAL ESSAY: "It is important simply as another evaluation tool."

INTERVIEW: Not required. For visitors, the Iowa Memorial Union House (close—on campus within the student union; $41.60) and Motel 6 (approximately three miles away; $21.95) are recommended.

ADMISSIONS TIPS: A common mistake is "not fully elaborating personal data in the personal statement."

CONTACT: Dennis J. Shields, Assistant Dean and Director of Law Admissions and Financial Aid

The College of Law is housed in a new $25 million law building, Boyd Law Building. This structure features state-of-the-art computer equipment, audio-visual technology, and three full-scale courtrooms. Iowa has one of the profession's few fully automated law libraries—a four-floor library with the tenth largest collection of law materials in the nation and one that provides private study carrels for all second- and third-year students.

The most cost-effective accommodations for a single student are renting a room in a house or sharing an apartment with roommates. For married students with or without children, it's the University Family Housing. On-campus housing is not guaranteed.

Before deciding whether to bring a car, consider the parking options for students: plug the parking meters at $.30 per hour, or pay a $40 monthly charge for a permit. There are 136 parking spaces available in the lot, which is exceeded by the total law student enrollment.

FINANCES

BUDGET	LOW	MEDIUM	HIGH
Tuition (Resident) **Tuition (Nonresi-dent)**	$2354 $7402	$2354 $7402	$2354 $7402
Books	$480	$480	$480
Living Accommoda-tions (9 months)	Shared Apt.* $1080	On-Campus $1670	One-Bedroom Apt. $3060
Food	Meal Plan (20/wk) $1250	Groceries $1500	Restaurants $1800
Miscellaneous	$1500	$1700	$1900
Transportation	Cambus** $0	Mass Transit $162	Car $600
TOTAL (R) TOTAL (NR)	$6664 $11,712	$7866 $12,914	$10,194 $15,242

* Shared House: $1350

** Campus (Campus Bus system) also runs from the University Family Housing to the main campus.

Employment During School: Not recommended during the first year. Work-study jobs are available for eligible students. Need-dependent jobs provide $3.50 an hour.

Scholarships: The school offers merit and need-based scholarships. Merit scholarships are contingent upon maintaining a certain GPA.

School Loan Program (Exclusive of Perkins Money): Yes. "The Iowa Law Foundation loan is supported by gifts to the Iowa Law Foundation by alumni and others. This loan is awarded based on the eligibility determined from the information provided by students on the Financial Aid Form (FAF) of the College Scholarship Service (CSS) of the College. The Iowa Law Foundation has an interest rate of 7%.

Students Requesting Aid: 90%; of these, 85% receive aid.

Student Indebted upon Graduation: 85%

Average Loan Indebtedness: N/A

ACADEMICS

During the first year there is an emphasis on "careful reading, close analysis, legal research, argumentation, and clear and precise writing." Classes are divided into sections of approximately thirty students for one course in the fall semester (or summer for accelerated students) and into sections of approximately twenty students for one course in the spring semester (or fall for accelerated students). Grades during this year are mandatorily curved.

During the second and third years, fact gathering, interviewing, counseling, drafting, transaction planning, negotiation, and litigation are dealt with. A diverse selection of courses is offered, including Economic Analysis for Lawyers, Law in American History, and Comparative Environmental Law. After a student has completed one half of the work towards a JD, he or she is eigible to participate in the College of Law Legal Clinic Program. Among the individuals that a student may represent under the supervision of attorneys are indigent clients in a wide variety of civil and criminal cases.

JOINT DEGREE PROGRAMS

JD/MBA joint degree programs are also available with more than sixteen other graduate departments and colleges, including Music, Computer Science, Religion, and Asian Civilization.

STUDENT LIFE

Students find the social life at Iowa to be satisfying. The Iowa Student Bar Association (ISBA) sponsors several events, including three law school picnics, a holiday party, an extensive intramural program, and "law school night" every Wednesday evening at the Airliner Bar on Clinton Street in downtown Iowa City.

PLACEMENT

300 corporations and/or law firms recruit on campus for summer and permanent jobs.

PREPARATION

The Placement Office prepares students through such means as videotaped mock interviews, interviewing techniques sessions, and résumé-writing seminars.

WHERE/WHAT GRADUATES PRACTICE

A. 7% Northeast; 3% South; 14% West Coast; 75% Midwest; 1% Other. (2% of students remain in the immediate vicinity of the law school within one year of graduation.)
B. 1% Solo Practitioner; 20% Small Firms; 20% Medium Firms; 20% Large Firms; 13% Clerkships; 1% Graduate Degrees; 1% Military; 12% Governmental Agencies; 6% Corporations; 6% Other.

500 WEST BALTIMORE STREET
BALTIMORE, MARYLAND (MD) 21201
(301) 328-3492

🍂 R E P O R T   C A R D 🍂

ADMISSIONS

SELECTIVITY 🎓 🎓 🎓 🎓

Applicants: 3150; Accepted: 750
Transfer Applications: 60; Accepted: 10
LSAT Mean: 39
GPA Mean: 3.3

ACADEMICS

Order of the Coif (1938)
Maryland State Bar Passage (first try): 85%
Faculty to Student Ratio: 1:16
Quality of Teaching: **B+**
Faculty Accessibility: **A**

PHYSICAL ENVIRONMENT

Location: Urban/Inner City
Safety: Fair–Marginal (Van Service-Escort
  Service)
HA: ♿ ♿ ♿ ♿ ♿

STUDENT ENROLLMENT

Class Size: 260
Women: 53%   Minorities: 27% (includes
  Asians)
Average Age of Entering Class: 26 (day); 30
  (evening)

PLACEMENT

REPUTATION: ★ ★ ★ ★

Recruiters: 150
Starting Salary Mean: $35,000+

FINANCES

Tuition: $4510 (R); $8202 (NR)
Average Total Cost: $11,560 (R); $15,252
  (NR)

STUDENT LIFE

RATING: ☺ ☺ ☺ ☺

After Hours: Bentley's

PROMINENT ALUMNI/AE

Include: N/A

Located in Baltimore, U. Maryland is walking distance away from federal and city courthouses and less than an hour's drive from the Capitol in Washington, D.C. Maryland gives students a broad range of educational opportunities and reflects four basic themes: knowledge, professionalism, perspective, and communication. Unlike many other law schools, admission to clinical or quasi-clinical offerings is not a privilege but is instead a requirement. As Director of Admissions James Forsythe explained, "The clinical law program affords students the opportunity to begin the transition from law school to law practice; from learning to be a lawyer to being a lawyer." The students practice under the supervision of full-time faculty members.

Of special interest is the school's diverse offerings of special programs. The new Law and Entrepreneurship program, through its core internship component, trains business lawyers to advise start-up and developing companies, primarily in the high-technology area. Its further purpose is to provide affordable legal services to high-tech companies in the Baltimore area. The school also provides a Law and Health Program, which offers nine courses dealing with law and health care. Students find that Maryland's strong alumni/ae network works to their advantage, helping them even further with placement. Recruiters are generally impressed with Maryland.

ADMISSIONS

CRITERIA

LEVEL 1: Grade Point Average; LSAT score(s)

LEVEL 2: Quality of undergraduate curriculum/course work completed; quality/reputation of college/university; work experience; recommendations; personal essay

MINORITY RECRUITMENT PROGRAM

Yes; conducted by visiting various colleges as well as by using the Law School Candidate Referral Service.

ABOUT THE APPLICATION

DEADLINE FOR FILING: 2/15

FEE: $25

LSAT: The school generally takes the average of applicant's scores. If you provide an explanation as to why there should be an exception made, the school will take this into consideration.

PERSONAL STATEMENT: This is your opportunity to tell the Admissions Committee what it is about yourself that you wish them to know. The ideas behind having an unstructured essay is to see how you as an individual interpret the question and decide what is most important about yourself.

INTERVIEW: Not required or recommended.

ADMISSIONS TIPS: The personal essay is your opportunity to be interviewed on paper. Maryland Law is an academic institution and therefore prefers letters of recommendation from academics (instructors) who know you well. If you have been out in the workplace for several years, you may also attach a résumé, not in place of the personal statement, but with it.

CONTACT: James F. Forsythe, Assistant Dean

PHYSICAL ENVIRONMENT

The law school is contained in a complex of buildings surrounding two inner court-yards, one of which is the famous Westminster Courtyard. The two wings of Lane Hall house classrooms, the moot court, administrative offices, student lounge, and faculty offices. The school's Clinical Program is here as well, and includes four law offices and a courtroom equipped with remote control video equipment that permits, with the client's consent, the student's activities to be taped for later critique and learning. The two wings of Lane Hall have recently been joined by a new student lounge. The Westminster Hall is used as a reading room for the adjacent Thurgood Marshall Law Library.

Students consider the area to be relatively unsafe. As one student described it, the school is located "downtown with both the glitz and the dregs of the inner city." There is an escort service, however. The handicapped accessibility is considered fairly good.

FINANCES

BUDGET	LOW	MEDIUM	HIGH
Tuition (Resident) Tuition (Nonresi- dent)	$4510 $8202	$4510 $8202	$4510 $8202
Books	$500	$500	$500
Living Accommoda- tions (9 months)	Shared House $2250	One-Bedroom Apt. $3150	On-Campus $3825
Food	Groceries $900	Cafeteria $1400	Restaurants $1800
Miscellaneous	$900	$1100	$1300
Transportation	Mass Transit $540	Car $900	Taxis $1800
TOTAL (R) TOTAL (NR)	$9600 $13,292	$11,560 $15,252	$13,735 $17,427

Employment During School: Only after first year. College work-study is available.

Scholarships: The school offers need-based and merit scholarships.

School Loan Program (Exclusive of Perkins Money): Yes; among others, emergency loans, Lewis D. Asper Fund, Ernan Harrison Loan Fund, and the Jeffrey I. Goldman Memorial Loan Fund.

Loan Forgiveness Program: No

Students Requesting Aid: N/A; of those requesting aid, 60% receive aid.

ACADEMICS

First-year courses are all required. Certain courses are also required of second-year students. Furthermore, in order to graduate you must take Professional Responsibility, at least one perspective course, and fulfill a writing requirement by preparing at least one paper that analyzes in depth a particular legal or law-related problem. Students warn that the grading system is a minus, and that it is virtually impossible to get higher than a 92. It has been also said that Income Tax is a required course, and many don't pass it the first time.

A wide range of elective courses are available and include Accounting, Admiralty Law, and Chinese Law. Seminars include Comparative Constitutional Law, Communications Law, and ethical and public policy issues of biotechnology. The school offers a wide variety of programs, including the Environmental Law Program. Through this program a broad curriculum of environmental courses has been developed. Seminars dealing with global environmental issues and environmental ethics, politics, and economics are offered. Students may also participate in an Environmental Clinic and an Environmental/Administrative Law Workshop.

The school takes the teaching abilities of its faculty very seriously, and students are required to evaluate faculty at the end of each semester. Students feel that the professors are generally caring and good, and as they have office hours, they are accessible.

JOINT DEGREE PROGRAMS

JD/MBA; also joint programs in Criminal Justice, Liberal Arts, Public Administration/Public Affairs, Psychology, and Social Work.

STUDENT LIFE

Students say that the atmosphere at Maryland is competitive. However, they "generally maintain good relations, despite the competition. You learn who will work with you and who won't." A variety of organizations exist at U. Maryland, including the Maryland Public Interest Project, the Maryland Environmental Interest Group, and the International Law Society.

Upperclass law students advise first-year students through the Student Volunteer Advisors organization. These meetings typically begin in the spring and summer with those students who have been accepted. In the fall semester, volunteers work with new students through their legal methods classes.

School-sponsored events include tropics parties, shows, and beer sales.

PLACEMENT

Students say that the Placement Office has good intentions, but seems to help only those who need it least, the top 10%, by steering them to local top firms. It is felt that more effort and practical assistance are needed for the 90% that make the 10% possible.

PREPARATION

The law school Career Services Office prepares students. A Minority Hiring Advisory Board was recently established.

WHERE/WHAT GRADUATES PRACTICE

A. 80% stay in the Maryland area. The percentages of where students practice outside Maryland are not kept. (95% responded to school's questionnaire.)
B. 45% Private Practice; 24% Judicial Clerkships; 17% Public Interest and Governmental Agencies; 5% Military; 4% Corporations.

UNIVERSITY OF MICHIGAN
Law School

311 HUTCHINS HALL
ANN ARBOR, MICHIGAN (MI) 48109-1215
(313)764-0537

REPORT CARD

ADMISSIONS
SELECTIVITY

Applicants: 5598; Accepted: N/A
LSAT: N/A
GPA: N/A

PLACEMENT
REPUTATION: ☆ ☆ ☆ ☆ ☆

Recruiters: 725
Starting Salary Mean: $57,808

ACADEMICS

Order of the Coif (1911)
Faculty to Student Ratio: N/A
Quality of Teaching: B+/A−
Accessibility: B

FINANCES

Tuition: $7000 (R); $14,800 (NR)
Average Total Cost: $15,115 (R); $22,915 (NR)

PHYSICAL ENVIRONMENT

Location: Medium-Sized City
Safety: Very Good–Good
HA: ♿ ♿ ♿ ♿

STUDENT LIFE
RATING: ☺ ☺ ☺ ☺

After Hours: Unos, Ashleys, Good Time Charlies, Full Moon Cafe, Rick's American Cafe

STUDENT ENROLLMENT

Class Size: 384
Women: 37%   Minorities: 12% (doesn't include Asians and Cubans)
Average Age of Entering Class: 25

PROMINENT ALUMNI/AE

Include: Clarence Darrow; Thomas Cooley

INSIDER INFORMATION

There are many excellent law schools in this country from which to choose. There are also many excellent public institutions that offer solid legal education at a more down-to-earth cost. When you combine these two criteria in your search for the best law education at the best cost, it points you in the direction of Michigan Law, a school with one of the most diverse student bodies in North America. Complete with Gothic architecture, the school's quadrangle, underground library, majestic reading room, and stained glass windows, Michigan's physical facilities are truly inspired. When asked what sets Michigan apart from other "top-tier" schools, Assistant Dean and Admissions Officer Allan Stillwagon replied, "The school's outstanding nationally and internationally recognized faculty, which has agreed that they will not represent clients for pay. The school's large endowment allows faculty to devote themselves to the traditional responsibilities of faculty who are not of counsel and who are available to their students."

Interestingly, Michigan may very well be the law school with the broadest national recruitment after graduation, partly because of its size and partly because few individuals come to Michigan with the intention of practing law in-state, with most spreading themselves out across the country. From a recruiter perspective, the school is often perceived as "a heavy hitter," with a stronger draw for Midwest firms because of its geographical location. Regardless of geographic positioning, many will identify the school as a "top five" and virtually none will exclude it from their "top ten list," but the majority of recruiters questioned place it somewhere between the two categories.

You might be surprised at such a diverse group of people living in a city like Ann Arbor, which students commonly cite as short on excitement, but the school brings together a highly eclectic group. In one student's words, "My first semester of law school I sat next to a lawyer from the People's Republic of China in Constitutional Law and worked out with a former Big Ten football player."

Students here find tolerance for a wide range of political and social views. Says one second-year student, "Being a minority in the legal profession is tough. Because so few minorities are of power in that profession, many of us are watched with intense scrutiny. We are to be 'examples' for our races. Yet, if we screw up, people point to us and say 'Told you they can't do it well,' or 'The only reason they are here is because of affirmative action.' Fortunately, the faculty/administration and fellow students are quite supportive." Some students add that they enjoy the open atmosphere, but it also creates a feeling of having to "walk on eggs" so as to make sure nothing you say is interpreted in the wrong way.

Faculty, many of whom have authored the casebooks read by law students throughout the country, are more accessible than students anticipated prior to attending. Most here believe that the quality of lectures ranges from the "truly moving, almost captivating legal discussions that don't just center around the law" to "some pretty boring ones." As is best expressed by a current student's own words, "Michigan is a law school where you [the applicant] can't go wrong. Everything's right there at your fingertips. It's a law students' law school." Among the top tier, Michigan's admissions is probably one of the least number-driven for approximately half of the chosen students, although strong academic promise is still an important criteria.

ADMISSIONS

CRITERIA

LSAT and analysis of transcript are considered of first importance. "Analysis, Analysis, Analysis," Assistant Director of Admissions Olivia Birdsall repeated, stressing that a mere review of the applicant's GPA would not be a sufficient determinant. The applicant's transcript is analyzed as to what courses actually were taken as opposed to what the individual's major was or what he or she received as an overall grade.

One half of the entering class is selected based on a calculation of the LSAT, GPA, and studies of the past performance of previous students at the law school. The other half is chosen from applicants whose grades and test scores qualify them for further consideration. These individuals are further judged by their intellectual attainments, nonacademic achievements, employment experience, and social background. Implicit in this method of selection is a slender preference for students who can demonstrate that they are more mature.

MINORITY RECRUITMENT

Minorities are strongly encouraged to apply and call upon the Assistant Dean for information and assistance. Black, Chicano, Native American, and many Puerto Rican applicants are automatically considered for a special admissions program designed to encourage and increase the enrollment of minorities.

ABOUT THE APPLICATION

DEADLINE FOR FILING: 2/15

FEE: $30

LSAT: "The test should be taken more than once only if the applicant believes that substantial improvement in performance can be achieved. If the test is taken more than once, all scores will be considered; the average score is most influential."

RECOMMENDED COURSES PRIOR TO MATRICULATING: "It is generally wasteful to study law as a preparation to study law." Good rigorous liberal education is very important to the full development of the law student and professional lawyer.

PERSONAL STATEMENT: Michigan's question is open-ended and Allan Stillwagon refers to it as a "prose Rorschach test" and adds that it is the applicants' chance to open themselves to the Admissions Committee. In the past, personal statements have been exceedingly variable with some students addressing philosophical dilemmas in relation to their course work, and others talking about why they want to be a lawyer. Stillwagon concedes that the latter approach is generally not the better one for students just out of college.

INTERVIEW: Not required or recommended, but applicants are free to visit the school and chat with admissions officers.

ADMISSIONS TIPS: You are urged to submit all of the required materials in the early autumn prior to the anticipated date of enrollment. Letters of recommendation should be mailed by the recommender directly to the law school. Under no circumstances should applicants include such letters with an application, even if the letter is sealed by the author.

CONTACT: Allan Stillwagon, Assistant Dean and Admissions Officer

Michigan, architecturally Gothic and ivy-covered, could very well be the most beautiful law school in the country. Shopping, football stadium, theaters, and restaurants are all within easy walking distance, and the main university student union is across the street. The law school's facilities are found to be excellent. The various law school buildings are laid out in a rectangular shape with a grassy quadrangle in the center. The classroom building and library make up one long side; an L-shaped law school dorm, the other long side and one end; and the dining hall and lounge the other short end. The campus is found to be relatively safe. An escort service serves U of M in general, but students don't find the need to use it since the law school is so self-contained. Some here don't find that the immediate surroundings of the school are worthy of the law school. "Ann Arbor is an appalling city—if excitement in the area is important to you, don't come to A^2. There is no legitimate theater." Many, particularly those from less urban environments would debate this characterization, adding that the university itself provides its own source of cultural diversions.

Most of the first-year students live in the law quad, also known as "The Lawyer's Club." Students line up housing early (February-March) for the following year, if they plan to move out of the dorm. However, it is felt that reasonable housing can be obtained at a later date. It just takes more looking. Approximately 300 students live in The Lawyers Club; the remaining 800 students live off campus in houses or apartments. Many students believe living on-campus is best in the first year because it gives students a "base of operations." Adds one student, "I know several first-year students who didn't live on campus, and they feel somewhat left out of the mainstream." Second- and third-year students live in apartments. As for eating accommodations, the meal plan is a better bargain because it is all you can eat, but groceries are considered better quality. Almost all housing is within walking distance of the school, minimizing transportation costs and the need for a car.

FINANCES

BUDGET	LOW	MEDIUM	HIGH
Tuition (Residents) **Tuition (Nonresi-** **dents)**	$7000 $14,800	$7000 $14,800	$7000 $14,800
Books	$515	$515	$515
Living Accommoda- **tions (9 months)**	Shared House/Apt. $2880	On-Campus $3960	One-Bedroom Apt. $4500
Food	Groceries $1800	Cafeteria $2000	Restaurants $4500
Miscellaneous	$900	$1200	$1750
Transportation	Walking/Mass Transit $405	Mass Transit $440	Car $620
TOTAL (R) TOTAL (NR)	$13,500 $21,300	$15,115 $22,915	$18,885 $26,685

Employment During School: Neither recommended nor prohibited. The college work-study enrollment program enables students to earn money working at one of a variety of jobs in the university community. Law students often work in the law library or as research assistants to law professors. Student Funded Fellowships (SFF), a student organization, helps provide summer fellowships for first- and second-year students who wish to work at summer public interest and public service jobs with little or no pay. The SFF Program works jointly with a full-time work-study program to supplement and extend funds available to students.

Scholarships: The school offers a multitude of scholarships. Law school grants are provided through the law school and university funds to minimize the educational debt of students who demonstrate financial need. Although there is no legal obligation to repay the funds, the law school hopes for an eventual donation, when the recipients are able to do so, of an amount at least equal to the assistance that they received.

School Loan Program (Exclusive of Perkins Money): Yes. At an interest rate of 7%, loans are awarded on a need basis after students have fully utilized federal loan programs. Repayment and interest begin one year after a student leaves the school.

Loan Forgiveness Program: Yes. The school's Debt Management Program is comprised of two principal interests: 1) assistance through law school loans to meet outstanding educational loan obligations and 2) eventual forgiveness of these special law school loans for those who remain in the program for the requisite period. These debts are reduced at a rate of 25% per year, up to a maximum of 100%, after ten years in the program for those under age forty and after four years for those forty and older. Graduates' income must not exceed $32,000 and must be from law-related work in a public interest position for a private firm or in a governmental service.

If someone asks you which "case club" you belong to, you might very well be talking to a fellow first-year student at Michigan. The Writing and Advocacy Program divides students into thirty-two case clubs of about twelve students each. Third-year students serve as the chief instructors and are titled senior judge, with second-year students assisting in the capacity of junior clerk. Each club is overseen by a professor who acts as its advisor. During the first year, besides a required set of courses, students are allowed an elective from courses like Blood Feuds, Law and Psychiatry, and Welfare Law. One section of students is chosen randomly and dubbed the "new section." For them, one or more of the normally required courses are shortened, and the second semester elective opportunity is eliminated to make room for two courses unique to the new section, Legal Process and Public Law. One quarter of each first class matriculates in early May. Most of the "summer starters" will have indicated a strong preference for admission to the summer session. However, others indicate no particular preference and some may initially have preferred to begin their work in the fall.

Second- and third-year students may take courses in other departments of the university and, with the approval of the Associate Dean, elect not more than six hours of credits in other departments in partial fulfillment of the JD requirement. Among other requirements, election must be limited to courses acceptable for graduate credit within the university. Students may also undertake an external studies program with a nonprofit organization or a governmental agency engaged in legal work. Course variety at Michigan is staggering, with opportunities to study Doing Business with China or English. Computers, including micro workstations, printers, and software are available to students, as well as courses such as the seminar in Communications Sciences and the Law, which addresses advances in the field of information technology.

People here are all very bright and want to do well, but they "compete much more with themselves than overly with other students." It has never been felt among students that any one was actively trying to sabotage another student's efforts. No one asks or knows what each others' grades are. They are not discussed. Michigan does not post class rankings or GPAs, and students are surprisingly noncompetitive. Students would like better course registration policies implemented for upperclass students. They feel there aren't enough opportunities to study the courses they want when they want them and also suggest adding more sections to popular classes, which would reduce class sizes from their current 90–100 level and help to create a less impersonal environment.

International and Comparative Law are among the school's strengths. Michigan has various clinical courses, including the Child Advocacy Clinic and the Environmental Law Clinic. Clinical Law I allows students to learn interviewing, motion practice, counseling, and research under faculty supervision. Students are also videotaped and critiqued in an intensive trial advocacy workshop in small groups. Michigan also allows for independent study.

Some may complain about the school's "impersonal feeling," but most here feel that if there's something you really want to do you can do it and, in that group, you will find a close group of friends. Says one, "You can't help that [the impersonal feeling] with large classes, but how could you possibly achieve such diversity in a class of one hundred people?"

JOINT/GRADUATE DEGREE PROGRAMS

Joint Programs: JD/MBA; JD/PhD (Economics); JD/MA (Modern Near Eastern and North African Studies); JD/MPP (Master of Public Policy); JD/MS (Natural Sciences); JD/AM (Russian and East European Studies); JD/AM (Political Science)
Graduate Degrees: LLM, MCL (Master of Comparative Law), and SJD (Doctor of Juristic Science). Concurrent graduate programs are also available, including History, Public Health, and Women's Studies. If admitted, the student may, after the completion of the first year of law studies, divide time between the law school and the concurrent program of study. An Overseas Travel Fellowship is available as well.

STUDENT LIFE

Considered excellent. In general, with most first-year students living in the law school dorm, people develop a wide range of friends—from classes, the dorm, and eating together in the dining hall. In addition, you meet a number of second- and third-year students from the dorm and dining hall. The Law School Senate sponsors social and sporting activities at least monthly. "Tremendous diversity and high quality of student body is Michigan's most redeeming attribute. Almost every student has had some unique experience or has some interesting facet in his or her background." Student organizations are continually forming, with a strong interest in intramural sports, including ultimate Frisbee.

PLACEMENT

Campus interviewers are not allowed to prescreen job candidates by GPA before interviewing them. By March at least two-thirds to three-fourths of all first year students have law-related summer jobs. Some here say that once you leave the Midwest you may find that you have to use your own "area ties," which is surprising given the school's strong placement record.

PREPARATION

The Placement Office prepares students through counseling, reference materials, and facilities for interviewing at the school. During the fall months, there is very active recruiting.

WHERE/WHAT GRADUATES PRACTICE

A. 17% Michigan, Illinois, California, D.C., New York, Ohio, Pennsylvania, and Minnesota. Chicago led urban employers, followed by D.C., Detroit, New York, L.A., and San Francisco.
B. 78% Private Practice; 10% Judicial Clerkships; 6% Governmental Positions; 6% Other.

290 LAW CENTER
229 19TH AVENUE SOUTH
MINNEAPOLIS, MINNESOTA (MN) 55455
(612)625-5005

❧ REPORT CARD ❧

ADMISSIONS
SELECTIVITY 🎓 🎓 🎓 🎓 🎓

Applicants: 2150; Accepted; N/A
LSAT Mean: 40   GPA Mean: 3.5

PLACEMENT
REPUTATION: ★ ★ ★ ★ ☆

Recruiters: 200
Starting Salary Median: $35,273

ACADEMICS
Order of the Coif (1915)
Minnesota Bar Passage (first try): 94%
Faculty to Student Ratio: N/A
Quality of Teaching: **B+**
Faculty Accessibility: **B+**

FINANCES
Tuition: $3916 (R), $7832 (NR)
Average Total Cost: $12,280 (R); $16,196
  (NR)

PHYSICAL ENVIRONMENT
Location: Large City
Safety: Fair
HA: ♿ ♿ ♿ ♿ ♿

STUDENT LIFE
RATING: ☺ ☺ ☺ ☺

After Hours: Bullwinkles, Grandma's

STUDENT ENROLLMENT
Class Size: 250
Women: 45%   Minorities: 16%
Average Age of Entering Class: 25

PROMINENT ALUMNI/AE
Include: Wendell R. Anderson, Governor and
  U.S. Senator; James H. Binger, CEO,
  Honeywell; A. W. Clausen, President of
  the World Bank and CEO, Bank America

INSIDER INFORMATION A distinguishing aspect of the school is its strong emphasis on clinical experience. Eleven clinical courses are offered in a wide range of subject matters, including domestic abuse, misdemeanor prosecution, federal taxation, and civil litigation. Although space is limited, approximately 85% of the graduates take at least one clinic. 55% of the student body participate in one or more courses that provide actual client representation.

Minnesota has been a pioneer in the development of computer-assisted instructional materials integrated into their law clinics. Students obtain legal experience while receiving immediate feedback through the use of computerized exercises, including interactive videodisc exercises. The school further emphasizes the use of computers in legal education through the use of its over 120 personal computers and computer-related course offerings are being expanded. The law school is home to the Center for Computer Assisted Legal Instruction (CCALI), a consortium that provides an information exchange for its over 120 member-schools and supports the authoring of instructional software for use on microcomputers.

ADMISSIONS

CRITERIA

LEVEL 1: Grade Point Average; LSAT score

LEVEL 2: Quality of undergraduate curriculum/course work completed; recommendations

LEVEL 3: Quality/reputation of college/university; work experience; personal essay

MINORITY RECRUITMENT PROGRAM

Yes

ABOUT THE APPLICATION

DEADLINE FOR FILING: 3/1

FEE: $20

LSAT: School takes the highest of applicant's scores, if raised by four points or more.

RECOMMENDED COURSES PRIOR TO MATRICULATING: N/A

PERSONAL STATEMENT: "It could push a 'borderline' candidate over into the 'admit' category."

ADMISSIONS TIPS: "Identify the 'right' law school and apply early."

CONTACT: Edward A. Kawczynski, Director of Admissions

Located on the West Bank of the university's Minneapolis campus, the law school is housed in its award-winning Law Center. This structure contains, among other things, classrooms, a law office for the school's clinical education program, two courtrooms, computer lab, and the placement and career planning office. Closed circuit television, which permits remote viewing of courtroom proceedings, and video recording equipment are available throughout the building. The structure is accessible to many university facilities, including a large athletic field that adjoins the law school.

5% of the students live in school-owned housing. The most cost-effective accommodations is an off-campus apartment for single and married students with no children. Married students with children are advised to consider an off-campus duplex or married student housing. A car is not recommended because the transportation system is excellent. It might be advisable, however, for second- and third-year students for transportation to clerkships.

FINANCES

BUDGET	LOW	MEDIUM	HIGH
Tuition (Resident) Tuition (Nonresident)*	$3916 $7832	$3916 $7832	$3916 $7832
Books	$400	$450	$500
Living Accommodations (9 months)	Shared House/Apt. $1575	One-Bedroom Apt. $4050	On-Campus $4116
Food	Groceries $1000	Meal Plan (21/Wk.)** $1764	Restaurants $3200
Miscellaneous	$1000	$1200	$1400
Transportation	Mass Transit $325	Bus/Car $900	Car $1170
TOTAL (R) TOTAL (NR)	$8216 $12,132	$12,280 $16,196	$14,302 $18,218

* The state of Minnesota has reciprocity agreements with North Dakota, South Dakota and Wisconsin.

** Cafeteria (nonmeal plan): $2000 (annual)

Employment During School: Not recommended for first-year students. Jobs are available for all students; these positions provide $8.00 an hour.

Scholarships: The school offers merit, minority, and need-based scholarships.

School Loan Program (Exclusive of Perkins Money): Yes. $1500 maximum per year. $5000 maximum can be borrowed over the entire three years. Interest charged: 3% in school; 6% out of school. Eligibility is need-based.

Loan Forgiveness Program: No

Students Requesting Aid: 85%; of these, 85% receive aid.

Students Indebted upon Graduation: 85%

Average Loan Indebtedness: $25,000

First-year students are required to take a certain set of courses. The Socratic method is prevalent in this year and throughout the three-year curriculum. The first-year class is divided into five sections of approximately fifty students each. Each of these divisions meet independently or with other sections for all first-year classes. During the legal research and writing, however, students meet in groups of sixteen or seventeen. Although they are required to take Professional Responsibility in their third year, upperclass law students have a wide selection of courses from which to choose. Specialization is permitted, and among the fields offered are Labor and Employment Law, International and Foreign Law, and Real Estate. Seminars are also offered and include such subject matters as Advanced Corporate Tax, Biomedical Ethics, and Divorce Negotiation and Planning. As noted before, the school has a diverse selection of clinical offerings. It further offers a lecture series and includes the Jurist-in-Residence Program, which has featured Sandra Day O'Connor.

U. Minnesota has a broad international curriculum and includes such programs as summer study-abroad programs in France, Sweden, and West Germany. There are also international scholars in residence and visits from foreign and American experts in International Law and Foreign Relations.

JOINT/GRADUATE DEGREE PROGRAMS

Joint Degrees: JD/MBA: JD/MPA (Master of Public Administration)
Graduate Degree: LLM

The student governing body of the law school is the Law School Council. The council coordinates many student services and organizations. It also publishes a school directory and sponsors many social functions throughout the school year. Student organizations to which it provides support include the International and Comparative Law Society, the Entertainment and Sports Law Student's Association, and the Minnesota Justice Foundation, which promotes and supports *pro bono* legal work in Minnesota.

Social functions sponsored by the school's Law Forum include the Barrister's Ball, the Law School Talent Show, and the Malpractice Party in conjunction with the University Medical School. As the main social and educational programmer for the school, the Law Forum also provides Friday Afternoon Forums, which allow students to meet law professionals in an informal social environment. This organization sponsors lectures featuring speakers of local and national importance.

PLACEMENT

96% of the students are placed within six months after graduation. Students are prepared by the Placement Office through various methods such as special seminars.

WHERE/WHAT GRADUATES PRACTICE

A. 8% Northeast; 4.5% South; 12.5% West Coast; 70% Midwest; 5% Other.
B. 0.5% Sole Practitioner; 18.7% Small Firms; 12.1% Medium Firms; 35.7% Large Firms; 18.7% Clerkships; 2.2% Graduate Degrees; 1.1% Military; 6.1% Governmental Agencies; 4.4% Corporations; 0.5% Other.

40 WASHINGTON SQUARE SOUTH, ROOM 419
NEW YORK, N.Y. 10012
(212) 998-6060

REPORT CARD

ADMISSIONS
SELECTIVITY:

Applicants: 7800; Accepted: 1200
Transfer Applicants: N/A; Accepted: N/A
LSAT Mean: 43   GPA Mean: 3.6

ACADEMICS
Order of the Coif (1959)
Faculty to Student Ratio: N/A
Quality of Teaching: B/B+
Accessibility: A-

PHYSICAL ENVIRONMENT
Location: Urban/Big City
Safety: Fair–Marginal
HA:

STUDENT ENROLLMENT
Class Size: 396
Women: 51%   Minorities: N/A
Average Age of Entering Class: N/A

PLACEMENT
REPUTATION:

Recruiters: 950
Starting Salary Range: $19,743–74,117

FINANCES
Tuition: $15,380
Average Total Cost: $27,455

STUDENT LIFE
RATING: ☺ ☺ ☺ ☺

After Hours: Jimmy Day's

PROMINENT ALUMNI/AE
Include: David F. Jordan, Magistrate, U.S. District Court, New York; Marjorie D. Fields, Judge, New York City Family Court

INSIDER INFORMATION

If ever there was a classic case of the Hertz-Avis situation among law schools positioned in the same major city, it would have to be between NYU and Columbia. But this law school Avis hasn't just tried harder than number one in town. NYU has used everything in its power—creating world-class facilities, offering astounding course selections ranging from courses in Artists, Authors, and the Law to Law and Economics, and seminars on the Law in Japan and Selected Topics in Talmudic Civil Law, and providing compassionate faculty members and a truly dynamic Placement Office—to attract the best and brightest applicants.

Students inside this traditional red brick complex near the perimeter of NYU's Washington Square campus often talk in reference to their nearby competitor, Columbia in almost challenging words, "Go over to Columbia. See what they tell you.

They'll tell you they wish they'd gone here." Indeed, with excellent placement capabilities (many say on par with or even superior to Columbia, particularly for first-year summer jobs), a wide array of clinical programs and course offerings, and not least of all a dynamic and surprisingly effervescent student body, NYU has risen with meteoric intensity aided by facilities including a magnificent, multi-tiered, paneled law library, and comparatively safe and affordable on-campus New York City housing.

"It's all that you would think law school isn't." This is a common sentiment among NYU law students. Students seemed rather laid-back. Adds one second-year student, "After you've been here, you realize the comparison between NYU and Columbia exists only in the minds of some of the applicants. Once you're here you forget about the other one [Columbia]."

NYU has an interesting program with an alternative to moot court known as the Lawyering Program, begun on a full scale in 1987. This program "teaches you more how to be a lawyer, as well as skills you need like negotiation, memo writing, and legal analysis. It allows a student the opportunity to take a case through from the beginning to the end, instead of giving one or two oral arguments." The school offers the added attraction of a pleasant and friendly atmosphere, in a city not known for its warmth, and numerous opportunities for job placement, both during and after you are here. "What you hear about here are the people who *don't* get jobs, because they are such a rarity."

Each year, a few "ROOTS," short for recipients of the Root-Tilden-Snow Scholarship, which awards two thirds of yearly tuition, regardless of need, renewable after the first year with satisfactory academic achievement, are awarded to students committed to practicing public interest law. These prestigious scholarships often lure applicants who were also accepted at Harvard, Stanford, or Yale. All of this has succeeded in pushing NYU into the awareness of recruiters from all parts of the country, many of whom feel that NYU students are interchangeable with their Columbia counterparts. They appreciate NYU students' enthusiasm for their school, but several top firms aware that NYU students get mostly Bs, are looking for a sprinkling of B+s and As in their grades.

ADMISSIONS

CRITERIA

All factors, including LSAT scores, GPA, quality of undergraduate course work completed, quality and reputation of school or university attended, personal essay, recommendations, and work experience, are considered level-one criteria and are given equal weight.

MINORITY RECRUITMENT PROGRAM

N/A

ABOUT THE APPLICATION

DEADLINE FOR FILING: 2/1

FEE: $45

LSAT: School decides on a case-by-case basis.

RECOMMENDED COURSES PRIOR TO MATRICULATING: No prescribed course of study recommended prior to attending.

PERSONAL STATEMENT: Limit it to one page. Be sharp, clear, and concise.

INTERVIEW: Not required or recommended.

RECOMMENDATIONS: Best to use academics as recommenders, particularly if you are coming straight out of college.

ADMISSIONS TIPS: Apply early. Pay close attention to detail. Set yourself apart through the personal statement, but try not to be gimmicky.

CONTACT: Nan McNamara, Assistant Dean for Admissions

PHYSICAL ENVIRONMENT

You are walking around the Washington Square campus asking for directions to the law school and every single student says, "It looks like a law school. You can't miss it. Just keep walking straight." Indeed, Arthur T. Vanderbilt Hall does look like a law school both outside and inside, with its red brick facade and sweeping staircases inside. The facility has just put on a new ten-million-dollar library, which is impressive by anyone's standards. The school is equipped with both WESTLAW and LEXIS. Students find the area around the school to be "surprisingly safe." "If you had come here three years ago, you would have been stopped by people selling drugs, but they've cleaned all that up."

NYU law students strongly recommend living in on-campus housing all three years, because it is reasonably priced and very close to the school. D'Agostino, or just D'Ag is recommended, because it is newer than Mercer and right behind the law school, although both housing facilities are considered accommodating. A car is looked upon more as a hindrance than a help, particularly with New York's subway and bus system. It might be recommended, however, for second- and third-year students for transportation to clerkships.

FINANCES

BUDGET	LOW	MEDIUM	HIGH
Tuition	$15,380	$15,380	$15,380
Books	$650	$650	$650
Living Accommodations (9 months)	D'Agostino/Mercer $7444 (includes food)	Shared Apt. (Q*) $4500	One-Bedroom Apt. (M)** $6750
Food	Meals (Included)	Groceries $2925	Restaurants $3315
Miscellaneous	$2500	$3500	$4500
Transportation	Mass Transit $500	Mass Transit $500	Car $1100
TOTAL	$26,474	$27,455	$31,695

* Q = Queens

** M = Manhattan

Employment During School: Work-study jobs are not available; most students choose outside work because these jobs pay better than work-study could.

Scholarships: The school offers merit and need-based scholarships.

School Loan Program (Exclusive of Perkins Money): Yes. NYU has several loan programs with varying terms and rates.

Loan Forgiveness Program: N/A

Students Requesting Aid: N/A; of those requesting aid, 80% receive aid.

ACADEMICS

"There's no reason to be miserable while you're in law school," says one second-year student here, and students feel that NYU lives up to this. Students are not overly competitive and the mean in most courses hovers around a B, although some students receive Cs, Ds, and very rarely Fs. The faculty are thought to be very good conveyers of information, but not all of them are inspiring as lecturers.

The First Year Lawyering Program, unique to NYU, involves a series of drafting exercises and is designed to develop legal writing and research skills. Students are mixed in their reaction to the program. "The first semester was pretty dry and boring. It picked up during the second semester." Teaching method ranges from Socratic small group learning to lectures. "It's a nice mix." "The first-year professors make a big effort to calm the students down, and after that, it becomes contagious." Students here find first-year professors more accessible than in any other year.

Competition at NYU "exists only among a few people who still have something to prove to themselves. Most of us get Bs, so there's no need to cut each other's throats."

The only requirements in second and third year are Constitutional Law, Professional Responsibility, Legal Institutions, and a writing requirement. Electives and seminars are praised by current students. A multitude of courses and clinical programs are offered, ranging from Advocacy of Clinical Case Clinic to Civil Rights Clinic and Corporation Counsel Litigation Clinic; many of these clinics have a fieldwork and seminar component and are praised by those who have participated. Not all students have been able to get into the clinic of their choice, however.

JOINT DEGREE PROGRAMS

Joint Degrees: JD/MA (History, Economics, French, Philosophy, Sociology); JD/MBA; JD/MPA (Master of Public Administration); JD/MUP (Master of Urban Planning); JD/MSW (Master of Social Work)

STUDENT LIFE

When the president of NYU's student association welcomed the incoming class, he said, "We have students from both the North and South . . . Shores of Long Island." In essence, it is a somewhat homogeneous group of students on paper, but each student is coming from a very different background. About half of the class has taken time off (usually a year or two) before entering. The students say they are like a family with "social events all of the time." Each year the school puts on a Law Revue spoofing life at NYU Law in order to let off steam.

PLACEMENT

"Excellent. They really go that extra mile, especially for students who don't have the higher grades/aren't at the top of the class." Many students are interested in the public sector, but the majority try for corporate work, because as one student puts it, "You have to pay back your loans somehow." Off-campus interviews available are based on students' geographic preferences. NYU's placement office is in the forefront of U.S. law schools, offering programs that facilitate recruiting for employers, such as through the "Résumés Only" service by which the office collects interested students' résumés at regular intervals and sends them to organizations that have indicated they will have jobs available.

PREPARATION

N/A

WHERE/WHAT GRADUATES PRACTICE

A. 67% stay within New York; 33% choose jobs outside of New York State; of this group, 7% California; 5% Washington, D.C.; 2.5% New Jersey; 3% Massachusetts.
B. 79% Very Large Firms; 12% Large Firms; 5% Medium Sized Firms; 4% Small Firms; 10% Federal Clerks; 1% State Clerks; 3% Government; 3% Public Interest; 0.5% Corporate In-house.

UNIVERSITY OF NORTH CAROLINA AT CHAPEL HILL
School of Law

VAN HECKE–WETTACH HALL
CAMPUS BOX 3380
CHAPEL HILL, NORTH CAROLINA (NC) 27599-3380
(919) 962-5106

🐦 R E P O R T   C A R D 🐦

ADMISSIONS
SELECTIVITY: 🎓🎓🎓🎓

Applicants: 3176; **Accepted:** 597
Transfer Applications: 28; **Accepted:** 3
LSAT Mean: 38   **GPA Mean:** 3.4

ACADEMICS
Order of the Coif (1928)
N.C. Bar Passage (first try): 92%
Faculty to Student Ratio: 1:20
Quality of Teaching: B/B+
Accessibility: B+

PHYSICAL ENVIRONMENT
Location: College Town
Safety: Good
HA: ♿ ♿ ♿

STUDENT ENROLLMENT
Class Size: 235
Women: 43%   **Minorities:** 12%
Average Age of Entering Class: N/A

PLACEMENT
REPUTATION: ★ ☆ ★ ☆

Recruiters: 450
Starting Salary Mean: $26,000 (R); $40,000 (NR)

FINANCES
Tuition: $962 (R); $6397 (NR)
Average Total Cost: $7758 (R); $13,193 (NR)

STUDENT LIFE
RATING: ☺ ☺ ☺ ☺

After Hours: Maria Kakis, Players

PROMINENT ALUMNI/AE
Include: Terry Sanford, U.S. Senator; Boyden Gray, Legal Counsel to President Bush; Steve Cowper, Governor, Alaska

INSIDER INFORMATION

If the term "bang for your buck" were applied to UNC law school, it would more likely be stated "explosion for your penny." Hands down UNC wins among the ultimate bargains in legal education today, especially for North Carolina residents. One-quarter of each entering class is made up of nonresidents, and applicants can obtain "Residency for Tuition Purposes" prior to applying by living in North Carolina for a full year with the intention of staying in the state. But Carolina is more than a bargain law school; it attracts a diverse and highly motivated student body who find wide-reaching placement opportunities without too much trouble, despite the Placement Office's current understaffing situation.

Interestingly, the school's proximity to Duke Law not only draws a sizable group of applicants who are "in the neighborhood" and decide to visit, but also brings in recruiters, particularly from the Northeast, who feel that they stand a better chance of pulling graduates up north, because there are fewer competitors.

For the most part, students agree that the faculty is composed of top-drawer professors who genuinely enjoy and some go so far as to say "love," teaching. Accessibility after class may not be quite what students here want, due mainly to the school's larger class sizes and the fact that some professors are not always approachable. Course variety has never been lacking, and several students felt there was so much variety that there were more courses available to them than were possible to fit into their three years.

Space, or the lack of it, is probably UNC's one major shortcoming. Students characterize the law school facility as overcrowded, with cramped quarters in the library, hallways, the snack area, and especially in parking facilities. Many agree that getting to school is "half the battle," because of the scarcity of parking spaces near the school. Yet, given what students here are paying in tuition and living costs, with few exceptions, they find they are getting more than their money's worth. So, if you're willing to put up with a tight fit in return for one of the best and most affordable legal educations money can buy, head in the direction of UNC School of Law. By all accounts, you'll be glad you made the trip.

ADMISSIONS

CRITERIA

LEVEL 1: Grade Point Average

LEVEL 2: LSAT score; diversity factors (e.g., minority status)

LEVEL 3: Quality of undergraduate curriculum/course work completed

LEVEL 4: Quality/reputation of college/university

LEVEL 5: Personal essay

LEVEL 6: Recommendations

LEVEL 7: Work experience

MINORITY RECRUITMENT PROGRAM

Yes, the Assistant Dean has primary responsibility for minority recruitment, but the Black Law Student Association and the faculty are extremely active in all phases of minority recruitment efforts.

A B O U T   T H E   A P P L I C A T I O N

DEADLINE FOR FILING: 2/1; rolling admissions

FEE: $35

LSAT: School takes the average of the applicant's scores.

PERSONAL STATEMENT: "The personal statement is most helpful in evaluating candidates who fall in the middle range of the applicant pool. A compelling, well-written essay from an applicant far below normal admission requirements will not, however, result in an offer of admission. Personal statements distinguish applicants in the competitive middle range."

INTERVIEW: Not required or recommended.

ADMISSIONS TIPS: "Apply early—by January 1. We are on rolling admissions and the class is generally filled by mid-March. Applicants should take the LSAT by December at the latest."

CONTACT: J. Elizabeth Furr, Assistant Dean

P H Y S I C A L   E N V I R O N M E N T

UNC Law is housed in Van Hecke–Wettach Hall on the edge of campus, which to most students resembles a high school. The building consists of two basic units and connecting bridges. The major student gripe at UNC tends to center around insufficient space in the hallways and the library. The area around the school is safe, and there is an escort service. Accessibility for the handicapped is considered fair.

A very small number of students live in on-campus housing, which is not guaranteed. The most popular form of student housing near the school is apartments. Students find that it is not difficult to locate suitable accommodations near UNC. The most cost-effective accommodations are for a single student, a shared apartment (although on-campus housing is cheaper, having no place to stay during breaks is a hinderance); for a married student with no children, student family housing (provided by the university); and for a married student with children, student family housing. A car is recommended because law students typically live off campus and need some mode of transportation if they wish to study at the law school in the evenings, after the buses stop running.

FINANCES

BUDGET	LOW	MEDIUM	HIGH
Tuition (Resident)† **Tuition (Nonresident)**	$962 $6397	$962 $6397	$962 $6397
Books	$700	$700	$700
Living Accommodations (9 months)	On-Campus $1539	Shared Apt.* $3222	Shared House** $3222
Food	Groceries $1524	Cafeteria*** $1524	Meal Plan (21/Wk.) $1600
Miscellaneous	$800	$1000	$1200
Transportation	Bus or bike $117	Car $350	Car $350
TOTAL (R) **TOTAL (NR)**	$5642 $11,077	$7758 $13,193	$8034 $13,469

† Estimated

* Student Family Housing: $2700

** One-Bedroom Apartment: $3222

*** Moderately priced restaurants: $1524

Employment During School: Not recommended. Work-study jobs are available for students. These jobs are open, with some based on need. Research assistantships are provided as well. Students receive $10,698 for a twelve-month appointment.

Scholarships: The school offers merit and need-based scholarships. Merit scholarships are not contingent upon maintaining a certain GPA.

School Loan Program (Exclusive of Perkins Money): Yes. $2500/year University Loan; 5% interest with no grace period upon completion of degree. Awarded based on need.

Loan Forgiveness Program: No

Students Requesting Aid: 80%; of these, 75% receive aid.

Students Indebted upon Graduation: 75%

Average Loan Indebtedness: Approximately $14,000

ACADEMICS

During your first year, you are split into sections of between sixty and ninety students, and you have a "small section" chosen at random from first-year courses, of between twenty-five to twenty-eight students termed "homeroom." The professor of this course also acts as your advisor. All first-year courses are required. Second- and third-year students take all electives, except a course in Professional Responsibility and a seminar. Certain second-year "foundation courses," including Business Associations, Constitutional Law, and Evidence are prerequisites for later courses, and recommended to facilitate taking more advanced courses. Third-year "foundation courses" include Professional Responsibility, Administrative Law, and Sales and Secured Transactions. Students here feel that there are more than enough electives offered with many problems stemming from fitting all of the electives they want to take into their three years at UNC. Grading is A–F, with pluses and minuses. Students have to maintain a GPA of C − to continue in school. Students find grades are "right on the money"—neither deflated nor inflated.

Faculty are outstanding regarding publishing and other scholarly interests, but students do not find them as effective when it comes to conveying information in an interesting manner. In few courses, students find that they have to teach themselves. Accessibility after class is mixed, depending on the instructor and the individual course. Most, however are available immediately after class.

UNC has two clinics and a nationally recognized trial advocacy program. The Clinical Experience Program consists of preliminary courses in rules of evidence and trial practice with mock trials and oral arguments. Students work with law enforcement officials, legal services agencies, and attorneys in North Carolina. Third-year students represent clients in landlord-tenant problems, divorces, and all phases of criminal practice, under supervision by practicing attorneys.

Star faculty include Paul Haskell (Trusts and Estates), Tom Hazen (Securities Regulation), Ken Wing (Health Law), Bill Turnier and Patricia Bryan (Tax Law), William Murphy (Labor), Daniel Pollitt (Constitutional Law), Robert Byrd (Torts), and Ken Broun (Evidence).

JOINT DEGREE PROGRAMS

JD/MBA; JD/MPH (Master of Public Health); JD/MAPPS (Master of Art and Public Policy Science, in conjunction with Duke); JD/MRP (Master of Regional Planning)

STUDENT LIFE

UNC schedules many social events, including Law Revue, Barrister's Ball, Orientation Pizza Lunch, and receptions after guest speakers. Competition is subtle but present; however, students generally welcome the chance to work with others. UNC's large class size allows students to form new groups at the school all the time. There is a wide range of special interest groups, including American Indian Law Students Association (AILSA); Second Careers in Law, for students who have at least five years of postgraduate work experience coming to UNC law school; and the Black Law Students Association. The North Carolina Lawyer's Research Service (NCLRS) is student run; it allows second- and third-year students to conduct research into current legal problems in the state of North Carolina.

PLACEMENT

Students find that the Placement Office could use more support personnel, but most agree that it does a fine job in bringing employers to the school. UNC is much stronger in the Southeast than in any other part of the country, but students have found placement in other parts of the country as well, most notably the Northeast. 95% of students are placed six months following May graduation.

PREPARATION

Students are prepared by the Placement Office through videotaped mock interviews, interviewing techniques sessions, and résumé-writing seminars.

WHERE/WHAT GRADUATES PRACTICE

A. 10% Northeast; 73% South; 1% West; 3% Midwest; 13% Other. (20% of the students remain within the vicinity of the law school within one year of graduation.)
B. 68% Private Practice; 2% Business, Legal; 8% Judicial Clerkships; 11% Government; 3% Military; 6% Public Interest; 1% Nonlegal Business; 1% Nonlegal unspecified.

357 EAST CHICAGO AVENUE
CHICAGO, ILLINOIS (IL) 60611-3069
(312) 908-0179

REPORT CARD

ADMISSIONS
SELECTIVITY:

Applicants: 3943; Accepted: 813
LSAT Mean: N/A   GPA Mean: N/A

PLACEMENT
REPUTATION: ★ ★ ★ ★

Recruiters: 550
Starting Salary Median: $62,000

ACADEMICS
Order of the Coif (1907)
Quality of Teaching: A –
Faculty Accessibility: A

FINANCES
Tuition: $14,382
Average Total Cost: $25,362

PHYSICAL ENVIRONMENT
Location: Large City
Safety: Excellent/Very Good (Escort Service)
HA: ♿ ♿ ♿

STUDENT LIFE
RATING: ☺ ☺ ☺ ☺

After Hours: Pippin's, Streeter's, Bar Review

STUDENT ENROLLMENT
Class Size: 220
Women: 11%   Minorities: 44%
Age Range of the Entering Class: 20–40

PROMINENT ALUMNI/AE
Include: Lowden (former governor of Illinois);
John Paul Stevens, Associate Justice of the
Supreme Court of the United States

INSIDER INFORMATION

From the average law applicant's vantage point, Northwestern is a diamond of a law school, set off by the brilliance of Chicago's "Gold Coast" and its own breathtaking and rather extensive physical facilities. Upon closer scrutiny, this "diamond" has a sizable number of flaws. First among these is NU's deep-rooted insecurity, resulting from its self-perceived reputation as a "fringe player" long known as a refuge for "top-tier rejects." Says one student here, "Northwestern deserves a better reputation than it has." And indeed, many recruiters, in the Chicago area in particular, have commented that, "although we might have a slight preference for Chicago, Northwestern turns out very polished graduates." It is only when you begin moving away from the school's Midwestern base that recruiter commentary is more varied.

Although Northwestern law students almost uniformly laud their faculty for their "outstanding teaching abilities and piercing insight into complex legal problems germane to our society," the school recently revealed its insecurities by commissioning its own study on areas, including "Median Items per Faculty Member, All Law Reviews," after receiving a less than satisfactory ranking in *U.S. News & World Report*. NU ran up a several-thousand-dollar tab in the process of proving its point. Few feel the self-commissioned study has served to help Northwestern's prestige, but students here have learned to live with their school's self-inflicted misery.

It's a misery of which they are largely undeserving. NU students are bright, motivated, and certainly as competitive, if not more so, than you will find at any top-tier school, and a tolerance for a wide number of political and/or other views is not only present but strongly encouraged. Of course, you will be hard pressed to find an NU student who doesn't allude to the school's hefty price tag. The Gold Coast provides a safe environment, but for those wishing to venture off-campus, affordable housing near the school is sparse, if not entirely absent. All of this complaining about costs and classes breeds what students feel is excessive whining among their classmates.

In the coming year, Northwestern will pull ahead of most of the top tier in one respect—they have raised their application fee from $50 to $75. Perhaps this is yet another case of the "diamond" proving its worth by raising its own price. After all, with the total costs of three years on a budget here easily going deep into five figures, one can't and really shouldn't suspect Northwestern Law School of being a high-priced cubic zirconium.

CRITERIA

LEVEL 1: Grade Point Average; quality of undergraduate curriculum/course work completed; quality/reputation of college/university; LSAT score; work experience; recommendations; personal essay

MINORITY RECRUITMENT PROGRAM

Yes. The Asian American Law Student Association has worked with the Admissions Office to further one of this organization's purposes—to increase the number of Asian-American law students at Northwestern University and in the legal community. An objective of the Black Law Students Association is to increase the number of black attorneys in the United States by encouraging interested black men and women to pursue a legal education.

DEADLINE FOR FILING: 10/1–2/15

FEE: $75

LSAT: School considers all scores, the circumstances surrounding each test experience, and the practical benefit to late scores resulting from prior exposure to the test.

RECOMMENDED COURSES PRIOR TO MATRICULATING: These courses include history, economics, anthropology, sociology, government, political science, philosophy, English, foreign languages, and public speaking.

PERSONAL STATEMENT: "We encourage you to discuss personal and professional goals that are important to you and to include information about your achievements."

INTERVIEW: The school does not conduct evaluative interviews, unless specifically requested by the Admissions Committee.

ADMISSIONS TIPS: "Applicants often believe that their prospects for admission are greater if they solicit letters of recommendation from judges or well-known public figures. Our experience has shown that many of these recommenders have only a passing knowledge of the applicant and therefore submit recommendations of little value. An applicant's most useful recommendations are from individuals who can offer sound judgments about the prospective student's qualifications for the study of law. For older applicants, GPA becomes less significant, and they may attach a résumé."

CONTACT: Susan Curnick, Assistant Dean for Admission and Financial Aid

PHYSICAL ENVIRONMENT

Located right on Chicago's Gold Coast, Northwestern's law school is probably in one of the safest areas of Chicago. Campus security can, however, provide you with escort service, if requested.

The school of law consists of a complex of buildings. The most recent addition, the Arthur Rubloff Building, was completed in 1984. The recently constructed Rubloff Hall doubled the library capacity as well as areas for students to study. The library is well equipped and includes both LEXIS and WESTLAW, though students feel that it might be nice to have more terminals. After first-year students are trained, they become excited about using the system and tie it up for second- and third-year students. An office tower above the southern end of the building is the national headquarters of the ABA, the American Bar Foundation, and the American Bar Endowment. Trial and appellate instruction are greatly facilitated by the school's two courtrooms, which are fully equipped with jury box, counsel tables, witness stand, and spectator seating.

Northwestern School of Law contains eight major classrooms, the largest of which, Lincoln Hall, was designed in the architectural style of the British House of Commons. Lowden Hall, a glass-enclosed atrium that connects the old and new buildings, serves as a student lounge. The lower level of Levy Mayer Hall has lockers, food and beverage dispensers, an eating area, and a television lounge.

Handicapped accessibility is considered very good, with easily accessible ramps and elevators, and wide hallways. However, Levy Mayer Hall doesn't have an elevator, although the administration has been known to make special arrangements for handicapped students.

There is student housing. In living off-campus, the closer you are to the campus the more you can expect to pay. Some students elect to live in apartments in Lincoln Park, which run around $500/month. Expect to pay heavily for convenience and luxury to the tune of $1000 + /month. The most popular form of housing is the dorms and shared apartments located nearby.

One generally has to commute in order to live in a shared house. Parking, however, is very expensive and difficult to get from the university. Few people have cars if they live near the campus, and walking is considered the best form of transportation. A car is not necessary due to the strong public transportation system near the school.

FINANCES

BUDGET	LOW	MEDIUM	HIGH
Tuition	$14,382	$14,382	$14,382
Books	$600	$600	$600
Living Accommodations (9 months)	Shared House $3825	On-Campus* $4050	One-Bedroom Apt. $7200
Food	Groceries $2160	Cafeteria $2160	Restaurants $4050
Miscellaneous**	$2000	$3000	$3750
Transportation	Mass Transit $500	Taxis $1170	Car $1215
TOTAL	$23,467	$25,362	$31,197

* Studio Apartment: $5850

** Students advise reserving money for extensive photocopying in addition to books and supplies.

Employment During School: Work-study jobs: each year a number of second- and third-year students are selected to serve as research assistants to individual members of the faculty. These appointments carry a modest stipend.

Scholarships: The school offers merit, need-based, and minority scholarships.

School Loan Program (Exclusive of Perkins Money): Yes. Interest free, sixty-day loans are available to any registered student under the university's Short Term Student Loan Program. Students, after completing a brief application, may receive immediate cash or a check to a maximum of $300. A student who has obtained one loan may not apply for a subsequent loan until the earlier loan has been repaid in full. Repayment of all loans made during the academic year must be made in full by the final day of class.

Loan Forgiveness Program: Yes. Loan Repayment Assistance Program (LRAP). LRAP is a loan repayment assistance program that provides interest-free loans to graduates who choose to pursue employment in the public interest, government, and academic sectors immediately following law school, or following a judicial clerkship. If the graduate works in a qualifying position for three years or more, the LRAP loan will be forgiven in part, and after a longer period, in full.

ACADEMICS

First-semester students receive what are called "shadow grades," which, in effect, means they have a "honeymoon period" during which they can adjust to the rigors of law school without the stress of grades. And, although students know their grades, they do not show up on transcripts. However, students feel that this actually increases the pressure on the second semester. "It doesn't just double the pressure on the second semester. It squares it."

Very few professors rely solely on the Socratic method for teaching, with the first year a mixture of Socratic/lecture, and the second and third years primarily lecture. The professors are more research- than real-world (practicing lawyer)-oriented. They are known to do a solid job of presenting material, and although each professor has a different methodology of presentation, they share the common ability to maximize their strengths and minimize their teaching weaknesses. That is, a professor who is a strong Socratic teacher sticks to this methodology; if not, the professor uses the lecture approach more. Faculty also care about what their students have to say in and out of class. Accessibility is outstanding, with almost all professors keeping an open door and several giving out home phone numbers.

Grading is done on an A–F system, with pluses but no minuses. The mean grade usually falls in the "B" range. There is no ranking of students. Admission to *Law Review* has been conducted in a variety of ways over the past years, one year cutting off at the top quarter of the class and having a writing competition among these students. Anyone not eligible by grades is able to "write their way on." Another method (to be used next year) will be a writing competition among the top quarter of the class by numerical grades; then, two-thirds of the evaluation will be based on the writing competition and one-third on grades. There are two journals and "if someone really wants to get onto a journal they can get on." Moot court has done well in the past and the school has a National Moot Court Team, an International Moot Court Team, and a moot court within the school.

NU offers an Extended Study Program that allows qualified students to take four years to complete the three-year course of study. No more than five students are admitted to the program.

JOINT/GRADUATE DEGREE PROGRAMS

Joint Degrees: JD/MM (Master of Music); JD/PhD
Graduate Degrees: LLM; SJD (Doctor of Juristic Science)

The law school's class size is fairly small, and students find that they know most of the people in their classes. Students characterize their classmates as from mostly upper-middle-class backgrounds with white-collar parents. The majority of the students are from the Midwest and several are from the East Coast. They have a wide spectrum of views and are tolerant of each other's beliefs. Some students elect to go to the Bar Review, where the students sample a different bar in the Chicago area once a week. Other activities are cocktail hours with faculty and the Booze Cruise on Lake Michigan.

Competitiveness varies with each class. "Some first-year classes share outlines; others guard them with their lives from those outside their study groups. After the first year, most students work cooperatively and work together well."

PLACEMENT

The Placement Office is considered excellent and very egalitarian in getting students jobs not based on grades. Students spread out all over the country from New York to L.A., Chicago, Indiana, Texas, and back. Placement is unquestionably national in its ability to locate employment for the school's graduates. There is no pre-screening for law firms recruiting on campus. Students rank their top selections, and the results are fed into a computer. Those students who rank a firm 1 (from 1–10 for that week) are given first priority and so on, until the number of slots for that firm fills up, with the rest being assigned randomly. The only problem with the Placement Office is that since it bends over backwards not to discriminate based on grades, it may be giving certain students, without a chance to get into a particular law firm, a false sense of hope.

PREPARATION

The placement office coordinates on-campus interviews, posts job information, holds seminars on professional opportunities, and conducts workshops on résumé preparation and job-search skills.

WHERE/WHAT GRADUATES PRACTICE

A. 11% Northeast; 3% Southeast; 72% Midwest; 5% Southwest; 7% Rocky Mountains/West; 2% Foreign.
B. 83% Private Practice; 2% Corporations and Businesses; 5% Government and Public Interest; 10% Judicial Clerkships.

P.O. BOX 959
NOTRE DAME, INDIANA (IN) 46556-0959
(219) 239-6626

REPORT CARD

ADMISSIONS
SELECTIVITY

Applicants: 2700; Accepted: N/A
LSAT Mean: 39   GPA Mean: 3.5

PLACEMENT
REPUTATION ☆ ☆ ☆ ☆

Recruiters: 300
Starting Salary Mean: N/A

ACADEMICS
Faculty to Student Ratio: N/A
Quality of Teaching: **A −**
Faculty Accessibility: **A**

FINANCES
Tuition: $11,905
Average Total Cost: $17,130

PHYSICAL ENVIRONMENT
Location: Urban/Small City
Safety: Good
HA: ♿ ♿ ♿ ♿

STUDENT LIFE
RATING ☺ ☺ ☺ ☺ ☹

After Hours: Coaches, Bridgets, Senior Bar

STUDENT ENROLLMENT
Class Size: 170
Women: 45%   Minorities: 9%
Average Age of Entering Class: N/A

PROMINENT ALUMNI/AE
Include: N/A

INSIDER INFORMATION

The oldest Roman Catholic law school in the United States, Notre Dame celebrated its 100th year of continuous operation in 1969. Its administration feels that the school draws its "inspiration" from two ancient traditions: the tradition of English and American law and the Catholic tradition.

"It might sound corny," one student said in describing one of the most memorable attributes of Notre Dame, "but the school is very close to its students. They really listen to the students." Students feel that ND law professors' top-notch quality adds to this value. It is felt that they are powerful and experienced in their field.

Students at Notre Dame are governed by the school's honor code, and have found that there is a healthy balance between academics and social life. They note that there is much more socializing at Notre Dame law school that they ever anticipated, "Wednesday night and Thursday night are virtually law school nights at the local bars."

The physical environment of Notre Dame is considered an asset as well. It was noted that, "this isn't a city school." The school is located on a big beautiful campus. The law school building was recently erected and the library expanded about three years ago. Although located in Indiana, Notre Dame is only one and a half hours from Chicago.

While placement is found to be very good in the Midwest, students feel that the school's national representation is weaker and that the office should try harder for the East Coast.

ADMISSIONS

CRITERIA

LEVEL 1: Grade Point Average; LSAT score; the maturing effect on an individual of spending years away from school; financial pressure requiring employment during the undergraduate years; significant personal achievement in extracurricular work at college; postcollege work experiences or military duty; unusual prior training that promises a significant contribution to the law school community; rising trend in academic performance versus solid but unexceptional work.

LEVEL 2: Economic disadvantages and ethnic minority background.

ABOUT THE APPLICATION

DEADLINE FOR FILING: 4/1

FEE: $40

LSAT: Considered to be a highly significant factor.

RECOMMENDED COURSES PRIOR TO MATRICULATING: Courses in philosophy, logic, and accounting. Intensive work in English composition is useful as well.

PERSONAL STATEMENT: Statement is required and is used as part of the evaluation process.

INTERVIEW: Not held for evaluative purposes. However, students have advised that it may be to your advantage to visit the school and ask to meet with the Dean of Admissions.

ADMISSIONS TIPS: "Applicants are urged to file an application even before receiving scores from LSDAS on the Law School Admission Test. This will expedite consideration by the Admissions Committee once the application is complete."

CONTACT: William McClean, Dean of Admissions

Notre Dame Law School is located at the entrance to the campus of the University of Notre Dame, a Holy Cross Institution. The law school is contained in a building with a Tudor Gothic exterior located at the entrance to the Notre Dame campus. The original building was recently refurbished and a major addition completed in 1987. The collection of the Kresge Law Library is made available to students twenty-four hours a day, seven days a week.

Facilities on the university campus include the Rockne Memorial and the Edmund P. Joyce Athletic and Convocation Center. The area is considered safe. The area is well-lit at night; an escort service is available; and there are patrol cars. Handicapped accessibility is considered very good, and there are ramps and elevators. It is felt that the highest rating for accessibility should not be given, however. Because the university campus is so large, the handicapped are not able to travel easily from one point to the other.

Although most students live off campus, there are a limited number of places available for single men and women on campus. Unfurnished two-bedroom, all-electric apartments close to campus are available for married students in University Village. Because the supply is limited, you are urged to act immediately upon acceptance if you are interested in this type of accommodation. A car is recommended because only a few of the available off-campus living accommodations are within convenient walking distance to the school. Bus service is, however, available between the university and South Bend and does stop in front of the campus.

FINANCES

BUDGET	LOW	MEDIUM	HIGH
Tuition	$11,905	$11,905	$11,905
Books	$450	$450	$450
Living Accommodations (9 months)	Shared House $150	Shared Apt. $250	One-Bedroom Apt. $4500
Food	Groceries $1560	Cafeteria $2500	Restaurants $3705
Miscellaneous	$1200	$1500	$1700
Transportation	Mass Transit $450	Bus/Car $525	Car $600
TOTAL	$15,715	$17,130	$22,860

Employment During School: Although the students are discouraged from working during the first year because of the academic rigor, the Notre Dame law student is encouraged to work during the summer months and, if necessary, work part-time during the second and third years of study. The law school has several jobs available to second- and third-year students. Other employment is available through the university's Financial Aid Office and there are resident assistantships. The assistantships cover room and board.

Scholarships: The school offers scholarships, which are awarded on the basis of demonstrated need and academic merit, and tuition grants, which are awarded to disadvantaged students on the basis of need and demonstrated ability to perform satisfactorily in the law school.

School Loan Program (Exclusive of Perkins Money): Yes. There are two privately sponsored loans.

Loan Forgiveness Program: No

Students Requesting Aid: N/A; of those requesting aid, 70% receive aid.

ACADEMICS

During the first year, students are taught primarily by the case method. All courses during this year are required. Second and third years are taught through the problem method, internship practice, and experience-based techniques. Students must take thirty credit hours of specified courses before graduating. Notre Dame Law School's curriculum includes legal research and writing courses all three years. First-year students develop a background in the technical use of the law library, take a rigorous legal writing course that prepares them for the writing demands of the legal profession, and, in the second semester, argue appellate moot court cases and assist clients in activities supervised by the Legal Aid and Defender Association. The writing and legal research program is elective in the second and third years of study.

Because the school's objective is participation by every student at every meeting of every class, it is committed to small classes, particularly in the second and third years. Formal instruction is supplemented with lectures, panel discussions by judges and practicing lawyers, and practice programs such as the moot (appellate) and practice (trial) courts. A year abroad through the London Program is available. Students may receive up to four credits for working for the Legislative Research Service, researching and writing legislative memoranda and participating in drafting bills for submission to state and municipal legislatures and Congress.

Students consider the professors very well informed on their subject matter. Many of them are coauthors of textbooks that the students use. They are also found to be very accessible. As one student said, "The doors are always open, and professors give out their home phone numbers." Star faculty include Patty O'Hart (Business Associations) and Robert Blakely (Criminal Law).

JOINT DEGREE PROGRAMS

Joint Degrees: JD/MBA; JD/degree in History; JD/degree in Engineering

STUDENT LIFE

Students feel that the social life at Notre Dame is very good. It was noted that "There is always someone who wants to go out. Wednesday night and Thurday night are virtually law school nights at the local bars." The Student Bar Association-sponsored parties are abundant. Class members appear to be very willing to help one another. This cooperation may be due in part to the fact that there is no calculation or publication of "ranking" or "class standing." Student organizations include the Social Justice Forum and the Women's Legal Forum.

PLACEMENT

PREPARATION

During the fall of each year, energies are devoted to a six-week on-campus interview program. The Placement Office staff is available for individual consultation on résumé preparation, job choice, and job-hunting techniques. Students report, however, that there are only two quick meetings on interviewing skills and most advising is accomplished through a yearly revised placement manual. These papers contain information on résumé writing and interviewing techniques, a list of recruiters, sample résumés, and a placement calendar. A source of placement help provided to the students is the Notre Dame Law Association, consisting of almost 5000 alumni/ae located all over the country.

WHAT GRADUATES PRACTICE

About 75% of graduates work in private firms and approximately 10% receive judicial clerkships.

78 NORTH BROADWAY
WHITE PLAINS, NEW YORK (NY) 10603
(914) 422-4212

REPORT CARD

ADMISSIONS
SELECTIVITY 🎓 🎓 🎓 ◀

Applicants: 2179 (full-time); **Accepted:** 594.
517 (part-time); accepted: 195
Transfer Applications: 29; Accepted: 2
LSAT Mean: 36   GPA Mean: 3.1

PLACEMENT
REPUTATION ☆ ☆ ☆

Recruiters: 42 (on-campus); 160 Inquiries
Starting Salary Median: $32,500

ACADEMICS
New York Bar Passage (first try): 76.5%
Faculty to Student Ratio: 1:22
Quality of Teaching: **B**
Faculty Accessibility: **B**

FINANCES
Tuition: $12,100 (full-time); $9076 (part-time)
Average Total Cost: $22,825 (full-time);
$19,801 (part-time)

PHYSICAL ENVIRONMENT
Location: Middle-Sized City
Safety: Good
HA: ♿ ♿ ♿ ♿

STUDENT LIFE
RATING ☺ ☺ ☺

After Hours: Oliver's

STUDENT ENROLLMENT
Class Size: 169 (full-time); 116 (part-time)
Women: 50% (day); 41% (evening)   **Minorities:** 11%
Average Age of Entering Class: 25 (full-time); 33 (part-time)

PROMINENT ALUMNI/AE
Include: N/A

INSIDER INFORMATION

When Pace Law School first appeared on the scene, White Plains was still in its developing stages with its chief advantage being that it was far enough outside of New York to be buffered from the city's frantic pace but also within easy reach. No one could have anticipated back then that White Plains would experience such a dramatic boom, causing those who had been away from the city for three or four years to stop in their tracks and ask themselves, "Is this the same city?" The same thing can be said of Pace Law School, whose popularity, if measured by percentage increase of applicants, has grown at among the highest rates in the country, with a near 50% jump in 1989 alone. The school has carved out several niches for itself with a respectable number of star faculty members positioned in the popular fields of Environmental Law, certificate programs in Environmental Law (1982), Health Law and Policy (1985), International Law (1987), and International Trade Law (1987). The option for students to graduate with a certificate in these specializations has enhanced their marketability among recruiters. Among the more encouraging signs of Pace's growth is the recent addition of Steven Goldberg, former Associate Dean of Minnesota, who has taken over as Pace's new dean.

Pace is a school with impressive tenacity. But like many younger law schools, which have strived to achieve so much in so short a time, the school has had some growing pains, primarily in the area of placement. Of those law firms/corporations that have been exposed to the school's graduates, there is no question as to recruiter satisfaction. Recruiters are beginning to think of Pace as more than just a commuter law school. Unfortunately, the school has spread its wings in the academic realm faster than it has in picking up nods from recruiters, who are as yet unfamiliar with their "product." However, there are strong signs of this situation improving, based on increased emphasis on placement with the recent addition of Diane McEvoy, Columbia's former director of placement, and visibly greater satisfaction with the Placement Office from students in more recent classes. Pace graduates tend to gravitate toward practicing law in small to very small firms in the Westchester/Connecticut area.

Those interested in Environmental Law and in gaining hands-on exposure through clinical programs in areas including Health Law should certainly consider Pace. As for the students the school attracts, Pace looks for diversity of backgrounds and it finds them. Recent classes include nurses, accountants, physicians, and a forest ranger. In the words of one third-year student, "This school, although young, is on the move up! It possesses a high-tier faculty. . . . The students are allowed to express their ideas. They are not spoon-fed, and professors enjoy students' challenging of their analysis of case law/interpretation."

ADMISSIONS

CRITERIA

LEVEL 1. LSAT score

LEVEL 2: Grade Point Average; graduate work

LEVEL 3: Quality of undergraduate curriculum/course work completed; graduate work

LEVEL 4: Quality/reputation of college/university; personal essay

LEVEL 5: Work experience; recommendations (useful for the awarding of merit scholarships and evaluating borderline applicants); writing skills as demonstrated by LSAT writing sample.

Note: "Legal study is a predominately academic endeavor. Although work experience may influence an admissions decision, it will not overcome unsatisfactory academic skills. Evidence of solid academic skills is vital."

MINORITY RECRUITMENT PROGRAM

Yes; all minority files are read by the Admissions Committee (composed of faculty and students). A variety of factors are evaluated. Students and faculty are available to talk to prospective and accepted applicants. Pace hosts a minority information day at which current students, faculty, and administration make presentations and speak informally about legal study and employment. Minority merit scholarships and minority need-based grants are awarded to admitted minority applicants.

ABOUT THE APPLICATION

DEADLINE FOR FILING: 3/15

FEE: $35

LSAT: School takes the average of the applicant's scores. The weight given to the scores depends upon the extent of the score differences. All scores are evaluated.

RECOMMENDED COURSES PRIOR TO MATRICULATING: Any course that develops an applicant's analytical ability in the areas of reading, writing, and speaking; these are not "major" specific. Some faculty recommend a philosophy course and an economics course that acquaints an applicant with a balance sheet and its related terminology and concepts.

PERSONAL STATEMENT: "The personal statement provides an applicant with the opportunity to explain any weaknesses/inconsistencies of their credentials and to balance them with strengths. It provides the committee a framework within which credentials may be evaluated. It is most important in borderline cases and in awarding of merit scholarships, as communication of spirit, self, and potential for contributions to the School of Law community are evaluated."

INTERVIEW: Not required or recommended, but the school does recommend a visit, including the opportunity to sit in on one or more classes. An interview is not used as part of the evaluation process unless one is required (e.g., handicapped students for whom LSAT may be waived). For visitors, the Marriot-Courtyard in Tarrytown has reasonable rates, but you'll need transportation (ten-to-fifteen-minute drive). Most convenient would be the Holiday Inn Crowne Plaza or the White Plains Hotel, from which the visitor can walk or take a bus or a taxi.

ADMISSIONS TIPS: "Applicants should type their personal statement, and devote attention to effective writing style, grammar, and punctuation. Quality, not quantity, is important. Accuracy and candor are essential."

CONTACT: Dorothy Umans, Assistant Dean

PHYSICAL ENVIRONMENT

Pace has an enviable location, as the only law school between Albany and New York City. White Plains not only is the seat of Westchester County government with city and county courts and a branch of the U.S. Federal District Court but is also near the headquarters, in Westchester County and nearby Connecticut, of several Fortune 500 companies.

Preston Hall, a Gothic structure housing classrooms, is in striking contrast to the school's spacious and modern law library. The area around the school is fairly safe, and an escort service is available. Handicapped accessibility is fair, and depending on need, arrangement may be made for an individual study area, audio-visual equipment, administrative assistance in securing public or School of Law financial support, or special examination conditions.

First-year day students are eligible for living on campus, but students advise against this option. Apartments are the most popular form of student housing and are found to be affordable, if a careful search is made prior to attending.

A car may be recommended. If the student lives on campus, a car is a luxury. Off-campus, many apartments in the area charge for parking. Street parking policies differ in the nearby communities. An express train ride to Manhattan for part-time employment or relaxation takes thirty-five minutes. Access to a car may become useful depending on where a student gains part-time employment during the academic year.

FINANCES

BUDGET	LOW	MEDIUM	HIGH
Tuition (full-time, day)	$12,100	$12,100	$12,100
Tuition (part-time, night)	$9076	$9076	$9076
Books	$775	$775	$775
Living Accommodations (9 months)	On-Campus $2800	Shared House $3600	One-Bedroom Apt. $5400
Food	Groceries $1200	Meal Plan (14/wk) $1400	Restaurant $3000
Miscellaneous	$1800	$2250	$2700
Transportation	Car $2700	Car $2700	Car $2700
TOTAL (FT)	$21,375	$22,825	$26,675
TOTAL (PT)	$18,351	$19,801	$23,651

Employment During School: Depends on such factors as year in school and hours. Work-study jobs are available for all students (not need-dependent). The approximate amount that students receive per hour in these jobs depends on the position.

Scholarships: The school offers merit, need-based, and minority scholarships. Merit scholarships are contingent upon maintaining GPA and rank requirements. These requirements depend on the type of scholarship. (*Note:* certain merit scholarships do not have performance requirements once the student is enrolled in law school.)

School Loan Program (Exclusive of Perkins Money): No

Loan Forgiveness Program: No

Students Requesting Aid: N/A

Students Receiving Aid: Although uncalculated, with the advent of Law Access and LALs, many students receive aid. All need-based packages require the awarding of Stafford Loans first; if additional need exists, students may be awarded a combination of grants, Perkins Loans, and work study. Merit scholarships are available to all and are awarded on the basis of credentials and projected contributions to the law school community.

ACADEMICS

Pace offers both a three-year day division and a four-year evening program, with the same professors teaching courses to both programs. In both programs, first-year courses are required. Second-year students are required to take Constitutional Law II, Federal Income Tax I, and Professional Responsibility. Upperclass elective courses are divided into various fields of concentration, including Administrative Law and Government Regulation, Environmental Law, and Intellectual Property. Several clinical and advocacy courses are also available and include Trial Practice, Criminal Law Clinics I and II, and an Appellate Litigation Clinic. The school offers special opportunities including judicial clerkships and the Pace Peace Center. Pace also offers a popular spring semester in London. Grading is from A–F with pluses and minuses.

Faculty here are characterized as very knowledgeable, and most have an open-door policy. Star faculty include Nicholas Robinson (Environmental Law), Richard Ottinger (Environmental Law), Willem Vis (International Commercial Law), Josephine King (Health Law), Stuart Madden (Products Liability), and Ben Gershman (Criminal Law).

JOINT/GRADUATE DEGREE PROGRAMS

Joint Degrees: JD/MBA; JD/MPA (Master of Public Administration)
Graduate Degree: LLM (Environmental Law)

STUDENT LIFE

Social life at Pace finds classes bonding and socializing with intramurals, dances, and picnics. Besides academic events, dances are held approximately three times a year. Most here feel that the best aspect of Pace is the "atmosphere," in which they do not have to look constantly over their shoulders to see if someone is trying to steal books or notes in order to get ahead. Competition is present but is both healthy and constructive among classmates.

PLACEMENT

Students find that over the past two years placement has dramatically improved, but some still feel that the "average" student is at times overlooked. Approximately forty-two employers participate in on-campus programs for permanent placement with the same number of employers participating on-campus for summer job placement.

PREPARATION

Students are prepared by the Placement Office through videotaped interviews with Pace graduates; an Alumni Advisor Program; résumé/cover-letter writing; interviewing workshops; individual counseling sessions; and panel presentations on different areas of practice. The Placement Office prepares numerous publications and resource materials, including placement newsletters for students and graduates.

WHERE/WHAT GRADUATES PRACTICE

A. 96% of students remain in the New York metropolitan area (NY, CT, NJ).
B. 2% Solo Practitioner; 52% Small Firms; 1% Medium Firms; 15% Large Firms; 3% Clerkships; 9% Governmental Agencies; 6% Corporations; 11% Other.

❧ R E P O R T   C A R D ❧

ADMISSIONS
SELECTIVITY 🎓🎓🎓

Applicants: 2328; Accepted: 1081
LSAT Mean: 36
GPA Mean: 3.07

ACADEMICS

Order of the Coif (1982)
California State Bar Passage (first try): 70.9%
California statewide average: 49%
Faculty to Student Ratio: 1:24
Quality of Teaching: **B+/B**
Faculty Accessibility: **A/A−**

PHYSICAL ENVIRONMENT

Location: Medium-Sized City
Safety: Good
HA: ♿ ♿ ♿ ♿

STUDENT ENROLLMENT

Class Size: 319 (full-time); 113 (part-time)
Women: 40.7%   Minorities: 8.3%
Average Age of Entering Class: 24 (full-
time); 29 (part-time)

PLACEMENT
REPUTATION ☆ ☆ ☆

Recruiters: 220
Starting Salary Median: $35,000

FINANCES

Tuition: $11,406 (day); $6753 (evening)
Average Total Cost: $24,290 (day); $19,997
(evening)

STUDENT LIFE
RATING ☺ ☺ ☺ ☺

After Hours: Tequila Willie's, Chevy's, Pine
Cove

PROMINENT ALUMNI/AE

Include: N/A

INSIDER INFORMATION Long before the Berlin Wall came tumbling down, Judge Gordon D. Schaber, McGeorge's dean, the Senior Dean in the United States, was giving speeches to the Hungarian Bar Association in Budapest. As Dean of Students Jane Kelso recounts, "They had to check the speeches and translations very carefully before anything was said." Today the school has a complete constellation of international programs in Salzburg, London, Vienna, and Edinburgh, as well as The Budapest/Vienna Institute on East/West Law and Relations examining East-West commercial and foreign policy as well as the legal and economic implications of expanding East-West trade. But knowing how far this school has come in so short a time, which many credit to Schaber, who transformed an unaccredited evening law school into a member of the coveted legal honorary society, Order of the Coif, you would expect this from McGeorge. It is a school that also lured Rear Admiral James L. McHugh, after he retired from his position as Judge Advocate General of the U.S. Navy, to become Associate Dean for Career Development.

For years McGeorge has been a lesser known commodity to East Coast applicants, who have recently heard the school's name mentioned with former faculty member, Supreme Court Justice Anthony Kennedy. This is a school willing to take more risks on its applicants than almost any other in the country, which accounts to a great extent for McGeorge's significant attrition rate. The school firmly believes that LSAT scores are only predictors of first-year success, and they have seen numerous instances of students who did not score well on the LSAT graduating in the top of their classes.

Most of the law schools you will visit will be composed of one or more buildings huddled together with law students scurrying to and about their law complex. McGeorge Law School isn't simply a cluster of buildings; it's a twenty-acre campus devoted solely to legal education. Of course, students here will still be scurrying to the school's spacious and well-equipped library, because at McGeorge hard work is more than a way of life, it's a means of academic survival. Grade deflation pervades most classes, with a "B −" average qualifying students for Dean's List.

McGeorge requires an above-average number of classes, which are now or may soon be required for the bar exam, and favors the quarter system, because it gives students more opportunity to take bar-like exams. Students characterize McGeorge's faculty as bringing with them years of experience in both public and private sectors. Many hold review sessions prior to exams, on weekends on their own time.

Recruiters familiar with the school's graduates, and their numbers are growing, consistently report that "McGeorge students are industrious and very hardworking." And with the exception of public interest and international law, students are very pleased with the school's placement capabilities.

ADMISSIONS

CRITERIA

LEVEL 1: Grade Point Average; quality of undergraduate curriculum/course work completed; LSAT score

LEVEL 2: Personal essay

LEVEL 3: Work experience; recommendations

LEVEL 4: Geographic and undergraduate institution diversity; extracurricular and community involvement.

MINORITY RECRUITMENT PROGRAM

Yes; as a part of the overall recruitment program with assistance from minority student organizations.

ABOUT THE APPLICATION

DEADLINE FOR FILING: None

FEE: $25

LSAT: School takes the highest LSAT score and the average of the LSAT scores, with the highest score given weight and all scores considered.

PERSONAL STATEMENT: Important in selecting from among applicants qualified on the basis of credentials (undergraduate record and LSAT); often useful in interpreting undergraduate transcripts or expanding on other information requested in the application form."

INTERVIEW: Not required or recommended, but available for counseling and information. Clarion Hotel, Holiday Inn (downtown), and Motel 6 (on 30th Street), all about ten to fifteen minutes by car from school, are recommended for visitors.

ADMISSIONS TIPS: "Most applicants furnish well-written, accurate, complete, and legible application materials, but failure to do so results in a negative first impression."

CONTACT: Jane Kelso, Dean of Students

PHYSICAL ENVIRONMENT

McGeorge, although affiliated with the University of the Pacific in Stockton, is approximately one hour away; this has been cited as the main reason why the law school has such a large campus. The law school is, in itself, its own university and because of its location fifteen minutes away from California's state capital, California's Third District Court of Appeal, and the U.S. District Court, students have excellent opportunities to observe the court systems and work in government.

Unlike other law schools, McGeorge students stay in apartments on campus, rather than dorm rooms. McGeorge offers its students furnished and unfurnished one-bedroom apartments, efficiency units, and town houses. The school is constantly building, and the school's new recreation center is underway. With a pool, Jacuzzi, basketball court, gym, and good weather year round, most could not refute that McGeorge's physical setting is among its best features.

The campus terrain is level, with most classrooms, library facilities, and student services on the first floor. Some on-campus apartments have been converted for handicapped use, and other accommodations are made as necessary.

Bringing a car is recommended because mass transit is not well developed in the area around the school.

BUDGET	LOW	MEDIUM	HIGH
Tuition (day) **Tuition (evening)**	$11,406 $6753	$11,406 $6753	$11,406 $6753
Books	$500	$500	$500
Living Accommodations	Shared House/Apt. $4500	On-Campus $5265	On-Campus $5265
Food	Groceries $1950	Groceries/Cafeteria $2925	Restaurants $3618
Miscellaneous	$2000	$2754	$3000
Transportation	Car $1800	Car $1800	Car $1800
TOTAL (day) TOTAL (evening)	**$22,156** **$17,503**	**$24,650** **$19,997**	**$25,589** **$20,936**

Employment During School: Yes. Work-study jobs are available for all students (not need-dependent). Over 400 students work in these jobs with salaries of about $10 an hour.

Scholarships: The school offers merit, need-based, and minority scholarships. Merit scholarships are contingent upon maintaining a 2.8 GPA.

School Loan Program (Exclusive of Perkins Money): No

Loan Forgiveness Program: Does not have, but is currently considering implementing one.

Students Requesting Aid: 89%; of these, 78% receive aid.

Average Loan Indebtedness: $55,000

"McGeorge is result-oriented—the school demands results for providing such an excellent environment, faculty, and facility. The major variable the school cannot provide is effort from the student—if a student is unwilling to work and take advantage of everything McGeorge provides to assist him or her in becoming a good lawyer, that student will probably become one of our attrition statistics, not a placement statistic."

Both first and second years are primarily required courses for McGeorge law students, which some here feel precludes their specializing and taking the electives that they want. Legal writing and research is a year-long course during the first year. Most courses use the Socratic method and moot court is conducted in the second year to provide advanced writing skills. The third year consists primarily of electives, with the exception of Remedies. Students find that scheduling, rather than course variety, is their chief difficulty, with most concurring that taxation and trial advocacy are strongest at the school.

McGeorge has had the good fortune of attracting numerous faculty members who are not simply well-published, but who also are strong teachers with a willingness to help students. Most faculty members give out their home phone numbers and post established office hours. Both Raymond Coletta (Property) and David Miller are cited by students as star faculty members. Students find that courses are both theoretical and "real world"-oriented. McGeorge's clinical offerings are far flung and number among the largest in the country.

If you have come to McGeorge without knowing the school's grading policies, you might be in for a shock when you find out your grades. Getting Bs and Cs is considered very good by students at the school. Some students advocate moving from a quarter into a semester system and expanding tests from 45 to 55 minutes and having fewer issues on each test.

JOINT/GRADUATE DEGREE PROGRAMS

Joint Degree: JD/MBA
Graduate Degree: LLM

Sacramento is California's state capital, and students feel that, although the program is rather rigorous, they do have time to get out. Adds one second-year student, "The school spends a high percentage of its money on student body functions and needs." As for competitiveness, most here agree that it is present but that students work together. "Academic pressure is high at McGeorge. Don't bother applying if you don't want to work; however, if you do, you'll likely find people pull together both academically and socially."

PREPARATION

McGeorge videotapes students in mock interviews, works with them on résumé writing, conducts job-search seminars, and provides individual counseling as well as bringing in outside speakers. The school sponsors a picnic for local firms. In one student's words, "I feel they [placement] do an excellent job of promoting the school and student. We have a fine on-campus interviewing program with numerous top firms from all over California and the U.S. coming to participate."

WHERE GRADUATES PRACTICE

3.9% Sole Practitioner; 56.2% Small Firms; 22.2% Medium Firms; 17.7% Large Firms.

3400 CHESTNUT STREET
PHILADELPHIA, PENNSYLVANIA (PA) 19104-6204
(215) 898-7400

REPORT CARD

ADMISSIONS
SELECTIVITY 🎓 🎓 🎓 🎓 🎓

Applicants: 4496; Accepted: 1107
LSAT Mean: 42
GPA Mean: 3.6

ACADEMICS
Order of the Coif (1912)
Faculty to Student Ratio: N/A
Quality of Teaching: **B+**
Faculty Accessibility: **A−**

PHYSICAL ENVIRONMENT
Location: Urban/Large-Sized City
Safety: Fair-Marginal
HA: ♿ ♿ ♿ ♿

STUDENT ENROLLMENT
Class Size: 289
Women: 39%   Minorities: 12%
Average Age of Entering Class: N/A

PLACEMENT
REPUTATION ★ ★ ★ ★ ☆

Recruiters: 600
Starting Salary Mean: New York: $77,263;
   L.A.: $63,500; Philadelphia: $59,000;
   Chicago: $65,000

FINANCES
Tuition: $13,980 (includes $620 university
   fee and $200 library fee)
Average Total Cost: $26,230

STUDENT LIFE
RATING ☺ ☺ ☺

After Hours: Cavanaugh's, Le Bus Cafe

PROMINENT ALUMNI/AE
Include: J. Harold Flannery, Associate Justice, Massachusetts Superior Court; John F.
   Rauhauser, Jr., Judge, Pennsylvania Court
   of Common Pleas

As you enter Penn Law School's main building, you immediately see students congregating around the Goat. No, the Goat is not a sacred herd animal cleverly smuggled inside the prison-tight security of the law school quadrangle. The Goat, named for the animal's statue donated by a Penn alumnus, is one of the many idiosyncrasies of this Ivy League law school known for its solid curriculum, well-organized Placement Office, and its outspoken and involved student body, some of whom are willing to campaign for heated issues such as the Women's Law Group in conjunction with Penn's People for Choice, or for themselves with picture/résumé election posters dotting the lounge's walls.

"It's the kind of law school where nobody on the outside has anything bad to say about it," says one second-year student. "The smallness of the classes is what makes Penn special. At least among second and third years." One woman feels the faculty bring with them a wide variety of sentiment and teaching styles. Few would argue with their professors' accessibility. "I was having trouble in a class and I called the professor at his office. 'I'm having some problems in your class. Do you mind if I come in to talk with you?' There was no problem at all."

Students are quick to point out the overcrowding problem, resulting from the unexpectedly large turnout—30% over a target number of 225—for the class of 1992. "It's just not meant for such a large class." Everything points to the fact that administrators are taking the proper steps to avoid this happening for the classes following, which should translate into an even more competitive admissions picture for hopeful applicants.

How does this new class cope with its overcrowded surroundings? The class, usually divided into two sections, is now split into three. Students also find the size manageable because of the camaraderie among their colleagues. Regardless of their class year, Penn students feel the edge has been taken off because "You work like hell to get in, but once you're here, the pressure eases up." Indeed, Director of Admissions Frances Spurgeon sums it up best, "Penn is one of the few law schools where it's possible to like law school." The school has no GPA or class rank; law review is achieved by "writing on;" and with from five to six hundred recruiters each year, and students averaging interviews comfortably in the double digits, virtually all students are placed doing "what they want to be doing where they want to be doing it." Recruiter satisfaction with Penn law grads is high on both coasts with comments ranging from, "steady if not the very top in performance," to "a rather exceptional group."

Penn was one of the pioneers in the integration of behavioral science and legal education. The school places an emphasis on public service/public interest, partially because of the dean's philosophy regarding these areas of the law. Some accepted students feel that Penn tends to look favorably on interest in public service among its applicants. Penn also offers a public service scholarship. Penn offers a loan forgiveness for students who choose to go into lower-paying public interest jobs; however, due to reported widespread dissatisfaction with the present system, an overhaul of this program is being reviewed by the student-faculty Freedom of Career Choice Committee.

The school's approach to learning the law weaves in elements from different cultures both here and abroad. Each year a limited number of students are able to take advantage of the school's FLAS Title VI Fellowships, which involve the training of students in Islamic social and legal systems, both on campus and in the Middle East.

Unfortunately, when blessings were being bestowed on law schools, location was not chief among them for Penn. West Philadelphia is a "safety-manageable" city if the proper precautions are taken, and with the school locked tighter than a drum, students find that they can make do. Penn's locale does have the added advantage of having other top schools within the University of Pennsylvania system, including the premier graduate programs at Wharton for business and Annenberg for communications.

Penn students are not only bright, ambitious, and hardworking, but they also have a sense of humor. This year the school is holding its First Annual Law School Ding Letter Contest. Categories included are Shortest Ding Letter, Longest Ding Letter, Most Pompous, Best Use of Euphemisms, Most Obviously a Form Letter, and Most Humorous. Only at an elite cluster of law schools, including Penn, can law students afford the luxury of laughing in the face of rejection. At other law schools, the "Dings" might be shuffled off into the nearest paper shredder.

ADMISSIONS

CRITERIA

Among "top-tier" law schools, Penn can certainly be thought of as one of the least "number-driven," and the Admissions Committee makes a concerted effort not to pick and choose based solely on applicants' LSATs and GPAs. Because of the overcrowding situation and the anticipated increase of close to 14% over last year's applicants, the school is likely to cut back on the number of students it admits and place a greater number on its waiting list.

MINORITY RECRUITMENT PROGRAM

Yes.

ABOUT THE APPLICATION

DEADLINE FOR FILING: 2/1

FEE: $45

LSAT: Penn takes the average of applicant's scores.

RECOMMENDED COURSES PRIOR TO MATRICULATING: No pre-law education is favored by the admissions committee.

PERSONAL STATEMENT: Many applicants tend to think of this as an opportunity to tell the Admissions Committee why they want to be a lawyer or attend law school. This is wrong. You should focus more on what makes you interesting and unique as opposed to other applicants. In essence, use this as a chance to give an interview on paper.

INTERVIEW: Not recommended or required.

ADMISSIONS TIPS: Don't send videotapes, senior papers, or other additional information to the school. It has a small staff that is overworked and doesn't have the time to read supplemental information for each applicant.

CONTACT: Frances E. Spurgeon, Assistant Dean for Admissions

PHYSICAL ENVIRONMENT

Given that the University of Pennsylvania was founded by Benjamin Franklin, you might be interested to know that Abraham Lincoln's bust sits on a pedestal as you ascend the staircase to the small but attractive law library. Unfortunately, the expanded first-year class has made many feel as if the school and its library are "bursting at its seams." The West Philadelphia area bordering the campus is not nice at all. The area gets worse to the north and west. The school is a campus within a city, and the campus is green and pretty. The law school itself is concentrated in a quad that is self-contained. It is a small community, but part of a larger university. The students find the campus facilities to be very accessible. Penn Law is only a few blocks from at least two facilities on campus. There are two gyms on campus, tennis courts, and an indoor swimming pool.

On-campus housing edges out apartments for popularity among first-year students, but second- and third-year students favor off-campus apartments. It isn't difficult to find suitable housing.

FINANCES

BUDGET	LOW	MEDIUM	HIGH
Tuition	$13,980	$13,980	$13,980
Books	$500	$500	$500
Living Accommodations (9 months)	Shared House $2250	On-Campus* $4500	One-Bedroom Apt. $5400
Food	Groceries $2500	Cafeteria $2800	Restaurants $3000
Miscellaneous	$3150	$3600	$4500
Transportation	Mass Transit $300	Car/Taxi $850	Taxis $2000
TOTAL	$22,680	$26,230	$29,380

* There may be a significant cost advantage in campus housing, which is probably due to a nine- rather than a twelve-month lease.

Employment During School: Possible, but only after the first year. Students may not work in excess of twenty hours a week while in attendance. There are jobs as research assistants to faculty members.

Scholarships: The school offers merit, need-based, and minority scholarships. Law Special Scholarships are available from general university funds and the Penn Public Interest Scholarship Program.

School Loan Program (Exclusive of Perkins Money): Yes. Some of these loans are conducted through the university's Penn Plan. Terms and interest on these loans vary.

Loan Forgiveness Program: Yes

Students Requesting Aid: N/A; of those requesting aid, 80% receive aid.

Average Loan Indebtedness: $45,000

ACADEMICS

First-year courses are all required, with the exception of one elective you will take in the spring semester. Legal writing taught during the first year is conducted by third-year students supervised by faculty members. It should be noted that many of those teaching the program, although not full-time faculty members, have come from teaching backgrounds, most notably the former headmaster of the Quaker School. Second- and third-year students are not required to take any other courses than the senior research and writing program. Students agree that course selection at Penn is "phenomenal when you can get them," including courses in Sports Law, Roman Law, Art Law, and United Nations Law. "Mini-courses," which are taught in one quarter of the school year are available, adding greater flexibility to the program. Reading courses are offered in order to bring in other instructional techniques besides the Socratic method.

The students here work well together and the atmosphere is amazingly relaxed for an Ivy League school. Penn does not rank the students, so they are not overly competitive. It is felt that people compete with themselves and not with their classmates.

All of the professors are good—obviously some are better than others—but this is more a function of personality than quality. The faculty is very willing to help. Although currently besieged because of the crowding, they make an extra effort to remain accessible. Penn prides itself on the integration of the law with tangential fields such as philosophy, economics, and the social and behaviorial sciences. The case method is used primarily in the first year, with a few faculty members gearing discussion around problems/discussions.

The Law School Clinical Programs Fund was established in 1985 to support expansion and enhancement of the clinical curriculum. There are many simulation courses in interviewing, counseling and negotiation, and pre-trial litigation.

JOINT DEGREE/SPECIAL PROGRAMS

Joint Degrees: JD/MBA (Wharton); JD/MA; JD/PhD

Special Program: University scholars at the University of Pennsylvania may apply after two years of the undergraduate program and pursue a joint BA/JD degree.

STUDENT LIFE

Social life is considered very good here. There are various off-campus parties, occasionally with other professional schools, and on-campus happy hours. Penn students appear to be "competitive in the healthiest way. Penn is very supportive and never cutthroat or backstabbing." 90% of the students are more than willing to help one another (i.e., lend notes, talk about class, direct another student to the best books or study aids, etc.).

PLACEMENT

There are opportunities in clinics, legal aid societies, clerkships, and research assistantships. Second-year students find Penn is much better at finding them summer jobs than it is for first-year students. Rank in class doesn't seem to be a major determining factor, and there is no pre-screening among employers. If a student can interview well, it appears to compensate for lackluster grades.

Students begin their introduction into placement in November of their first year with an appraisal of the job market. They are videotaped and given mock interviews.

Students are able to use the Placement Office's phone to make calls to judicial clerkships/public interest employers, provided that they report back to the school what they have learned, so there is responsibility associated with this. Students who do not have the financial means may also use the school's phone to call employers.

Sign-up for placement is achieved through computer request, and spots are based on student preference. The intimate atmosphere in the school at large also exists in the Placement Office, which maintains an open-door policy to all students.

WHERE/WHAT GRADUATES PRACTICE

A. 79.4% Northeast; 4.6% Southeast; 6% Great Lakes and Plains; 10% West.
B. 77.6% Private Practice; 0.5% Public Interest; 2.4% Business Concerns; 1.4% Government; 16.7% Judicial Clerkships; 1.4% Academic.

UNIVERSITY OF PITTSBURGH
School of Law

3900 FORBES AVENUE
PITTSBURGH, PENNSYLVANIA (PA) 15260
(412) 648-1412

❧ REPORT CARD ❧

ADMISSIONS
SELECTIVITY 🎓 🎓 🎓 🎓

Applicants: 1634; Accepted: 580
Transfers Applications: N/A; Accepted: N/A
LSAT Mean: 37
GPA Mean: 3.3

ACADEMICS
Order of the Coif (1927)
Pennsylvania Bar Passage (first try): 91%
Faculty to Student Ratio: 1:23
Quality of Teaching: B+
Faculty Accessibility: B+

PHYSICAL ENVIRONMENT
Location: Urban
Safety: Fair
HA: ♿ ♿ ♿ ♿ ♿

STUDENT ENROLLMENT
Class Size: 234
Women: 50%   Minorities: 10%
Average Age of Entering Class: 25

PLACEMENT
REPUTATION ☆ ☆ ☆ ☆

Recruiters: 160
Starting Salary Median: $36,000

FINANCES
Tuition: $6830 (R); $10,920 (NR)
Average Total Cost: $14,115 (R); $18,205
(NR)

STUDENT LIFE
RATING ☺ ☺ ☺ ☺

After Hours: Peter's Pub, Caleco's, Zelda's,
CJ Barney's, Doc's Place, Mitchell's, The
Balcony, Metropole, or the giant Sports Bar

PROMINENT ALUMNI/AE
Include: Richard Thornburgh, Attorney
General of the United States, former
Governor of the State of Pennsylvania;
Orrin Hatch, United States Senator, Utah;
Derrick Bell, former Dean of Oregon
School of Law

INSIDER INFORMATION Pitt Law School is a good example of a law education that not only allows its students to have their cake and eat it, but also, from the money they save on tuition and the relatively low cost of living in Pittsburgh, allows them to afford another slice. There are those here who feel the school attracts an inordinate number of students driven to a shiny BMW and a condo with a skyline view. Perhaps, but Pitt also has ensured that a good number of its students are dedicated to the public service partially through its programs and mainly from the dynamic faculty it has succeeded in attracting. Students here point to a "young core of Yale-type professors" who care more about serious legal issues and bring that into the class.

By most accounts, Pitt's program excels in social issues law including the legal rights of the disabled and elderly. The school recognized early on that it was important to teach the law not as an isolated discipline, but as related to other fields of study. The school has joint degree programs with Katz Graduate School of Business, the Graduate School of Public and International Affairs, and the Graduate School of Public Health, as well as with schools at nearby Carnegie Mellon.

For those who have qualms about attending law school in Pittsburgh, you should know that most students feel that Pittsburgh has a great deal to offer in terms of culture and entertainment, not to mention a fairly cheap cost of living. Placement at the school is exceptional, with between 97–98% of students placed by the time bar results are available. Recruiters' perceptions of the school's grads have been very respectable with most placing Pitt students at above average levels in legal research and writing abilities.

ADMISSIONS

CRITERIA

LEVEL 1. Grade Point Average; quality of undergraduate curriculum/course work completed; LSAT score

LEVEL 2: Quality/reputation of college/university; minority status; recommendations; personal essay

LEVEL 3: Work experience

LEVEL 4: Recommendations

MINORITY RECRUITMENT PROGRAM

Yes; The Admissions Office coordinates minority programs. The Black Law Students Association is very active in this effort. In addition, a special section of Legal Research and Writing has been established to support this program.

ABOUT THE APPLICATION

DEADLINE FOR FILING: 3/1

FEE: $20

LSAT: The school takes the highest of applicant's scores.

RECOMMENDED COURSES PRIOR TO MATRICULATING: Courses that strengthen communications skills, critical writing, speech; also logic, philosophy, and government.

PERSONAL STATEMENT: "The personal statement is very revealing in terms of preparation, presentation, writing ability, and individuality. A poorly written personal statement of an otherwise competent applicant can negatively affect the decision."

INTERVIEW: Not required or recommended. For visitors, Holiday Inn/University Center (412) 682-6200; Litchfield Towers Residence Hall/Pitt Dorms (available only from May–August) (412) 648-1206; and Howard Johnson in Oakland, five blocks from campus, (412) 683-6100 are recommended accommodations.

ADMISSIONS TIPS: "1) Apply early and continue to monitor the [application] file. 2) Visit the law school, sit in on classes, and talk to current students; 3) Visit the Placement Office in order to gain statistical information on placement, geographic areas, bar passage rate, and employment opportunities."

CONTACT: Fredi G. Miller, Director of Admissions

PHYSICAL ENVIRONMENT

The school building is in excellent condition, having been built about fifteen years ago. Says one student about the school's facilities, "A dreary physical building designed to induce depression during Pittsburgh's many gray days." There are no problems with overcrowding; each student gets his or her own locker and mailbox. The school has an impressive courtroom, and faculty offices are highly accessible. Two of the classrooms are very large, making it somewhat difficult to hear what faculty are saying.

"Pittsburgh is an excellent, affordable, cultured city in which to go to school, with a very active business, corporate, and legal community." Many students (44% of graduating class) come to the school and decide to stay after graduation. A car is not recommended. Parking on the campus is very limited, and most students rely on public transportation. Cars can be parked at apartments and used for pleasure, but for school, they are not essential. The best living accommodations for a single student is sharing an apartment (sharing list provided to first-year students); for a married student with no children, an apartment in the neighborhood surrounding the university within walking distance or bus ride; for a married student with children, an apartment in a surrounding neighborhood that provides quality education, day care, and private and public schools.

FINANCES

BUDGET	LOW	MEDIUM	HIGH
Tuition (Resident) Tuition (Nonresident)	$6830 $10,920	$6830 $10,920	$6830 $10,920
Books	$400	$400	$400
Living Accommodations (9 months)	Shared House $2250	Shared Apt. $2700	One-Bedroom Apt. $3150
Food	Groceries $1950	Restaurants $2535	Groceries/Cafeteria $3315
Miscellaneous	$900	$1200	$1500
Transportation	Bus $280	Bus/Car $450	Car $650
TOTAL (R) TOTAL (NR)	$12,610 $16,700	$14,115 $18,205	$15,845 $19,935

Employment During School: Recommended only after first year. Work-study jobs are available for all eligible students. Students receive $3.70 to $4.10 an hour.

Scholarships: The school offers merit and need-based scholarships. Merit scholarships are contingent upon maintaining a 3.0 average.

School Loan Program (Exclusive of Perkins Money): No

Loan Forgiveness Program: No

Students Requesting Aid: 50%; of these, 30% receive aid.

Average Loan Indebtedness: $35,000

ACADEMICS

Students find that Pitt's "curriculum [is] strongest in Labor Law, Social Issues Law (Elderly and the Law, Literature and the Law, Gender Issue Law) and lacking in Entertainment Law or a wide variety of Constitutional Law courses." A new group of younger faculty, described as "Yale types," are encouraging students to look beyond the "trade school" aspect of a legal education. This "new blood" are "fun, liberal, and interesting." Consistency level isn't there, but the worst of them is rated by students as "C or C+."

Strong faculty-student relationship. Alumni/ae upon returning to the school often comment that they still contact their former teachers for advice and simply to talk. The program is traditional as well as offering a good selection of courses. The faculty have very impressive credentials, particularly in publishing. However, students wish that some of these faculty members would place a greater emphasis on teaching.

JOINT DEGREE PROGRAMS

Joint Degrees: JD/MPA; JD/MBA; JD/MUP (Master of Urban Planning); JD/MPIA (Master of Public and International Affairs); JD/MS. Many programs are joint with Carnegie Mellon.

Students find the social life fair, although it gets rather competitive around job placement times. The SBA sponsors a wide variety of events. Said one third-year student, "Unfortunately first-year sections are rather isolated from each other, so if you get stuck with a bad section you are basically socially dormant until second year."

The Placement Office is outstanding. Two dedicated professionals willingly assist students in placement throughout the legal arena—corporate, big and small firms, public interest, or governmental agency. The problem lies in the general focus being Pittsburgh. This seems to be changing as more N.Y., D.C., and Philly firms come in for placement. The outstanding individual attention aids those students in search of jobs in faraway places.

PREPARATION

Students are prepared by the Placement Office through mock interviews, résumé-writing seminars, and having their interviews videotaped. There are interview skills workshops for both on-campus and call-back interviews, networking and job-hunting strategy sessions, and guest (on-campus recruiters) speakers at interviewing strategy workshops. One student here feels that placement is "very good with traditional legal jobs, but could improve with nontraditional careers." Students wish the school would do more to assist those not in the top 25% of class. Students in this group are easily placed, others may have a harder time, but within a few months of graduation, the vast majority of the class is placed, and to most students' satisfaction.

WHERE/WHAT GRADUATES PRACTICE

A. 92% Northeast; 2% South; 1% West Coast; 5% Midwest.
B. 2% Sole Practitioner; 23% Small Firms; 10% Medium Firms; 26% Large Firms; 13% Clerkships; 1% Graduate Degrees; 2% Military; 13% Governmental Agencies; 7% Corporations.

UNIVERSITY OF PUGET SOUND
School of Law

950 BROADWAY PLAZA
TACOMA, WASHINGTON (WA) 98402
(206) 591-2252

REPORT CARD

ADMISSIONS
SELECTIVITY 🎓🎓🎓

Applicants: 1167; Accepted: 672
Transfer Applications: 23; Accepted: 6
LSAT Range: 35–37
GPA Mean: 3.2

ACADEMICS

Faculty to Student Ratio: 1:22
Quality of Teaching: A–/B+
Faculty Accessibility: A

PHYSICAL ENVIRONMENT

Location: Urban
Safety: Good–Fair
HA: ♿ ♿ ♿ ♿ ♿

STUDENT ENROLLMENT

Class Size: 251 (full-time); 65 (part-time)
Women: 48%   Minorities: 14.2%
Average Age of Entering Class: 30

PLACEMENT
REPUTATION ☆☆☆

Recruiters: 125–150 per year, with an
    additional 500 corporations/firms actively
    soliciting job applicants via the school's
    monthly *Job Board* newsletter.
Starting Salary Median: $28,268

FINANCES

Tuition: $9750 ($325 credit/first year)
Average Total Cost: $16,050

STUDENT LIFE
RATING 😊 😊 😊

After Hours: The Spar, The Judicial Annex,
    Engine House Number 9

PROMINENT ALUMNI/AE

Include: N/A

INSIDER INFORMATION In one Puget Sound third-year student's words, "The University of Puget Sound School of Law operates like a family where family members support each other. It begins at the admissions stage and continues through the entire law school career to the placement phase." Although it graduated its first class a little over twenty-five years ago, Puget Sound has made significant strides, particularly with Washington recruiters who feel as one hiring partner says, "The school has really pulled itself up and we're looking to them more and more for quality attorneys with strong writing capabilities." Recruiter satisfaction with student writing may be attributed to Puget Sounds' legal writing program which was profiled as one of the most ambitious in a recent issue of the *Student Lawyer* published by the ABA/Law Student Division.

The University of Puget Sound places teaching commitment and aptitude as its primary consideration in granting tenure to professors. Numerous faculty are engaged in research and many have come from large law firms, small practices, and public service and have been prosecutors, adding a real-world dimension. Students have been mixed regarding faculty quality, most feeling they are good conveyers of information, and a few believing that some attempt to intimidate the students. The school's Flex Schedule allows students to take courses from 8 a.m. to 10 p.m., twelve months a year, affording students greater opportunities for working while attending law school. Students also have different entry options including full-time summer entry; full-time fall entry; part-time summer entry, and part-time fall entry.

Among its more interesting features is a broad range of students with many older students, aged from twenty to fifty-nine years, as well as the highest law school minority enrollment in the Northwest. According to Puget Sound's Executive Director of Admissions, Jennifer Freimund, the school does not cut applicants by LSAT and GPA because it believes there are a lot of qualified individuals with lower quantitative credentials who will turn out to be fine lawyers. The school has an Alternative Admissions Program for 10% of each entering class, and among those considered are students who are at historic disadvantage, the physically disabled, older applicants, and students whose achievement may not be reflected in "the numbers." So, if you're finding that your scores may not be all that you hoped for on the LSAT, but you have a solid record and/or you're older and want to work while studying at a law school "on its way up," consider the University of Puget Sound School of Law.

ADMISSIONS

CRITERIA

LEVEL 1: Grade Point Average; LSAT score; work experience; personal accomplishments, which may or may not include work-related accomplishments.

LEVEL 2: Quality of undergraduate curriculum/course work completed; quality/reputation of college/university; recommendations; personal essay

MINORITY RECRUITMENT PROGRAM

Yes; conducted by Admissions Office, Candidate Referral Service, Minority Student Groups, and Minority Attorney Groups.

ABOUT THE APPLICATION

DEADLINE FOR FILING: 5/1

FILING FEE: $30

LSAT: School takes your highest score but does not ignore the lower score.

RECOMMENDED COURSES: Courses that require the use of analytical, written, and verbal communication or logic skills.

PERSONAL STATEMENT: Very important in determination of admissions. "We strongly consider writing ability when we evaluate an applicant's file. A strong, well-written personal statement can have a significant impact on the Admissions Committee's assessment."

INTERVIEW: Not required or recommended. For visitors, La Quinta, Tacoma Dome Hotel, Motel 6, Executive Inn Nendel's Motor Inn, Sheraton/Tacoma Hotel, and Keenan House (bed and breakfast) are recommended.

ADMISSIONS TIPS: "We recommend that the applicant spend time ensuring that the personal statement is well written and has no grammatical, spelling, or typographical errors. We also recommend that they select recommenders who are either former instructors or current professional colleagues. Evaluations from personal or family friends are not as helpful. We also encourage applicants to submit a work and/or volunteer experience vita. Finally, we recommend early application."

CONTACT: Jennifer Freimund, Executive Director of Admissions & Financial Aid

PHYSICAL ENVIRONMENT

Of all the law schools in the Northwest, U. Puget Sound, situated in a four-building complex in downtown Tacoma, is one of the few true law centers. Norton Clapp Law Center is home to the Washington State Court of Appeals, the Federal Public Defender, numerous private law firms, and other law-related enterprises. Says one second-year student, "The school's facility is great. The opportunities for hands-on experience are incredible." Norton Clapp is fully accessible for the handicapped, and the area around the school is comparably safe for an urban environment, with a parking garage for students' cars. A car is recommended.

Best living accommodations for a single student is sharing a house/apartment; for a married student with no children, a one-bedroom apartment; for a married student with children, a larger apartment.

FINANCES

BUDGET	LOW	MEDIUM	HIGH
Tuition (annual first year*)	$9750	$9750	$9750
Books	$550	$550	$550
Living Accommodations (9 months)	Shared House/Apt. $1575	Shared House** $1800	One-Bedroom Apt. $2340
Food	Groceries $1350	Groceries/Cafeteria $2200	Restaurants $3500
Miscellaneous	$900 (annual)	$1100 (annual)	$1300 (annual)
Transportation	Mass Transit $270 (bus pass)	Car/Bus $650	Car $750
TOTAL	$14,395	$16,050	$18,190

* Tuition is three-tiered, in an effort to alleviate annual tuition increases. 1st Year: $325/credit; 2nd Year: $305/credit; 3rd Year: $305/credit; Transfer: $305/credit.

** Studio $210/month

Employment During School: Only after first year. Work-study jobs are available for all students (not need-dependent).

Scholarships: The school offers merit scholarships to top 30–35% of students. Merit scholarships are contingent upon staying in the top third of the class.

School Loan Program (Exclusive of Perkins Money): No

Loan Forgiveness Program: No

Students Requesting Aid: 85%; of these, 84% receive aid.

Students Indebted upon Graduation: 84%

Average Loan Indebtedness: $35,000

Note: The university as a whole has made a commitment to increase its scholarship base by 1% of tuition per year. It currently allocates 6% of overall tuition per year to scholarships; next year it will allocate 7% of tuition for scholarships.

Special: University scholars, a program starting in 1990, which pays for qualified candidates to come to campus and be interviewed. Granting of the scholarship, which pays full tuition for all three years plus a stipend of $5000 for each year of study, is based on GPA/LSAT scores as well as nonstatistical factors and a personal interview. At present, it has not been determined whether or not recipients of the scholarships will be required to perform public interest law after graduation.

ACADEMICS

The first year is highly traditional, with required courses, plus a highly regarded one-year legal writing program. Upperclass requirements include Constitutional Law I and II, Evidence, Legal Writing II, Professional Responsibility, Persuasive Writing and Oral Advocacy, and one of the school's Philosophical/Historical/Theoretical courses. Puget Sound has a good variety of course offerings in such areas as Chinese Law, which examines Chinese attitudes towards the law, Soviet Law, and Street Law, which involves teaching the law to high school students. Environmental Law is considered among the school's strengths.

Puget Sound has an Externship Program whereby students are able to design their own programs with faculty approval and work in areas such as public agencies or courts for three or four credits. Students are quick to mention their school's grading policy, which is rather low, with the average pegged at a C+. Students find this puts them at a disadvantage with recruiters who are unfamiliar with the grading policy.

Faculty are generally regarded as accessible both after class and at other times. Whether they combine legal scholarship with legal application tends to depend on the professors. Says one third-year student, "Some [faculty] are very good at making you think while conveying the necessary doctrine. Others don't just hide the ball, they don't even bring it to class. This is especially frustrating in upper-level courses." UPS has a number of cocurricular opportunities both on and off campus including Law Review and Moot Court.

STUDENT LIFE

Students find that because there is a substantial number of older, somewhat more mature students in their classes, there are few instances of overt competitiveness or cutthroatism. UPS law students subscribe more to the belief that law school is a shared experience to be met as a collective and to come out from as a stronger individual. Among the school's extracurricular organizations is INN OF COURT, where senior trial attorneys, young lawyers, third-year law students, and judges discuss a number of legal issues affecting members of the bar and bench.

PLACEMENT

Some students find that the Placement Office caters to the students who need it least, particularly the top 10% and those on Law Review, but most find that the office is amiable, well organized, and willing to lend support when needed. 89% of graduates were placed within six months of graduation; 95% were placed within one year.

PREPARATION

Workshops include résumé writing and cover letter, interviewing techniques, employer's perspective, and professional dress. Workshops offered include Choices in Traditional Practice; Gateways to Practice, which deals with daily issues; Nuts and Bolts of Small and Solo Practice; and Small Town Law Practice.

WHERE/WHAT GRADUATES PRACTICE

A. 2.1% South; 90.3% West Coast; 5.5% Midwest; 2.1% Other (20% remain within immediate area/city within one year after graduation; 70% remain in the state).
B. 3% Sole Practitioner; 30.9% Small Firms; 3% Medium Firms; 16% Large Firms; 9.2% Clerkships; 2% Graduate Degrees; 2% Military; 17% Governmental Agencies; 9% Corporations; 4.6% Public Interest; 3.3% Other.

UNIVERSITY OF SAN DIEGO
School of Law

ALCALA PARK
SAN DIEGO, CALIFORNIA (CA) 92110
(619) 260-4528

REPORT CARD

ADMISSIONS
SELECTIVITY

Applicants: 3570; Accepted: 1138
Transfer Applicants: 45; Accepted: 15
LSAT Mean: 37 GPA Mean: 3.3

ACADEMICS
California Bar Passage (first try): 75.1%
(Statewide Average: 72.2%)
Faculty to Student Ratio: N/A
Quality of Teaching: **B**
Faculty Accessibility: **B**

PHYSICAL ENVIRONMENT
Location: Medium-Sized City
Safety: Good
HA:

STUDENT ENROLLMENT
Class Size: 256 (full-time); 86 (part-time)
Women: 44% Minorities: 15%
International Students: 6%
Average Age of Entering Class: 24 (day); 29
(evening)

PLACEMENT
REPUTATION ☆ ☆ ☆

Recruiters: 200
Starting Salary Median: $38,000

FINANCES
Tuition: $10,300 (full-time day); $7300
(part-time evening)
Average Total Cost: $18,050 (full-time day);
$15,050 (part-time evening)

STUDENT LIFE
RATING ☺ ☺ ☺ ☺ ☾

After Hours: Rusty Pelican, O'Connell's,
Nico's

PROMINENT ALUMNI/AE
Include: Robert F. Adelizzi, President, Home
Federal Savings & Loan; Hon. H. Lawrence
Garrett III, Secretary of the Navy; Hon.
Patricia D. Benke, California Court of
Appeals

INSIDER INFORMATION

If you didn't know better as you stepped out of your car, you might think you had ended up at Disney World rather than the USD School of Law. Students here praise their school for more than its Eden-like environment, which overlooks Mission Bay and the San Diego Presidio. Faculty use the Socratic method to generate thought and preparedness rather than as a means to frustrate and intimidate their class. Of particular interest are USD's Immigration International and Environmental Law clinics, its summer abroad program and Diversity Qualified Admissions Program.

Students felt that the administration was unsympathetic to student needs, including adequate parking, and merits provided a sounding board but no action. Others stated, however, that during the most recent school year the law school intensified its efforts to get students involved in the proper administration of the law school.

232 UNIVERSITY OF SAN DIEGO

Student at USD have expressed some misgivings about placement opportunities. The school's "outreach" program should remedy this situation. One California recruiter comments about USD law grads, "We have had enormous success assimilating attorneys from USD into our program with an exceptionally low attrition rate. Their work is excellent, and their ideas on an ideal firm and practice are closely aligned with our own, thus accounting for the low turnover rate."

ADMISSIONS

CRITERIA

LEVEL 1: Grade Point Average; LSAT score

LEVEL 2: Personal essay; diversity in background

LEVEL 3: Quality of undergraduate work; reputation of college/university

LEVEL 4: Work experience

LEVEL 5: Recommendations

MINORITY RECRUITMENT PROGRAM

Yes.

ABOUT THE APPLICATION

DEADLINE FOR FILING: 2/1

FEE: $35

LSAT: The school takes the average of applicant's scores.

PERSONAL STATEMENT: "The personal statement may push a 'borderline' or wait-listed candidate into the 'admit' category."

RECOMMENDED COURSES PRIOR TO MATRICULATING: Courses that will develop writing, logic, and analytical skills.

INTERVIEW: Not required or recommended. EZ-8 Mission Valley (619) 291-8282 and EZ-8 Old Town (619) 692-1288 are recommended accommodations if visiting.

ADMISSIONS TIPS: "1) Apply early in the admissions process. Know all deadlines. 2) Try to take the LSAT before February, so that your file will be complete early. 3) Make sure your application is complete and signed, as it will not be reviewed until it is complete."

CONTACT: Cindy C. Butler, Director of Admissions

PHYSICAL ENVIRONMENT

USD Law School is contained in a three-building complex of Spanish architecture in the center of the University of San Diego campus. More Hall is the major classroom facility. Adjacent to More Hall is the law library, which is being renovated in 1990. A third building is dedicated to the law school's research centers: the Center for Public Interest Law, the San Diego Law Center, and the Patient Advocacy Law Clinic.

The University Center has been designed to be the university's campus "living-room." It contains among other things, formal and informal dining areas, a game room, and a television lounge. On the university campus, the students have access to the university sports center, which contains a heated Olympic-sized pool, a large gymnasium, and a weight room.

USD maintains two graduate student apartment complexes. Due to the limited number of these units, on-campus housing is not guaranteed. Apartments are distributed by lottery. Oakwood Apartments and Prado Apartments are both located in San Diego and provide what the school considers to be suitable off-campus housing.

The main law school building has an elevator and one wheelchair-accessible restroom. Both buildings are accessible by ramps in front and by ground-level entry on the side. Parking spaces in the front and on the parking-lot level are reserved for handicapped parking. Although a car is recommended, parking for students will be greatly enhanced once a parking structure is built on campus.

FINANCES

BUDGET	LOW	MEDIUM	HIGH
Tuition (full-time day)	$10,300	$10,300	$10,300
Tuition (part-time evening)	$7300	$7300	$7300
Books	$550	$550	$550
Living Accommodations (9 months)	Shared House* $3285	On-Campus $3600	One-Bedroom Apt. $5535
Food	Groceries $2000	Groceries $2000	Restaurants $3600
Miscellaneous	$800	$1000	$1200
Transportation	Car $600	Car $600	Car $600
TOTAL (FT day) TOTAL (PT evening)	$17,535 $14,535	$18,050 $15,050	$21,785 $18,785

* Shared Apartment: $3510

Employment During School: Recommended if studies allow the time. School provides both need-based and non-need-based jobs. The positions pay $6.50 to $7.50 an hour.

Scholarships: The school offers merit and need-based scholarships. Merit scholarships are awarded to those in the top 15–20% of the class.

School Loan Program (Exclusive of Perkins Money): Yes. The school offers a Tuition Credit Loan Program. The amount awarded is similar to the Perkins—generally in the $1000–2000 range per year. Eligibility is similar to the Perkins as well. The interest rate is 7%. Repayment starts one year after completion.

Loan Forgiveness Program: No

Students Requesting Aid: 70-75%; of these, 75% receive aid.

Students Indebted upon Graduation: 75%

Average Loan Indebtedness: N/A

ACADEMICS

USD has a large number of required courses both during the first year, which is all required, and the second year, which allows room for some electives. The third year is all electives, with the exception of Professional Responsibility. Lawyering skills are integral to the program and are taught in both the first and second years. Students find that Lawyering Skills II builds well on what they learn in the first year, further strengthening their written and oral communication skills.

USD law students are highly mixed regarding their faculty, many arguing that their faculty are made up from both practicing attorneys and judges along with academicians. Faculty stars include Kenneth Culp Davis, Bernard Siegan, and Herbert Peterfreund.

The general sentiment among students is that the school adeptly combines research and real-world elements of legal instruction. Specifically, students praise the school's clinical programs in Immigration and Environmental Law. Course variety does not seem to be the problem as much as scheduling, which many, particularly evening students, feel is unfair, forcing them to take day classes during their graduating year although many of them work. Conversely, day students often are forced to take evening courses. Students may accelerate the completion of their degree requirements by attending summer sessions. Normally one semester, in either day or evening division, may be saved by attending two summer sessions. Summer abroad programs in England, France, Ireland, Mexico, Poland, and the USSR are available.

JOINT/GRADUATE DEGREE PROGRAMS

Joint Degrees: JD/MBA; JD/MIB (Master in International Business); JD/MIR (Master in International Relations)
Graduate Degrees: Master in Comparative Law; LLM

STUDENT LIFE

One of the strongest features of USD is its students, who regard their classmates as professional and including only a few "cutthroats" who have been known to rip pages from books in the library during exam time. Student organizations include the Black Students Association and Asian Pacific Student Association. The Student Bar Association sponsors social events and guest speakers and provides assistance to first-year students. Students say that if you like outdoor sports, you're in luck.

PLACEMENT

Students praise the Placement Office's "outreach" program. The school has groups of employers from select states, often from firms in neighboring states, which interview on campus each semester. 92% of the class are placed within one year after graduation.

PREPARATION

The Placement Office prepares students through videotaped mock interviews with alumni/ae recruiters, workshops with panels of law firm recruiters, and individual counseling sessions on résumé development and job-search strategy.

WHERE/WHAT GRADUATES PRACTICE

A. 7% Northeast; 2% South; 75% West Coast; 16% Midwest. (38% remain in the immediate area/city within one year after graduation.)
B. 0.6% Sole Practitioner; 38.2% Small Firms; 12% Medium Firms; 30% Large Firms; 3.1% Clerkships; 14% Governmental Agencies; 1.1% Corporations; 1% Public Interest.

UNIVERSITY OF SOUTHERN CALIFORNIA
The Law Center

UNIVERSITY PARK
LOS ANGELES, CALIFORNIA (CA) 90089-0071
(213) 743-7331

REPORT CARD

ADMISSIONS
SELECTIVITY 🎓🎓🎓🎓

Applications: 3450; Accepted: 640
Transfer Applications: 100+; Accepted: 10
LSAT Mean: 42   GPA Mean: 3.5

ACADEMICS
Order of the Coif (1929)
California Bar Passage Rate (first try): 86.4%
   (ABA Statewide Average: 72.2%)
Faculty to Student Ratio: 1:11
Quality of Teaching: B+
Faculty Accessibility: A−/B+

PHYSICAL ENVIRONMENT
Location: Urban/Very Large City
Safety: Marginal–Poor
HA: ♿ ♿ ♿

STUDENT ENROLLMENT
Class Size: 185
Women: 43%   Minorities: 26% (includes
   Asians)
Average Age of Entering Class: 25

PLACEMENT
REPUTATION ★★★★

Recruiters: 350–400
Starting Salary Mean: $52,500

FINANCES
Tuition: $15,316
Average Total Cost: $25,626

STUDENT LIFE
RATING ☺ ☺

After Hours: West side of L.A. near UCLA

PROMINENT ALUMNI/AE
Include: Malcolm Lucas, Chief Justice,
   California Supreme Court; David Eagleson,
   Associate Justice, California Supreme
   Court; Marcus Kaufman and Joyce
   Kennard, both Associate Justices, California
   Supreme Court

INSIDER INFORMATION

It is late fall. While many other parts of the nation are suffering from cold rainy weather, a relaxed group of USC law students are sitting outside on the cement steps leading up to the law center in ninety degree sunshine talking casually about law and life in general. Another group is stretched out on park benches arranged around a fountain immediately in front of the modern USC law center. Inside the law center, affixed to a bulletin board is a poster of "L.A. Law's" Leyland McKenzie urging onlookers to do *pro bono* work.

The USC campus is a 150-acre educational park, only three miles south of the Los Angeles Civic Center. Its location in the downtown area, however, makes it a big safety concern of the students. All of the students we spoke to told us that they preferred not to live in the school's housing, the Law House, because it was not safe to travel from the accommodations to the law center.

USC prides itself on being a small school and providing its students with individualized attention. During the fall semester, first-year students are invited to luncheon with the faculty and later to a dinner with the faculty at the dean's home. Later in the spring, they attend a luncheon for students and alumni and are paired with a graduate practicing in the field in which they are interested.

Despite the very high cost of attending USC students have noted that the Financial Aid Office has been generous in providing loans, scholarships and grants. "The school teaches you to be a lawyer," one student stated. USC is known for its international and entertainment law. Students attend several schoolwide events each year, including the Roth Lectureship, which brings an eminent jurist and scholar to the campus in the fall. The law center has established formal faculty exchanges with law schools in among other areas, Israel, England, and China. Numerous courses and clinical experiences are offered as well.

Students are satisfied with the placement opportunities here, and the fact that there is "tremendous networking with alumni" was noted. Recruiters, particularly along both coasts, are satisfied with USC student's presentation skills, both oral and written.

ADMISSIONS

CRITERIA

LEVEL 1: Grade Point Average; LSAT score; quality of undergraduate curriculum/ course work completed; quality/reputation of undergraduate university/college attended

LEVEL 2: Recommendations; personal essay; "The diversity a student can contribute to the law center student body."

LEVEL 3: Work experience

MINORITY RECRUITMENT PROGRAM

Yes; all minority associations assist with recruitment of quality minority applicants.

ABOUT THE APPLICATION

DEADLINE FOR FILING: 3/1

FEE: $35

LSAT: The school takes the average of the scores unless the second score well exceeds the first score and an explanation is given.

RECOMMENDED COURSES PRIOR TO MATRICULATING: Any courses that would develop the applicant's writing and analytical skills.

PERSONAL STATEMENT: "The personal statement is important to the extent that it illustrates the level of the applicant's writing and analytical skills and addresses specific points on the application.

INTERVIEW: Not required or recommended. University Hilton is located across the street from the campus for those who wish to visit.

ADMISSIONS TIPS: 1) Applications should be completed on a timely basis, prior to deadline if possible. 2) Personal statement should address any noticeable discrepancies in the academic record. 3) Applicant, if at all possible, should include one or two academic recommendations.

CONTACT: Diana Beyer, Director of Admissions

PHYSICAL ENVIRONMENT

The law school portion of this compact campus is contained in a modern building that is currently undergoing renovations. The school is located in downtown Los Angeles. Safety is an important concern here. All of the students spoken with stated that, while it was relatively safe to stay within the confines of the campus, beyond the perimeter was unsafe. Because of that, students did not recommend staying at Law House, the school's dormitories that are located a couple of blocks from campus. Approximately 25% of USC law students live in on-campus housing during the first year. Students are not guaranteed on-campus housing. The most cost-effective accommodations for a single student are a shared apartment, for a married student, with or without children, an off-campus apartment.

Both students and the administration recommend bringing a car. Los Angeles is a sprawling city, and the campus is some distance from a number of popular locations and suburbs.

FINANCES

BUDGET	LOW	MEDIUM	HIGH
Tuition	$15,316	$15,316	$15,316
Books	$600	$600	$600
Living Accommodations (9 months)	Shared Apt. $4000	One-Bedroom Apt. $5000	On-Campus $6500
Food	Groceries $1620	Meal Plan $2200	Restaurants $2800
Miscellaneous	$1000	$1700	$3000
Transportation	Car $810	Car $810	Car $810
TOTAL	$23,346	$25,626	$29,026

Employment During School: Not recommended during first year. During second and third year, OK. Work-study jobs are available to eligible students. These need-dependent positions pay $9.00 an hour.

Scholarships: The school offers merit and need-based scholarships. Merit scholarships are not contingent upon GPA.

School Loan Program (Exclusive of Perkins Money): Yes. The loans are only available after all other possibilities have been exhausted (i.e., student must first take all other available loans [Stafford, Perkins, SLS, Law Access], and since these are almost always enough to meet their expenses, the only time law center loan funds are used is when they are turned down for the other loans.

Loan Forgiveness Program: Yes; for the first three years of eligible employment, the law center advances funds in the form of a loan to assist the graduate in making higher loan payments. After three years in eligible employment, this loan is forgiven in part, and after six years it is forgiven entirely.

Students Requesting Aid: 70 + %; of these, 70% + receive aid.

Students Indebted upon Graduation: 65%

Average Loan Indebtedness: $25,000

ACADEMICS

The first year consists of eight required courses. Other than taking Professional Responsibility and an upper division writing requirement, second- and third-year students may choose from a wide variety of electives, ranging from Law and Aging to Legal Aspects of Motion Picture Production. Most students take nearly all of the basic courses given in these years. Included in their education are seminars, clinical instruction and supervised writing and editing opportunities. Two types of clinical courses are available: those that provide training through simulation and those that permit the student actually to practice law under the supervision of an attorney. Clinical offerings of the latter category include the Post Conviction Prisoners Project and the Public Interest Law Project. A judicial Law Clerk internship is offered as well in which the student is assigned to state and federal judges to do legal research and other duties.

Class size is relatively small and is divided into three sections. Faculty are considered well informed and accessible. Star faculty include Dean Jerry Wiley (Torts) and Irwin Chermerinsky (Civil Procedure, Federal Torts).

JOINT DEGREE PROGRAMS

Joint Degrees: JD/MBA; JD/MBT; JD/MSW; JD/MPA (Master of Public Administration); JD/PhD (Economics); JD/MA (Religion); JD/MA (Industrial Relations); JD/MA (Communications Management); JD/MA (Economics)

The Entertainment Law Society, the Environmental Law Society, and the International Law Society are some of the organizations at USC. Students do not stay around the campus after dark, but meet at places near UCLA.

91% of the class of 1988 had jobs at the time of graduation.

PREPARATION

Students are prepared through workshops and seminars featuring attorney panelists; individual sessions with the placement director; videotaped mock interviews critiqued with the student and placement director; and numerous reference and publication guides on résumé writing, areas of practice, and interviewing techniques.

WHERE/WHAT GRADUATES PRACTICE

A. 83% of students practice law on the West coast.
B. 27% Small Firms; 33% Medium Firms; 35% Large Firms; 2% Clerkships; 7–8% Governmental Agencies; 2% Corporations; 2% Public Interest.

STANFORD UNIVERSITY
Stanford Law School

CROWN QUADRANGLE
STANFORD, CALIFORNIA (CA) 94305-8610
(415) 723-4521

REPORT CARD

ADMISSIONS
SELECTIVITY 🎓 🎓 🎓 🎓 🎓

Applicants: 5253; Accepted: 465
LSAT Mean: 43   GPA Mean: 3.65

PLACEMENT
REPUTATION ☆ ☆ ☆ ☆

Recruiters: 600
Starting Salary Mean: N/A

ACADEMICS

Order of the Coif (1912)
California Bar Passage (first try): 86%
  (ABA State Average: 72.2%)
Faculty to Student Ratio: N/A
Quality of Teaching: B+
Faculty Accessibility: A

FINANCES

Tuition: $14,168
Average Total Cost: $24,334

PHYSICAL ENVIRONMENT

Location: Small City
Safety: Very Good
HA: ♿ ♿ ♿ ♿

STUDENT LIFE
RATING ☺ ☺ ☺ ☺ ☺

After Hours: The Dutch Goose, the Tied
  House, Applewood Inn

STUDENT ENROLLMENT

Class Size: 170
Women: 42%   Minorities: N/A
Average Age of Entering Class: Over 50%
  out of college for over two years.

PROMINENT ALUMNI/AE

Include: Pamela A. Rymer, Judge, U.S.
  District Court, California; Philip M. Saeta,
  Judge, Superior Court of California, Los
  Angeles County

INSIDER INFORMATION

If Shangri-La had established a law school, it might have been like Stanford, if they were lucky enough. "Stanford is a law school with a human face. If you want to receive an excellent legal education in a personal, friendly, and supportive environment where people of all positions know and care about each other, I am convinced that there is no better place than Stanford," says one third-year student here interested in pursuing a future career in public service. Or, if you're interested in working for one of the several hundred recruiters lined up to lure Stanford grads away from public interest jobs you will seldom be disappointed—everyone at Stanford Law School gets job offers and good ones at that. Recruiters from all parts of the country remark on the stellar performances among Stanford Law grads. Says one particularly impressed Midwest recruiter, "They're virtually the only law school we've seen where you just can't lose by hiring any of them [the students]."

And although you might think that, with a grading system that separates students by tenths of a point, i.e., 3.2 versus 3.3 as a grade, there would be some competition, this is not the case at Stanford Law. In fact, talking about grades, and/or the fact that you came to the school with something particularly impressive in your background are taboo topics at this school. Course offerings are almost too diverse, with so little emphasis placed on traditional law courses that students recently had to fight to get Copyright Law, causing the school to bring in an adjunct professor in the same semester that Global Warming and Subordination were offered. Says one student referring to Stanford's course offerings, "Stanford tends to deemphasize the 'meat and potatoes' in favor of dessert."

"In one of our first-year courses, we had a woman professor who had never taught at Stanford before. She addressed all of us [the students] by Ms. and Mr., relying on her experiences at Harvard. Finally, after a few weeks, one student got up and said, 'Will you please call us by our first names?' After that she did. All professors call the students by their first names, and many of the students call the professors by their first names as well." This goes for both inside and outside of class, and students have no trouble locating faculty members as mentors.

Some here feel that Stanford Law "has been turned into a giant hot tub" with emotionality highly encouraged among classmates and in class discussion. "People tend to argue issues using their experiences and little else." And Stanford provides more than enough opportunities for students to study and indulge themselves in the beauty of their surroundings. "That's the difference between Stanford and Harvard and Yale. People here have alternatives to studying." Alternatives include tennis courts, a golf course, and the chance to get a tan while their Northeast Coast counterparts fight off frostbite.

"If you have the initiative and you are willing to work you can do it. You won't face the bureaucratic obstacles as at other law schools, perhaps because the school is on the less tradition-bound West Coast. The school's Public Interest Fund didn't have enough money. Students approached Dean Brest for matching funds, and he challenged them to raise money from law firms. The school matched the money dollar for dollar." Stanford may break some traditions, but it has put in place one of its own: a tradition of "painless legal study," where the graduates coming out are as satisfied, if not more so, than the ones going in.

ADMISSIONS

CRITERIA

LEVEL 1: LSAT and GPA

Stanford uses an index made up of factors including GPA, LSAT, and quality of the undergraduate university(ies)/college(s) attended by the applicant. Students above the Index number designated by the school are automatically accepted. Applicants in a specified range are in consideration, and applicants below a specified number are automatically not in consideration for admission. Geographical diversity is not considered a strong factor in determining applicant selection. For older applicants, it is important to tell the school "what you've been doing since graduating from college." Sending a résumé is optional. Stanford has rolling admissions.

MINORITY RECRUITMENT PROGRAM

Yes; the Admissions Office personnel, including a minority student recruitment assistant, the Minority Recruitment Committee, and the local Black Law Students Association chapter conduct the program.

ABOUT THE APPLICATION

DEADLINE FOR FILING: 3/1

FEE: $50

LSAT: Judged on a case-by-case basis.

RECOMMENDED COURSES PRIOR TO MATRICULATING: None.

PERSONAL STATEMENT: Applicants are encouraged to describe, in about two pages, how factors, including advanced studies, significant work experience, publications, extracurricular or community activities, and cultural or political projects relate to their law school studies or their careers.

INTERVIEW: Interviews are not part of the admissions process.

ADMISSIONS TIPS: Although the deadline for applications is March 1, the Admissions Committee begins consideration of applications in January. It is therefore to your advantage to have your file completed as early as possible, preferably by February 1.

CONTACT: Sally Dickson, Assistant Dean

PHYSICAL ENVIRONMENT

Situated in Palo Alto, thirty-five miles south of San Francisco, the law school is located at the center of the university campus in the Crown Quadrangle, a modern four-building complex. The complex includes the Crown Library, classrooms, a moot courtroom, offices and meeting rooms for faculty and student organizations, a student lounge and snack bar, and Kresge Auditorium and Mark Taper Law Center, a recreation and meeting facility opened in 1987.

You might be surprised to find out how expensive off-campus housing is at Stanford. However, the school has Crothers Hall, an on-campus dormitory that is located one block away. Stanford "is an insulated campus" where people can ride bicycles, play softball, etc.; it is rather idyllic. Stanford has a Disability Resource Center, and is considered very good for the handicapped. The large size of the campus may create some problems. The school is willing to accommodate individual students' needs. This past year the school library set up a machine on which a quadriplegic student was able to work using his mouth.

Stanford provides housing for nearly 50% of its graduate students. Housing is guaranteed to all new matriculating students who apply by a specified date (for 1989-90, May 15) and are willing to live in any residence for which they are eligible. The university is also generally able to meet the housing demand of continuing graduate students willing to live in any graduate residence. Crothers Hall is a coed dorm for single graduate students located two blocks from the law school and adjacent to the Mark Taper Law Student Center. Although law students are given priority there, Raines House, fully furnished, fully equipped, and also on-campus, is preferred and hard to get. Married couples, with and without children, are eligible for housing in Escondido Village, a 3500-resident campus community. This area has, among other things, an elementary school, several nursery schools, and childcare programs on the grounds. Palo Alto is its own thriving legal community and is "just far enough away (forty minutes to an hour) from San Francisco but isn't really a suburb." Students strongly recommend taking a car to school.

FINANCES

BUDGET	LOW	MEDIUM	HIGH
Tuition (annual first year)	$14,168	$14,168	$14,168
Books	$840	$840	$840
Living Accommodations (9 months)	Shared Apt. $4500	On-Campus $5256	One-Bedroom Apt. $5400
Food	Groceries $1000	Cafeteria $1750	Restaurants $3000
Miscellaneous	$900	$1700	$3000
Transportation	Bike/Car $450	Car $620	Car $620
TOTAL	$21,858	$24,334	$27,028

Note: A program of financial assistance exists for those students who choose to spend a summer in unpaid or low-paying service work. The school needs to publicize and emphasize fellowship opportunities.

School Loan Program (Exclusive of Perkins Money): Yes. Stanford Law School has a limited amount of loan funds. Interest is waived while the borrower is a student.

Loan Forgiveness Program: Yes, Public Interest Low Income Protection Plan (PILIPP) for graduates who take low-paying, public interest jobs and have substantial educational debt.

Subject to the availability of funds, the school will lend to eligible applicants money to help meet monthly education loan payments. If the graduate stays in a low-paying, public interest job for a period of years, a portion of the law school loans may be forgiven.

Students Requesting Aid: N/A

Average Loan Indebtedness: N/A

ACADEMICS

First-year students break up into sections of sixty people with one small section of about twenty. Because the small sections rotate, students get to know their classmates. Unlike other law schools, Stanford helps ease the transition for first-year students, who are often intimidated upon entering.

There is a lot of simulation in the classes, and Stanford uses some adjunct professors from law firms in the Bay Area. The Socratic method is minimal, and when it does exist, it is relaxed. In most classes, students can say they are not prepared or "Pass." Even in classes with cold calling, if professors see that a student is uncomfortable with a question, they will ask someone else. Constitutional Law is particularly strong. Other special study programs include Law and Business, Public Interest Law, Law and Economics, Comparative and International Law, and Public Policy and Administration. As far as taking classes outside the law school, it is somewhat difficult because students in the school you're trying to get a course in are able to sign up first, with the exception of JD/MBAs.

Clinical opportunities are good because students have access to East Palo Alto, where the school has the East Palo Alto Community Law Project, which has significant funding from the school. Students do landlord/tenant and small claims work as well as TRO (temporary restraining orders). There's a professional full-time staff of lawyers at the clinic. Students receive credit for the clinics they participate in.

Law Review is open, indicative of the lack of competitiveness at Stanford. Anyone who wants to come out for the Review can participate in a workshop that begins before the first week of classes. There is no quota set on the number of students who can be admitted; the only requirement is that their work must meet Review standards. The Review is interested in attracting students of color and has a positive commitment to this. One student's work is not compared to another's; it is judged on its merits.

Some of the most exciting professors are the adjuncts. Many find the faculty as a whole somewhat "spotty," although there are ways to avoid these professors who tend to be caught up more in research and writing than in teaching. Student-chosen faculty stars include: Barton Tomson, a specialist in Environmental Practices which teaches what you need to know about Environmental Law and weaves in practical experience, allowing participation in a legislative hearing on acid rain, Michael Wald (Child Custody), and Barbara Babcock (Criminal Procedure). There is dialogue between students and faculty, and the administration is sensitive to students' wishes for high-quality teaching. "It's a good school to be a student in. If you want to effect change, you can put together a coalition of students and you know you're going to be listened to." Such a group of students is currently attempting to modify the school's loan forgiveness program.

JOINT/GRADUATE DEGREE PROGRAM

Joint Degrees: JD/MBA; JD/MA; JD/MPA. The school has also established programs with the departments of economics, history, and political science. Students may also develop individual programs with other university departments and divisions, including communication, Latin American studies, sociology, and health services.
Graduate Degrees: JD; JSD; MLS; JSM

There are many student organizations including Women of Stanford Law and the Stanford Law and Technology Association. Says one third-year student, "There is a real tendency to turn the school into a 24-hour hot tub. Emotionality is indulged, even encouraged. This tendency can be distracting, but then again, it does make for a humane environment." The students here absolutely do not play competitive games with each other. Outlines are readily shared. Groups of law students will socialize together without being exclusionary and cliquey. The Bridge, a student-operated peer counseling group, is available to the student body.

Students give placement the highest possible ratings and the Placement Office a 6 or 7 on a scale of 10, with many feeling that the number of recruiters coming to the school is more indicative of Stanford's name and reputation than of the efforts of the Placement Office. Not too many students seem to take advantage of the Career Service Office's relatively limited preparation. However, Career Services does a good job of facilitating interviewing and has also manifested its commitment to public interest opportunities.

Each fall the school hosts a Public Interest Law Week, with information sessions as well as job interviews. Stanford also works with other Bay Area law schools to host the Public Interest Job Fair in February. School-sponsored programs and panels feature attorneys working in various positions. Programs feature different types of practices as well as current issues.

WHERE/WHAT GRADUATES PRACTICE

A. 61% California; 11% New York; 7% Washington, D.C.
B. 50% Law Firms; 20% Judicial Clerkships; 10% Nonlaw, Public Interest, Government, or Post-graduate Education; 5% Business; 15% Other.

SYRACUSE UNIVERSITY
College of Law

SUITE 212
SYRACUSE, NEW YORK (NY) 13244-1030
(315) 443-1962
FAX 315-443-9568

REPORT CARD

ADMISSIONS
SELECTIVITY

Applicants: 2146; Accepted: 915
Transfer Applicants: 13; Accepted: 2
LSAT Mean: 35   GPA Mean: 3.3

ACADEMICS

Order of the Coif (1952)
NYS Bar Passage (first try): 54%
Faculty to Student Ratio: 1:19
Quality of Teaching: **B**
Faculty Accessibility: **B**

PHYSICAL ENVIRONMENT

Location: Medium-Sized City/College Town
Safety: Good–Fair
HA:

STUDENT ENROLLMENT

Class Size: 251 (full-time); 4 (part-time)
Women: 43%   Minorities: 5%
Average Age of Entering Class: 24

PLACEMENT
REPUTATION ☆ ☆ ☆

Recruiters: 122
Starting Salary Mean: $42,000

FINANCES

Tuition: $12,680
Average Total Cost: $21,730

STUDENT LIFE
RATING ☺ ☺ ☺

After Hours: Roman's, Faegan's

PROMINENT ALUMNI/AE

Include: Joseph R. Biden, Jr., U.S. Senator;
Tarky J. Lombardi, Jr., New York State
Senator; Alfonse D'Amato, U.S. Senator

Solid as a rock. Syracuse Law School has long been known as a rock solid school where applicants who were left out in the bitter cold by more competitive admissions at "name" schools sought refuge, put in three tough years, and came out with a solid, if not golden, credential. But after close to one hundred years of sound standing with relatively small movement, recent Dean Michael Hoeflich has begun to chart a course for what was once a sedentary school and, according to students here, the direction is upward.

Even when Hoeflich first took over, students were buzzing about the changes going on. Said one second-year student, "He's shaking things up, but that's exactly what this school needed." Adopting the credo, "Innovation building on tradition," Hoeflich has set out to merge the basic building blocks of legal education with innovative programs combining law, technology, and management; a legal history component; and emphasizing international law and offering a degree specialization in this area.

Most students concur that the faculty's strength at Syracuse lies more in their accessibility than in their teaching abilities, though there are few complaints. Recruiters have noted the new dean's presence and have found most recent graduates recruited highly motivated and personable.

ADMISSIONS

CRITERIA

LEVEL 1: Grade Point Average; LSAT score

LEVEL 2: Quality of undergraduate curriculum/course work completed

LEVEL 3: Quality/reputation of college/university

LEVEL 4: Recommendations; personal essay

LEVEL 5: Work experience

MINORITY RECRUITMENT PROGRAM

Yes; conducted through the Admissions and Financial Aid Office and the Faculty Committee on Minority Recruitment, with assistance from the Director of Student Affairs.

ABOUT THE APPLICATION

DEADLINE FOR FILING: 4/1

FEE: $35

LSAT: The school takes the average of applicant's scores in the majority of cases.

RECOMMENDED COURSES PRIOR TO MATRICULATING: Logic, reasoning, philosophy, and writing courses.

PERSONAL STATEMENT: "It provides us with information about the applicant's background and experiences. It also allows us to evaluate the applicant's writing skills. A striking essay might allow a 'borderline' candidate to move into the 'admit' category."

INTERVIEW: Not required or recommended. If visiting, the Sheraton University Inn, Genesee Inn, The Hotels at Syracuse Square, The Quality Inn, and the Holiday Inn have been suggested.

ADMISSIONS TIPS: 1) Pay attention to deadlines for both admissions and financial aid. 2) Begin the application process early. 3) Be patient!

CONTACT: Cheryl Ficarra, Director of Admissions

PHYSICAL ENVIRONMENT

The college of law complex is made up of three connected buildings, Ernest I. White Hall, Arnold M. Grant Auditorium, and the H. Douglas Barclay Law Library. The law library has been constructed most recently, and students find it suits their needs regarding both space and resources. The area surrounding Syracuse Law varies greatly in safety depending on which bordering area you are in. Syracuse offers on-campus housing, which is recommended for first-year students (45% live on campus) to get to know one another. After that, most upperclassmen feel it's best to move off campus for better bargains. Both students and the administration recommend bringing a car to school because it facilitates travel through Syracuse, although finding on-campus parking can be very difficult.

FINANCES

BUDGET	LOW	MEDIUM	HIGH
Tuition	$12,680	$12,680	$12,680
Books	$650	$650	$650
Living Accommodations (9 months)	Shared Apt. $2700	On-Campus $3300	One-Bedroom Apt. $4050
Food	Groceries $1600	Meal Plan (19/wk) $2400	Restaurants $3000
Miscellaneous	$1600	$1800	$2000
Transportation	Bus $360	Car/Bus $900	Car $1215
TOTAL	$19,590	$21,730	$23,595

Employment During School: Possible, but it depends on the individual. Work-study jobs are available for all students (not need-dependent).

Scholarships: The school offers merit, need-based, and minority scholarships. Merit scholarships are contingent upon maintaining a 3.0 GPA on a 4.0 scale.

School Loan Program (Exclusive of Perkins Money): No

Loan Forgiveness Program: No

Students Requesting Aid: 65%; of these, 75% receive aid.

Average Loan Indebtedness: $36,000

ACADEMICS

The organizational unit for the first year is the "law firm," consisting of thirteen students per unit with a teaching assistant and faculty member. This organization unit is used to hone lawyering skills in client interviewing and negotiation, as well as computer skills. All first-year classes are required. Second and third years offer complete elective opportunities, with the exception of one course in Criminal Law during second year, Professional Responsibility second or third year, and a two-semester writing course usually taken third year. Competition among students is present and at times intense, particularly during the first semester.

Students have found that the school's clinical opportunities are better and more comprehensive than they had expected before attending and are among Syracuse's best features. There are clinics for the homeless and for struggling artists as well as opportunities to work with a public interest law firm in the city of Syracuse.

Star faculty include Robert Anderson (Land Use), L. Frederick E. Goldie (International Legal Studies), Michael H. Hoeflich (Legal History), and William M. Wiecek (Public Law & Legislation, History).

JOINT DEGREE PROGRAM

Joint Degrees: JD/MBA; JD/MPA; JD/MS

STUDENT LIFE

Students find the social life at Syracuse good. There are several student organizations available at the College of Law, including the Student Senate at the heart of the school's student government, the Communications Law Society, and the Legislative Service Bureau. Many social events are organized by the school, including ski trips, bar nights, picnics, and a well-attended formal in the winter. The atmosphere is considered fairly competitive. As one student has stated, "If they [the students] have to, they will work together, but there is still one-upmanship in the air."

PLACEMENT

At Syracuse, students want employment ASAP. That doesn't just mean as soon as possible but also stands for the school's Alumni/Student Advisor Program which is spoken of very highly by students.

94% of students are placed six months after graduation.

WHERE/WHAT GRADUATES PRACTICE

23% Very Small Firms (2–10 Attorneys); 12.5% Small Firms (11–25 Attorneys); 10% Medium Firms (26–50 Attorneys); 7.5% Large Firms (51–100 Attorneys); 18% Very Large Firms (100 + Attorneys); 2% Business/Industry; 15% Government; 11% Judicial Clerkships; 2% Public Interest.

UNIVERSITY OF TEXAS AT AUSTIN
School of Law

727 EAST 26TH STREET
AUSTIN, TEXAS (TX) 78705
(512) 471-8268

❧ REPORT CARD ❧

ADMISSIONS
SELECTIVITY 🎓 🎓 🎓 🎓

Applicants: 4206; Accepted: 953
Transfer Applications: N/A; Accepted:12
LSAT Median: 40
GPA Mean: 3.5

ACADEMICS
Order of the Coif (1926)
Texas Bar Passage (first try): 82.97%
Faculty to Student Ratio: 1:29
Quality of Teaching A−/B+
Faculty Accessibility: B

PHYSICAL ENVIRONMENT
Location: Large City
Safety: Good
HA: ♿ ♿ ♿ ♿

STUDENT ENROLLMENT
Class Size: 559
Women: 42%   Minorities: 20%
Average Age of Entering Class: 26

PLACEMENT
REPUTATION: ★ ★ ★ ★ ⯪

Recruiters: 550
Starting Salary Median: $49,500

FINANCES
Tuition: $3100 (R); $5800 (NR)
Average Total Cost: $10,032 (R); $12,732
  (NR)

STUDENT LIFE
RATING: ☺ ☺ ☺ ☺ ☺

After Hours: Posse East, Trudy's, Crown and
Anchor Pub

PROMINENT ALUMNI/AE
Include: James Baker III, U.S. Secretary of
State; Lloyd Bentsen, U.S. Senator, Texas;
Robert Strauss, former Chairperson, Demo-
cratic Party

"I am graduating this semester, and I am absolutely sure that I made the correct decision when I decided to attend the University of Texas Law School—next to choosing my wife, the best decision that I ever made." It's hard to dispute testimony like this, particularly in the light of most students' positive input about their school, which is undeniably among the best values in legal education in America. Many here feel that the large number of students in each class affords greater diversity and provides more chances for support during stressful times. One third-year student did counter that "the large class size of between 1300–1500 students makes it virtually impossible to know everyone even in three years, and occasionally there are classes of 90–100 students with only 1 or 2 familiar faces." But in an effort to counteract the feeling of what many here liken to swimming alone upstream in a sea of people, UT places students in what are commonly known as TQs, comprised of 25 first-year students and a third-year student who teaches the group legal writing. The group also acts as a social and emotional support network throughout the first year.

As a result of the large classes, there are many organizations designed to serve special interest: Thurgood Marshall Legal Society, Women's Legal Caucus, and many others, including an outstanding extracurricular advocacy program conducted through the student-run organization, Board of Advocates. The BOA sponsors many mock trials (simulated jury trial) and moot court (simulated appeal) competitions throughout the year, which are judged by local attorneys from Austin, Dallas, San Antonio, and Houston. For those interested in pursuing a career in litigation, it can "put students light-years ahead of their peers."

Reasons for the school's successes: Very strong alumni/ae network and a dean who cares as much for the concerns of students as for fundraising.

Students don't think you can get a better education anywhere for your dollar. The school is constantly improving itself with better faculty members, more faculty members, and better facilities.

ADMISSIONS

CRITERIA

LEVEL 1: Grade Point Average; LSAT score

LEVEL 2: Quality of undergraduate curriculum/course work completed; quality/reputation of college/university

LEVEL 3: Personal essay

LEVEL 4: Work experience

LEVEL 5: Recommendations

MINORITY RECRUITMENT PROGRAM

Yes; most recently, the Admissions Coordinator, members of Project Info (minority recruitment), the Student Recruitment and Orientation Committee, faculty, and staff traveled to over ninety events in cities across Texas and the nation to recruit outstanding minority and Anglo students to the University of Texas School of Law.

ABOUT THE APPLICATION

DEADLINE FOR FILING: 2/1

FEE: $25

LSAT: The school takes the average of applicant's scores.

RECOMMENDED COURSES PRIOR TO MATRICULATING: The school advises pre-law students to emphasize courses that 1) require rigorous analysis including mathematics, philosophy, the natural sciences, engineering, economics, and the empirical social sciences; 2) require the students to write and to revise their writing in response to criticism (i.e., social sciences and humanities); and 3) develop ways of thinking that have been widely applied to legal problems (e.g., moral philosophy or ethics).

PERSONAL STATEMENT: "Candidates with certain undergraduate grade point averages and LSAT scores will automatically receive offers of admission. The Admissions Committee then reviews all of the remaining applicants for evidence of other factors that might indicate the candidate's ability to succeed at the law school. Personal statements are not required but will be considered as one of the many factors in the Admissions Committee's decisions."

INTERVIEW: Not required or recommended. If visiting, the Brook House Bed and Breakfast Inn, 609 West 33rd Street (512-459-0534); McCallum House Bed and Breakfast, 613 West 32nd Street, (512-451-6744); and Rodeway Inn-University, 2900 North IH 35, (512-477-0473) have been recommended.

ADMISSIONS TIPS: "It is essential that applicants read the application/bulletin carefully. The LSAT must be taken by December for applicants to be considered for either the May or August entering class. Applicants should enclose the proper application fee; no personal checks are accepted (nor is cash). Additionally, applicants sometimes fail to indicate their choice of the May or August class. Applications from previous years are not accepted. Any of these circumstances may result in the application being sent back to the applicant."

CONTACT: Yvette Gale Scott, Admissions Coordinator

PHYSICAL ENVIRONMENT

The students feel that although Austin is a big city, it has "a small-town feel to it." At this moment, the school is within three miles of the airport. This is subject to change, however. A new airport will be built elsewhere in the next five to ten years. The school has very good accessibility to campus facilities and is within walking distance of the gymnasium and swimming facility.

The university campus is very large, but the law school is much less imtimidating. The law school located on the northeast corner of the campus, so it's somewhat removed from the main campus. Overall, the facilities are found to be excellent. The law school is housed within two interconnected buildings, Townes Hall and a 1980 addition, Jesse H. Jones Hall. Together these structures contain the law library, classrooms, seminar rooms, student lounges, student organization areas, storage lockers, Placement Office, clinical education area, and faculty offices. The area has many trees and hills. The building is accessible to the handicapped. There are ramps, elevators, electric access doors, and handicapped parking. Safety is considered good. There is a brand new, well-lit parking garage and an escort service.

Housing is not difficult to find and the most popular form of accommodations appears to be apartments. The most cost-effective accommodations are a shared apartment for a single student, an apartment for a married student with no children, and married student housing for a married student with children.

A car is not recommended. A shuttle bus service is operated for students, faculty, staff, and their dependents and is provided on all official registration, class, and final exam dates of the main university. In addition to UT shuttle bus routes, students are entitled to service on all Capital Metro buses.

FINANCES

BUDGET	LOW	MEDIUM	HIGH
Tuition (Resident)	$3100	$3100	$3100
Tuition (Nonresident)	$5800	$5800	$5800
Books	$550	$550	$550
Living Accommodations (9 months)	Shared Apt. $2400	On-Campus* $3000	Shared House $4500
Food	Groceries $900	Meal Plan (20/wk)** $1682	Restaurants $3000
Miscellaneous	$1000	$1200	$1400
Transportation	Shuttle Service $0.00	Car/Bus $500	Car $600
TOTAL (R)	$7950	$10,032	$13,150
TOTAL (NR)	$10,650	$12,732	$15,850

* One-bedroom apt. $3150

** Cafeteria Not on Meal Plan

Employment During School: Only after first year. Work-study jobs are available (need-based, not need-dependent).

Scholarships: The school offers merit, need-based, and minority scholarships. Merit scholarships are contingent upon students' being in good standing (maintaining a 65).

School Loan Program (Exclusive of Perkins Money): Yes. The University of Texas School of Law Emergency Student Loan Program provides loans up to $1000 to law students on an emergency basis. Loans must be repaid in three months.

Loan Forgiveness Program: No

Students Requesting Aid: 67%; of these, "everyone who applies for financial aid receives some form of assistance."

Average Loan Indebtedness: $18,000

ACADEMICS

During the first year, a faculty member in each section is designated the academic faculty advisor. Before the end of this year, one faculty member in each section advises you on course selection in the second year. Additional counseling is available from the assistant dean of student affairs. The students interviewed found the faculty in general, competent. The quality of the lectures was excellent overall. The students find that the professors have an open-door policy and are required to have office hours.

In order to graduate, upperclassmen must take and pass one writing seminar. Other than this requirement, second- and third-year students may select from a wide array of courses including Law and Higher Education, Regulation of Broadcasting, Water Law, and Legal Medicine. Seminars are limited to twelve students. The Law School has a professorial exchange program with Queen Mary College, The University of London. Clinical education courses are available for credit, including Inmate Assistance Program, Children's Rights Clinic, Criminal Defense Clinic, Elder Law Clinic, Mental Health Clinic, Juvenile Justice Clinic, and Federal Appellate Advocacy.

Students are eligible to participate in the Texas Law Review on the basis of high academic achievement and demonstrated written proficiency.

JOINT/GRADUATE DEGREE PROGRAMS

Joint Degrees: JD/MBA, JD/MPA
Graduate Degrees: LLM, MCL

STUDENT LIFE

Although the social life at UT is considered good and the atmosphere is relaxed, grading causes competition. It is felt, however, that after the first year the competitiveness is markedly reduced. Students will work together, but it is not essential. Especially during the first year, the student should be wary of relying on someone else's work, because new law students have no way to evaluate its quality effectively.

There are many student organizations. Furthermore, the University of Texas has an outstanding extracurricular advocacy program through the student organization, called the Board of Advocates, which sponsors several moot court and mock trial competitions throughout the school year. Sponsored parties include Spring Fling, Fall Drunk, and Welcome Back Keggars.

PLACEMENT

This school's Placement Office is considered excellent, and the $25/year fee is well worth it. 98% of the students are placed after graduation.

The school's work opportunities are also desirable, as local firms in town pay second- and third-year students well. Austin has an abundance of lawyers—many part-time clerkships are available during the school year. Also, Austin is the state capital, so legislative and state agencies hire many clerks, particularly the Attorney General's Office.

PREPARATION

The Placement Office prepares students through mock interviews. These interviews are conducted by practicing attorneys from local firms and are critiqued by those attorneys to the student at the end of the interview.

WHERE/WHAT GRADUATES PRACTICE

A. 3% Northeast; 8% South; 7% West Coast; 4% Midwest; 78% Texas (Of the 1988 graduates, 18.3% practiced in Austin, 66.3% practiced in Dallas, Fort Worth, Houston, and San Antonio.)
B. Less than 1% Solo Practitioner; 31% Small Firms; 19% Medium Firms; 39% Large Firms; 9% Clerkships; less than 1% Graduate Degrees; less than 1% Military; less than 1% Governmental Agencies; less than 1% Corporations.

TULANE UNIVERSITY
School of Law

JOSEPH MERRICK JONES HALL
TULANE UNIVERSITY
NEW ORLEANS, LOUISIANA (LA) 70118-5670
(504) 865-5930 [5932]

REPORT CARD

ADMISSIONS
SELECTIVITY 🎓 🎓 🎓 🎓

Applicants: 2450; Accepted: 900
Transfer Applications: 45; Accepted: 20
LSAT Mean: 37
GPA Mean: 3.2

ACADEMICS
Order of the Coif (1931)
Louisiana Bar Passage (first try): 70–90%
Faculty to Student Ratio: 1:26
Quality of Teaching: B+
Faculty Accessibility: B

PHYSICAL ENVIRONMENT
Location: Medium-Sized City
Safety: Fair
HA: ♿ ♿ ♿ ♿

STUDENT ENROLLMENT
Class Size: 305 (full-time)
Women: 40% Minorities: 18%
International: 2%
Average Age of Entering Class: 24

PLACEMENT
REPUTATION: ☆ ☆ ☆ ☆

Recruiters: 200–250
Starting Salary Median: Approximately
$40,000

FINANCES
Tuition: $14,230
Average Total Cost: $21,662

STUDENT LIFE
RATING: ☺ ☺ ☺ ☺ ☺

After Hours: The Boot, The Maple Leaf

PROMINENT ALUMNI/AE
Include: Several federal judges, including
John Minor Wisdom; Robert Harling,
author of *Steel Magnolias*; John Weinmann,
Ambassador to Finland

INSIDER INFORMATION

As one southern recruiter very familiar with Tulane's graduates has stated, "Tulane scores highly with a great number of recruiters on 'team playership' abilities. Exceptional. Of all the schools at which we recruit, the Tulane students seem to be the most willing to 'jump in' to any project or function. Great attitudes and flexibility—probably their most distinctive trait."

Admiralty research is unparalleled . . . "We sense that their students are receiving improved litigation research skills. We have found top quality problem-solvers at Tulane. Not only are they fine legal scholars, but they have the spark we are looking for in a new lawyers."

Often regarded as the premier law school in Louisiana by both students and recruiters, Tulane has an enviable position, particularly within its geographical region. What sets this school apart are its young, productive faculty, who are also good and committed teachers, and the opportunity it provides students who wish to engage in the serious study of comparative law. This school has one of the more diverse student bodies in the country based on gender and ethnic and geographical background. Tulane now has clinical programs in eight areas. It further has an active public-interest bent, including a community service obligation that all students must fulfill, a Public Interest Law Foundation supported by students and the administration to provide summer fellowships for public interest jobs, and a loan forgiveness program. The school's international connections are strong.

ADMISSIONS

CRITERIA

LEVEL 1: Grade Point Average; LSAT score

LEVEL 2: Personal essay; diversity factors (e.g., minority status)

LEVEL 3: Recommendations

LEVEL 4: Quality of undergraduate curriculum/course work completed; quality/reputation of college/university

LEVEL 5: Work experience

MINORITY RECRUITMENT PROGRAM

Yes; conducted through the Admissions Office with the help of a minority assistant dean.

ABOUT THE APPLICATION

DEADLINE FOR FILING: 5/1

FEE: $30

LSAT: The school takes the highest of applicant's scores.

PERSONAL STATEMENT: "It can sway us one way or the other in marginal cases, of which we have hundreds."

INTERVIEW: Not required or recommended. For visiting applicants, there are usually on-campus accommodations available in dorms and campus apartments. Off-campus: Parkview Guest House, Columns Hotel, St. Charles Inn, Ramada Inn, Prytania Inn, and Quality Inn-Maison St. Charles are recommended. (Indicate you are a guest of Tulane and get a special rate.)

ADMISSIONS TIPS: "Answer all the questions. Don't leave any gaps or unanswered questions about 1) what you've been doing each year, and 2) any irregularities. Don't try to hide things—be honest. Make sure Law Services has your entire file (e.g., all transcripts). Don't expect Law Services or the law schools to which you apply to be clairvoyant."

CONTACT: Susan L. Krinsky, Associate Dean

PHYSICAL ENVIRONMENT

Tulane Law is located on a large, beautiful uptown campus on lush grounds dotted with many oak trees. The school buildings are old and majestic. However, students find the library somewhat cramped. A new university athletic center, opened in fall 1988, is two blocks away from the law school. The infirmary is one block away and the Records Office is one block away.

Although it is convenient to have a car, it is difficult to find parking on campus or close to the law school. Public transportation is very good. Although the area surrounding the school is residential and filled with old homes, shops, and restaurants, some students comment that it is not very safe. An escort service is available.

Handicapped accessibility is considered good. There is a ramp and an elevator to facilitate students in wheelchairs.

Apartments are the most common and most cost-effective form of housing with a one-bedroom apartment costing $250–350/month. Students say that it is not difficult to locate housing, and thousands of apartments are available.

FINANCES

BUDGET	LOW	MEDIUM	HIGH
Tuition	$14,230	$14,230	$14,230
Books	$450	$450	$450
Living Accomodations (9 months)	Shared Apt. $2475	One-Bedroom Apt. $2700	On-Campus $3600
Food	Groceries $1400	Cafeteria/Restaurants $2000	Meal Plan $2100
Miscellaneous	$800	$1000	$1200
Transportation	Mass Transit $1000	Car/Trolley $1282	Car $1580
TOTAL	$20,355	$21,662	$23,160

Employment During School: Allowed but not recommended. Work-study jobs are available for students. If enrolled in work study, you must have a need. The amount received depends on the type of job and the year in school—for clerical/receptionist about $5 an hour, more for research assistants, and $10 an hour for tutors.

Scholarships: The school offers merit and need-based scholarships. Very few are pure merit, however. About 90% of the total scholarships are need-based. Merit scholarships are contingent upon maintaining a 3.0 GPA.

School Loan Program (Exclusive of Perkins Money): Yes. The school provides $1000 a year ($3000 for three years), with 6% interest. Loan is need-based for students who aren't eligible for other loans.

Loan Forgiveness Program: Yes. Tulane has become the fifteenth law school in the country and the only one in the South to enable its students to pursue legal careers in the public interest regardless of salary considerations by helping qualifying graduates, starting with the class of 1988, to pay back law school educational debts. This loan forgiveness program will cover all students earning less than the entry salary for federal lawyers (now approximately $24,000 a year) in public interest or government work and will relieve them of all debt burden in excess of 6% of their disposable income.

Students Requesting Aid: 65%; of these, 100% receive aid.

Students Indebted upon Graduation: 80%

Average Loan Indebtedness: N/A

ACADEMICS

The first year consists entirely of required courses. Every first-year student takes at least one of these courses with approximately 35 to 40 classmates. In addition, each student is given instruction in legal research and writing in groups of 10 to 12 with a regular faculty member and a third-year instructor or senior fellow assigned to each group.

Second- and third-year students have complete flexibility with the exception of the course in Professional Responsibility. At least fifteen clinical courses are provided, including Administrative Advocacy Seminar and National Labor Relations Board Placement. The school has hosted 450 admiralty lawyers from around the world for an intense three-day program on the state of products liability in the maritime context.

Second- and third-year students are permitted to register in other departments of the university for one course per semester, without additional charge, on consent of the vice dean. No credit will be awarded towards the JD, but course titles and grades received will appear on your transcript.

Grading is A − F with plusses but no minuses. There is a curve; if the class is about thirty-three people, 50 − 55% must get B or better, which, students comment, is in sharp contrast to nearby neighbor Loyola.

Opportunities are provided for students to spend a semester away from campus engaging in an activity for which credit is granted. Typically, ten hours of credit are granted for a semester spent at organizations including the National Wildlife Fund and the Reporter's Committee on Freedom of the Press.

Tulane also offers a summer program and sponsors programs in five other locations each year, including Cambridge, England; Grenoble, France; Jerusalem, Israel; and Crete.

Students recommend that you take law courses such as Labor or Business Law if possible as an undergraduate as well as writing/composition. You should "be able to write well." Another tip is to study, then discuss in small groups, to organize your oral skills. It also helps later when under the time pressure of exams. Star faculty include Catherine Hancock (1st-year Constitutional Law and Constitutional Criminal Procedure), Oliver Houck (Environmental Law), David Gelfand (Civil Rights), and Gary Roberts (Sports Law).

JOINT/GRADUATE DEGREE PROGRAMS

Joint Degrees: BA/JD; BS/JD; JD/MBA; JD/MHA; JD/MSPH; LLM/MSPH; MCL/ MA (Latin American Studies).
Graduate Programs: LLM; Master of Comparative Law; Master of Laws of Admiralty; LLM in Energy and Environment; SJD; MCL - MA in Latin Studies; LLM (International Law).

The social life at Tulane is excellent. Tulane recently had an unusually large class; although it was targeted to be 265, it turned out to be 305. Students have class officers who are allocated money for parties. There are generally 7 or 8 class-wide parties per year, including TGIF keg parties and "a rowdy Louisiana-style poster-crammed buttons-and-slogan election for student bar officers."

Students are competitive, but do not appear cutthroat. The students do help each other, but only in small cliques formed in the first year. Prominent guest speakers are invited to the scool. Student organizations include Class Actions Incorporated, the Tulane Environmental Law Society, and the Sports and Entertainment Law Society.

97% of Tulane graduates are placed within nine months of graduation.

PREPARATION

The Placement Office prepares students through videotaped mock interviews. Résumés are required as part of the legal research and writing project. There are workshops on cover letters, interviewing, and different practice settings. There are also individual (one-on-one) meetings to devise strategy and plan job searches.

WHERE/WHAT GRADUATES PRACTICE

A. 9.6% Northeast; 80.5% South; 3.4% West Coast; 4.6% Midwest; 1% Foreign. 42.3% remain within immediate area/city within one year after graduation.
B. 2.8% Sole Practitioner; 25.7% Small Firms; 7.1% Medium Firms; 26.4% Large Firms; 16% Clerkships; 0.5% Graduate Degrees; 0.5% Military; 13% Governmental Agencies; 5% Corporations; 4% Public Interest.

80 NEW SCOTLAND AVENUE
ALBANY, NEW YORK (NY) 12208
(518) 445-2326

 REPORT CARD

ADMISSIONS

SELECTIVITY

Applicants: 2077; Accepted: 826
Transfer Applications: 26; Accepted: 11
LSAT Mean: 37
GPA Mean: 3.2

ACADEMICS

N.Y.S. Bar Passage (first try): 85 – 90%
Faculty to Student Ratio: N/A
Quality of Teaching **B**
Faculty Accessibility: **B**

PHYSICAL ENVIRONMENT

Location: Urban/Middle-Sized City
Safety: Fair–Good
HA:

STUDENT ENROLLMENT

Class Size: 330 (full-time)
Women: 45%   Minorities: 10%
Average Age of Entering Class: N/A

PLACEMENT

REPUTATION: ☆ ☆ ☆

Recruiting Firms: 117
Starting Salary Mean (medium firms):
$35,500

FINANCES

Tuition (three-tiered):
First Year and Transfers: $11,700
Second Year: $10,500
Third Year: $10,200
Average Total Cost: $17,525

STUDENT LIFE

RATING: ☺ ☺ ☺ ☺

After Hours: Student parties, QE2, Lark
Tavern, Quintessence

PROMINENT ALUMNI/AE

Include: William B. McKinley, President of
the United States; David J. Brewer, U.S.
Supreme Court Justice

One of the oldest law schools in the country, Albany found itself in a rut for several years with alumni/ae recruiters advising potential applicants that they should come only if they want to work in the Albany area. But with an aggressive dean, a newly built library and moot court center, and a strong goal to turn an already strong regional (Northeast) reputation into a more nationally based and recognized law school, that rut may well be a thing of the past. These days, Albany's problems stem more from having too many students accept their admissions offers than from overcoming any regional biases in attracting applicants.

Recently, Albany has begun to prove its "push outward" by attracting top New York City law firms to recruit its students by screening potential applicants before interviews. Recruiters commend the school for its solid curriculum and down-to-earth graduates. "But like most law schools," says one third-year student, "Albany is what you make of it. Placement is there to help (you), but it's you who have to show the initiative and scout for jobs. They aren't going to hold your hand." Students would also like to see more interaction with the school and nearby Albany Medical College, which is also a part of Union University.

Albany Law offers the advantage of being a small school situated in the seat of New York State government, which is where many students find internships and jobs. Students find the faculty good in terms of both quality of lectures and accessibility. One student added that the recent influx of new faculty members has led to more concern for students and livelier discussions in class. Due to its high passage rate on the New York State Bar Exam, Albany has been thought of as a school that teaches for the Bar, but students concur that Albany provides a solid grounding in legal fundamentals with a healthy sprinkling of cutting-edge classes.

ADMISSIONS

CRITERIA

LEVEL 1: Grade Point Average; quality of undergraduate curriculum/course work completed; quality/reputation of college/university

LEVEL 2: LSAT Score

LEVEL 3: Work experience; recommendations; personal essay

MINORITY RECRUITMENT PROGRAM

Yes. The Black Law Student Association works in conjunction with the Admissions Office to recruit at various law school forums and fairs as well as to visit undergraduate schools. They also utilize the Law School Admissions Service Candidate Referral System.

ABOUT THE APPLICATION

DEADLINE FOR FILING: 4/15

FEE: $50

LSAT: School takes the highest of the applicant's scores.

RECOMMENDED COURSES PRIOR TO MATRICULATING: English literature/composition, history, government, economics, philosophy, logic, mathematics, and accounting.

PERSONAL STATEMENT: "The Admissions Committee reviews all parts of an application. Their primary objective is to determine if the candidate has the potential to be successful at our law school as demonstrated by their academic credentials, i.e., undergraduate work, LSAT. The letters of recommendation, personal statements, and other materials submitted by the applicant are important in borderline cases."

INTERVIEW: Not required or recommended. If you are visiting the school, however, Days Inn (518) 459-3600, Turf Inn (518) 458-7250, and Econo Lodge (518) 456-8811 are recommended.

ADMISSIONS TIPS: "Apply in the fall, rather than the spring; take the LSAT in the fall, rather than February or June; make sure the application is signed and the application fee and LSDAS matching form are included when submitted to law school." Candidates who have been out of school for some time would also benefit by enclosing a résumé with their application.

CONTACT: Dawn M. Chamberlaine, Director of Admissions and Financial Aid

PHYSICAL ENVIRONMENT

Although Albany Law School is part of Union University, it is about 25-minute drive to the undergraduate campus in Schenectady. There are athletic facilities within ten blocks of the school, including a YMCA and a health club. Students find that the school's location in downtown Albany provides excellent opportunities for inexpensive housing near the school in reasonably safe areas. The school has an escort service to the back parking lot, and most students have not had any major safety problems.

Housing is not guaranteed in the law school dormitory, which is shared with the medical school, so those interested in on-campus housing should apply early. However, any student who gets dormitory accommodations for the first year is guaranteed a space in the dorm for all three years. Students feel that the dormitory may be a good place to make friends during your first year, but it is best to move out after that because of the easy availability of low-rent apartments near the school. An average shared apartment costs between $150–250 a month. 12% of the students live in school-owned housing.

The most cost-effective accommodations are for a single student, a two- or three-person shared apartment; for a married student with no children, a one-bedroom apartment; and for a married student with children, a two- or three-bedroom apartment.

The law school itself is housed in an interconnected complex of older stone buildings and beautiful, newly constructed library, which has a full-time librarian to assist students with the school's computer services, which include both LEXIS and WESTLAW. The law school is within easy reach of a fairly reliable bus system, but students feel that a car is "a good thing to have . . . especially if you want to get away to go skiing for the weekend." Albany assesses the needs of each handicapped student and accommodations are made. The school is currently in the process of purchasing equipment to assist its visually impaired students.

Albany itself is in the midst of a revitalization program, with a multi-million dollar civic center recently completed. There are numerous cultural and entertainment facilities, including those in nearby Saratoga. Given its proximity to Boston and Manhattan and its relatively low crime rate and cost of living, Albany Law School's location may be one of its most attractive features.

FINANCES

BUDGET	LOW	MEDIUM	HIGH
Tuition (annual first year)*	$11,700	$11,700	$11,700
Books	$500	$500	$500
Living Accommodations (9 months)	Shared House/Apt. $150/month, $1350 (annual)	On-Campus $1500 (annual)	One-Bedroom Apt. $250/month $2250 (annual)
Food	Groceries $70/month $630 (annual)	Groceries/Cafeteria $2300	Restaurants $2750
Miscellaneous	$800 (annual)	$1000 (annual)	$1200 (annual)
Transportation	Mass Transit $25/month, $225 (annual)	Car/Bus $500 (annual)	Car $600 (annual)
TOTAL	$15,205	$17,500	$19,000

* In an effort to alleviate annual tuition increases, tuition is three-tiered: first year and transfers: $11,700; second year: $10,500; third year: $10,200.

Employment During School: Only after first year. Work-study jobs are available for all students (not need-dependent).

Scholarships: The school offers merit, need-based, and minority scholarships. Merit scholarships are contingent upon staying in the top 25% of your class.

School Loan Program (Exclusive of Perkins Money): Yes. A total of $2000, over three semesters is available; need-based. Interest is 8%.

Loan Forgiveness Program: School does not now have one, but is considering implementing one.

Students Requesting Aid: 85%; of these, 75% receive aid.

Average Loan Indebtedness: $25,000

ACADEMICS

Albany Law School offers a traditional three-year program that can be stretched to four years for those with special needs. The first year consists of basic courses that are designed to acquaint the student with "legal thinking." The remaining two or three years are designed to further define legal goals, although students are not required to declare a concentration. A research paper is required for graduation; this paper may be completed in a number of ways, including writing a publishable paper as a member of Law Review, writing a paper through faculty guidance, or writing a paper for any course, if approved by a faculty member. A strong feature of the program is the emphasis on small group learning and individual attention. Most classes, particularly in the first year, are taught using the Socratic method.

Students do not find their courses difficult as much as time consuming, due to the heavy amounts of reading required. Some students warn against buying used books because previous owners often have written in them. Buying any commercial outline, such as Nutshells or Gilberts as well as Sum and Substance tapes, is recommended for those who want to do well. There is a competitive atmosphere at the school, but students are not cutthroat; they are simply concerned with succeeding in their own right.

The faculty receive mixed reviews from students. First-year students have nothing but glowing comments about the faculty, and many remark how accessible the professors are. Both second- and third-year students also note that the faculty is accessible and are frequently found talking with students in the school's cafeteria. Second-year students feel that their professors are excellent "teachers," and third-year students find that the faculty has improved in teaching quality due to an influx of new faculty members.

JOINT DEGREE/SPECIAL PROGRAMS

Joint Degrees: JD/MBA (St. Rose); JD/MBA (RPI); JD/MPA (SUNY/Albany); JD/MBA (Union College)
Special: Combined undergraduate six-year programs are also available in conjunction with Union College, RPI, the University of Albany, the College of St. Rose, and Russel Sage.

STUDENT LIFE

Students find the social life at Albany Law School adequate. There is a Halloween party as well as a "Half-Way There" party held during the third semester ("only three semesters to go"). Several students have taken time off prior to entering the law school and, although most of the students are from New York State, many have attended colleges in other parts of the country, so there is a diversity in the student body.

PLACEMENT

Students think that the placement office is well organized and that it has improved during the past year.

PREPARATION

Students are prepared by the placement office through videotaped interviews and résumé-writing seminars.

WHERE/WHAT GRADUATES PRACTICE

A. 93% Northeast; 5% South; 1% West Coast; 1% Midwest.
B. 48% Small Firms; 10% Medium Firms; 10% Large Firms; 6% Clerkships; 1% Graduate Degrees; 1% Military; 16% Governmental Agencies; 4% Corporations; 4% Other.

VANDERBILT UNIVERSITY
School of Law

NASHVILLE, TENNESSEE (TN) 37240
(615) 322-6452

❧ R E P O R T   C A R D ❧

ADMISSIONS
SELECTIVITY 🎓 🎓 🎓 🎓

Applicants: 1500; Accepted: 480
Transfer Applications: 25; Accepted: 6
LSAT Mean: 40
GPA Mean: 3.5

ACADEMICS
Order of the Coif (1948)
Tennessee Bar Passage (first try): N/A
Faculty to Student Ratio: 1:18
Quality of Teaching: A−
Faculty Accessibility: A

PHYSICAL ENVIRONMENT
Location: Medium-Sized City
Safety: Good–Fair
HA: ♿ ♿ ♿ ♿

STUDENT ENROLLMENT
Class Size: 180
Women: 37% Minorities: 6%
Average Age of Entering Class: 27

PLACEMENT
REPUTATION: ★ ★ ★ ★ ☆

Recruiters: 619
Starting Salary Median: $51,000

FINANCES
Tuition: $13,500
Average Total Cost: $20,950

STUDENT LIFE
RATING: ☺ ☺ ☺ ☺

After Hours: San Antonio Taco Company,
Gold Rush, Bluebird Cafe

PROMINENT ALUMNI/AE
Include: N/A

INSIDER INFORMATION

When northern applicants contemplating crossing the Mason-Dixon line peruse a list of high-prestige law schools, they may zero in on Duke, Virginia, perhaps Emory, or UNC. Let the fact be known, there is another jewel of a law school waiting to be discovered. Unlike Duke or Virginia, "Vandy," as its students often refer to it, has never leapt out at applicants from the Northeast considering law schools, which is rather surprising in light of what this small-sized, megawatt powerhouse has to offer.

Students here find that because the second- and third-year courses are electives, they have ample opportunities to pursue any area of the law that interests them. Open-door policy is religiously followed by the faculty, with many attending the students' TGIF parties and as one third-year student puts it, "If the door is closed, just knock, and you're in." Vanderbilt not only offers superior general legal education but specialty programs in the areas of international law and intellectual property.

More than 700 employers from around the country visit the campus to hire students for both summer and permanent associate positions. The school also has a thriving clinical program that incorporates its close working relationship with the Public Defender, Legal Services, and Juvenile Court.

Congenial and warm are the two words most often used to describe the social and academic atmosphere at the school. Though some feel that because of the high caliber of students attracted to the school they are inherently competitive, there have been few instances of overt acts of competitiveness such as tearing pages from required texts and "any written work is ruled strictly by the Honor Code, which is taken very, very seriously." Nashville, Tennessee's capital, offers numerous opportunities for involvement in the state legislative process, and with RCA, Columbia, and other recording labels based here, it makes for an exciting and vibrant array of musical entertainment.

Among recruiters, students at Vanderbilt consistently scored high in team playership, research, and oral and written presentation skills. "The graduates of this school are polished, team players with good research skills." From what a substantial number of recruiters have indicated, it appears that once they discover just how good Vanderbilt students are, they keep coming back for more. If you are considering Vandy, and have outstanding academic credentials, consider applying for the John W. Wade Scholarship, which is worth $45,000 towards your three years of study.

ADMISSIONS

CRITERIA

LEVEL 1: Grade Point Average; LSAT score

LEVEL 2: Quality of undergraduate work; reputation of college/university; recommendations; personal essay

LEVEL 3: Work experience; extracurricular activities

MINORITY RECRUITMENT PROGRAM

Yes, conducted through Black Law Student Association (BLSA). The school also visits many campuses and law days to recruit minority students.

ABOUT THE APPLICATION

DEADLINE FOR FILING: 2/1

FEE: $40

PERSONAL STATEMENT: The personal statement may "help a candidate whose 'numbers' are below normal requirements and can be persuasive in moving an applicant up in the evaluation process."

INTERVIEW: Not required or recommended. When visiting, request a student host. The Hampton Inn–Vanderbilt and the Holiday Inn–Vanderbilt are both recommended accommodations.

ADMISSIONS TIPS: "Observe deadlines; write the personal essay carefully and thoroughly; request information on any program or activity that will make the choice of a law school better informed."

CONTACT: Anne N. Brandt, Director of Admissions

PHYSICAL ENVIRONMENT

One Vanderbilt third-year student feels that the physical building is the school's weakest point. "We are bursting at the seams for more classroom, library, and faculty space. Nevertheless, the current structure suits our needs for the time being. Plans are in the works for a substantial addition to the law school." About 10% of students live in on-campus housing, which is not guaranteed. Nashville itself serves a rapidly growing backdrop to the law school with a reputation as the Athens of the South with a vast number of colleges and universities of which Vanderbilt is unmistakably most recognizable.

Vanderbilt is largely a pedestrian campus with a heavy emphasis on landscaping. The school is located at the fringe of the downtown area of Nashville. The majority of students find reasonably priced housing and bring a car. "I walk as do many students, but all's cheap in Nash." Still, other students and the administration suggest bringing a car because public transportation is limited to buses. Safety around the law school is good during the day but questionable at night. Accessibility for the handicapped is good and the school is working to make it even better.

FINANCES

BUDGET	LOW	MEDIUM	HIGH
Tuition	$13,500	$13,500	$13,500
Books	$500	$500	$500
Living Accommodations (9 months)	Shared Apt.* $2025	On-Campus $3600	One-Bedroom Apt. $3600
Food	Groceries $675	Cafeteria $3000	Restaurants $3600
Miscellaneous	$1900	$2700	$3500
Transportation	Bus $500	Bus/Car $650	Car $750
TOTAL	$19,100	$23,950	$25,450

* Shared House: $150–200

Employment During School: Not recommended during the first year. During the second and third years, if necessary, with local law firms. Work-study jobs are not available.

Scholarships: The school offers merit and need-based scholarships. Merit scholarships are not contingent upon GPA.

School Loan Program (exclusive of Perkins Money): Yes. Vanderbilt Loan offered to students with financial need, instead of Perkins, when Perkins funds are not available. The maximum amount is $4000 at 7% interest, six-year-repayment plan.

Loan Forgiveness Program: Yes; limited program. The Dean's Award is made to graduating students who are entering public service.

Students Requesting Aid: 67%; of these, 67% receive aid.

Students Indebted upon Graduation: 67%

Average Loan Indebtedness: $30,000

ACADEMICS

One third-year student feels "[Vanderbilt is the] best place to go to law school. Very laid back. You can always get notes when you miss a class. Faculty [are] fairly young and excited about teaching. Come here for Top Ten academics and #1 atmosphere!" The first year consists of a required curriculum, which students find well taught and fast-paced, with most teachers using the case method. Class sizes are small enough so that the students have ample opportunity to know their classmates and have individual attention from faculty. Second- and third-year students are basically free to take electives. Many students are drawn to the school's highly regarded *Vanderbilt Law Review* and *Vanderbilt Journal of Transnational Law*. By and large students find the curriculum at Vanderbilt to be keeping pace with the legal profession. The curriculum includes courses like The Law of Work, Corporate Finance, and seminars on Soviet Law, Bioethics, and Immigration Law.

"Our faculty are second to none. They are demanding yet fair. One look at our course selections and you'll see that courses are offered in virtually all important areas of the law. The open-door policy is religiously honored by the faculty. Many come to our TGIF's." Faculty are highly regarded, although a few newer faculty have been known to be less than up to Vanderbilt's high teaching standards. These same individuals have improved immeasureably after their first year at the school. Faculty stars include John W. Wade and Harold G. Marieu.

JOINT DEGREE PROGRAMS

Joint Degrees: JD/MBA; JD/M. Div.

STUDENT LIFE

"I considered a lot of schools before I chose Vanderbilt, and I am very satisfied with my choice. The atmosphere here is congenial, and, since the classes each year only have 180 members, it is easy to get to know your classmates as well as students in other years. The social life the school encourages is probably one of the reasons the school is so friendly with weekly Black-acres, Holiday Parties (Halloween), a formal Barrister's Ball, and the Annual Quasi-Olympics. "We all work hard and afterwards play hard together. There are some cutthroats in each class, but peer pressure usually gets them to be not quite adversarial in the classroom."

"Students here are very helpful. It only gets tight around here around exam time and when grades are distributed."

PLACEMENT

Students speak highly of the school's Placement Office and many find that it does a good job with national private firms but is weaker in the areas of public interest and corporate placement. 93.4% of the class of 1989 was placed before graduation.

Vanderbilt's summer opportunities are far-flung. Many students, particularly first-year students take advantage of summer internships with government offices or the judiciary to gain experience and academic credit.

PREPARATION

Students are given résumé-writing advice through the Placement Office on a one-on-one basis. Interview advice and techniques are provided by handouts, in small seminars, and by student committees. A first-year recruiting program is conducted on campus (ninety firms) giving actual interview experience. If additional help is needed a videotape is made.

WHERE/WHAT GRADUATES PRACTICE

A. 22.5% Northeast; 51.3% South; 17.1% West Coast; 8.5% Midwest; 0.6% Foreign. (15% of graduates remain in the immediate vicinity one year after graduation.)
B. 12.1% Small Firms; 19.1% Medium Firms; 44.4% Large Firms; 15.6% Clerkships; 1.3% Graduate Degrees; 0.6% Military; 2.4% Governmental Agencies; 1.9% Corporations; 2.6% Public Interest.

UNIVERSITY OF VIRGINIA
School of Law

NORTH GROUNDS
CHARLOTTESVILLE, VIRGINIA (VA) 22901
(804) 924-7351/7805

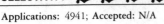

ᕫ REPORT CARD ᕫ

ADMISSIONS
SELECTIVITY 🎓 🎓 🎓 🎓 🎓

Applications: 4941; Accepted: N/A
LSAT Median: 41.3 (92nd percentile)
GPA Mean: 3.53

ACADEMICS

Order of the Coif (1909)
Quality of Teaching: B
Faculty Accessibility: B+

PHYSICAL ENVIRONMENT

Location: College Town
Safety: Good
HA: ♿ ♿ ♿ ♿ ♿

STUDENT ENROLLMENT

Class Size: 393
Women: 38%   Minorities: 7.4% (only in-
cludes black students)
Average Age of Entering Class: 24

PLACEMENT
REPUTATION ☆ ☆ ☆ ☆ ☆

Recruiters: 805 (On-campus Interviewers)
Starting Salary Mean: N/A

FINANCES

Tuition: $4116 (R); $8976 (NR)
Average Total Cost: $11,416 (R); $16,276
(NR)

STUDENT LIFE
RATING ☺ ☺ ☺ ☺ ☺

After Hours: C. Barrister Ball (winter), softball league, bar review, "The Corner," The
Virginian, Sloan's

PROMINENT ALUMNI/AE

Include: John Carro, Judge, New York
Supreme Court, Appellate Division; George
Herbert Goodrich, Associate Judge, Supe-
rior Court, District of Columbia

INSIDER INFORMATION

Virginia has recently been in the national spotlight both for its hosting of the Educational Summit and because of the Wilder election; this may have added some fuel to UVA's growing popularity. This has increased markedly over last year, with the school already mailing out 20,000 applications for this year.

Virginia law students tend to possess fully thought out, sometimes passionate, and very often polarized, opinions about their school. "Virginia is not what you might expect from a law school. The people here are REAL . . . . You don't look at anyone and suspect them of backstabbing."

The Honor System, which strictly forbids lying, cheating, or stealing, permeates every aspect of Virginia's law school. As a result of the school's "B Mean" (most people get Bs), and since there is no ranking, people will not "ice you out" of study groups. "Most people will help you out by lending notes to you or recommending a good supplement." Adds another, "UVA has a balance that few schools achieve . . . . Academics compete with social life and athletics for primary focus. If you like to remember what it's like to be a human being and a law student—this is the place for you." Counted among Virginia's strengths is also a growing International Law Program.

Some students refer to the school as the "University of Chicago of the East" due to its conservative faculty, which students criticize for lacking critical legal scholars and praise for their "growing effort to be more accessible to students." Virginia students also bemoan their school's heavily stressed Law and Economics perspective as well as its paucity of clinical opportunities for credit. Says one student, "The Family Law Clinic and Criminal Practice Clinic (both of which are partially simulated) accommodate very few students." Students are also quick to mention that a "Southern-gentleman" attitude pervades the administration, and there have been isolated incidents of male chauvinism within the school. But some say that this is changing, particularly within the faculty, where students find professors using women in their examples more and more. It has been felt that the friction between faculty and students is slowly easing up, and many point to such programs as the Student-Bar-Association-sponsored "Take a Professor to Lunch."

By all accounts, the Placement Office at UVA is among the most efficiently run in the country, with more recruiters making their pilgrimage to recruit Virginia students than go to most other law schools in the country. Recruiters' high regard for UVA grads at firms both large and small across the country is nothing short of phenomenal. According to one hiring partner at a New York firm, "We've never seen anything like UVA law grads. They're bright, articulate, and very hard-working." Many other New York, L.A., and other firms across the country have similar opinions and comments.

Given that Virginia is among the top values of national law schools, especially for the significant number of "one-year miracles" who moved to Virginia one year before entering so that they could take advantage of the school's in-state tuition, anyone considering law school should give serious consideration to Virginia. If you do feel that this might be the place for you, request a personal interview; they are evaluative and are offered on campus. Make certain that you schedule as far in advance as possible.

ADMISSIONS

CRITERIA

Unlike other state schools, Virginia has a higher number of nonresidents, primarily because it attempts to be more national and due to the number (11%) of "one-year miracles." The school places academic record and LSAT on the same level; however, it should be noted that a poor record will rarely be compensated for by a strong LSAT score.

LEVEL 1: LSAT and GPA. 80% total weight on these two factors. Takes into consideration the strength of your course work and where the degree was completed.

LEVEL 2: Other factors such as "the maturing effect on an individual of some years away from formal education; a rising trend in academic performance versus solid but unexceptional work; financial pressure requiring employment during the undergraduate years, etc."

MINORITY RECRUITMENT PROGRAM

Yes; through the Black Virginia Law Students Association.

ABOUT THE APPLICATION

DEADLINE FOR FILING: Rolling Deadline: January 15

FEE: $40

LSAT: The school generally takes the average of applicant's scores. However, if there is a wide discrepancy of more than four or five points, the school will probably give more weight to the higher score.

PERSONAL STATEMENT: Broad essay. What you choose to write about and how well your essay is written are important to the Admissions Committee. Make sure it is limited to 250 words and that you only write on one side of the page.

INTERVIEW: This is your chance to clear up any ambiguities in your academic record. You will have to travel to the campus. It is the policy of the Admissions Committee to grant an interview to any applicant who requests one. If you are a marginal applicant seriously considering the school and feel you come across well in an interview, it is advisable to request an interview as soon in the admissions process as possible.

RECOMMENDATIONS: Should come from an instructor who knows your work well. Recommendations from upper-level courses in your major are generally better.

ADMISSIONS TIPS: According to Assistant Dean Stokes, it is very important that applicants review the application carefully and begin answers to required questions on the application itself. Applicants who attach separate sheets may run the risk of having associated materials lost.

CONTACT: Jerome W. D. Stokes, Assistant Dean

PHYSICAL ENVIRONMENT

The law school's buildings are tan brick and modern, and the school is separate from the main campus. However there is an abundance of facilities, all within a very short ride on the university bus, as well as an excellent athletic facility within walking distance. The campus is beautiful in the spring. Handicapped accessibility has recently been addressed by the administration, resulting in almost complete accessibility for the physically challenged.

The area around the school is described as safe, and one students attributes this to the Honor System on the UVA campus, which greatly reduces the number of undergraduate pranks. The student dorm is across from the law school, and despite its being very inexpensive (less than $200/month) students do not recommend it because of cramped quarters (you have to share a bedroom). It is not difficult to find inexpensive housing in Charlottesville, with two-bedroom apartments renting for $465/month, or a little more than $230 per person. It is even possible to get housing under $150/month if you look hard and early enough. Students recommend bringing a car because Charlottesville can get pretty small, and there are so many other places to go, such as Monticello and Richmond, Virginia.

FINANCES

BUDGET	LOW	MEDIUM	HIGH
Tuition (Resident) Tuition (Nonresident)	$4116 $8976	$4116 $8976	$4116 $8976
Books	$550	$550	$550
Living Accommodations (9 months)	On-Campus $1800	Shared House $2250	One-Bedroom Apt. $2700
Food	Meal Plan $1350	Groceries $1800	Restaurants $2700
Miscellaneous	$1600	$1800	$2000
Transportation	School Bus $0.00	Car/Bus $900	Car $1800
TOTAL (R) TOTAL (NR)	$9416 $14,276	$11,416 $16,276	$13,866 $18,726

Employment During School: Possible, but it depends on the individual. Work-study jobs are available for all students (not need-dependent).

Scholarships: The school offers merit and need-based scholarships.

Summer Savings Expectancy: Students are expected to work each summer in order to make up part of the following year's expenses. Students working in public service will have a lower savings expectancy.

Students Requesting Aid: N/A

Average Loan Indebtedness: N/A

ACADEMICS

First-year classes are primarily taught by the Socratic method, followed by two years of a mixture of Socratic method, small group discussion, and seminars. The first year is divided into sections of thirty-two students, and a faculty advisor, although students are not limited to that professor for advising. Students take classes with their sections and some classes with one or two other sections. The students are not "cutthroats," and many students feel it's best not to "kill yourself because you'll probably end up getting a "B" anyway."

The faculty are, for the most part, spoken highly of in terms of knowledge and preparation, though students would like to see more diversity in the faculty—i.e., more women and minority faculty members. A few students have mentioned that faculty quality varies from "stars who will really knock you out of your chair with their wit, and others who are simply appalling." Most faculty members go out of their way to be accessible; a few, however, are known to be very intimidating. Their home phone numbers are published in the directory, and several professors stick around after classes or at the cafeteria in back of the school. There is an SBA-sponsored "Take a Professor to Lunch" program whereby students are reimbursed for taking faculty members to lunch. This is designed to encourage student-faculty interaction.

The clinical program is not as fully developed as students would like, primarily because it awards no credits. There are opportunities, under the aegis of a professor, to work with post-convictions and to argue the case on appeal to the Virginia Supreme Court. The Legal Assistance Society also has a program whereby students help migrant farm workers who are living in substandard housing (covered with flies, no running water) by drafting complaints.

Moot court is extremely popular, with an Oral Advocacy during the first year, which 95–96% of the students volunteer to take part in. Second year is Moot Court Competition, which can last up to two semesters (covering four different briefs). The school also sends teams to both national and international moot court competitions. Law Review admits students based on grades (B+/A−) in addition to a two-phase writing process consisting of a canned ten-page paper and a more creative exercise. Each of the journals hold writing competitions for admission. About one in three students do get on if "you're a good enough writer." *The International Law Journal* is thought of very highly by students.

JOINT-GRADUATE DEGREE PROGRAMS

Joint Degrees: JD-MA, JD-MBA, JD-MP, JD-MS

Graduate Degrees: JD, LLM, SJD, LLM

STUDENT LIFE

The class is 55% Virginia residents, but that number includes a number (approximately 11%) of "One-Year Miracles"—people from other states who have obtained residency by living in Virginia one year before applying to the school. There are numerous activities sponsored by the school, including the Barrister's Ball, the Bar Review (sampling different bars in the area), and parties at students' houses/apartments. Overall students find there is an opportunity to voice your opinion, be it through the Black Virginia Law Students Association (does minority recruitment for the school as well) or Virginia Women (very active).

PLACEMENT

We cannot overemphasize the efficiency of the Placement Office. It is felt that more recruiters visit this school than any other in the country (second to Harvard). The first year is more difficult but it is getting better (60% of first-year students will be getting placement for summer).

Placement is good if you want to work with a firm—more difficult for public sector. UVA has a great record at getting first-year students a job. They also have a student-funded fellowship program to help students who want to work in the public sector.

WHERE/WHAT GRADUATES PRACTICE

A. 20.6% Washington, D.C.; 7.8% New York; 4.8% Richmond, VA; 2.8% Norfolk, Virginia; 2.5% Chicago; 2.5% Boston; 2.0% Northern Virginia; 1.8% Raleigh; 1.5% Atlanta; 1.5% Philadelphia; 1.5% Dallas; 1.5% Seattle; 1.5% Charlottesville; 47.7% Other.
B. 75% Small and Very Large Firms, 13% Judicial Clerkships, 4% Government/Public Interest, 8% Other.

WAKE FOREST UNIVERSITY
School of Law

P.O. BOX 7206 REYNOLDS STATION
WINSTON-SALEM, NORTH CAROLINA (NC) 27109
(919) 761-5430

REPORT CARD

ADMISSIONS
SELECTIVITY 🎓 🎓 🎓 🎓

Applicants: 1476; Accepted: 452
Transfer Applications: 19; Accepted: 4
LSAT Mean: 38   GPA Mean: 3.33

ACADEMICS

North Carolina Bar Passage Rate (first try): 89%
Faculty to Student Ratio: 1:18
Quality of Teaching: A−/B+
Faculty Accessibility: A

PHYSICAL ENVIRONMENT

Location: Small City
Safety: Good
HA: ♿ ♿ ♿ ♿

STUDENT ENROLLMENT

Class Size: 160
Women: 44%   Minorities: 10%
Average Age of Entering Class: 24.3

PLACEMENT
REPUTATION ☆ ☆ ☆

Recruiters: 202 (on-campus)
Starting Salary Median: $38,605

FINANCES

Tuition: $9650
Average Total Cost: $17,525

STUDENT LIFE
RATING ☺ ☺ ☺

After Hours: Penelope's, Corbin's, Ziggy's— listen to bands/drink beer, Village Tavern, "The Yuppie Place to Eat and Drink Beer," Michael's on Fifth Street.

PROMINENT ALUMNI/AE

Include: Joseph Branch, retired Chief Justice, North Carolina Supreme Court; Rhoda Billings, former Chief Justice, North Carolina Supreme Court; Robert Morgan, former U.S. Senator, North Carolina

INSIDER INFORMATION

As one Wake student says, "Wake stresses the importance of providing clients with the very best that you can, in terms of legal counsel. So, doing things thoroughly and with an eye for effectiveness and detail is stressed. . . . Wake seems to keep the right perspective, having a great Business/Transaction/Tax focus, but also an outstanding program for litigation hopefuls!"

Most students feel that the school's physical appearance is its chief drawback. Wake will have a new professional center completed by 1992. The school makes a strong use of computers, and students have complete access to them. It is also felt that the school should upgrade its facilities by expanding the size of the current building as well as acquiring additional resources in the law library and should place a greater emphasis on national rather than regional law.

Faculty are praised for versatility in teaching styles as well as their ability to merge practical and theoretical aspects of the law. They are highly accessible. "By and large professors are very helpful outside of class. . . . There is a cameraderie at Wake that enables students to go to their professors with questions about most any topic—academia-related or life-related." Counters another, "Students do not receive enough active counseling concerning class selection." Improved channels between faculty and students in this area may see more students participating in clerkships, trial practice courses, and business drafting courses. The courses are offered, but many students select "Bar Topics" instead.

Placement at the school is strongest in the South, particularly in Florida, Virginia, Georgia, North Carolina, and Washington, D.C.; it does not have as strong a pull in the North. Recruiters questioned about the school's graduates were satisfied with the majority of students that they interviewed.

Wake is very strong in trial and appellate advocacy, as well as a leader in legal computer technology. A unique aspect of the school is that all first-year classes are limited to about forty students in each section. The Legal Research and Writing Program is taught by full-time faculty with sections of about twenty students. Wake Forest, in conjunction with the North Carolina State Bar, with Interest of Lawyers' Trust Accounts (IOLTA) funds, now provides public service internships for summer associates. This program is administered by the Placement Office.

ADMISSIONS

CRITERIA

LEVEL 1: LSAT score(s)

LEVEL 2: Grade Point Average

LEVEL 3: Quality of undergraduate curriculum/course work completed

LEVEL 4: Personal essay

LEVEL 5: Recommendations

LEVEL 6: Quality/reputation of college/university

LEVEL 7: Work experience

MINORITY RECRUITMENT PROGRAM

Yes. Minority students accompany recruiters on individual school or graduate and professional day forums.

ABOUT THE APPLICATION

DEADLINE FOR FILING: 3/15

FEE: $35

RECOMMENDED COURSES PRIOR TO MATRICULATING: Advanced English courses that require significant writing, accounting, history, and logic. Any course that develops thinking, reading, and writing abilities.

LSAT: The school takes the average of the LSAT scores unless there is an explanation or valid reason for not using the lower score.

PERSONAL STATEMENT: As to its importance, the personal statement can help applicants but they "would still have to be in the 'ballpark,' " statistically.

INTERVIEW: Not required or recommended. The school does attempt to accommodate anyone who wishes to visit. Wake Forest encourages applicants to visit, sit in on classes, speak with students, and tour the facility.

ADMISSIONS TIPS: "Timely application. Follow-up when notified an item is missing from their file. Timely filing of the appropriate financial aid form so that the applicant, if accepted, will know his/her eligibility for aid."

CONTACT: Melanie E. Nutt, Director of Admissions and Financial Aid

PHYSICAL ENVIRONMENT

Physical appearance may not be Carswell Hall's greatest strength, but Wake has set a new professional center in motion that has been projected for completion in 1992. One third-year student adds, "Wake Forest needs to improve its physical facilities; while the school has an excellent faculty and student body, they are packed into an undersized building."

Winston-Salem may not be all that you want if you're used to and enjoy New York or L.A., but it certainly has its own brand of charm, with a warm, small-town feeling. Housing is cheap relative to other cities, and students here do not appear to have major concerns with safety problems. Students recommend bringing a car because public transportation in the area is not the best.

FINANCES

BUDGET	LOW	MEDIUM	HIGH
Tuition	$9650	$9650	$9650
Books	$450	$450	$450
Living Accommodations (9 months)	Shared Apt. $1980	Shared House $2250	One-Bedroom Apt. $3150
Food	Buying Groceries $975	Meal Plan $2025	Restaurants $2025
Miscellaneous (including transportation)	$2500	$3150	$3900
TOTAL	$15,555	$17,525	$19,175

Employment During School: Not in the first year. Work-study jobs are available.

Scholarships: The school offers merit and need-based scholarships. Merit scholarships are contingent upon maintaining a B average.

School Loan Program (Exclusive of Perkins Money): No

Loan Forgiveness Program: No

Students Requesting Aid: 75%

Students Indebted upon Graduation: 75%

Average Loan Indebtedness: $35,000

ACADEMICS

Your first-year courses at Wake are all required, as are Evidence, Professional Responsibility, and Constitutional Law in subsequent years. Wake's strength lies in its ability to teach "real-world" courses. In Real Property Security, one student was able to walk away with a "nuts and bolts" understanding of mortgages, but also took with her an understanding of the academic issues, discrepancies, and conflicts. Course variety has not been a problem for students, and the school offers many courses in areas from Business Practice to Public Practice. "I wish I could fit them all into my schedule."

The clinical program, open to third-year students, integrates a criminal law element that overlaps for six weeks with a civil segment. Lawyering skills, including interviewing, negotiation, discovery, and counseling, are taught with the participation of the community's judges and lawyers. Wake also has a very strong array of trial advocacy programs, including trial simulations, the Clinical Program, moot court, and the Student Trial Bar. Some students believe that clinical training should begin earlier, as this second-year student states, "Students should be assigned individually to local attorneys while they are 1Ls [first-year students] to research and write a memo and possibly to see the case handled from start to finish! I think having that practical perspective would be very helpful to first-year students. Note that the practice and procedure classes and judicial clerkships for upperclassmen give them that perspective.

Students find their professors to be very current with the law as well as cognizant of its historical foundation. There is a good blend of academia and practical aspects of the law. Faculty are always receptive. Although professors have set office hours, most here agree that there exists a genuine "open-door" policy, and with a few exceptions, faculty are considered strong conveyers of information.

JOINT DEGREE PROGRAMS

Joint Degrees: JD/BA; JD/MBA

STUDENT LIFE

Wake stresses a feeling of compassion for other students; upperclassmen take time out of their schedules to advise and hold seminars for first-year students. Wake Forest students are drawn from a variety of backgrounds, from the Ivy League to West Point and students who attended Wake Forest as undergrads. They present a striking breadth of interests, including journalism displayed through the school's publication, *Heresay*. Wake Forest has a chapter of the Black Law Students Association, the Federalist Society, and a Law Students Civil Liberties Chapter. Legal fraternities, Phi Alpha Delta, Phi Delta Phi, and Delta Theta Phi also have chapters at the school.

PLACEMENT

"As with most all law schools, I believe, the effectiveness of Placement rests in the Law Review/Moot Court students. They're sought-after students regardless of how many firms visit any campus. . . . The opportunities are there, but Placement can't work miracles. If the interviewer doesn't think you 'mesh' with the firm—that's it." Other students find that the school's Placement Office devotes too much of its attention to firm recruiting and should more heavily promote other options such as public interest, government, and corporations. 93% of students are placed after graduation.

PREPARATION

For the most part students are pleased with their preparation, which begins first semester, first year and includes résumé writing, interviewing techniques, and video-taped mock interviews.

WHERE/WHAT GRADUATES PRACTICE

A. 8% Northeast; 82% Southeast; 1% West Coast; 9% Midwest (15% remain in the area one year after graduation).

B. .02% Sole Practitioner; 66% Firms (No breakdown); 12% Clerkships; .01% Graduate Degrees; .02% Military; 7% Governmental Agencies; .04% Corporations.

UNIVERSITY OF WASHINGTON
School of Law

316 CONDON HALL, JB-20
SEATTLE, WASHINGTON (WA) 98195
(206) 543-4550

REPORT CARD

ADMISSIONS
SELECTIVITY 🎓🎓🎓🎓

Applicants: 1438; Accepted: 432
LSAT Mean: 41   GPA Mean: 3.5

ACADEMICS

Order of the Coif (1924)
Washington Bar Passage (first try): 86%
Faculty to Student Ratio: 1:15
Quality of Teaching: B+
Faculty Accessibility: B+

PHYSICAL ENVIRONMENT

Location: Large City
Safety: Fair
HA: ♿ ♿ ♿ ♿ ♿

STUDENT ENROLLMENT

Class Size: 150
Women: 45%   Minorities: 12%
Average Age of Entering Class: N/A

PLACEMENT
REPUTATION ☆ ☆ ☆ ☆

Recruiters: 140
Starting Salary Range: $21,000–52,000

FINANCES

Tuition: $2600 (R); $6500 (NR)
Average Total Cost: $8579 (R) $12,992 (NR)

STUDENT LIFE
RATING ☺ ☺ ☺ ☺

After Hours: N/A

PROMINENT ALUMNI/AE

Include: N/A

INSIDER INFORMATION Situated on the shores of Lake Washington in residential Seattle, "The U Dub" is surrounded by mountains and salt and fresh water. Characterized as the "most livable city in the United States," the "Emerald City" provides a multitude of legal opportunities for U. Wash's graduates. Recruiters praise the University of Washington School of Law. One, in particular, stated that the school provided, "excellent academic training that is practice-oriented. We find the University of Washington graduates know the Pacific Northwest and come to our firm with the training and capability to help us serve our clients." This training is made possible in part by the school's wide variety of specializations, which include Commercial and Corporate Law, Property, Public and Regulatory Law, Perspective Courses, and International and Comparative Law. Other specializations are those dealing with Procedure and Advocacy and Lawyering Skills.

U. Wash further offers a good selection of seminars that deal with diverse topics ranging from Ocean Policy to Indian Law to the International Protection of Human Rights.

The school's extracurricular activities further enhance its students' practical experience. The International Law Society, the Federalist Society, the Juris Club, the Law, Science, and Technology Society, and the Christian Legal Society all host regular lunches and informal discussions with invited guests who are experts in relevant areas of law. Another distinguishing aspect of the University of Washington is the extensive opportunity it offers for small-group and individual research. The diverse student body comes from eighty-one different colleges and universities.

ADMISSIONS

CRITERIA

LEVEL 1: Grade Point Average; LSAT score

LEVEL 2: Quality of undergraduate curriculum/course work completed; quality/reputation of college/university; recommendations; nature and attainment of advanced degree; the applicant's post-college experience as it relates to the applicant's academic potential; any substantial changes in the applicant's health or economic position as they affect academic performance; variations in the level of academic achievement over time.

LEVEL 3: Special consideration given to applicants who are members of racial and ethnic minority groups that have been subject to long-continued, pervasive discrimination sanctioned by the legal system, and that otherwise would not be meaningfully represented in the entering class.

MINORITY RECRUITMENT PROGRAM

Yes. The Minority Law Students Association (MLSA) is active in efforts to recruit students for the School of Law, and it extends an invitation to all prospective minority students to visit the school and ask questions about the law-school experience.

ABOUT THE APPLICATION

DEADLINE FOR FILING: 2/1

FEE: $35

LSAT: The school will take the average of applicant's scores.

RECOMMENDED COURSES PRIOR TO MATRICULATING: No required undergraduate program; however, courses that provide facility in reading, writing, and speaking the English language, creative reasoning, and logic and critical understanding of human values and institutions are recommended.

PERSONAL STATEMENT: "If you have a history of poor test-taking skills, you may want to include a brief explanation in your personal statement."

RECOMMENDATIONS: The strongest recommendations are those submitted by a teacher who knows your work well and can give a well-substantiated assessment of your academic potential.

INTERVIEW: Not part of the admissions process. You may, however, wish to visit and meet with the admissions staff to have any questions answered.

ADMISSIONS TIPS: "If you have a history of poor test-taking skills, please submit any appropriate documentation, including prior SAT scores," and an explanation.

CONTACT: Director of Admissions

PHYSICAL ENVIRONMENT

The University of Washington School of Law is contained in Condon Hall, which was built in 1974. This building is three blocks from the main campus and houses classrooms, student lounge, and locker areas, offices for faculty, administration, student organizations, and the Marian Gould Gallagher Law Library. Students also have access to the twenty other libraries of the university. The school is considered very accessible to those who are handicapped. The law school computer lab located next to the library includes fifteen IBM computers and is open evenings and weekends. Mercer Hall, a residence hall for graduate students, is located near the law school.

FINANCES

BUDGET	LOW	MEDIUM	HIGH
Tuition (Resident) **Tuition (Nonresident)**	$2061 $6474	$2061 $6474	$2061 $6474
Books	$498	$498	$498
Living Accommodations (9 months)	On-Campus $2700	Shared House $3150	One-Bedroom Apt. $4500
Food	Groceries $900	Restaurants $1350	Meal Plan $1800
Miscellaneous*	$600	$800	$1000
Transportation	Bus $495	Car $720	Cabs $1350
TOTAL (R) TOTAL (NR)	$7254 $11,667	$8579 $12,992	$11,209 $15,622

* Includes Accident and Health Insurance

Employment During School: Because of the heavy work load, employment during your first year is strongly discouraged.

Scholarships: The school offers scholarships.

School Loan Program (Exclusive of Perkins Money): N/A

Loan Forgiveness Program: N/A

Students Requesting Aid: N/A; of these, 75% receive aid.

Average Loan Indebtedness: N/A

ACADEMICS

University of Washington places great emphasis on gaining experience in analyzing cases, statutes, and other legal materials. The school does not only stress Washington State Law. The school is on the quarter system and new students enter only in the autumn quarter. First-year students are required to take a specific set of courses. Classes are broken down into small sections of fewer than thirty students during the fall and winter quarters. Basic Legal Skills, which is taught in sections of approximately twenty-five students, is taught the entire year.

Second- and third-year students find that they have great flexibility in choosing their courses and are only required to take Professional Responsibility and Analytic Writing. Specializations include Labor Law, Tax Law, International Law, Environmental Law, and the Law of Sex and Race Discrimination.

Clinical and Trial Advocacy Programs are also offered, and students may earn credit for working as judicial, legislative, agency, or public-interest externs. Faculty members generally have an open-door policy and are considered to be above average conveyors of information.

JOINT/GRADUATE DEGREE PROGRAMS

Joint Degrees: JD/MBA; JD/PhD; JD/MPA; JD/Economics; JD/International Studies

Students can coordinate a concurrent degree with the School of Law and any of the ninety other departments in the Graduate School of Arts and Science.

Graduate Degrees: LLM and PhD (both in Asian Law and Law and Marine Affairs)

Student organizations include the Student Bar Association, the Law Women's Caucus, and the Washington Law Student. These organizations sponsor regular forums and speeches on topics of interest to law students. As for the school's highly competitive reputation, many students here find that it is largely undeserved. "You have to help each other in order to make it through."

PREPARATION

The Placement Office prepares students by counseling them on résumé-writing and job-hunting techniques and arranges special group programs. A book of placement information and advice is published for first-year students at the start of the school year. Speaker programs are sponsored by the Placement Office as well.

WHERE/WHAT GRADUATES PRACTICE

A. 80% stay in the state of Washington. Remaining graduates take positions in Alaska; California; Washington, D.C.; Hawaii; Illinois; Maine; Nevada; New York; Ohio; Oregon; Pennsylvania; and Vermont.

B. 50% Private Practice; 6.1% Business and Industry; 14.3% Government; 8.2% Judicial Clerkships; 5.4% Public Interest; 1.3% Academic.

❧ R E P O R T   C A R D ❧

ADMISSIONS
SELECTIVITY 🎓 🎓 🎓 🎓 ◗

Applicants: 2366; Accepted: 649
Transfer Applications: 34; Accepted: 1
LSAT Mean: 40   GPA Mean: 3.20

ACADEMICS
Order of the Coif (1981)
Virginia Bar Passage (first try): N/A
Faculty to Student Ratio: N/A
Quality of Teaching: A/A−
Faculty Accessibility: A/B+

PHYSICAL ENVIRONMENT
Location: Small Town
Safety: Very Good
HA: ♿ ♿ ♿ ♿

STUDENT ENROLLMENT
Class Size: 199
Women: 48%   Minorities: 12%
Average Age of Entering Class: 24

PLACEMENT
REPUTATION ☆ ☆ ☆ ☆

Recruiters: 240
Starting Salary Mean: $38,200

FINANCES
Tuition: $3668 (R); $8894 (NR)
Average Total Cost: $13,242 (R); $18,468
(NR)

STUDENT LIFE
RATING ☺ ☺ ☺

After Hours: Paul's "Deli"; The Green Leafe;
The Second Street Cafe; Barrett's

PROMINENT ALUMNI/AE
Include: N/A

William and Mary's Marshall-Wythe College of Law may have been the first college to offer professional training in the law back in 1779, but as the school moves into the 1990s M-W has introduced some of the most innovative ideas in legal education. Foremost among these is the school's recently introduced Legal Studies Program, "the student's first window on the legal profession." From your very first day at M-W you will assume the role of counselors-at-law and begin to learn the real meaning of the phrase "a life in law." The organizational unit of the program is the law office, with each first-year student becoming one of a small group of approximately fifteen associates and remaining a part of that office for his or her first two years. A faculty member and a carefully selected third-year student are partners in the firm who provide guidance to new associates. To provide realism every office is located in and uses the law of an actual jurisdiction, currently including Virginia, New York, Pennsylvania, Ohio,

Illinois, and California. During the two-year life of the program, students are introduced to the whole range of required lawyering skills: interviewing and counseling; negotiating; research and writing memoranda; drafting documents, opinion letters or briefs; and arguing cases at trial on appeal, through "hands-on" experience representing simulated clients. First-year students tend to bemoan the program's heavy work load, but once second-year students get into the trial stages of the program, they feel that the hard work is definitely worth it.

In one student's words, "Marshall-Wythe generates synergy—in short there's a lot happening here." The Institute for Bill of Rights Law, a think tank, attracts the best constitutional scholars from around the country as well as U.S. Supreme Court Justices and British High Lords for symposia and lectures. However, M-W is not a huge law school, and consequently, students find that it offers few esoteric courses. Most feel M-W's strengths lie in Constitutional Law. Some here wish it would offer more "nuts and bolts" courses, but there are many of these in the school's tax program. Because of the school's small size, there are very few "specialized" courses (i.e., Sports Law), and when they are offered, it is somewhat sporadically. Students who take all of their "suggested courses" second year, including Federal Tax Law, Trusts and Estates, and Corporations, may miss out on certain electives.

Marshall-Wythe fosters a close faculty-student relationship. Most faculty give out home and work numbers and don't mind students asking questions in the hallways.

During the beginning of first year, students are broken up into groups of fifteen to twenty and are assigned both a student and faculty advisor. Although students are ranked and Law Review is staffed half on grade-ons and half on write-ons, students are competitive only with themselves.

William and Mary is a harmonious school, rich in its acceptance of diversity in views. On Martin Luther King Day, BLSA sponsors an awareness program with individuals speaking on a number of different topics; there is singing, and faculty and students are involved. It isn't difficult to change residency, but approximately 70% of the class is made up of Virginia residents.

Placement is very aggressive, well organized, and will assist students with a variety of career options. It has produced great results, increasing the school's popularity with recruiters. Recruiters who come to the school generally will come back again, because the students they have recruited present outstanding written communication skills.

ADMISSIONS

CRITERIA

LEVEL 1: Grade Point Average; quality of undergraduate curriculum/course work completed; quality/reputation of college/university; LSAT score

LEVEL 2: Work experience; recommendations; personal essay

LEVEL 3: Personal interview

OTHER: Important factors in admissions are extra-curricular and community activities, diversity, and residency.

MINORITY RECRUITMENT PROGRAM

Yes. The Admissions Office personnel including a minority student recruitment assistant, and the combined efforts of a Minority Recruitment Committee and the local Black Law Students Association chapter conduct the program.

ABOUT THE APPLICATION

DEADLINE FOR FILING: 3/1

FEE: $20

LSAT: The school takes the average of applicant's scores.

RECOMMENDED COURSES PRIOR TO MATRICULATING: Courses that have and develop analytical reasoning, research, and writing skills.

PERSONAL STATEMENT: "The personal statement is an opportunity to present additional information, not required to complete the application, that applicant wishes to contribute. The content and presentation become a part of the material that is evaluated."

INTERVIEW: Not required or recommended. New or additional information provided during a personal interview may be used and may contribute to the decision. Prospective students may contact the Office of Admissions for assistance in setting up visits. Cost-effective lodging includes Econo-Lodge, 1413 Richmond Rd. (804) 229-8551; Econo-Lodge, 505 York St. (804) 220-3100.

ADMISSIONS TIPS: "Be sure to read and follow the specific steps outlined in the printed application procedures. Because our application deadline is March 1, candidates planning to apply during their senior year may wait until the senior year fall grades are recorded to submit their transcript to Law Services for their summary evaluation."

CONTACT: Faye F. Shealy, Associate Dean

PHYSICAL ENVIRONMENT

In 1980 the law school moved to a new building located adjacent to the headquarters of the National Center for State Courts and a quarter of a mile from the campus of the College of William and Mary. The campus, which includes approximately 1200 acres, including Lake Matoaska and picturesque College Woods, is about 150 miles from Washington, D.C.

After being there for three years, some students find that Williamburg, being a small tourist town, "can get worn out" but others counter, "It's a great area to be going to school in." There are a lot of theaters near the school, and Richmond is only forty-five minutes away. Safety is good near the law school with escort services on an informal basis. Physical facilities are good, but the popularity of the school has increased, causing some crowding problems in the library.

The college offers apartment-style living on a limited basis to graduate students. On-campus housing is not guaranteed for law students, many say that living off campus is probably your best bet anyway, because housing is not expensive in the area surrounding the school. A car is recommended due to the distance between the law school and the main campus, and for access to nearby larger cities.

Students feel that the physical facilities should be expanded, especially the library. In the words of one current student, "As the school grows in popularity, the classes grow. This is a positive change but must be accompanied by growth in the facilities."

FINANCES

BUDGET	LOW	MEDIUM	HIGH
Tuition (Resident) **Tuition (Nonresident)**	$3668 $8894	$3668 $8894	$3668 $8894
Books	$600	$600	$600
Living Accommodations (9 months)	On-Campus $1800	Shared House/Apt. $3600	One-Bedroom Apt. $4000
Food	Groceries $1600	Meal Plan $1774	Restaurants $5460
Miscellaneous	$1500	$3000	$4000
Transportation	Car $600	Car $600	Car $600
TOTAL (R) TOTAL (NR)	$9768 $14,994	$13,242 $18,468	$18,328 $23,554

Employment During School: Only recommended in the summer. Work-study jobs: Summer jobs are available (need-dependent); up to forty hours in the summer.

Scholarships: The school offers merit and need-based scholarships. Merit scholarships are not contingent upon maintaining a certain GPA.

School Loan Program (Exclusive of Perkins Money): No.

Loan Forgiveness Program: No

Students Requesting Aid: 80%; of these, 33% receive aid.

Average Loan Indebtedness: N/A

ACADEMICS

First-year courses are required. The required Legal Skills Program begins this year, as well, covering such areas as negotiating, counseling, drafting, and interviewing. Students take Legal Skills I and II in the first year and Legal Skills III and IV in the second year. What makes Legal Skills III and IV interesting is that they are taught primarily through small student "law firms." Current student reaction to the Legal Skills Program has been that the first year is of questionable value, but second year more than makes up for it, and the entire program is rewarding once you've made it through. To help students choose from the electives offered, a faculty advisor is assigned. Third-year students have a writing requirement that can be satisfied by a seminar or courses in independent legal writing.

Although Marshall-Wythe provides approximately eleven clinical or practical courses, students have asked that this number be increased. This type of course includes Juvenile Law Clinic, Attorney General Practice Clinic, and an Employee Relations Clinic, but the clinics are limited in size, and only a few students can participate. Students can, however, organize their own work experience and receive credit, if the job is not compensated.

The faculty is know for its sensitivity to students' concerns. Class lectures are lively and often result in challenging debate. Students can approach faculty without reserve to discuss personal concerns as well as to work out unclear issues. The faculty is often seen at student events. Faculty stars include Fred Lederer (Trial Practice and Evidence), Walter Felton (Criminal Law), and Jayne Barnard (Corporations, Debtors/Creditor).

JOINT/GRADUATE DEGREE PROGRAMS

Joint Degree: JD/MBA
Graduate Degree: Graduate Tax Program

STUDENT LIFE

There is a wide variety of organizations, including the Student Bar Association, Law and Medicine Club, International Law Society, Law School fraternities, and the student chapter of the Association of Trial Lawyers of America. Each class has a different overall group personality. Every effort is made to accommodate student-run events.

PLACEMENT

Individualized career planning is emphasized. Throughout the law school career, the students are offered a structured series of programs. These sessions include panel presentations by participating attorneys representing a broad range of locations and types of employers, judicial clerks offering insights about clerkship application and selection, and practitioners providing tips for successful interviewing and productive summer clerkship experiences. Other topics include nontraditional careers, solo practice, and opportunities in law enforcement, the federal government, the military justice system, and substantive specializations. The school also has off-campus interview programs.

Students feel that the Placement Office is outstanding. Dean Kaplan works with students individually and collectively. He also provides a broad range of employment options from large firms to public-interest practice.

WHERE/WHAT GRADUATES PRACTICE

A. 40% Northeast; 43% South; 7% West Coast; 6% Midwest; 4% Other. (7% of students remain in the immediate vicinity of the law school within one year of graduation.)
B. 1% Solo Practitioners; 12% Small Firms; 16% Medium Firms; 31% Large Firms; 14% Clerkships; 11% Governmental Agencies; 7% Military; 3% Corporations; 1% Graduate Degrees; 3% Other.

UNIVERSITY OF WISCONSIN
Madison Law School

232 LAW SCHOOL
MADISON, WISCONSIN (WI) 53706
(608) 262-2240

ᐭᐠ REPORT CARD ᐭᐠ

ADMISSIONS
SELECTIVITY 🎓 🎓 🎓

Applicants: 2482; Accepted: 552
Transfer Applications: 52; Accepted: 11
LSAT Mean: 38   GPA Mean: 3.45

ACADEMICS
Order of the Coif (1908)
Wisconsin Bar Passage Rate (first try): N/A;
  students in Wisconsin have the "Diploma
  Privledge" exempting them from the bar.
Faculty to Student Ratio: 1:20.6
Quality of Teaching: A –
Faculty Accessibility: B

PHYSICAL ENVIRONMENT
Location: Large Campus (law school is in
  center of campus)
Safety: Excellent–Very Good
HA: ♿ ♿ ♿ ♿ ♿

STUDENT ENROLLMENT
Class Size: 268 (full-time); 17 (part-time)
Women: 44%   Minorities: 12% (does not
  include Asians)
Average Age of Entering Class: 25

PLACEMENT
REPUTATION ☆ ☆ ☆ ☆

Recruiters: 275
Salary Mean: $39,885

FINANCES
Tuition: $3046 (R); $8622 (NR)
Average Total Cost: $9967 (R);
  $15,112 (NR)

STUDENT LIFE
RATING ☺ ☺ ☺ ☺ ☺

After Hours: Bucks, Whitehorse Inn

PROMINENT ALUMNI/AE
Include: N/A

INSIDER INFORMATION It may not be situated in a mega-city like New York or Los Angeles, but make no mistake, Wisconsin is a trendsetter in legal education, boasting clinics including the ILDP Legal Defense Program, where students control the entire defense case from start to finish under an attorney's supervision, advanced courses, and most recently, computerization of the library. Starting next year students will be able to check out laptop computers from the library with modem/telephone hookup access to the WESTLAW/ LEXIS terminals. Wisconsin Law is an interdisciplinary law school, where many faculty have joint appointments with the Political Science department and the medical school, and are active in the instruction of labor law in conjunction with the School For Workers. The school boasts a strong criminal justice program, which includes two large clinical programs. Wisconsin's General Practice course, taught to second-semester third-year students by practicing attorneys who come in teams of four for one week at a time, has been used as a model in U.S. legal education.

The University of Wisconsin's Chancellor Donna Shalala is found to be wholly receptive to law students' needs and suggestions. And when Wisconsin students ask for changes in their school, they put their money where their mouth is. In fact, to guarantee that their library was upgraded, students voluntarily increased their own tuition $500 out-of-state and $400 in-state, with the proviso that the funds were to be earmarked for their law library. They raised $350,000 in the process.

As a large school with large classes, Wisconsin offers a good diversity of students ranging from firemen, nurses, professors, and this year, a first-year student who is a state senator. First year there is one small group section of twenty-five to thirty students (though targeted for twenty), for one of the required courses, such as criminal law. Students are given a midterm exam in that small section class so that they can get a "feel" for taking law school exams, and many professors either deemphasize or entirely disregard the results of the exam. Faculty are knowledgeable with a mixture of teaching styles and personalities, including those who are somewhat standoffish and those who will walk with you to the student union to discuss a question. Regardless of personality makeup, all of them will make an effort to meet with you, especially if you have made an appointment.

Wisconsin placement is strong. Because of its proximity to the seat of state government as well as numerous courts, the school adds new dimensions to the term "live learning." Recruiters are genuinely pleased with Wisconsin students, but some coastal recruiters feel they don't have a strong chance of attracting Wisconsin grads so they don't make use of on-campus interviewing.

Students are quite willing to stretch themselves to make their and others' activities successful. Each year the school cosponsors a mixer, known as Malpractice, with the medical school. This affair had a turnout of 400–500 law students alone last year, filling the entire student union. There is also a more formal Barrister's Ball and organized receptions for visiting faculty members. Transition into law school is eased for first-year students with an orientation and a week of planned parties.

As one Wisconsin administrator says of his school, "Wisconsin is serious but unpretentious. . . .It's a Garrison Keillor [*Lake Wobegon Days*] midwestern law school with a 'don't blow your own horn' kind of attitude." For this reason, you may find that Wisconsin's application literature doesn't come off as persuasively glossy as at other top-tier law schools, but don't let that stop you from applying, particularly if you are a Wisconsin resident, who make up approximately 75% of the school's enrollment.

ADMISSIONS

CRITERIA

LEVEL 1: GPA (60%), includes a quality of undergraduate school attended and course selection; LSAT (40%).

LEVEL 2: Personal Statement: Stress what it is about yourself that makes you able to contribute to and benefit from the law school. This is also a chance to display diversity.

LEVEL 3: Recommendations.

A completed application is reviewed by a member of the school's Admissions Committee. Using a prediction index produced by a formula involving your GPA and LSAT, the committee may find you to be outstandingly qualified, in which case an acceptance will be sent without further screening. If you appear to "represent an unacceptably high academic risk because of low academic credentials not counterbalanced by other factors, you will be sent a letter of denial. If you fall somewhere in the middle, you may be placed in the "hold" category and so notified. Applicants placed in "hold" are not further reviewed until all files have been initially reviewed. Hold files are then reviewed by the entire committee using both academic and non-academic factors. Non-academic factors are given primary emphasis.

Academic Factors are evaluated as follows:

1) *Trend of College Grades: Although poor college grades changing to very strong performance in later college years can be a plus, a gradual rising trend is not considered significant.*
2) *Letters of Recommendation: These are not required, but most students send between three and four. They are not counted very heavily but may play a role in the case of marginal applicants.*
3) *Graduate Study: Strong graduate work, plus a strong LSAT score, may override a weaker GPA. Graduate study may also provide a favorably interesting background.*
4) *Time Interval between College Graduation and Application to Law School: One year out of college, plus strong recent LSAT, may override weaker GPA. Experience may be a favorable non-academic factor as well.*
5) *Quality of Applicant's College: Convincing evidence considered.*
6) *College Grading and Course Selection Patterns: Transcripts are examined individually.*
7) *Outside Work while in College: Heavy workload may override weaker GPA.*
8) *Writing Sample from LSAT: The school receives this and weight is given to it.*

Nonacademic Factors that demonstrate diversity include: 1) minority status; 2) unusual cultural background; 3) geographical diversity; 4) Wisconsin residency (higher standards are imposed on nonresident applicants); 5) acceptance in a prior year; 6) diversity of experience or background; 7) diversity of stated professional goals; 8) women.

MINORITY RECRUITMENT PROGRAM

Yes.

ABOUT THE APPLICATION

DEADLINE FOR FILING: 2/1

FEE: $20

LSAT: The school takes the average of applicant's scores, unless there has been a significant time lapse between scores, in this case they will give more weight to the more recent score.

RECOMMENDED COURSES PRIOR TO MATRICULATING: There is no required course of study.

INTERVIEW: Not a part of the admissions process. If an informational interview is conducted, no written record of it is made.

PERSONAL STATEMENT: Although not required, strongly recommended. Admissions consider this a very important component of the admissions package, which serves as the "interview in writing." The question is open-ended, and it is up to you to decide what about yourself is important for the Admissions Committee to know. If you have any discrepancies in your record, you should put them here. Be concise.

ADMISSIONS TIPS: As noted before, while it won't totally outweigh academic factors, diversity is an important nonacademic determinant. It therefore should be emphasized through the personal statement. According to Admissions Officer, Mary Duckwitz, "Many applicants procrastinate." All applications postmarked after the deadline are returned.

CONTACT: Mary Duckwitz, Admissions Officer

PHYSICAL ENVIRONMENT

Built in 1964, the law school building is a five-floor atrium located halfway up Bascom Hill. The library is nothing to write home about, but locked carrels are available to some graduate students in law and special research. Nearly all of the law school's facilities are accessible to the handicapped.

FINANCES

BUDGET	LOW	MEDIUM	HIGH
Tuition (Resident) **Tuition (Nonresident)**	$2617 $7762	$2617 $7762	$2617 $7762
Books	$600	$600	$600
Living Accommodations (9 months)	On-Campus $1800	Shared Apt. $2800	One-Bedroom Apt. $4000
Food	Groceries $1200	Groceries/Restaurants $2000	Restaurants $3500
Miscellaneous	$1000	$1500	$2500
Transportation	Bus $350	Car/Bus $450	Car $620
TOTAL (R) TOTAL (NR)	$7567 $12,712	$9967 $15,112	$13,837 $18,982

Employment During School: First-year students are warned not to carry the double load of part-time work and law studies. It is also not encouraged for second and third years, but understood that it may be necessary. A number of law firms and state offices regularly hire students for part-time work. A limited number of research assistantships are available to second- and third-year students with outstanding academic records. Employment is also available in the Law Library. About twenty upperclass law students with good academic records are employed each year as instructors in the first-year Legal Writing Program; if you are a nonresident, you receive a remission of nonresident tuition as well as a salary.

Scholarships: The school offers merit and need-based scholarships.

School Loan Program (Exclusive of Perkins Money): No

Loan Forgiveness Program: N/A

Students Requesting Aid: N/A

ACADEMICS

Wisconsin is considered to have one of the most innovative, liberal law school programs and is a leader in most areas. Although first-year students are required to take a certain program of courses, second- and third-year students have considerable flexibility. Instruction techniques tend to rely more heavily on the Socratic method first year. For second- and third-year students, many faculty teach using internally generated course materials, many of which are photocopies and reflect the particular interests of the individual instructor. Legal Writing is taught in sections of between fifteen and twenty students by a staff of two practicing attorneys and an instructor with a background in English, as well as by selected second- and third-year students who have also taken Advanced Legal Writing.

The curriculum is divided into subject matters, including Administrative and Legislative Process, Business Organization and Regulation, Property and Natural Resources, and Practical Skills and Related Subjects. You will find that most of the school's courses are not "black letter" but rather teach you how to research and make arguments.

Grades are force-averaged to an 82; often an 85 is the highest grade awarded, with 90s a rarity. Law Review is composed of two groups. "Grading on" is accomplished by being in top 10 (number not percent) out of 350. Writing on is also possible.

Clinical programs offered at the law school include the Center for Public Representation, which deals with the representation of traditionally underrepresented groups; the Judicial Internship Program; the Labor Law Clinical Program; the NAACP Legal Defense and Education Fund Summer Internships Program; and the Public Intervenor's Program, which deals with environmental law. You have to interview to get into the clinics, but it is rare that anyone is denied access. Special programs include the Criminal Justice Program and the Legal Assistance to Institutionalized Persons Program, which offer you the opportunity to resolve legal problems for inmates in Wisconsin state and federal prisons and patients in state mental health institutions.

Wisconsin students who wish to stay in-state are able to practice without taking a bar exam through "The Diploma Privilege". A small number of part-time students attend during the day, stretching out the degree time from three to six years.

Star faculty include Richard Delgado (Civil Procedure I & II, Racism on Campus Seminar) and Stephen Herzberg (Criminal Procedure).

JOINT/GRADUATE DEGREE PROGRAMS

Joint Degrees: JD/MPA; JD/Library and Information Services; JD/Ibero-American Studies; JD/PhD
Graduate Degrees: LLM; SJD; MLI (Master of Arts or Master of Science in Legal Institution)

STUDENT LIFE

In explaining the extent of the social life at Wisconsin, one student stated, "Wisconsin is not known for its parties for nothing." There are many organizations dedicated to providing social functions. Minority groups sponsor events as well. The Student Bar Association sponsors various social events. The association maintains a book mart that provides students with books and other supplies at a discount and with funds for student activities.

PLACEMENT

Students are very satisfied with the Office of Career Services. However, it is felt that the help is available if you ask; if you don't, no one will go out of their way. Placement starts for most after the first year, though students can get involved with it on their own earlier if they take the initiative. Some feel that Placement could be stronger and inform first-year students more of their alternatives and help with résumé writing. Second-year students select computerized systems where students request appointments with four firms who come to interview for that week. Sometimes students don't get an interview, but the school sends their résumés to the firm anyway. In one case the firms called a student back on their own for an interview. By the end of the year, 97% of UW-Madison's graduates had found jobs.

WHERE/WHAT GRADUATES PRACTICE

A. 61.5% Wisconsin; 81.9% Midwest (including Wisconsin); 10% Northeast (includes D.C.); 2.8% South; 2.1% West; 1% Southwest/Mountain.
B. 2.6% Self-Employed; 24.2% [2-10 Lawyers]; 15% [11-25 Lawyers]; 9.8% [26-50 Lawyers]; 10.5% [51-100 Lawyers]; 27.5% [100+ Lawyers]; 10.5% Unknown; 5.7% Corporate Business; 6.1% Public Interest; 10.3% Government (includes general and prosecution); 10.1% Judicial Clerkships; 6.1% Military.

CAMPUS BOX 1120
ONE BROOKINGS DRIVE
ST. LOUIS, MISSOURI (MO) 63130-4899
(314) 889-4525

REPORT CARD

ADMISSIONS

SELECTIVITY 🎓 🎓 🎓 🎓

Applicants: 1499; Accepted: 729
Transfer Applicants: 6; Accepted: 1
LSAT Mean: 34
GPA Mean: 3.26

ACADEMICS

Order of the Coif (1924)
Faculty to Student Ratio: 1:20
Quality of Teaching: A
Faculty Accessibility: A+

PHYSICAL ENVIRONMENT

Location: Large City
Safety: Good
HA: ♿ ♿

STUDENT ENROLLMENT

Class Size: 235
Women: 45%   Minorities: 6%
Average Age of Entering Class: 23

PLACEMENT

REPUTATION ☆ ☆ ☆ ☆

Recruiters: 170
Salary Range: $19,000–75,000

FINANCES

Tuition: $14,200
Average Total Cost: $22,720

STUDENT LIFE

RATING ☺ ☺ ☺

After Hours: Tom's, Soulard (a collection of
blues bars), Red Sea, House of Jamaica

PROMINENT ALUMNI/AE

Include: William Webster, Head of the CIA;
Clark Clifford, Secretary of Defense during
Johnson Administration

INSIDER INFORMATION

There is a cohesive atmosphere at Washington University. The school provides its students with a very qualified faculty, representing a wide variety of viewpoints and areas of expertise. Washington stresses theoretical law but seeks to provide a fine advocacy program as well. Its philosophy is based on close contact and free exchange of ideas between professor and student. These professors are not blind to publication needs, but emphasis is clearly on teaching and student association. Even the physical setup, with faculty offices distributed throughout the library, encourages free contact. Learning just begins in the classroom and is extended to practical application through the critical clinical courses in which at least four faculty members members actively participate. Students have an opportunity to work on two nationally recognized legal publications: the *Law Quarterly* and the *Journal of Urban and Contemporary Law*.

Students feel that the physical structure needs reconsideration. The facilities used are not adequate to handle the ordinary class size of 210, let alone the last year's overenrollment of 228. Be advised that admission standards will be more stringent, due to Washington U's desire to revise the entering class size back down to 210.

CRITERIA

LEVEL 1:   Grade Point Average; LSAT score; quality of undergraduate curriculum/ course work completed; quality/reputation of college/university. The school uses an index number [(10 × GPA) + LSAT].

LEVEL 2:   Diversity factors (e.g., minority status); recommendations; work experience (this factor is more important for those individuals who have been out of school five to ten years).

DEADLINE FOR FILING: Modified Rolling Admissions (starts September 1)

FEE: $45

LSAT: All scores are looked at, but for purposes of computing your "index," multiple scores will be averaged.

PERSONAL STATEMENT: The personal statement can push a "borderline" applicant into the "admit" category.

INTERVIEW: Will not be used for evaluative purposes.

ADMISSIONS TIPS: "The personal statement is your written interview. Don't be cute and write about your goldfish or your Miami Drug Bust. Tell us why you're qualified" and give compelling demonstration that you have a grasp of the concepts, of your committment, and that you write well. (Take LSAT in June or September/ October of year in which you apply. Submit application early because school uses a modified rolling admissions process.)

CONTACT: Kip Darcy, Director of Admissions

PHYSICAL ENVIRONMENT

Located on the western edge of St. Louis, the law school is housed in the Mudd Law Building. The Freund Law Library occupies a significant portion of the first and second levels of this structure.

The primary business district is located seven miles from the university. Handicapped accessibility is known to be poor. Ramps are in the process of being put in. Safety is considered fairly good. The area is well lit, a university escort service is available, and there are patrol cars.

No school-owned housing is available to the students and the most cost-effective accommodations are shared apartments. A car is recommended, because, although there is a bus system, there is no subway or light rail system. A car is not a necessity, but students with cars get to enjoy more of the metro area.

FINANCES

BUDGET	LOW	MEDIUM	HIGH
Tuition	$14,200	$14,200	$14,200
Books	$800	$800	$800
Living Accommodations (9 months)	Shared Apt. $2025	Shared House $2520	One-Bedroom Apt. $3825
Food	Groceries $2500	Cafeteria $3000	Restaurants $4000
Miscellaneous	$1200	$1700	$2500
Transportation	Mass Transit $300	Bus/Car $500	Car $700
TOTAL	$21,025	$22,720	$26,025

Employment During School: Neither recommended nor discouraged.

Scholarships: The school offers merit, need-based, and minority scholarships. A first-year scholarship is awarded on the basis of merit to students with outstanding academic records. The Scholars in Law Program and the Olin Fellowship for Women are offered as well.

School Loan Program (Exclusive of Perkins Money): Yes. Emergency Loan and Washington University Loan, which is merit-based.

Loan Forgiveness Program: No, but school is looking into this.

Students Requesting Aid: N/A; of those requesting aid, 70% receive aid.

Average Loan Indebtedness: N/A

ACADEMICS

All first-year courses are required. Case-study and Socratic methods are primarily used during this time. Upperclass law students are required to take a course in Professional Responsibility and two writing courses. A broad range of courses are offered, including Chinese and Soviet Law, Commercial Fraud, and Partnership Taxation. Many of these classes are small. The Applied Lawyering Skills Program provides students with practical experience through clinical courses, internships, and externships. Simulation and theory courses dealing with such topics as Pretrial Practice and Procedure, Business Planning and Drafting, and Criminal Justice Administration are included. Through internships, students may work in private and governmental law offices, state and federal courts, and congressional offices. These clinics include the State Criminal Defense Clinic and the Judicial Clerkship. A Congressional Clinic in Washington, D.C. is also offered to third-year students in the spring semester.

Opinions concerning lecture quality vary. Some students find that the professors are excellent in their particular area, while others are great lecturers in general. Other classmates note that some professors still lack good lecture style. Most of the professors have been very accessible after class. Star faculty include Frank Miller (Criminal Procedure), David Becker (Property), and Kathleen Brickey (Corporate and White Collar Crime).

JOINT/GRADUATE DEGREE PROGRAMS

Joint Degrees: Six combined degree programs are available, including Asian Studies, Political Science, Health Administration, and Social Work.

Graduate Professional Programs: LLM (Taxation); LLM (Urban Studies); LLM/JSD; MJS (Master of Judicial Studies).

STUDENT LIFE

Social life is good at Washington U, and the atmosphere is generally noncompetitive. It is found, however, that the school can "take on the feel of a commuter school with students coming for class, studying, and leaving; never taking advantage of the extracurricular activities available through small, but active, school organizations." Student groups include the Student Bar Association, the Pro Bono Association, and the Devil's Advocate.

PLACEMENT

Students express satisfaction with placement opportunities. One student noted, "The Placement Office is making a serious effort to increase our name recognition on the East Coast. In my case it was a successful effort." Local firms are required to interview all students who sign up. Firms outside of St. Louis can screen job applicants, so it is quite a bit tougher to get out-of-town interviews.

PREPARATION

Students are prepared by the Career Services Office through individual and group counseling for résumé preparation, interviewing techniques, and job-seeking strategies. Programs are sponsored, and alumni/ae are invited to participate in discussions. Programs include "The Job Hunt, Strategy in Job Hunting and Interviewing" and "Mock Interviews for First-Years."

WHERE/WHAT GRADUATES PRACTICE

1% Sole Practitioner; 28% Very Small Firms (2–10 attorneys); 19% Small Firms (11–25 attorneys); 13% Medium Firms (26–50 attorneys); 29% Large Firms (51–100 attorneys); 10% Very Large Firms (100+ attorneys); 12% Clerkships; 1% Military; 12% Governmental Agencies; 9% Corporations; 3% Public Interest.

YALE UNIVERSITY
Law School

P.O. BOX 401A, YALE STATION
NEW HAVEN, CONNECTICUT (CT) 06520
(203) 432-4995

❧ REPORT CARD ❧

ADMISSIONS
SELECTIVITY 🎓 🎓 🎓 🎓 🎓

Applicants: 4660; Accepted: 394
LSAT Mean: 44
GPA Mean: 3.78

ACADEMICS
Order of the Coif (1919)
Faculty to Student Ratio: 1:8.5
Quality of Teaching: B+/A−
Accessibility: A

PHYSICAL ENVIRONMENT
Location: Urban/Medium-Sized City
Safety: Marginal–Poor
HA: ♿ ♿ ♿ ♿

STUDENT ENROLLMENT
Class Size: 179
Women: 40% Minorities: 20%
International: 3.4%
Average Age of Entering Class: 24–25

PLACEMENT
REPUTATION ☆ ☆ ☆ ☆

Recruiters: 412 on-campus requests
Starting Salary Mean: $58,000

FINANCES
Tuition: $15,015
Average Total Cost: $23,375

STUDENT LIFE
RATING ☺ ☺ ☺

After Hours: The Graduate Student Professional Center at Yale (GYPSY)

PROMINENT ALUMNI/AE
Include: William Butler, former general counsel, Environmental Defense Fund; Gus Speth, President of World Resources Institute

INSIDER INFORMATION

"My first semester I met a person who herded cows in Zimbabwe, an air traffic controller from New York City, and someone who had written a book." In light of their accomplishments, people here are very modest. Adds another, "It's a school for self-discovery. People at this school care. There is very little external competition, but internal competition is fierce. Pressure exists [here] because of the people the school attracts, even though there aren't as many hoops as at other schools. When people see one they're going to put themselves through it."

Yale law students are not just talented in the law, but in diverse ways. Many of them have interests tangential to the law. Students take exams after Christmas vacation and four days later start the second semester. Clinics are so popular that there is oversubscription. However, since first-year, first-semester students aren't able to take clinic, whoever doesn't get a clinic first-year, second-semester has priority for second-year, first-semester.

The Yale Law Journal is the only journal at the school that is competitive, with students being required to give a writing sample. Student organizations are born all the time at the school, and there are a remarkable number considering the small size of the student body. First Generation Professionals is a support group for law students who are the first in their families to attend professional school or college. SAGE, Students Against Graduating Early, is for older students.

Yale's strongest feature may be that it is a school that not only allows but also helps its students' dreams come true. Anything students want to do they can from starting a journal or club to taking a semester at another law school for a different perspective or an intensive semester abroad. Yale has far less red tape than other schools. Constitutional, Property, Criminal, and International Law are considered strong. Public service is strongly encouraged. The school has a free phone at the Placement Office for students to call public service organizations, and a good number of Yalies go on to public service. Recruiters are impressed with the students they see from Yale, but as one puts it, and many agree, "It's a tight pull. They have such a small class with so many going into clerkships that it's not easy getting them." Consequently, when law firms do get Yale graduates, they try to keep them.

The school offers a two-week shopping period so that students can sit in on classes (after required classes), and decide what they want to drop and add. This helps students make sure they study with the professors they really want. There is a sprinkling of the Socratic method among the faculty, but few adhere to it strictly. Students would like to see more informal interaction between students and faculty.

As for the area around the school, "You go to Yale in spite of New Haven, certainly not because of it," though it provides students with excellent chances to work with the underprivileged in need of legal services.

Yale is a school that fosters personal and intellectual growth. Due to the school's segregation from the undergraduate school, social life can be problematic at times and a car is recommended. An expensive car is not a good idea, because there have been problems with break-ins among students who don't park in pay lots.

ADMISSIONS

As one of the two or three most selective law schools in the country, the Admissions Committee at Yale has a formidable task choosing among highly qualified applicants, many of whom have superior LSAT scores and GPAs. Although the school has high mean scores for both GPA and LSAT and the great majority of accepted applicants have scores in the top 10% of both factors, each year applicants with numbers below these means are accepted. A significant number of students are accepted from Yale and Harvard undergraduate, due in part to the fact that these schools provide the most applications—238 from Harvard and 237 from Yale (one of the first years there were more applicants from Harvard than Yale). Students are accepted from other undergraduate schools as well. Admissions Committee members who have worked at other law schools are often amazed at the quality of many of the students the school has to turn down.

CRITERIA

LEVEL 1: Grade Point Average; quality of undergraduate curriculum/course work completed; quality/reputation of college/university; LSAT score; work experience, recommendations; personal essay

OTHER: Important factors in admissions are extracurricular and community activities, diversity, and residency.

MINORITY RECRUITMENT PROGRAM

Yes. The school uses the Minority Candidate Referral Service and hosts a recruitment weekend in late March sponsored by the school and various minority student associations.

ABOUT THE APPLICATION

DEADLINE FOR FILING: 2/15

FEE: $45

LSAT: Whether or not the school takes the average or the highest of applicant's scores depends on individual cases.

RECOMMENDED COURSES PRIOR TO MATRICULATING: Courses that have and develop analytical reasoning, research, and writing skills.

PERSONAL STATEMENT: Required essay and an optional statement. School encourages the applicant to take advantage of both, but certainly make sure you do the short essay. Regarding this essay's evaluation, the admissions reader may ask: 1) Was it funny? 2) Was it insightful? 3) Did it show that the applicant thinks well? 4) Did it show that the applicant is compassionate or has a breadth of interest? The faculty like it to be topical. They do not want it to be "bureaucratic."

Says Admissions Director Jean Webb, "The required essay and optional statement are there to benefit the applicant. We strongly encourage that you take advantage of both." As to experiences when writing the personal statements, she adds, "People coming out of college tend to give sterotypical reasons for wanting to become a lawyer." However, for older applicants who have had unusual life experiences, she encourages them to elaborate on the reasons that drew them to the study of law. **Important:** Often people assume that the two essays should be related or that one should be an extension of the other. It is important for the applicant to differentiate the two pieces of writing, taking into account that they serve two different purposes. As for what the school looks for in an essay, "We don't know what we're looking for, except for excellence. When we see it we know it." Clearly, typing the application is better than handwriting. As to submitting outside materials, the feeling among the Admissions Committee is that substance is preferred over gimmicks. People who have unusual life experiences should bring this out through the essay.

INTERVIEW: Not required or recommended. However, students are welcome to visit the school.

RECOMMENDATIONS: The school prefers two letters of recommendation from faculty from upper-level courses. These professors should be fully acquainted with the applicant; this is especially important for applicants who attended larger universities where faculty members may not be as familiar with students in introductory courses.

ADMISSIONS TIPS: The school requires two letters of recommendation, and it is preferred that these recommendations come from academics, preferably in the applicant's major. Graduate work is considered an enhancement rather than a substitute for undergraduate work. In getting recommendations it is important to get recommenders who know your work rather than "name" faculty with whom you have taken a course. These individuals generally tell the Admissions Committee little more than can be ascertained from reviewing the applicant's transcript. For students who have transferred during college, recommendations should come from faculty in upper-level courses at current university/college, with the possible exception of mentors who may have played an important role in the decision to transfer. Students who have been out of school for several years can also use employers for recommendations.

CONTACT: (Ms.) Jean K. Webb, Director of Admissions

PHYSICAL ENVIRONMENT

New Haven cannot be considered one of Yale's chief drawing cards, with a relatively high crime rate near the school and a renting market that strongly favors landlords, because of the scarcity of suitable living accommodations in good areas near the school. Yale Law School offers its students an attractive facility, which is slated for expansion. Handicapped accessibility is considered above average, and the building is fully equipped, with accommodating the physically challenged a priority.

Housed inside the Sterling Law Quadrangle is the YLS Early Learning Center which, students feel, adds a special dimension to the school as well as making life easier for students with children. Students recommend living in the dorm first year and moving off for the second and third years.

FINANCES

BUDGET	LOW	MEDIUM	HIGH
Tuition	$15,015	$15,015	$15,015
Books	$550	$550	$550
Living Accommodations (9 months)	Shared Apt. $2475	On-Campus $2810	One-Bedroom Apt. $3600
Food	Meal Plan $1390	Groceries/Cafeteria $2000	Restaurants $2600
Miscellaneous	$1000	$1500	$2000
Transportation	Walking/Mass Transit $500	Car $1500	Car $1500
TOTAL	$20,930	$23,375	$25,265

Employment During School: Allowed but not recommended.

Scholarships: The school offers both scholarships and fellowships.

Loan Forgiveness Program: Yes, Career Options Assistance Program. It provides grants to cover the shortfall between graduates' educational loan payments and what graduates can afford to pay from relatively modest incomes. For participants with annual incomes under $28,000, the law school assumes repayment of the entire annual obligation for all educational loans. Participants with income over $28,000, are expected to contribute 25% of the income in excess of that amount toward repayment.

Students Requesting Aid: N/A; of those requesting aid, 66.7% receive aid.

Average Loan Indebtedness: N/A

ACADEMICS

The first semester of your first year holds the bulk of requirements for law students. In one of the required courses of your first term, you are assigned to a seminar, usually of not more than seventeen people. This small group is the class where you will be taught legal research and writing, which are integrated with regular course work. Besides required courses, you must take Criminal Law Administration I, three units of supervised analytic writing, and write a substantial paper of at least two units. Students can take students activities for a credit, and there appear to be few obstacles to taking courses in the other schools at Yale, which include the Yale School of Organizational Management.

Faculty are considered highly accessible and very much into the theoretical aspects of the law. Sometimes you may not see as much black letter law as you may want, but as one faculty member told a student here, "The skills you are getting here will show up five to seven years down the road." The immediate security of black letter law is replaced by deep, thoughtful analysis.

A highly unusual program at the school is the Masters Program in Legal Studies (MSL) to better educate journalists who write on legal issues. Students are not able to get into the JD program through this program. First year is the traditional first year of law school.

Grades are in the form of Honors/High Pass/Low Pass/Fail.

JOINT/GRADUATE DEGREE PROGRAMS

Joint Degrees: JD/MA; JD/MPPM (Master of Public and Private Management); JD/PhD; JD/DCL (Doctorate in Civil Law)
Graduate Degrees: LLM; JSD; MSL (Master Of Studies in Law/Fellowship in Law for Journalists)

STUDENT LIFE

New Haven may not be the most socially active area in the country to attend law school. However, students find cultural opportunities both within the Yale University community and the law school itself. There is a regular train to New York City. Yale's Social Committee is run by students who organize parties and a weekly happy hour. Two or three films a week are presented by the Yale Law School Film Society and other university film societies. Cultural resources at the university include the Art Gallery, the Peabody Museum of Natural History, and the Yale Symphony, as well as the Yale Center for British Art.

PLACEMENT

Placement at Yale fosters student employment in both private and public sectors. A large percentage of graduates opt for judicial clerkships, and there are a good share of students who pursue careers with mega-firms. The school offers a voluntary Job Match Program whereby first-year students may be "matched" for summer jobs with a minimum of interviewing.

Yale cosponsors numerous job fairs for public interest positions as well as an international job fair. Students have workships on interview skills, and they are free to meet with two placement counselors. As to recruiter selection, each week students hand in a list of employers along with their geographical preferences and schedule of classes. These factors are input into the office's computer and, based on this, the school schedules interviews with recruiters. Recruiters are given students' résumés to prep one week prior to coming on campus, but they are not permitted to use the résumés to screen out potential candidates.

Placement at Yale, as at all law schools, works best for students who have a sense of direction. For this group of individuals, the placement rate is virtually 100%.

WHERE/WHAT GRADUATES PRACTICE

A. 60% Northeast; 11% South; 9% Midwest; 19% West Coast; 1% Foreign.
B. 42% Firms (includes large, medium, and small firms with the majority of students in this group accepting jobs with large firms, though many times they are in a branch office not large in itself but associated with a megafirm); 1% Corporate/Business; 2% Government; 45% Judicial Clerkships (both state and federal); 3% public service (students pursuing jobs in this area are given use of the school's phone); 1% Teaching; 6% Other (includes fellowships, graduate school, military, writing).

55 FIFTH AVENUE
NEW YORK, NEW YORK (NY) 10003
(212) 790-0274

REPORT CARD

ADMISSIONS

SELECTIVITY

Applicants: January: 182, **Accepted**: 61;
May: 126, **Accepted**: 70; September:
2400, **Accepted**: 836
Transfer Applications 7; **Accepted**: 5
LSAT Mean: 39
GPA Mean: 3.2–3.3

ACADEMICS

New York State Bar Passage (first
try): 72%

Faculty to Student Ratio: N/A

Quality of Teaching: **A –**

Faculty Accessibility: **A**

PHYSICAL ENVIRONMENT

Location: Urban/Large City

Safety: Fair–Good (Security Guards)

HA:

STUDENT ENROLLMENT

Class Size: January: 52; May: 51;
September:245 (all full-time)

Women: 50% Minorities: 6%

Average Age of Entering Class: January; 28,
May: 26; September: 23

PLACEMENT

REPUTATION

Recruiters: 120

Salary Range (medium firms): $23,000–
75,000

FINANCES

Tuition: $11,825

Average Total Cost: $24,773.50

STUDENT LIFE

RATING

After Hours: McSorley's, The Lone Star,
Pappa's Place, Cedar's Tavern

PROMINENT ALUMNI/AE

Include: Geoffrey Goldfeder, NYC
Councilman; Ivan Tillem, Philanthropist
and businessman; Sandra Feuerstein (Judge,
Nassau County)

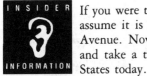

INSIDER INFORMATION

If you were to judge Cardozo simply by its exterior, you would safely assume it is located in one of the many office buildings lining Fifth Avenue. Now, step inside that same building, ride the elevator up, and take a trip inside one of the unique law schools in the United States today.

By possessing an intuitive sense of what a law school should be and do for its students, Cardozo has succeeded in a little over fourteen years, in doing what some in the legal profession may have thought impossible. In the school's earliest years, Cardozo volunteered its students to firms as interns. As Acting Director of Admissions, Anita Walton puts it, "They had nothing to lose, so they tested our students." The recruiters liked what they found with the students they tried. Gradually, those same recruiters came back to hire graduates of the law school that had been shrewd enough to entice potential employers by providing Cardozo students' services for a nominal fee. The school's positive reputation has also entered into the admissions arena, propelling Cardozo's mean LSAT to just below what is commonly referred to in admissions as "the 40 threshold."

As you pass through Cardozo's floors, you will be alerted to the school's affiliation with Yeshiva by the presence of mezzuzahs on the door frames of the offices, male students wearing yarmulkes and *maskgiock* who bring kosher food over from Yeshiva for the law school's vending machines. Cardozo also attracts many students who aren't Jewish. As for the school's physical environment, there is little "campus life" and no on-campus housing, and many students share the sentiment that "you are on your own as far as living is concerned." But Cardozo is also a warm school, where students are competitive with their classmates but still willingly help one another. Because it is a commuter school, student life revolves around academics, but there are occasional student-sponsored events.

Cardozo is a young school whose standards have skyrocketed. Without any doubt, Cardozo's greatest strength lies in its faculty who by all accounts are not only excellent conveyors of information but are also very accessible to students. The faculty includes Telford Taylor, chief U.S. prosecutor at the Nuremburg War Crimes Trials, and Leon Wildes, who defended Yoko Ono and John Lennon, teaches Immigration Law.

The school has a "two-pronged approach," providing both a solid theoretical background in the classroom and opportunities for practical experience in internships, clinical programs, and other work experiences. One of the advantages of Cardozo's being a young school is that its curriculum is both flexible and responsive to the marketplace in such ways as by offering courses in real estate law.

Most recently the school has added the Affordable Housing Clinic and the Program in International Law and Human Rights. The Samuel and Ronnie Heyman Center on Corporate Governance has held conferences on "High Leverage, Low Protection: The Two-Sided Problem of Corporate Debt" and "Trading Claims and Bankruptcy." The Howard Squadron Program in Law, Media, and Society, inaugurated in 1990, will strengthen the school's highly respected Entertainment/Communication and Arts and the Law Programs; speakers for the program include media/communication leaders Leonard Tisch and Rupert Murdoch.

ADMISSIONS

CRITERIA

LEVEL 1: Grade Point Average; quality of undergraduate curriculum/course work completed; quality/reputation of college/university; LSAT score

LEVEL 2: Work experience; personal essay

LEVEL 3: Recommendations

MINORITY RECRUITMENT PROGRAM

Yes; Through a special Candidate Referral Service using Law Schools Data Assembly Service (LSDAS), letters, and phonathons from minority organizations; files are shared with entire Faculty Committee on Admissions.

ABOUT THE APPLICATION

DEADLINE FOR FILING: 4/1

FEE: $40

LSAT: School takes the highest of the applicant's scores, although they do look at all scores.

RECOMMENDED COURSES PRIOR TO MATRICULATING: "None—just pick an undergraduate discipline that you enjoy and do well. We do put an emphasis on 'progressive' work experience."

PERSONAL STATEMENT: "Next to the LSAT, GPA, and College information, this is probably the most important part of the application, particularly for older, non-traditional students. We are interested in knowing about the student—what makes them 'tick' and what distinguishes them from all the other applicants."

INTERVIEW: Not required or recommended.

ADMISSIONS TIPS: "Use your personal statement wisely! We want to know about you, not about legal theory or about your poor academic performance your freshman year [do that on a separate sheet]. Also, please do not send term papers—we usually do not have the time." **ADDITIONAL TIP** The more an applicant can distinguish him or herself the more it is to their advantage. Interviews are not required or encouraged unless the circumstances are highly unusual. Minority students are granted interviews. Few transfers are accepted each year. Students must be in the top 10–25% of class. There are no cutoffs. The school is looking for students who will give more to society than simply going into a top law firm.

CONTACT: Anita T. Walton, Acting Director of Admissions

PHYSICAL ENVIRONMENT

Cardozo, housed in an office building, borders on Greenwich Village near many restaurants, parks, theaters, and bars. Although there is no campus, students can use the nearby YMCA/YWCA for free; the New York Health and Racquet Club is around the corner. Restaurants are very expensive, as are living accommodations near the school. Students find Cardozo is easily accessible by subway, PATH train, and bus. Safety is good by New York City standards, due to a high concentration of students in the area of the school. Although there is no cafeteria, the students have a lounge and vending machines. Accessibility for handicapped students is excellent in all but one classroom, and classes here can be moved, if a handicapped student is unable to participate in this room.

No on-campus housing is available for students, and the most common type of housing is sharing an apartment. The cost of a one-bedroom apartment is approximately $1200 a month. You have to weigh the cost of transportation against cheaper housing outside the city versus the more expensive apartment prices in Manhattan. The school's library is closed on Saturdays, which students find somewhat inconvenient. A car is not recommended, because there is good public transportation, the cost of car insurance is very high, and there's no parking in the area of the school.

FINANCES

BUDGET	LOW	MEDIUM	HIGH
Tuition	$11,825	$11,825	$11,825
Books	$800	$800	$800
Living Accommodations (9 mo)	Apt. (Q) $4500	Shared Apt. (M) $7650	One-Bedroom (M) $10,800
Food	Groceries $1800	Groceries/Vending $2250	Restaurants $3600
Transportation	Walking/Mass Transit $400	Mass Transit $448.50	Taxis/Mass Transit $700
Miscellaneous	$100/month, $900	$200/month, $1800	$300/month, $2700
TOTAL	$20,225	$24,773.50	$30,425*

M = Manhattan, Q = Queens

* Note: It is difficult to determine high end, because it is literally limitless in New York. You must weigh whether or not you want to live near the school and save on commuting or take PATH trains from New Jersey (stops about two blocks away) or the subway (also two blocks away) from buroughs, save on rent, and pay extra transportation costs.

Employment During School: Recommended. Work-study jobs are available for eligible students during the summer. These jobs are federal, need-based financial aid programs and pay $4.50 an hour.

Scholarships: Need-based scholarships are available.

School Loan Program (Exclusive of Perkins Money): Yes; the Cardozo Financial Assistance Program. Cardozo makes loans based on financial need, academic standing, and availability of funds. The money is applied to a student's tuition accounts in two equal installments on a per-semester basis. During the borrower's attendance at Cardozo, no interest accrues or is charged. During the first year after leaving Cardozo, only interest is charged; thereafter, the loan principal and interest are to be paid in equal installments over seven years. The interest rate for these loans is currently 7%.

Loan Forgiveness Program: Does not have, but currently considering implementing one.

Students Requesting Aid: 70%; of these, 65% receive aid.

Students Indebted upon Graduation: 65%

Average Loan Indebtedness: $65,000–70,000

ACADEMICS

During the first year, all courses are required. The second and third years are primarily elective, with the exception of a course on Professional Responsibility and an upper-level writing requirement, which students don't feel is that difficult to satisfy. Electives are extensive with courses including Intellectual Property, Publishing Law, Human Rights Law, and Professional Sports Law. Depending on your interests, you can take traditional courses or more theoretically based law courses.

Faculty stars include Barry Scheck (Hedda Nussbaum's lawyer, Criminal Law Clinic), Drucilla Cornell (Jurisprudence), David Rudenstine (Constitutional Law), Monroe E. Price, Dean (Entertainment Law, American Indian Rights), and Malvina Halberstam (International Law). Students find that they are good teachers and conveyers of information, as well as accessible; they are known to give out their phone numbers to students. Grades are curved to approximately a B−, with very few As and very few failures. Students recommended the following study methods: Don't allow supplements to supplant texts. Keep up with the work. Utilize briefing and outlines in the beginning of each course.

Students find that the strongest aspect of Cardozo is that it offers so many work experience/internships and clinics with five clinics and several intensive trial programs. Cardozo also has a strong reputation for Arts and Entertainment Law.

SPECIAL PROGRAMS

Cardozo offers an Accelerated Entry Plan (AEP) under which qualified students may enter the law school after the third year of undergraduate study, or through which college graduates may complete the law degree requirements in two and a half years.

STUDENT LIFE

Cardozo students have long been characterized as highly competitive on the verge of cutthroatism. In reality, about half of the class is very competitive, but a friendly competition exists. The social life at the school is not very active because it is primarily a commuter school. There is, however, a newly formed Student Bar Association and several other activities scheduled by students. New York offers limitless cultural opportunities, but, in the words of one student, "You worry all week about the cost of this and the cost of a can of soda, and then you blow it in one night at a night club." Mostly students here do things on their own.

PLACEMENT

Students find the Placement Office adequate in its ability to find them employment. Although it best serves students at the top of the class, a conscientious effort is made to help all students regardless of grades. 94% of the Cardozo students are placed after graduation.

PREPARATION

Students are prepared through videotaped mock interviews, individual counseling sessions, panel discussions on various areas of professional opportunities, and seminars on interviewing techniques.

WHERE/WHAT GRADUATES PRACTICE

A. 95% Northeast; 1% South; 1% West Coast; 1% Midwest; 2% Other.
B. 1% Solo Practitioner; 20% Small Firms; 6% Medium Firms; 22% Large Firms; 4.5% Clerkships; 1% Graduate Degrees; 6.5% Governmental Agencies; 8% Corporations; 8% Public Interest; 8% District Attorney.

LIST OF CONTRIBUTORS

We gratefully acknowledge the information, support, and guidance we have received from the following individuals. We also wish to thank the hundreds of contributors who wished to remain anonymous.

Chris Adams
Christy Adams
Tana M. Adde
Erin Ahearn
Mark C. Allen
Mitzi Alsparigh
Theresa Amato
Cindy Ambrose
Carlton Ammons
Dave Anderson
Jim Anderson
Leslie B. Anderson
Tina Antonik
Norman Aranda
Adrian Armstrong
Anna Assimakopoulos

Dawn Thomas Baggett
Olen M. Bailey, Jr.
Lawrence M. Baker
Todd Baldwin
Sam Barker
Sue Barker
Jaynelle Bell
David A. Benfield
Dudley Bertram
Victoria E. Biedebach
Ann Marie Black
Edward A. Boling
Eric Braverman
Bernardean Broadous
David J. Brymesser
Suzanne Butwin
Nona Byington

David Neal Calvillo, CPA
Laurie Cambra
Patricia Canavan
Claudia Cantarella
Jeffrey R. Capwell
Donald Carey
Michael Carithers
Teri Carr
Cliff L. Carter
Jose Castaneda
Cheryl Collins
Blaise William
    Constantaares
Drew Cooper
Diane Costa

Kevin G. Cravens
Carla D. Crouch

Daniel L. Darlow
John T. Davis
Diane Davison
Paul A. Deas
John Sabine DeGroote
Scott Doggett
Kelly J. Doherty
Charles Durant

Diana Edensword
Diana Edmiston
Douglas Elcock
Sandee Espy
Geoffrey Eustis
Christina Ewing
Darryl L. Exum

Shari Feemster
Kary M. Ferguson
Robert D. Fish
June Fledman
Joseph J. Fonseca
Laura E. Forester
Jeffrey Frankel

Brian Gearinger
Sheryl Gittlitz
Randi Goda
Mathew D. Goetz
Marjory Goldberg
Jonathan Goldstein
Marcelle Gorelick
Eric Gould
Louis W. Grande, Jr.
David C. Greenberg
Evan Greenberg
David Earl Griffith
Glenn A. Gulino

Jack Hagerty
Jill I. Hai
Lily Hamrick
Tom Hanusik
Marc Hardestu
Cyndy Harnett
David A. Hawley
Jenny Hebert

Kirk D. Hendrick
Frederick J. Henley, Jr.
John Henry
J.A. Herman
Thomas D. Herndon
Cheryl Hesse
Tiana M. Hinnant
Jennifer Hooker
Brad Houston

John J. Igliozzi

Amy Jackson
Pam Jackson
Doug Jacobson
Gerald Jeegar
Frank M. Jenkins III
Lloyd G. Johnson
Susan H.R. Jones
Jonathan A. Judd

Kenneth S. Kawabata
Henderson Kearney
John Keating
John P. Kepich
Julie Klahr
Barbara Klotz
R. J. Kobylak
Kathryn Kohlman
Jeffrey Koppele
Douglas Krabbenhoft
Christopher E. Krafchak
Joseph J. Krasovec
William H. Kuntz

Brian Lamb
Andy Laszlo
Kathryn Jane Monson
    Latour
Craig C. Lebamoff
Conrad Christopher Ledoux
Catherine A. Lee
Lauren Lemmon
Robert A. Lester
Jodi Lolik
Teresa Lozano

Jeff Majzoub
Lisa Mandel
Richard Marasse

Patricia J. Mastnanni
Carolyn Matheson
Andrew R. McCumber
Pete McCutchen
Mary Porter McKee
Phillip McKinney
Gordon Shane McNeill
Noah D. Mesel
Ken Metzner
Dianne E. Miller
Cheryl D. Mills
Gina Maria Monforte
Jim Monroe
Carol H. Morita
Lynne Harns Moss
Robin C. Murray-Gill

Anni Najem
Stefan M. Nathanson
Brent T. Neck
Barbara Nelson
Eric L. Nesbitt
Sherri Netburn
Mark Neustadt
Ed Newcomer, Jr.
Caroline Newkirk
Mathew S. Nosanchuk
Philip W. Nykyforuk

Steven D. Olmstead
Ailish O'Connor
Eileen O'Neill
Rhonda Ores
Beverly Ann Ortega
Andrew M. Ostrognai

William J. Paris
Carrie Pastor

Mel Patterson
John A. Patti
Chandra E. Pezzullo
Dan Poliak

Debbie E. Queen

John Rabalais
Janice Rauen
Jacqueline Raznik
Denise K. Reinsch
Stephen Reynolds
Adrienne Rice
Beth Rickher
Debra Kimbriel Rittiluechai
Scott E. Roderick
Julian Rodriguez, Jr.
Tatiana Roodkowsky
Paul Rosenberg
Laura Rothschild
Maryrobin Rurney

Judi Sanchez
Ed Sasaki
Melissa Scanlan
Betsy Scherl
Susan Scuderi
Ellen Seats
William G. Shaw
Katherine Sher
Irene Shin
Jack Sigman
Donald K. Slaughter
Mark Sligh
Daurean G. Sloan
Stephanie Smith
R. Adrian Solomon

Matthew Sons
Stephen Spencer
Frank Stambaugh
Steven W. Starke
Martha Steinman
E. W. Stephenson-McEwan
Micki S. Stern
Randi Sue Stock
Charla Stratton
Andrea J. Sullivan

Thomas Talor
Fran Tankersley
Walter Taylor
Louis Theros
Ernest Tigano
Toby Tyler, Jr.

Linda Vita Velez
George F. Voinovich
Eugene Volokh
Michele M. Volpe

Michael E. Waller
Jennifer C. Warren
Laura Beth Washburn
Tracie L. Washington
Stephen Wederoth
Catherine Welsh
Dennis Wetta
Samuel C. Wisatzkay
David E. Wolf
Steve Wood
Drew H. Wrigley

Kurt Zimmerman
Michael F. Zullas